A Natural History of the Intermountain West

Grasslands to mountains, northern Arizona, pencil on paper, 2004, Gwendolyn Waring.

# A Natural History
## of the Intermountain West

*Its Ecological and Evolutionary Story*

Gwendolyn L. Waring

THE UNIVERSITY OF UTAH PRESS
*Salt Lake City*

The Defiance House Man colophon is a registered trademark of the
University of Utah Press. It is based upon a four-foot-tall, Ancient
Puebloan pictograph (late PIII) near Glen Canyon, Utah.

15  14  13  12  11        1  2  3  4  5

LIBRARY OF CONGRESS CATALOGING-IN-PUBLICATION DATA
Waring, Gwendolyn L., 1952-
  A natural history of the intermountain West : its ecological and
evolutionary story / Gwendolyn L. Waring.
      p. cm.
  Includes bibliographical references and index.
  ISBN 978-1-60781-028-5 (pbk. : alk. paper)
  1. Natural history—Great Basin.  I. Title.
  QH104.5.G68W37 2010
  508.79—dc22

                        2010039654

All figures, unless noted otherwise, by Gwendolyn Waring.
Frontispiece: Gwendolyn Waring

Figure 3.7 (lower image) published with the permission of
S. B. Vander Wall and Oxford University Press. It was previously
published in R. M. Lanner, *Made for Each Other: A Symbiosis
of Birds and Pines* (Oxford University Press, 1996).

Figure 4.2 (lower section) published with the permission of the
Ecological Society of America.

Figure 5.4 published with permission of K. Dial and T. Vaughn, the
American Society of Mammologists, and Allen Press, Inc.

Printed and bound by Sheridan Books, Inc., Ann Arbor, Michigan.

*For Phoebe*

# Contents

# Figures

## Tables

# Color Plates *(following page 72)*

# Preface

This world is all about change. The plants and animals described in these chapters have been evolving and migrating endlessly through time, a fact I find somewhat comforting as we head into a pretty uncertain future. Studies indicate that some species are already migrating to higher ground, though others, such as the golden frog of Costa Rica, could not ascend high enough and have already gone extinct. As one who knows the texture of the meadows where I live—meadows that I have looked on with love for thirty years—I don't want them to change, but changing they are, and right before our eyes.

This book is a testament to natural selection and evolution, miraculous forces of the natural world that constitute a large part of my religion. It is also a testament to the tenacity of life on this planet. There are countless examples of explosions of species and subspecies, varieties and types, in every chapter of this book. Life forms are constantly arising, and each one is a wonderful experiment.

One of the most exciting aspects of writing this book has been learning about the Pleistocene, the last period of major cold and glaciation that ended only 12,000 years ago. Its effects on the land are still conspicuous because it was the most recent major climatic event. In the West we have a special record of the enormous and rapid changes that occurred in western ecosystems during the Pleistocene's last major glacial period, the Wisconsin Glacial Episode. This record is available for two reasons: because the West is so dry, and because of packrats (*Neotoma* spp.), which like so many of the species described in this book occur only in western North America and Central America. Packrats construct large nests, called middens, out of pieces of surrounding plants. The nests are thus durable records of local plant communities dating back more than 50,000 years. Thousands of packrat middens have been studied, and along with fossil pollen from lake cores, they have revealed a great deal about this region's prehistory.

They show that the ranges of plant and animal communities have been surprisingly dynamic, with enormous forests of ponderosa pines, for instance, disappearing and then quickly reforming.

This book describes the geological formation of the West and how plants and animals have come to live in this young, rocky region, which encompasses the Great Basin, the Colorado Plateau, and the Southern Rockies. The first chapter, on geology, focuses on the complexity of landforms in the West, how they came to be, and how that complexity influences the resulting life forms. Chapter 2 focuses on the water in the West's two great drainage systems, the Great Basin and the Colorado River basin, both of which have a greater proportion of endemic fishes than any other basin in North America. Chapter 3 discusses the West's young mountain chains, which concentrate water and in some cases support alpine tundra and enormous coniferous forests. Plants and animals have traveled back and forth along these north-south-oriented mountains for millions of years as climates have changed. This is true for the nearly twenty-five alpine species found on the San Francisco Peaks of Arizona that also occur in the Arctic. Chapters 4 through 6 examine the West's forests, woodlands, and grasslands. Enormous ponderosa pine forests occur throughout the West, yet this species may have migrated or shifted its range back into its current distribution from low-elevation Pleistocene refugia only within the last 10,000 years. The pinyon-juniper woodlands also have a dynamic and somewhat enigmatic history. Grasslands arose throughout the world during the dry Miocene epoch (23 to 5 Ma), quickly leading to the evolution in North America of an astounding diversity of grazing mammals, including the horse. Although these ancient grasslands have always been assaulted by herbivores, the intense cattle-grazing practices of the last 150 years have transformed them.

The "cold desert" is discussed in chapter 7. This dry corridor extends from northern Arizona to British Columbia, inland from the coastal mountains that cast long rain shadows, and is so named because its winter temperatures drop below freezing. It is a land of shrubs whose populations, which extend as far as the eye can see, are well adapted to life in this beautifully spare land. Finally, a few flowers that are relatively common in the West are described in chapter 8. Their stories are improbable, and many require complex interactions with pollinators and herbivores to survive.

The scientific research on western ecosystems is exciting. The stories of plants and animals and processes are stranger than fiction. I feel very privileged to present so many of these stories in this book, and I am indebted to the scientists who talked with me about their cutting-edge research on everything from penstemon evolution to the restoration of natural conditions in western forests. There is great thinking going on here in the West, and my hat goes off to these scientists for showing us how magical this world really is.

# Acknowledgments

I would especially like to thank Larry Stevens, Gerald Smith, and John Spence for their major contributions to the chapters on geology, water, and the cold desert. Special thanks also to my sister, Linda Poché, for helping to bring this book into its final form. Thanks to Winnie Taney for editing with the sharp eyes of a naturalist and a grammarian. Many, many thanks for the editorial contributions of Brad Baxter, Julio Betancourt, Ronald Blakey, William Bowman, Neil Cobb, Frank DeCourten, Jeffrey Eaton, Marylou Fairweather, Thomas Fleischner, Peter Fule, Scott Hodges, Will Moir, Nancy Morin, Ronald Lanner, Russell Monson, Michael Ort, Ken Paige, Gordon Pratt, Peter Price, Sara Rathburn, Nancy Riggs, John Paul Roccaforte, Katrina Rogers, Thomas Sisk, Michael Wagner, Justen Whittall, Andrea Wolfe, and James A. Young.

I want to thank E. Durant McArthur and James Young for expressing great faith in and hope for the future of these western ecosystems.

For great conversations and information I also thank Scott Anderson, Sue Beard, Robert Behnke, Matthew Bowker, David Breshears, Bryan Brown, Jean Chambers, Michael Collier, Leland Dexter, Dick Fleishman, William Friedman, Joseph Hazel, Rich Hereford, Leo Hickey, Richard Hofstetter, Tiffany Knight, George Koch, Bill Liebfried, Jim Mead, Courtney Meier, Jeffrey Mitton, Margaret Moore, Jodi Norris, Joel Pederson, Barbara Phillips, Robin Tausch, Bill Vernieu, Bob Webb, and Tom Whitham.

Huge thanks to University of Utah editors Reba Rauch, Jessica Booth, and Glenda Cotter for making it all possible.

Big thanks to Christina Norlin for making the maps so cool.

Special thanks to Susan Beard and Kathryn Petersen, librarians at Northern Arizona

University, for finding so many obscure books and papers.

Great thanks to my family, Linda, Rob, Star, Dana, and Annie, and friends. Special thanks to my mother, Gwendolyn S. Waring, for loving life so much.

Very special thanks to Frances B. McAllister for her generous financial support of this project.

# CHAPTER 1

# How the Rocky West Formed and How It Shapes Western Ecosystems

## GWENDOLYN WARING AND WAYNE RANNEY

Western North America acquired its mountainous shape and colorful rocks over the course of hundreds of millions, even billions, of years through a series of remarkable processes. The geologic formation of the West involved two separate and distinct episodes: a long period of deposition when its rocks were formed, and a shorter, more recent period during which they were uplifted and shaped by erosion (Fig. 1.1). These formative geological processes also shaped western life forms. This chapter describes how the various rocks were formed, how the land was shaped by tectonics and erosion, what environments once existed here, and how geology has so profoundly influenced the evolution and distribution of the plants and animals that have inhabited this land. Today the greatest levels of biological diversity in North America are found in the West.

The story begins with the formation of the West's foundation or "basement." In the Grand Tetons of Wyoming, the basement rocks are about 3 billion years old and date back to when the southern edge of the continent was located near present-day northern Colorado. About 1.75 billion years ago, two or more tectonic plates carrying chains of volcanic islands collided with North America as they drifted in from the south. These islands progressively became "sutured" onto the continent's edge, pushing some rocks deep into the crust (Ilg et al. 1996). These

1.1. Topography of the contiguous United States, 1:3,500,000, 1990. Note the pronounced geographic deformation of the West. Courtesy of the U.S. Geological Survey.

**TABLE 1.1.** GEOLOGICAL TIME LINE FOR THE WESTERN UNITED STATES

| Period | Epoch | Beginning of Interval | Events |
|---|---|---|---|
| Quaternary | Holocene | 10,000 years ago | Δ Ponderosa pine and other plants migrate back to higher elevations and latitudes.<br>Δ Warming, drying trend.<br>Δ Euro-Americans settle in the West. |
| | Pleistocene | 1.6 Ma | Δ Major glaciation worldwide, causing plant and animal migrations and flooding.<br>Δ Humans evolve. |
| Tertiary | Pliocene | 5 Ma | ~ 3 Ma, the south-north American land bridge allows intercontinental floral and faunal interchange. |
| | Miocene | 22 Ma | Δ Grasslands spread throughout the world during a warm, dry climate, followed by an explosion of grazing mammals, including horses.<br>Δ Sierra Nevada, Cascades, and Great Basin form, contributing to drying of the Intermountain West.<br>Δ Colorado Plateau uplifts.<br>Δ Upper and lower Colorado River basins connected. |
| | Oligocene | 34 Ma | Δ ~30 Ma, change from shortening to extension of western North American plate, causing further extension of the Great Basin. |
| | Eocene | 55.8 Ma | Δ Warming climate; subtropical flora makes it to Alaska.<br>Δ Earliest ponderosa pine, British Columbia. |
| | Paleocene | 66 Ma | Δ Age of mammals. |
| Cretaceous-Tertiary Boundary | | 65.5 Ma | Δ Extinction of dinosaurs.<br>Δ Laramide Orogeny produces the Rocky Mountains…again. |

became the Southwest's basement rocks and so extended the size of the continent. These crystalline rocks underlie most of Utah, Colorado, New Mexico, and Arizona, but they are exposed only in the bottoms of the deepest canyons, such as Arizona's Grand Canyon (Plate 1), Westwater Canyon in Utah, and the Black Canyon of the Gunnison in Colorado. These oldest rocks include metamorphic schist and gneiss, and igneous granite. Where exposed, their hardness makes river canyons narrow and steep, and

few plants can colonize their sheer walls and rocky slopes.

These tectonic collisions also warped the western landscape into an ancient mountain range that existed for several hundred million years. But by 750 million years ago (Ma), a great rifting or splitting event affected the entire West. By about 525 Ma, rifting and erosion had lowered the American Southwest to near sea level, and sediment of mostly marine origin accumulated in the area for the next 210 million

**TABLE 1.1. CONTINUED**

| | | |
|---|---|---|
| Cretaceous | 144 Ma | Δ Sevier (Nevada) Orogeny.<br>Δ Evolution of flowering plants and pollinators; age of dinosaurs. |
| Jurassic | 213 Ma | Δ Age of reptiles.<br>Δ Morrison Formation forms from floodplain sediments. |
| Triassic | 251 Ma | Δ Continental deposits form, including Chinle Formation from rivers, and Navajo Sandstone from dunes.<br>Δ Earliest dinosaurs.<br>Δ Formation of deserts.<br>Δ Breakup of Pangea into Gondwanaland and Laurasia, and then into modern continents.<br>Δ Evolution of pines before breakup of Laurasia. |
| Permian | 299 Ma | Δ Formation of red beds.<br>Δ Frequent western orogeny. |
| Mississippian | 360 Ma | Δ ~350–250 Ma, the Ancestral Rocky Mountains form. |
| Devonian | 416 Ma | Δ Antler Orogeny; subduction along Pacific coast. |
| Silurian | 440 Ma | Δ First land plants and insects. |
| Cambrian | 544 Ma | Δ ~525 Ma, lowering of western North America leads to several hundred million years of deposition of marine and coastal sediments. |
| Precambrian | 4600 Ma | Δ ~1175 Ma, portion of western North America attaches south of present-day Wyoming.<br>Δ ~ 3950 Ma, oldest sedimentary rocks form; first single-celled organisms. |

*Source*: Geological Society of America website, http://www.geosociety.org/science/timescale

years (Plate 2). The seas left resistant layers of coastal sandstone and offshore limestone and dolomite that can be found across much of the West today. The Redwall Limestone is 500 feet thick in the Grand Canyon (Middleton and Elliott 2003) and is present in the Northern Rockies as well (where it is known as the Madison Limestone). The Tapeats Sandstone in the Southwest (called the Flathead Sandstone up north) formed along a beach in a nearshore environment (Table 1.1). All totaled, between 2,500 and 5,000 feet of marine and coastal deposits (and even more in the Great Basin) were laid down over this immense amount of time. Limestone is especially durable in the modern arid environment and forms the backbone of many mountain ranges in the Great Basin. As with the basement rocks, canyons cut into limestone are generally narrow and steep, which limits the development of riparian plant communities.

By about 315 Ma, the long period of marine sedimentation ended as the crust of western North America became slightly elevated by tectonic movements (Blakey 2003, Blakey and Ranney 2008). At first, as the more continental depositional environment began, marine and continental deposition events traded off, as revealed along the San Juan River in southeast Utah, where 800 feet of the alternating gray marine limestone and red continental mudstone and sandstone of the Honaker Trail Formation reflect this transitional process (Plate 3; Baars and Stevenson 1986).

During the next 220 million years, continental environments shaped the West, with sediment accumulating in two highly generalized environments: fluvial (river) and eolian (dunes) (Plate 4). Deposits derived from dominantly fluvial environments include the Organ Rock, Moenkopi, Chinle (Plate 5), Moenave, Kayenta, and Morrison formations. These deposits were derived from rivers emanating from the region's highlands, including the Ancestral Rocky Mountains in Colorado (part of which is known as the Umcompahgre Uplift), the Mogollon Highlands in southern Arizona, and even the southern Appalachian Mountains (Riggs et al. 1996). Formations that were deposited in desert dune environments include the Cedar Mesa, Coconino, De Chelly, Wingate, Navajo, and Entrada sandstones. The winds that delivered this voluminous sand blew in from the north and west, and the deposits reflect the arid conditions that existed then. The dramatic colors of these continental deposits are due to trace amounts of red iron oxide on the surface of individual sand grains (Plate 6; Ranney 2010). Minerals such as mica and hornblende supplied the iron to the otherwise white sand after being eroded from the granite of nearby mountain ranges.

Shallow seas occasionally encroached on the edges of these continental settings, leaving marine deposits known today as the Pedregosa, Kaibab, and Carmel formations. By the Cretaceous period, however, an incursion of the Great Western Interior Seaway advanced upon the landscape, depositing the Dakota Sandstone and the Mesa Verde Group in nearshore and shallow marine environments. The great coal deposits in the West are Cretaceous in age and formed in the backwater swamps adjacent to this shoreline. Fossils of the dinosaurs that lived in these swamps are still being unearthed in Grand Staircase–Escalante National Monument in southern Utah.

As the continental deposits were forming in the West, the enormous supercontinent of Pangea was breaking up, and its pieces—today's continents—were moving toward their modern positions. Pangea broke first into the subcontinents Gondwanaland and Laurasia. This momentous event began in the Triassic, about 210 Ma, and continued during the Jurassic period, between 200 and 144 Ma (Dickenson 1989). Research on the breakup of these continents has revealed where many plant groups originated and how their ecological traits determined whether they would be confined to the new continents or move beyond them. Today nearly all of the world's pines, with their heavy seeds, occur only in the Northern Hemisphere, on continents that once made up Laurasia, which is where they originated. Grasses, on the other hand, have seeds that are dispersed easily by wind and animals, allowing them to colonize all of the modern continents even though they arose much more recently than pines, and long after the breakup of Pangea.

As North America drifted toward its

modern position, collisions with tectonic plates transformed its western edge from a large seaway into tremendous mountains. The topography we see today began to form about 70 Ma, as North America collided with the Farallon plate, compressing the West. The plate may have subducted at a shallow angle beneath North America, further crumpling the West's surface and uplifting the Rocky Mountains and the Colorado Plateau (Dickenson 1987). This mountain-building event is known as the Laramide Orogeny (70 to 40 Ma), named for the Laramie Basin of Wyoming, whose fossil-rich sediments reveal when this uplift occurred.

During this time, the landscape of western North America became progressively warped and uplifted between the coast and the emerging Rockies. Traces of this event can be found in the many monoclines, or folds, of the Colorado Plateau, including Comb Ridge, Waterpocket Fold, and the East Kaibab Monocline (which elevated the Kaibab Upwarp near the future Grand Canyon). Significant uplift of the Colorado Plateau certainly occurred during the Laramide, although more recent uplift (between 15 and 5 Ma) may also have contributed to the region's high elevation. The plateau is a large and relatively undeformed region spanning much of the Four Corners states; an explanation of why it escaped the ravages of crustal deformation found in adjacent areas remains elusive for research geologists.

In the midst of these physical changes, the climate became very warm and humid during the Eocene epoch (about 55 to 37 Ma). The earth experienced its "thermal maximum" during this time, with temperatures 15°F warmer than today, due in part to increased volcanic activity worldwide. Angiosperms (flowering plants) expanded

their range dramatically, and subtropical plants grew as far north as Alaska, replacing long-established pines throughout much of the West. Warmth and humidity were followed by the cool, dry conditions of the Oligocene epoch (37 to 23 Ma). Increased aridity resulted in the formation of the world's first grasslands. The combination of extensive mountain building and a drying climate led to a great diversity of species in the West, many of which are endemic, meaning they occur nowhere else on earth.

By 17 Ma, the compressive forces that had uplifted the Rockies and the Colorado Plateau changed to forces of extension, setting the stage for a different kind of mountain building (Fiero 1986, Huntoon 2003). Faulting stretched the Great Basin landscape to double its original width and gave rise to the sparsely populated Basin and Range geologic province. The stretching caused a series of north-south, fault-blocked mountains separated by low basins. This event resulted in the general lowering of the Great Basin (even though mountains were formed) and created the lowest elevations found in North America. The region has more than a hundred landlocked basins, and many of these were the sites of Pleistocene lakes ~2.6 million to 10,000 years ago. It is not surprising that the Great Basin drainage system has a large proportion of endemic fishes, though its intense aridity has limited numbers of species overall due to a long history of extinctions.

On the heels of the expansion of the Great Basin, western ranges such as the Sierra Nevada and Cascades rose up adjacent to the Pacific coast. The rise of these coastal ranges cast a broad rain shadow across the West and sealed its fate as an arid region. The Sierra Nevada began its long rise in the

Cretaceous, with a renewed uplift between about 20 Ma and 12 Ma. The volcanoes in the Cascades, to the north, became active only in the last 5 Ma. With the creation of this more modern landscape, the Colorado River drainage came into existence, draining the Rocky Mountains of their snowmelt and carving many canyons in the sedimentary rocks of the Colorado Plateau.

The climate during the Pleistocene, which included the last ice age, had profound effects on the West. Plants and animals were driven southward thousands of miles seeking warmer refuges from glaciers, cold weather, and wetter than normal conditions, and then rebounded during warming interglacial phases. Relicts of these events abound in the West and include arctic species that have persisted in high mountains as far south as Arizona. Pleistocene glaciers advanced and retreated many times, sculpting the western mountains and carving deep river canyons (Ranney 2005). As many as fifteen to twenty glacial phases occurred during the 2 million plus years of the Pleistocene, with the glacial phases lasting about ten times longer than interglacial phases.

Enough water was tied up in ice to lower the sea level by more than 300 feet (Van Devender 1995). The Late Pleistocene and the dry period since have given rise to many new habitats and species.

The land and climate of the West continue to evolve, and change, it seems, is the only constant in the West. I am fascinated by how quickly enormous changes have occurred. For example, it appears that ponderosa pine, the most widespread pine in western North America, largely disappeared from the West during the last glacial phase of the Pleistocene and only reappeared in the last 10,000 years to form enormous forests. According to data from packrat nests, ponderosa only returned to Montana from southwestern refugia within the last 1,000 years. Given recent predictions of global warming, ponderosa pine might just keep on moving north, where it originated during an earlier time. With climate change upon us, these dynamic and fascinating processes are reshaping the world as we know it. No one knows for sure where things are headed, but it is certainly going to be interesting.

# CHAPTER 2

# *Precious Water in the West*

Water is the bottom line. In the West, places with water—whether springs, streams, rivers, or lakes—are where living things congregate (Plate 7).

Earth's wonderful freshwater evaporates off the surface of the oceans and condenses into clouds. These wet air masses rising off the vast Pacific Ocean are pushed eastward, releasing most of their moisture as they are forced up over the mountains. The air cools with the climb, causing water to precipitate from cloud vapor, resulting in either rain or snow. Ultimately, this water runs down from the mountains in rivers and streams, seeps through cracks into underground aquifers, flows to the oceans, or evaporates.

Most precipitation in the West comes in the form of wet winter storms that move from the northern Pacific through most of the region, and summer monsoons that move north from the Gulf of California and the Gulf of Mexico through the Southwest and much of the Southern Rockies.

WHY THE WEST IS SO DRY

Most of the western United States is regarded as semidesert or desert because it receives less than 10 inches of precipitation annually *and* its precipitation levels are exceeded by evaporation, or water loss, as water turns to vapor and disappears (Fig. 2.1). Dry areas such as the Great Basin often receive less than 4 inches of precipitation annually. Higher-elevation regions, including the Rockies, typically receive more than 30 inches of precipitation per year. Potential evaporation rates in northern Utah exceed 50 inches per year, and evaporation is even greater in the southern deserts. It's this combination that defines a desert. There are areas in the eastern and northwestern United States that have much greater annual evaporation rates than the arid West (e.g., 36 inches in eastern pine forests and river bottomlands, and 60 inches for Pacific Douglas fir forests), but because these rates do not exceed precipitation levels, most of the East and the Northwest are lush—hardly desertlike. While Hillet Doleib, Sudan, in Africa, annually receives about 30 inches of rain, far more than the western United States, its rain falls mainly in summer and is evaporated away by high temperatures; hence, this area appears just as arid as other places in North Africa that have a tenth of the precipitation (Warner 2004).

Several features converge to make the West so dry. First, the Intermountain West and the Rockies lie far inland from the oceans and gulfs that surround the shores of western North America—too far away to benefit from their moisture. Other inland continental deserts occur in central Asia and sub-Saharan Africa.

Perhaps an even greater cause of aridity is the north-south orientation of nearly all western mountains, including the coastal Cascades and Sierra Nevada, the intermountain plateaus and ranges, and the Rocky Mountains. These mountains prevent the flow of moist Pacific air from moving inland, resulting in rain shadows. What little moisture does make it beyond the coastal ranges is gradually siphoned off as the air masses rise again and again over the intermountain ranges and plateaus, and finally the Rockies (Fig. 2.2).

After modeling precipitation patterns in areas with mountain barriers and then "removing" the mountains, Broccoli and Manabe (1992) concluded that without these mountain barriers, places such as the Canadian prairie would receive three times the amount of precipitation they currently do lying in the rain shadow of the Canadian Rockies. The largest arid regions in North America, Asia, and South America are all within the rain shadows of major mountain ranges. These include the Eurasian deserts from Russia to Mongolia, and the Monte

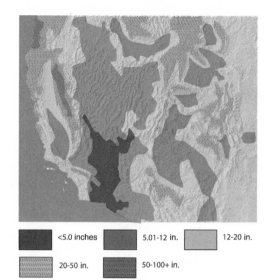

| | | |
|---|---|---|
| ■ <5.0 inches | ■ 5.01-12 in. | ▨ 12-20 in. |
| ▨ 20-50 in. | ▨ 50-100+ in. | |

**2.1.** Approximate annual precipitation in the western United States. Lower-elevation regions receive the least moisture.

and Patagonian deserts of South America. Finally, as warmed and drier air currents descend the lee side of western mountains, they are less likely to support further precipitation and more likely to suppress storm development (Warner 2004).

Fortunately, parts of the West get a fair amount of rain from summer monsoons that draw moisture from the Gulf of California and the Gulf of Mexico. Because this moisture is drawn from south to north, it is not blocked by the mountains, but monsoon circulations are still greatly influenced by both the Rockies and the Colorado Plateau, which help to draw monsoon moisture up from the southern gulfs. The same is true in Asia, where the Tibetan Plateau causes the northward expansion of the south Asian monsoon over India (Warner 2004).

These storms are characterized as monsoons because they occur only in the summer and because temperatures are highest immediately before their onset (Broccoli and Manabe 1992). The warming of the land surface relative to the sea surface pulls moisture

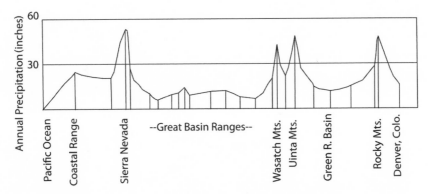

**2.2.** Annual precipitation levels across the western mountains and lowlands. Adapted from Bailey 1941.

inland. The southern Colorado Plateau, including northern Arizona, receives up to half of its annual precipitation from these storms, which are most active in July and August (Barrow et al. 1998). It is common in places such as Flagstaff, Arizona, for everyone to start grumbling about the heat in late June and watching the skies for the monsoon's characteristic thunderhead clouds. The effects of the North American monsoon storms diminish to the north, and the northern Colorado Plateau and Great Basin receive relatively little summer precipitation.

The Southwest's monsoon season is fairly predictable, although the amount of measurable rain can vary widely. Some plants on the southern Colorado Plateau are entirely adapted to these summer rains, whereas many plants that lie beyond the monsoon's reach, such as those of the Great Basin, respond most strongly to winter precipitation.

Once the West receives its small amounts of precipitation, a combination of sunny days, poorly developed soils, sparse vegetation cover, consistent winds, and moderate to high temperatures results in high rates of evapotranspiration, which is the vaporization of water from land and water surfaces (bare soil, lakes, rivers, springs) and

from living plants. Of course, evaporation is greatest in the summer heat, but even in winter significant evaporation occurs due to sublimation, in which snow evaporates directly into vapor rather than melting into water first. Clear, cloudless skies from dawn to dusk are characteristic of desert climates around the globe, with most deserts of the western United States receiving more than 80 percent of all possible sunshine during the summer (Petersen 1994).

## BIG WATER OF THE PAST

It is always pleasing when living in an arid land to imagine the cooler, wetter periods of the past. Water and ice were far more abundant in the West during the Pleistocene, and both worked to sculpt mountains and create soil, sometimes through cataclysmic floods that had profound effects on the biological structure of the land. As many as fifteen to twenty glacial phases occurred during this time. Drier and warmer periods, similar to today's climate, only occurred about 6 percent of the time during the last 340,000 years (Van Devender 1995). During the last glacial maximum, up to 32 percent of the globe was covered by ice (Sharp 1988). The North American ice sheet, at its largest, covered most of Canada and was thousands of feet thick (Sharp 1988). Even in the Southern Rockies, glaciers exceeded half a mile in thickness (Barnosky et al. 1987). Higher-elevation regions of the Colorado Plateau supported valley glaciers and small ice caps during the final phase of the Pleistocene (Marchetti et al. 2005). The alpine glaciers in the San Francisco Peaks near Flagstaff and in the White Mountains on the Arizona/New Mexico border marked the southern edge of glaciation in North America. These two ranges, as well as the La Sal Mountains in Utah and Grand Mesa in west-central Colorado, had at least several glacial advances. The flat top of Boulder Mountain, Utah, was glaciated during the Late Pleistocene, and outlet glaciers flowed over the summit, carving broad glacial valleys (Marchetti et al. 2005). Because so much water was bound up in ice, Pleistocene climates were dry and dusty during some of the coldest times, and sea level may have been 300 feet lower than it is today (Petersen 1994).

Today the glaciers of North America are associated with the Western Cordillera, which includes the Pacific and Rocky Mountain ranges (Meier 1990, Hambrey and Alean 2004). The largest glaciers occur in the Northern Rockies, in Canada and Alaska, but glaciers are also found farther south, in the Rockies of Montana, Wyoming, and Colorado. Glaciers also occur on volcanic peaks in Washington and in California's Sierra Nevada.

When the massive Pleistocene glaciers began to melt throughout the world at the end of the period, about 15,000 years ago, enormous lakes formed, and spectacular

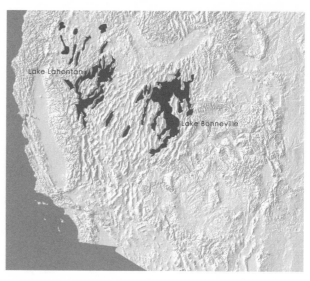

**2.3.** Approximate distribution of lakes formed in the Intermountain West during the Late Pleistocene.

flooding occurred (Fig. 2.3). Imagine landscapes utterly saturated and running with enormous volumes of water set free from ice. In some cases, snowmelt feeding into established drainages caused catastrophic flooding that significantly altered the landscape.

During the last glacial period, a lobe of the Laurentide ice sheet blocked the course of the Clark Fork River in western Montana. This ice dam created an enormous lake, referred to as Lake Missoula, estimated to have had a volume of water comparable to that of Lake Erie and Lake Ontario combined. When this ice dam broke apart toward the end of the Pleistocene, it caused one of the largest and most scouring floods ever known to have occurred. Water from melting ice began to cut a channel through the glacier, gradually growing until the dam collapsed into a massive flood. In as little as two or three days as much as 600 million cubic feet per second (cfs) of water blasted westward at up to 60 miles per hour through a mile-wide canyon in the glacier (Parfit 1995, Herget 2005). The water was more than 1,500 feet deep (Parfit 1995), and

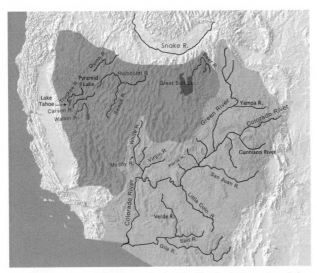

**2.4.** Major rivers of the Great Basin (darkly shaded area) and the Colorado River basin.

phases, refilling Lake Missoula (Sharp 1988).

Today Utah's Great Salt Lake is 30 feet deep and occupies 1,000 square miles, but during the Pleistocene, its predecessor, Lake Bonneville, was 1,000 feet deep. As it reached its greatest extent about 15,000 years ago (Fig. 2.3), a rapid incision of the alluvial fan that separated the Bonneville Basin and the Snake River system occurred, with as many as 15 million cfs of water pouring into the Snake River (O'Connor 1993). The corridor for this flood included the Bear River drainage (Fig. 2.4) and Red Rock Pass, between the Bannock and Portneuf ranges. Red Rock Pass is considered to have been a weak point in the lake's northern alluvial border. Along its way through this river system, the Lake Bonneville flood also breached a lava dam and emptied the Pleistocene lake known as American Falls. Sections of the Snake River canyon were greatly enlarged by this flood, and like the flooding from Lake Missoula, it created extensive scablands.

3,000 square miles of the Columbia Plateau were inundated by this glacial flood. Large, scoured areas extended from Montana to Washington and Oregon. The rich loess soils that had capped the Columbia River lavas—nearly 200 feet deep—were washed away as the flood scoured the land right down to underlying basalt. These areas are called the Scablands, and today the landscape is a mosaic of scoured bedrock with intermittent patches of soil. Loess soils—some of the richest on earth—are derived from the glacial erosion of bedrock (Sharp 1988). Where these soils stayed in place, in eastern Washington, they support some of the most productive wheat fields in the country (Sharp 1988).

The flood carved passages up to three-quarters of a mile long in canyon floors and deposited huge loads of debris. Boulders from as far away as Idaho and Montana are found in Oregon, and it is thought that they were carried by icebergs during this flood (Parfit 1995). This flooding process occurred forty or more times throughout the Pleistocene's glacial and interglacial

Enormous floods also occurred elsewhere in the West (e.g., Birkeland 1968, Rathburn 1993), in Scandinavia, in the Hindukush Mountains of southern Asia, and in the Altai Mountains of Siberia, where floods may have been even larger than the Lake Missoula flood (peak discharge of ~636 million cfs); boulders more than 40 feet wide were transported on chunks of glacier ice, or "ice rafted," during flooding there (Herget 2005). Undoubtedly many other such events occurred, but without leaving clear records.

In the Southwest, rivers swelled enough toward the end of the Pleistocene to move large river cobbles hundreds of miles and to cause significant downcutting of channels. Pleistocene river cobbles from nearby mountains are found on large outwash terraces along the Green and Colorado rivers, suggesting very high discharges between 13,000 and 11,000 years ago (Webb et al. 2004). In fact, glacial melting may have caused significant downcutting through these canyons (Webb et al. 2004), including that of the Paria River, a tributary of the Colorado River (Fig. 2.4). According to Webb et al. (2001), flood deposits indicate that the bedrock channel of the Paria River may have been downcut as much as 60 feet in 20,000 years due to large Pleistocene flows. Glacial melt flows in the Colorado River may have reached 1 million cfs and deepened Glen Canyon to a depth of 800 feet within the last 500,000 years (Ranney 2005). Even part of the English Channel is thought to have been deepened by Pleistocene flooding (Herget 2005).

## Glaciers

Though shrinking rapidly today, glaciers still store most of the earth's freshwater, equivalent to about sixty years' worth of precipitation over the entire globe (Meier 1990). About 10 percent of the earth's surface remains covered by glacial ice, including both poles, Greenland, and various mountain regions throughout the world. Many of these glaciers are remnants of the extensive Pleistocene ice sheets.

Ever since the Little Ice Age of the eighteenth and nineteenth centuries, most of the world's glaciers have been receding. Some lost up to half of their mass in the twentieth century, and others disappeared (Meier 1990, Hambrey and Alean 2004). Glaciers in Africa and South America are disappearing particularly quickly, which will create major problems for large cities such as La

Paz, Bolivia, and Lima, Peru, which rely on these sources for drinking water, agriculture, and hydroelectric power (Hambrey and Alean 2004). In the Swiss Alps, the elevation above which glaciers are maintained is expected to rise by about 1,000 feet by 2035, at which time half of Switzerland's glaciers will be gone.

Some towns still receive their municipal water from glacial melt. Boulder, Colorado, for example, receives much of its water from Arapahoe glacier. In the late 1800s, Boulder purchased the watershed that includes this glacier and began to build reservoirs to catch its seasonal runoff. This watershed now covers 3,695 acres and includes thirteen reservoirs and natural lakes, but Arapahoe was reclassified as a snowfield in 1998 due to its shrinking size.

Ice loss in Greenland and Antarctica is occurring faster than was previously predicted (Rignot et al. 2008). Antarctica holds 90 percent of the world's ice, but the rate at which this ice mass is being lost has increased by 75 percent over the last ten years. If the entire Antarctic ice sheet melted, a volume of water greater than 7 million cubic miles would be added to the oceans. This would submerge many major cities, including London, New York, Buenos Aires, Calcutta, Shanghai, and Tokyo (Hambrey and Alean 2004).

Glaciers not only store freshwater but also helped to form soil in many parts of the world through abrasion of underlying rock surfaces. Glaciers in the western mountains still cause considerable erosion in the headwaters of streams (Foxworthy et al. 1988).

## Groundwater in Aquifers and Springs

Not including the water held in glacier ice, groundwater is thirty to forty times more plentiful than surface freshwater (Robson and Banta 1995).

There are five main aquifers or groups of aquifers that underlie most of the Southern Rockies and the Intermountain West in rock cavities and fractures (Robson and Banta 1995): the Basin and Range aquifer of the Great Basin and southern Arizona, the Colorado Plateau aquifer, the Rio Grande aquifer in northern New Mexico and southern Colorado, the massive High Plains aquifer that extends from Texas to South Dakota, and the Denver Basin aquifer along the eastern edge of the Colorado Rockies. Each regional aquifer is composed of many subaquifers. The Basin and Range and Colorado Plateau aquifers underlie most of the Great Basin and Intermountain West (Fig. 2.5). There are also many smaller, shallower groundwater sources in the region called *perched aquifers* that typically discharge only the current year's accumulation of precipitation.

The major western aquifers are found in fractured, consolidated rock layers or unconsolidated rocks such as clays and gravels. The Basin and Range, Rio Grande, and High Plains aquifers all occur in unconsolidated rock. Aquifers in the Great Basin often occur in basin-fill deposits of unconsolidated gravels, sands, silts, and clays that have eroded and washed down from the surrounding ranges. Some aquifers are bounded by these surrounding ranges, while others flow between them (Winograd and Thordarson 1975).

The Colorado Plateau aquifers lie in moderately to well-consolidated sedimentary rocks. They are classic aquifers—underground basins of water in caverns or fractured rocks. The four major aquifers in the Colorado Plateau group are separated from one another by thick, impermeable rock such as the dense Mancos and Chinle shales and Moenkopi sandstones. The Coconino–De Chelly aquifer is one of the most extensive, lying in Early Permian rocks (~280 Ma) that extend 1,000 feet below the surface. Groundwater in this aquifer generally flows toward lower-elevation discharge areas along the Colorado and Green rivers and their tributaries. Water from the Redwall aquifer, as well as some from the Coconino–De Chelly aquifer above it, feeds springs issuing from the Mississippian Redwall Limestone in the Grand Canyon. Fractures and channels in the rocks between the Coconino–De Chelly aquifer and the Redwall Limestone, and within the Redwall itself, provide conduits for this groundwater (Plate 8).

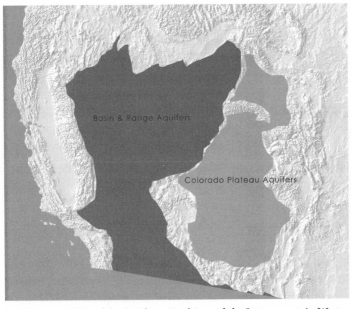

Basin & Range Aquifers

Colorado Plateau Aquifers

2.5. Major aquifers of the Southern Rockies and the Intermountain West.

The source of nearly all groundwater is rain and snow, and yet only about 5 percent of annual precipitation recharges aquifers (Robson and Banta 1995). In the closed Great Basin, up to 16 percent of annual precipitation recharges local and regional groundwater systems. Winter snowfall is the greatest source of recharge in higher-elevation watersheds (Jewett et al. 2004), but summer monsoon storms also provide some aquifer recharge on the Colorado Plateau.

The water in these aquifers can be thousands of years old. Within Grand Canyon, where numerous springs discharge from the Redwall Limestone, some springwater has been estimated to be between 1,500 and 3,000 years old (Monroe et al. 2005). A deep aquifer at Great Sand Dunes National Monument in south-central Colorado has water that has been carbon 14 dated at nearly 30,000 years old (Rupert and Plummer 2004). Water deep in the lower end of the Mohave River basin in southern California may be even older (Izbicki and Michel 2004).

*Springs*

Springs are a significant form of groundwater discharge. In many parts of western North America, they are the most reliable water sources and often feed into surface streams and lakes (Weixelman et al. 1996, Minckley and Unmack 2000, Stevens and Meretsky 2008). Because springs are often isolated and the only water source in parts of the West, they support a disproportionate number of plant and animal species, many of which are threatened and endangered.

The faulted rocks of the West provide more opportunities for water to discharge from aquifers, and there are far more springs there than in the flatlands of the Great Plains (Stevens and Meretsky 2008). Oregon has a higher density of springs per square mile than any other state, followed closely by Arizona. Kansas has the fewest springs of any state west of the Mississippi River.

Springs in the West include hot springs, hillside springs, limnocrene (or pool-forming) springs, hanging gardens, and rheocrene (or channel floor) springs (Stevens and Springer 2004). Hot springs are particularly common in areas such as Yellowstone National Park because volcanic and seismic activities are more recent and still occurring. The stretching of the Great Basin has produced a great many geothermal springs. Hillside springs are those emerging from slopes that are not subject to scouring floods. Limnocrene springs have large pools of open water, such as Montezuma's Well in central Arizona or the many springs in Ash Meadows, Nevada. Hanging gardens form where springs flow out of overhanging cliffs. Rheocrene springs are also common, but intense flooding of the channel floor limits the species associated with them.

For more than a hundred years, Flagstaff derived up to 70 percent of its municipal water from a lake and springs in the nearby San Francisco Peaks. Today, with a population of about 60,000 and still growing, the city receives less than 25 percent of its water from these sources. The rest comes from wells that have been drilled at the rate of nearly one every two years over the last twenty years. A changing and drying climate, along with population growth, has increased the demand for groundwater. Fortunately, Flagstaff is situated above the extensive Coconino aquifer.

## SURFACE WATER

Nearly all western rivers originate in the Rockies, the coastal ranges, and the mountains of the Intermountain West. Mountains concentrate water.

Surface water comes from precipitation (rain, snowmelt), glacial melt, and springs issuing from groundwater sources. In the Intermountain West, this water collects in the Colorado River basin and Great Basin. The former drains to the sea, while the latter is a closed, landlocked system (Fig. 2.4).

*The Great Basin*

The Great Basin's watershed extends from the Sierra Nevada in California to the Wasatch Range in eastern Utah, and from Oregon to southern Nevada. Nearly all of the water drains into Utah and Nevada. As a landlocked system, this vast region of closed basins is very different from that of the Colorado River, which used to flow into the Gulf of California before so many demands were made on it. The Great Basin is comprised of more than a hundred separate north-south-trending basins that receive seasonal runoff from surrounding mountains (Fig. 2.4). Although these basins are dry most of the year, ephemeral lakes do form in them (McMahon 2004). The longest river in the Great Basin, the Humboldt, runs about 300 miles, only a fraction of the Colorado's 1,400 miles.

The rivers and streams of the Great Basin ultimately become losing systems as they enter and infiltrate alluvial fans, where all surface water evaporates, is transpired by plants, or percolates into aquifers (Jewett et al. 2004). Not surprisingly, the hydrology of the Great Basin is highly complex due to its many basins and internal drainage (Mifflin 1988). Local flow regimes within basins are characterized by surface and groundwater discharges that vary greatly by season, and there is little or no transfer of water between basins (Jewett et al. 2004).

The Great Basin encompasses nearly 200,000 square miles, including most of Nevada, the western third of Utah, and smaller portions of California, Idaho, Oregon, and Wyoming. The mountain ranges in the central Great Basin are characterized by many small watersheds (less than 40 square miles) that terminate in alluvial fans flanking the many intermountain basins (Miller et al. 2004). Precipitation ranges from about 30 to 40 inches in the highest mountains, to less than 5 inches per year in the driest western region (DeCourten 2003). Melting of winter snowpack leads to increased stream flow during springtime. As spring runoff decreases, groundwater becomes the primary source of stream flow (Jewett et al. 2004).

The lakes and rivers of the Great Basin are still classified according to which lake system they belonged to during the Pleistocene (Houghton 1994). The Lake Lahontan system includes the westernmost set of lakes and rivers that once fed or lay within that massive Pleistocene lake (Figs. 2.3, 2.4). It covered 8,600 square miles at its maximum stage, some 13,000 years ago (DeCourten 2003). Its rivers include the Truckee, Carson, and Walker rivers, all of which descend from the east side of the Sierra Nevada (Fig. 2.4). The longest and most complex basin is that of the Humboldt River, which carries water from the East Humboldt, Ruby, Independence, Toiyabe, Shoshone, and Santa Rosa mountains to the southwest, with most water ending up in the Humboldt Sink (Houghton 1994). Most of the basins associated with these rivers are now fairly dry due to water diversions. Exceptions include Pyramid and Walker lakes and, of course, Lake Tahoe.

Lake Tahoe appears much the same as it has for thousands of years, covering 193 square miles and having a depth greater than 1,630 feet (Houghton 1994). More than sixty creeks and drainage basins supply water to the lake. Its only outlet is the Truckee River, which flows northeastward to Pyramid Lake (Fig. 2.4). Along its 140-mile course there are sediment terraces 20 to 30 feet above the river that may reflect flows during Pleistocene times.

The dramatic Pyramid Lake lies in an alkali flat within Nevada's Black Rock Desert (Plate 9). Its basin is over 25 miles long and varies from 4 to 11 miles wide. Pyramid Lake was the deepest point of Lake Lahontan, measuring some 900 feet below the surface (DeCourten 2003). Like most Great Basin lakes today, it is a losing system, with tributaries contributing less and less water over time. Its dramatic rock outcrops are composed of tufa, a durable calcium carbonate ($CaCO_3$) precipitated from supersaturated waters entering the cold lake from springs (Houghton 1994). Despite high salinity, Pyramid Lake supports several endemic fishes.

The Humboldt River travels 300 miles and drains the largest watershed in the Great Basin, about 16,600 square miles (Fig. 2.4). The Humboldt is the only permanent stream that flows through the Great Basin (DeCourten 2003); however, because the region it drains is one of the driest in the Intermountain West, the Humboldt is characterized by very low stream flow relative to the size of its watershed (Miller et al. 2004). The river's average annual discharge is less than 400 cfs, based on a ninety-seven-year average, and it empties into the saline Humboldt Sink only in years with higher than average precipitation.

Death Valley, at the southwest edge of the Great Basin, is a deep and narrow trough along the southwest border of Nevada. It is recent in origin, having formed within the last several million years as a result of faulting (Houghton 1994). During the Pleistocene it received considerable flow from many

rivers, including the Owens River to the north and the Mohave and Amargosa rivers to the south. Today the Amargosa River and springs such as those in Ash Valley supply water to Death Valley (Houghton 1994, Bushman et al. 2010). Although intermittent, the river continues to flow through Amargosa Canyon, where it supports a small riparian habitat. The Amargosa River's intermittent flow results from its water traveling underground in some reaches, as also occurs in a number of other Basin and Range rivers (Houghton 1994). Farther along its course, the Amargosa becomes highly saline, prompting Hubbs and Miller (1948) to refer to it as "an artery of salt running through the desert." It enters Death Valley from the south and flows northward, disappearing underground in Badwater Basin (the lowest point in North America at 282 feet below sea level), where it feeds the aquifer that is the remnant of a prehistoric lake. During the Pleistocene, Lake Manly filled the lower part of Death Valley and spanned some 90 miles, with a depth of 600 feet (La Rivers 1994, DeCourten 2003). Many of its terraces can still be seen today. With its extensive faulting, Death Valley hosts many thermal, often saline springs that support several endemic fish whose distributions reveal much of the history of this region's waterways.

The Lake Bonneville drainage system included nearly all of the northeastern Great Basin during the last glacial phase of the Pleistocene about 16,000 years ago (Fig. 2.3; Houghton 1994). Lake Bonneville was the largest of the pluvial lakes, up to 1,000 feet deep and covering some 20,000 square miles (DeCourten 2003). It was a freshwater lake, fed mainly by runoff from the Wasatch and Uinta mountains (DeCourten 2003). As many as seven separate sub-basins were connected into Lake Bonneville (Sacks 2002).

The Great Salt Lake, at 1,700 square miles, is the largest salt lake in North America, and yet it is only one-fourteenth the size of Lake Bonneville (Fig. 2.4). It now lies in the salt desert left behind by Lake Bonneville (Plates 10 and 11), and it is saltier than the world's oceans. The salinity of its waters reaches more than 25 percent when lake levels are low, making it uninhabitable for most creatures other than salt-tolerant brine shrimp, brine flies, and algae. A railroad causeway separates the northern and eastern portions from the main body of the lake, creating less-saline sections that provide critical habitat for millions of shorebirds and waterfowl.

The Bear, Weber, and Jordan rivers, which drain the northern portion of the Wasatch Range, are the main tributaries of the Great Salt Lake. The Sevier River drains the southern end of the Wasatch Range and feeds Sevier Lake, which is dry in some years. During the Pleistocene, this river system flowed into Lake Bonneville.

Although the Lake Lahontan and Lake Bonneville systems encompassed many enormous lakes and rivers, only smaller and more isolated lakes formed in the central Great Basin during the Pleistocene (DeCourten 2003). This may have been due to the closer proximity of Lake Lahontan and Lake Bonneville to larger mountain ranges and their snowmelt, and to their lower elevation (DeCourten 2003). Today drainages of the central Great Basin are often characterized as "sterile basins" because so few fish are associated with their few springs (Houghton 1994).

Last but not least, in the southeastern corner of the Great Basin in Nevada, the pluvial White River drains the eastern slopes of White Pine Ridge near Ely and travels southeast, where it connects with the Muddy River and then the Colorado River

in Lake Mead (Fig. 2.4). Large sections of its 200-mile course are dry today, but the White River flowed all the way to the Colorado River during the Pleistocene. And even though it occurs in the Great Basin, its endemic fishes are more closely related to Colorado River fishes, further revealing the importance of its earlier connections during the Pleistocene (Miller 1961).

Today there are few surface water connections between the Colorado River basin and the Great Basin. The same is generally true for groundwater, though there are exceptions, including several basins near the Ruby Mountains in central Nevada from which groundwater drains south into the Colorado River (Winograd and Thordarson 1975).

### The Colorado River Basin

The Colorado River starts in lakes in both the Rocky Mountains of Colorado and the Wind River Range in Wyoming, and travels in a southwesterly direction for more than 1,450 miles to the Gulf of California. The Colorado River drainage basin covers more than 246,000 square miles, the seventh largest of North American rivers (Fig. 2.4). Before it was dammed, the Colorado carried 1.4 to 4.3 cubic miles of water each year to its delta in Mexico.

This immense drainage basin cuts through many undeformed sedimentary layers across the Colorado Plateau. Through a combination of faulting, uplifting, and the erosive power of running water, geologic layers more than a mile deep are exposed at points along the Colorado River's journey to the sea.

Major tributaries of the Colorado River include the Green, Gunnison, Yampa, and Dolores rivers in Colorado; the Escalante and Virgin rivers in Utah; the San Juan River in Colorado, New Mexico, and Utah; and the Little Colorado River in Arizona (Fig. 2.4). The Green River is the Colorado's largest and longest tributary, contributing nearly half of its total flow. (Political considerations resulted in naming the combined rivers the Colorado rather than the Green.)

Despite large runoff flows, the Colorado River basin is considered one of the driest in the world (Stanford and Ward 1986). Although 75 percent of its water comes from snowmelt in its mountainous headwaters, most of the catchment basins lie in semiarid desert. Evaporation rates at lower elevations are very high, with as much as 5 feet per year evaporating from the surface of Lake Powell in southern Utah (Andrews 1990).

There are also heavy demands on the Colorado River, making it one of the most regulated rivers in the world (Blinn and Poff 2005). Today there are forty large dams along the Colorado, and their reservoirs collectively hold 59 million acre feet of water, with Lake Powell and Lake Mead holding 50 million acre feet (Mueller and Marsh 2002). More than 60 percent of runoff is used for irrigation (Blinn and Poff 2005). Diversions carry water to many western cities, including Denver, Phoenix, and Tucson.

The formation of the Colorado River drainage basin is a highly controversial topic that may never be resolved. It does appear, though, that by about 5 Ma a river was flowing from the Colorado Rocky Mountains to the Gulf of California (Ranney 2005, Spencer et al. 2008). There are four main hypotheses about its formation: (1) channel development occurring in an upstream fashion through headward erosion, capturing other streams along the way (stream piracy); (2) formation of multiple regional lakes that ultimately carved connecting channels; (3) an initial flow from west to east before the river reversed to its present east-west

direction; and (4) significant deepening of parts of the river system during the Pleistocene due to enormous glacial melt flooding (Ranney 2005). Recent DNA studies of Colorado River basin fishes have revealed distinct differences between upper and lower basin fishes that put the date of connection between the two basins at about 5 Ma (Spencer et al. 2008). We may never know whether one or all of these theories are relevant to the Colorado River basin's formation, but the debate is fascinating.

When talking about the Colorado and other western rivers, you almost have to have two separate conversations: one about how things used to be, and one about how they are today. Western rivers have been utterly transformed by humans and their technology. Heavy river regulation, and especially damming, has had largely negative effects on this ecosystem, though some surprising and positive effects have also occurred. Dams have blocked the movement of water, sediment, plants, and animals, and have altered water temperatures and chemistry, resulting in additional ecological changes throughout the system.

Before much of the Colorado River was dammed starting in the 1930s, major springtime floods roared through the canyons between April and June as mountain snowpack melted. In addition to enormous volumes of water, these floods also carried sediment and organic material that revitalized river channels and beaches. These seasonal floods historically had an average peak of about 86,000 cfs, yet often exceeded 100,000 cfs (Johnson 1990). Historical floods in 1884 and 1921 carried up to 210,000 cfs and 170,000 cfs, respectively (Fig. 2.6; Topping et al. 2003). After floodwaters receded each year, flows were less than 8,000 cfs (Topping et al. 2003). There were also large

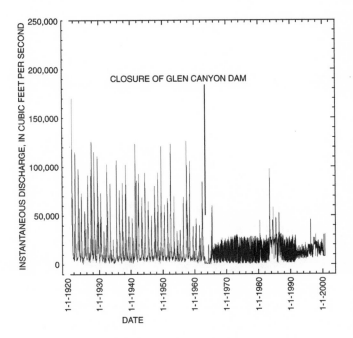

**2.6.** Annual high flows in the Colorado River in Grand Canyon, 1920–2000. Note the sharp drop in flows following the completion of Glen Canyon Dam in 1963, and then the post-dam flood spike in 1983. Courtesy of Topping et al., U.S. Geological Survey, 2003.

97,000 cfs through the dam's generators, outlet jets, and spillways (Fig. 2.6). This event provided an opportunity to see what flooding was like before the Colorado was dammed. More than 50 percent of the shoreline vegetation was scoured away (Stevens and Waring 1988), and because the dammed river was running clear and sediment-hungry, the 1983 flood also stripped fine sediments such as silts and clays away from beaches, leaving behind only coarse sand.

Before it was dammed, the Colorado River had some of the most sediment-laden waters in North America. Its average annual sediment load before construction of Glen Canyon Dam was nearly 91 million tons (Topping et al. 2003). Although most of the Colorado's water comes from headwaters near the crest of the Rocky Mountains, most of its sediment load—made up of silts, clays, and sands—comes from lower, drier parts of the basin (Wolman et al. 1990). While the arid Colorado Plateau below the mountains encompasses 37 percent of the basin's total drainage area, it delivers just 15 percent of the total runoff, but over 80 percent of the sediment (Blinn and Poff 2005). Most of the sediment is from tributaries in southeastern Utah, northeastern Arizona, and northwestern New Mexico, all in the center of the Colorado Plateau (Andrews 1990). The most conspicuous sediment sources are the soft shales and mudstones of the Wasatch, Mancos, Morrison, Chinle, and Moenkopi formations (Wolman et al. 1990).

floods in 1957 and 1958 (125,000 and 108,000 cfs, respectively). On occasion, flooding from summer monsoon rains can also occur. As destructive as it can be, flooding is a critical natural disturbance that keeps river systems healthy.

Glen Canyon Dam, completed in 1963, has limited the downstream flow of water in the Colorado River, holding most of it back in Lake Powell, which provides water storage and hydroelectric power for western states (Fig. 2.6). Nevertheless, the Colorado River below Lake Powell also flooded in 1983, nearly thirty years after it was dammed! A combination of El Niño effects, the recent filling of Lake Powell in 1980, and above-average snowpack in the Rockies converged to create pre-dam-like flooding in this regulated system. With the reservoir overfilling and enormous runoff still expected, the Bureau of Reclamation released as much as

**2.7.** Delta formation near Hite, Utah, where the upper Colorado River meets the slack water of Lake Powell, 1998. All of the land in the foreground is composed of sediment deposited by the Colorado River. Courtesy of William Vernieu, U.S. Geological Survey.

One tributary of the Colorado, the Paria River, has at times carried a greater concentration of suspended sediment than any other river in North America; concentrations of up to 2 pounds of sediment per quart make its water hypersaturated. The Paria River drains about 1,400 square miles of sedimentary rocks in southern Utah and northern Arizona, and most of its headwaters originate in soft Tropic Shale (Fig. 2.4; Webb et al. 2001).

Sediment loads carried by flooding are larger in western streams because the West is a dry region with sparse vegetation and often poorly developed soils, especially at lower, drier elevations, leading to greater erosion (Fisher 1995). The smaller amount of sediment carried in eastern rivers is attributed, in part, to the erosion-resistant nature of the Canadian Shield through which they travel (Meade et al. 1990).

Most of the sediment now carried by the Colorado River settles out where it meets the slack water of reservoirs such as Lake Powell and Lake Mead, which have formed behind the dams. Between 1935, when Hoover Dam was completed on the lower Colorado, until Glen Canyon Dam was completed in 1963, the annual sediment accumulation rate in Lake Mead from the upper Colorado River was 91,450 acre feet (Lara and Sanders 1970). By 1964, 2,720,000 acre feet of sediment had accumulated in the form of massive deltas. Enormous deltas also formed where the Colorado River and its tributaries meet Lake Powell (Fig. 2.7). Where these deltas of sediment have become established, extensive and diverse riparian communities have quickly formed, at least when lake levels are high enough. These deltas are made up of clays and silts so fine that they are difficult to get off your shoes. With their smaller diameter, they bind both water and fine nutrients, resulting in beaches that are ideal for rapid plant establishment and growth. Beaches in the Grand Canyon, however, have been stripped of fine sediment by the river, leaving mainly coarse sand that holds little water or nutrients and quickly blows away.

**2.8.** Coyote willow colonizing a beach in the Grand Canyon, 1992. Courtesy of Larry Stevens.

animals, providing water, food, and habitat for species as diverse as lizards and desert bighorn sheep. The basis for this diversity starts with riparian plants such as willows and cottonwoods, which are fast-growing and highly productive.

At the higher elevations in the Colorado Rockies and the Wind River Range in Wyoming, there is little difference between plant communities along headwater streams and those occurring away from streams since there is more water throughout. Riparian and montane plants readily mix at these cooler, wetter elevations. In these mountainous areas, spruce, fir, aspen, narrowleaf cottonwood, water birch, willow, wild rose, and currant occur together, along with meadows of grasses, sedges, and forbs. The same species are found along stream headwaters in the Great Basin (Weixelman et al. 1996, Chambers and Miller 2004).

Farther downstream, in the semiarid basins across the Colorado Plateau and the Great Basin, riparian plants differ entirely from neighboring desert plants. Coyote willow (*Salix exigua*; Fig. 2.8), which is dominant along shorelines, cannot live more than about 6 feet above a stream channel (Weixelman et al. 1996). Their dependence on water prevents riparian plant communities from spreading very far from the shoreline, resulting in thin, green lines of vegetation crossing through an increasingly arid landscape. The surrounding desert plants are also limited in their range; they are

Because sediment is no longer being replaced in reaches below the dams, beaches are becoming smaller and disappearing. The suspended sediment load of the Colorado River below Glen Canyon Dam has declined by as much as 95 percent (Andrews 1990). The annual sediment load in the Colorado River through Grand Canyon has declined from 91 million tons to about 12 million tons, with the latter coming from the Paria and Little Colorado rivers, which occur below Glen Canyon Dam (Andrews 1990).

## Riparian Communities

The ecological importance of riparian, or shoreline, ecosystems in the arid West cannot be overstated (Carothers et al. 1979). These ecosystems are bastions of biodiversity, more so than any other in the West. While riparian habitats encompass less than 1 percent of western land, they support many plant and animal species, and they are systems at risk (Webb et al. 2007, Baker et al. 2004, Niemeyer and Fleischner 2005, Malanson 1993, Bennett and Simon 2004). Riparian habitats also support numerous upland intolerant of water, and for them the shoreline is too wet.

It is downstream, as these rivers become larger, that they really assert themselves on riparian ecosystems. In the Colorado River drainage basin, especially before damming, rivers picked up mass and volume as many drainages converged, leading to large-scale seasonal flooding events. Prior to damming, there was little vegetation along the Colorado in Grand Canyon because powerful spring floods scoured plants away (Waring 1996a). The disturbance caused by these powerful floodwaters constituted a strong form of natural selection for river-dwelling plants and animals.

Riparian ecosystems are strongest and healthiest with occasional flooding. The plants are adapted to being underwater for long periods of time and to being beaten up or pulled up from time to time by intense flooding, with perhaps some part reestablishing on a riverbank downstream. Floodwaters rejuvenate riparian ecosystems by bringing in much needed fine sediment, nutrients, and water. These pulses of resources and disturbance allow riparian plants to grow vigorously. Floods open up ecosystems, permitting the establishment of new plants that need open, sunny beaches. It is no coincidence that coyote willow and Fremont cottonwood release their seeds as spring floods subside.

## Plant Communities and Bedrock Type

Plant communities along the Colorado River vary from mile-wide riparian forests to thin strands of coyote willow—and everything in between. The size of each community is determined by the type of rock the river is passing through. This was true before the Colorado was dammed, and it is still the case today. Generally speaking, riparian plant communities along the Colorado are more extensive where the river and its tributaries travel through sandstone, which is a softer sedimentary rock that is easily eroded by wind and water. Rivers can carve sandstone into wide, low-gradient floodplains, allowing the river to spread out and move through more slowly. When floodwaters slow down in such settings, valuable sediment is deposited, and where it accumulates, colonizing plants are able to persist and thrive. Enormous stands of vegetation can develop in such floodplains, including large stands of coyote willow, forests of Fremont cottonwood, and thickets of Goodding willow. By contrast, hard limestones and crystalline strata such as basalt and schist force the river to carve narrower, steeper canyons. Floodwaters move faster, carrying all the sediment downstream, and colonizing plants are typically washed away (Fig. 2.9). Riparian trees are rare in such settings (Stevens et al. 1995). There are several great examples of this process where the Colorado River passes through sandstone and then immediately through a layer of limestone. The associated riparian plant communities are abruptly transformed from large stands of trees into thin lines of vegetation (Fig. 2.9).

Glen Canyon is gone now; it lies behind Glen Canyon Dam, under 500 feet of water in Lake Powell. Before the dam was completed in 1963, the Colorado's floodwaters moved gently through the sandstone of Glen Canyon and then picked up the pace and raged through the limestone of Grand Canyon just downstream. According to a biological survey conducted in the 1950s to record what natural resources would be lost due to damming, Glen Canyon hosted extensive stands of riparian vegetation (Flowers 1959), including coyote willow, Goodding willow, seep willow, tamarisk, and arrowweed.

Most of Glen Canyon's riparian communities ranged in width from 10 to 60 feet, but where side canyons entered, they became dense jungles more than 200 yards across. In places, shrubs and trees reached 40 feet in height. Then, as today, coyote willow was the most abundant riparian plant. Its trunks regularly grew to 2 to 4 inches in diameter, and occasionally up to 11 inches. The areal extent of these communities, the large size of coyote willow, and the presence of Goodding willow trees all indicate that these were stable communities despite annual flooding. Gerald Smith, a member of the team that conducted the survey, recalls that getting from the shoreline to the uplands of Glen Canyon was very difficult due to the dense stands of riparian plants (personal communication, 2006).

Historical aerial photographs show that in contrast to Glen Canyon, there was very little riparian vegetation in Grand Canyon, just downstream (Turner and Karpiscak 1980, Waring 1996a,b, Webb 1996), because spring floodwaters reaching 85,000 cfs or more raged through the steep, narrow limestone canyon in most years, scouring away the streamside vegetation.

Glen Canyon is carved through soft Triassic sandstones, including Navajo Sandstone, while Grand Canyon rocks at river level are predominantly harder limestones and crystalline rocks. Consequently, the river's gradient in Grand Canyon is about four times steeper than it was in Glen Canyon (0.004 feet versus 0.00115 feet per yard). Its channel was about half as wide (240 versus 490 feet), and it had nine times greater stream power than in Glen Canyon (Mackley 2005).

The San Juan River below Bluff, Utah, travels through a wide floodplain cut into Navajo Sandstone and then into a steep, narrow limestone canyon. The upper floodplain is a mile wide in places and is often covered with a dense cottonwood forest. The San Juan River moves through it as a calm,

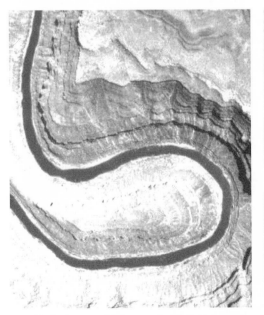 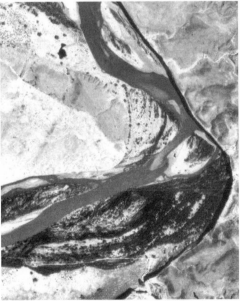

**2.9.** Aerial photos of the San Juan River in southeastern Utah showing sparse riparian vegetation in a narrow limestone canyon (*left*) versus dense riparian vegetation growing in a wide, flat sandstone floodplain, 1990s. Courtesy of the U.S. Geological Survey.

flat river, but just downstream the river drops into a steep, narrow limestone canyon exposed in the Monument Upwarp. Here there are no cottonwoods, only a thin strandline of coyote willow (Fig. 2.9).

## PLANTS AND DAMS

The effects of dams on riparian ecosystems have been largely, though not entirely, negative. The shorelines of the Colorado River in Grand Canyon were kept clear of streamside plants until the completion of Glen Canyon Dam, after which riparian vegetation increased by more than 160 percent (Waring 1996a, b).

Before the Colorado was dammed, perennial plants were found only above the annual flooding zone. Western honey mesquite trees are known to have persisted there for more than 500 years (Hereford et al. 1996). These plants are now perched high and dry, 30 feet above the river, and western honey mesquite and catclaw acacia persist only because their long taproots can still access the water table. Although they are not replacing themselves above the old flood zone, their offspring are gradually colonizing the current shoreline. The nitrogen-fixing habits of legumes such as mesquites and acacias contribute nitrogen to soils that now receive few nutrients from the river due to a lack of flood-related sediment deposition.

Prior to construction of Glen Canyon Dam, there were as few as ten marshes along the Colorado River in Grand Canyon. Following damming and a reduction in scouring floods, more than 1,100 riverside marshes had formed by 1991 (Stevens et al. 1995). Marshes, which are among the most productive habitats in the world (Sigler and Sigler 1996), are found along western rivers, and in Grand Canyon they form where fine sediment and nutrients accumulate

along backwater or eddy sections and wide stretches with a low gradient (Stevens et al. 1995). Plant diversity is greatest in marshes, and common species include cattails, sedges, rushes, and common reed. Diversity of marsh plants can be as high as about 5 species per 3 square feet; however, without periodic flooding disturbance, one species or another will come to dominate, and marsh diversity will decline (Stevens et al. 1995). Many animals, including the endangered willow flycatcher, are highly dependent on river marshes. Some people consider the increase of resources such as marshes as some compensation for the loss of habitat upstream in Glen Canyon (Risser and Harris 1989).

Coyote willow clones, or thickets, respond to reduced flooding disturbance by becoming larger and more heavily branched. A study comparing coyote willow clones on dammed and undammed rivers in California showed that on the dammed river there were fewer, though larger clones, reflecting a decline in the genetic diversity of coyote willows (Douhovnikoff et al. 2005). These larger coyote willows may be less genetically diverse, but they provide more abundant resources and habitats for many animals.

Post-dam floods, when they do occur, reveal a great deal about how natural flooding once affected these ecosystems. The flooding in Grand Canyon in 1983 was reminiscent of pre-dam floods and yet very different in some ways. A sequence of photos taken at 43-mile sandbar along the dammed Colorado River provides a good example (Figs. 2.10, 2.11). This sandbar became heavily vegetated because of a lack of flooding for nearly twenty years. In June 1983 a massive flood scoured away the entire sandbar, which is precisely what happened to shoreline vegetation every year before the river

**2.11.** The 43-mile sandbar in 1991 (*top*) and in 2005, after flooding and recolonization by tamarisk and coyote willow. Courtesy of Larry Stevens.

**2.10.** Effects of flooding at the 43-mile sandbar along the Colorado River in Grand Canyon: *top to bottom*, in June 1980 the sandbar was heavily vegetated with coyote willow (*Salix exigua*), seep willow (*Baccharis salicifolia*), and cattail (*Typha latifolia*); in June 1983 the sandbar was flooded and scoured; by August 1984 the sandbar had been redeposited. Courtesy of Larry Stevens.

was dammed. Receding floodwaters deposited new sand, and by August 1984 the sandbar had formed again (Fig. 2.10). Colonization of this sandbar by plants has been poor, even after more than twenty years, because the sand that rebuilt it was much coarser and drier than what was deposited in pre-dam days (Fig. 2.11). This has kept native coyote willow from recolonizing most of the beach that it had previously dominated (Larry Stevens, personal communication).

Riparian trees such as Goodding willow and Fremont cottonwood are thought to require wet, nutrient-rich soils to establish and grow as quickly as they do, but a dendrochronological study (tree ring analysis) of Goodding willow in Grand Canyon (Waring 1996a, b, Mast and Waring 1996) found that, in fact, most individuals living along the Colorado River today became established after the river was dammed in 1963, and *especially* after the 1983 post-dam flood (Fig. 2.12). This is a very encouraging finding, though Goodding willow populations are still at risk. One of the few species of tree willows in the southwestern United States, Goodding willow grows to 50 feet and may live more than a hundred years. These days, forests of Goodding willow occur where the Colorado River runs into the slack water of Lake Mead, where massive deposits of fine sediment settle into large deltas that are ideal germination habitats (Plate 12). These willow forests are unique in the West, especially given the region's considerable loss of riparian habitats.

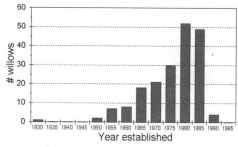

Goodding Willows Establishment

**2.12.** A dense young forest (*left*) of Goodding willow (*Salix gooddingii*) in a delta formed where the Colorado River meets Lake Mead, 1996. The graph (*right*) shows that after the Colorado River was dammed in 1963, Goodding willow were still able to establish in these rich, lower delta soils in 1980 and 1985, years with post-dam flooding. Courtesy of Gwendolyn Waring and the U.S. Geological Survey.

## OTHER PLANTS

At lower elevations in the Colorado River drainage basin, the most common woody shoreline species are willow, alder, water birch, Fremont cottonwood, box elder, Goodding willow, seep willow, arrowweed, desert olive, western honey mesquite, and nonnative tamarisk and Russian olive. Deltas and marshes along the lower Colorado are colonized by cattail, bulrush, sedge, and common reed, which provide critical habitat for many birds.

Of course, many other native plants live in riparian zones along smaller streams or in side canyons, such as the beautiful redbud, native grape, and an enormous variety of shrubs, herbs, grasses, and wetland species. Stevens and Ayers (2002) reported that nearly half of the plant species in Grand Canyon are found in or on the edge of riparian habitats.

Willow and cottonwood are among the most important riparian plants in the West. They are also abundant through temperate portions of the Northern Hemisphere. Some willows extend into the mountains of North America and the Arctic. Willow and cottonwood are tied closely to perennial water sources at lower elevations, but at higher elevations they can occur along intermittent streams. There are about twenty species of willow in Utah; at least sixteen of them have ranges that extend from the Arctic and Canada to Mexico (Welsh et al. 1993). Many of these are upland species that have migrated down through the Rockies, often from populations at higher latitudes throughout the Northern Hemisphere.

Willow and cottonwood are dioecious, meaning female and male flowers are produced in separate plants. Willow are commonly pollinated by bees (Stevens 1985), while cottonwood flowers are wind pollinated (Welsh et al. 1993). Willows are important colonizing species in riparian habitats. Their small, short-lived seeds are typically released as spring floods subside in the West. They are geared to colonize newly flooded, wet beaches that are sunny and recharged with fine-grained sediment and nutrients, as in the pre-dam days. With these resources, willow and cottonwood have phenomenal growth rates. Stems of establishing plants easily grow more than 3 feet during a single growing season. Because they are so productive, willows support a greater diversity of animals than most other plants (Southwood 1961). Willows, in particular, were very successful in colonizing glacier-worked soils as Pleistocene glaciers retreated.

Willows are renowned for being tolerant of high concentrations of trace elements such as copper, lead, nickel, arsenic, cadmium, and zinc, all of which can increase in soils due to mining and industrial activities (Hansen and Massey 1999). Apparently, willows are able to concentrate these metals in their roots, which prevents their translocation through the plant. It is thought that this mechanism evolved to protect the trees' photosynthetic ability from damage by floodplain contaminants. Coyote willow is also tolerant of low levels of salinity, which may explain why it is so common along drainages in the Great Basin.

Coyote willow is the most common willow at lower elevations (below 7,000 feet) along Colorado River basin and Great Basin rivers. It is also one of the most widespread willows in North America. Its distinctive clonal growth form, which is unusual in willows, contributes enormously to its great success along lower-elevation rivers and streams that experience the greatest flooding. A coyote willow clone produces a diffuse system of wandlike stems that may colonize an entire beach (Fig. 2.8). Clones of up to 1,000 square feet have been found (Douhovnikoff et al. 2005). This species is shallow-rooted and, consequently, readily scoured away by floodwaters, but even a small piece of a stem can establish itself and colonize a new beach. I saw this firsthand along the Colorado River following flooding in 1983. A lone coyote willow growing out of a newly scoured, large beach was excavated and found to have been established by a 6-inch piece of beaver-cut stem that had been deposited by the flood. Similarly, if even a small portion of a clone remains along the back of a beach following flooding,

new underground stems, or rhizomes, are quickly sent out toward the shoreline, somehow sensing the direction of the water. This also occurred along the Colorado after the 1983 flood. A beach covered with coyote willows was scoured away and was then re-formed with deposited sand. Lines of willow stems advanced from the back of the beach toward the shoreline at a rate of 30 feet per year (Stevens and Waring 1988).

Few western willow species reach the abundance of either coyote willow or Goodding willow. Arroyo willow is an upland species that often dominates drainages above 7,000 feet. At first glance an arroyo willow appears to be a series of large shrubs or subtrees, but as revealed in an excavation in a northern Arizona drainage, many of the "shrubs" are actually branches of a form that resembles an underground tree (Craig et al. 1988). It may be that such an enormous underground form helps to hold water in intermittent western streams and hold the plant in place during severe flooding.

Cottonwoods in the West occur in floodplains and the side canyons of large rivers, although rarely in limestone canyons. Like willows, cottonwoods are typically short-lived, rarely exceeding 100 years in age. Within that time, however, they can become very large, reaching more than 50 feet in height with enormous trunks and canopies. Fremont cottonwoods (Fig. 2.13) are most common at lower elevations in the Southwest. At higher elevations and latitudes, narrowleaf cottonwood and black cottonwood are more common.

Seep willow is a composite shrub that favors rocky shorelines along rivers in the Colorado River drainage basin and in the southern Great Basin. Through the rocky, soil-limited reaches of Grand Canyon's deep gorges, seep willow is often the only shoreline plant to be found. There are at least three species in Grand Canyon.

Long-leaf brickellbush is one of the only riparian plants seen in the dry canyons of Arizona, Utah, Nevada, and California where streams flow only intermittently (Fig. 2.14). This small shrub with its distinctive white bark has its own niche in such western canyons because of its ability to tolerate both extended dry periods *and* violent flash floods. Often brickellbush may have a rather flattened and beat-up appearance, indicating that a flash flood with lots of water and debris has recently passed through.

**2.13.** A forest of Fremont cottonwood (*Populus fremontii*) along the San Juan River, Sand Island, Utah.

## Nonnative Plants

Today, the world is being overrun by nonnative plants. They are particularly common in riparian habitats, and their ecological impacts can be enormous (Stevens and Ayers 2002). Tamarisk, or salt cedar (Fig. 2.15), and Russian olive were

**2.14.** Brickellbush (*Brickellia longifolia*), Grand Canyon, Arizona. Brickellbush is one of the few riparian shrubs that can tolerate intermittent flooding with scouring damage and then prolonged drying.

both introduced into North America from the Middle East in the early 1800s for bank stabilization (they have strong root systems), as wind breaks, and as ornamental plants. They both escaped cultivation and have been aggressively colonizing western riparian habitats ever since. Both species now have extensive distributions along rivers and streams in western North America.

Tamarisk is often more common than native coyote willow at lower elevations in the Colorado River drainage basin. An individual tamarisk may produce more than

150 million seeds annually (Stevens 1989). Its feathery leaves readily secrete and concentrate salts in underlying soils, making them uninhabitable for native plants. Few insects feed on tamarisk, except for a sap-sucking leafhopper that was inadvertently introduced with it from the Middle East. This lack of herbivores means that as tamarisk comes to dominate shorelines in dense thickets, the resources offered to animals by native plants diminish, though there are exceptions (discussed further below). Tamarisk, like all riparian plants, evapotranspires

**2.15.** Nonnative tamarisk (*Tamarix* sp.) in bloom. Also known as salt cedar, it was introduced from the Middle East in the late 1800s and quickly spread throughout the West. Courtesy of Larry Stevens.

more water through its leaves than do upland plants. Dense stands of tamarisk can lower water tables associated with intermittent streams and dry up springs. Its strong root systems harden or stabilize shorelines, especially along dammed rivers, so that river channels become entrenched and cease to meander. This limits riparian plants to even narrower distributions along rivers and streams. Although tamarisk is a highly invasive species, it is replaced on occasion by coyote willow, which simply sends runners out in front of it along the Colorado River, and by seep willow along the lower San Juan River and in Cataract Canyon (Stevens 1989; Waring, personal observation, 1995; Webb et al. 2004).

As tamarisk has become widespread along western rivers, it is increasingly used by several native bird species, including the endangered southwestern willow flycatcher. Having lost much of its native habitat, this bird, along with a growing number of obligate riparian breeding species, now preferentially nests in tamarisk (Brown and Trossett 1989).

The only other good thing to say about tamarisk is that it's not as bad as Russian olive. Even fewer insects, except for pollinators, feed on Russian olive than on tamarisk. Russian olive has only a very transient group of plant-feeding insects associated with it. Along the San Juan River, coyote willow was found to support eight times more insect herbivore species, and ten to twenty times more herbivores than Russian olive (Waring 1993). Not surprisingly, there are fewer bird species and smaller bird populations associated with Russian olives than with native trees along the Snake River in Idaho (Brown 1990). This difference is most pronounced during the breeding season, when insect densities are also highest on native plants. Russian olive has overtaken the banks of much of the San Juan River in Utah in less than thirty years, and this transforming invasion is ongoing throughout the United States (Knopf et al. 1988). Many attributes make Russian olive successful along today's dammed rivers. Because it is a nitrogen-fixing species, it can grow more quickly than native plants, and it produces an abundance of very large and durable seeds that are dispersed by the river and by birds. Its seedlings are shade tolerant, so it can establish under native plant canopies and quickly overtop them.

## Shoreline Animals

In the West, animals, like plants, concentrate along the shorelines of rivers and streams to a stunning degree. This is due not just to the presence of water itself, but also to the great productivity of riparian vegetation.

Insects on riparian plants are diverse and abundant, and represent important resources for the invertebrates and vertebrates that live along rivers and streams, as well as for visiting animals. Coyote willow foliage on the San Juan River produced more than twenty herbivorous insect species per one hundred sweeps with a sweepnet (Waring 1993). There are also large numbers of invertebrate predators and parasites associated with these herbivores, resulting in complex communities.

Riparian mammals include beavers, otters, muskrats, and bats. Beavers feed on the bark of both willow and cottonwood. They also girdle and down large cottonwood trees, often killing them, in an effort to grind down their indeterminant teeth. Beavers are widespread throughout North America, and their habit of killing selected tree species and damming streams can transform riparian forests (Johnston and Naiman 1990, Mortenson et al. 2008). In the Colorado River basin, they exhibit highly flexible behavior as to where and how they construct their dens. Along smaller streams in the system, such as Spencer Canyon in the lower Grand Canyon, they dam channels and convert desert streams into lush jungles of vegetation, at least until large floods occur. Along the mighty Colorado River, they simply build dens in banks along the shoreline (Waring, personal observation).

Lizard populations are largest along Colorado River shorelines in Grand Canyon, with numbers diminishing away from the river and into desert vegetation (Warren and Schwalbe 1988). Tree lizards, western whiptail lizards, desert spiny lizards, and side-blotched lizards are most common. It seems likely that the increase in vegetation along

the river since damming has contributed to this trend.

Cottonwood and willow communities along Arizona and California rivers have the highest bird diversity of all desert vegetation types (England et al. 1984). A study of bird populations along the Verde River in central Arizona reported the highest population densities for noncolonial nesting birds in North America (Carothers et al. 1974). In southwestern deserts, 77 percent of the 166 breeding bird species are at least partially dependent on riparian habitats (Johnson et al. 1977).

### Animals and Dams

Damming of the Colorado and other western rivers has created new and unprecedented resources for birds and other animals. While waterbirds such as mallards, northern pintails, gadwalls, northern shovelers, and blue-winged teals typically breed in lakes and potholes of the midcontinent prairies (Gammonsley 1996), the impoundment of western rivers has created some new and substantial habitats for them. Many waterbirds now overwinter and breed along the dammed Colorado River (Stevens et al. 1997). These species occurred there only infrequently prior to the dam because the river was too muddy and turbulent to support aquatic plants and insects.

The deltas that have formed where the Colorado River and its tributaries meet the large reservoirs behind the dams have become important riparian habitats for birds. Such deltas and associated riparian ecosystems have formed across the Southwest (Brown 1989, 1995). These deltas have been colonized by huge stands of native willow, marsh species, and nonnative tamarisk, and they have, in turn, been colonized by a great diversity of birds (Figs. 2.7, 2.12; Brown 1995). A study of breeding birds in the early 1990s determined that each year between 12,000 and 19,000 individual breeding birds may occupy more than 3,000 acres of such habitat at the top of Lake Mead (Brown 1989, 1995). Densities of nesting birds in forests of mature native willows and other plants were extremely high (1,764 and 1,840 individuals per 100 acres in 1993 and 1994, respectively) and comparable to the highest densities ever reported for noncolonial nesting birds, such as the 847 pairs per 100 acres estimated in riparian cottonwood forests along the Verde River of central Arizona (Carothers et al. 1974). These stands of vegetation and their associated bird communities became established on upper Lake Mead deltas within less than ten years.

On Lake Roosevelt in Arizona, lake levels fell in the 1990s, and large stands of tamarisk formed on exposed siltbanks. Within a few years, these stands were colonized by the endangered southwestern willow flycatcher and other species. By 2002, these stands supported the largest known nesting population of willow flycatchers in the Southwest (more than 100 nesting pairs [Bryan Brown, personal communication]). The cyclic nature of these lake levels renders these phenomenal resources highly dynamic and, sadly, ephemeral.

In wet years, breeding waterbirds also nest opportunistically, and successfully, in smaller ephemeral lakes such as those that form in basalt basins along the southern edge of the Colorado Plateau near Flagstaff and the White Mountains in Arizona (Gammonsley 1996). Very high numbers of breeding waterfowl were observed in the early 1990s after several years of above average precipitation. In drier years, migrating waterfowl simply use this area as a stop-over on their way to more reliable water sources for breeding in the Plains states.

## OTHER RIPARIAN HABITATS

Springs flowing from aquifers are hotspots for biodiversity. Stevens and Ayers (2002) reported that 11 percent of the more than 1,500 plant species in the Grand Canyon region are found only at springs. Undisturbed low-elevation springs in the Southwest commonly support 500 to 1,000 times more plants and animals than adjacent uplands. More than a third of the region's aquatic bugs and beetles are found only at springs (Stevens and Polhemus 2008). The Grand Canyon Wildlands Council (2010) has reported that bird and butterfly diversity and abundance are up to 300 times greater at springs; 35 species of birds, sometimes in large flocks, were found visiting Cliff Spring in less than an hour of observation. Virtually every bird species in the area came to water there. In times of drought, springs also serve as refugia as other aquatic habitats dry up.

Hanging gardens occur in permeable sandstones along rivers that have cut through the Colorado Plateau (Plate 13). The distributions of plant species in these unusual gardens tell their own stories about the plateau's history (Spence 2008). Hanging gardens typically form in spring-fed cliff faces or undercut alcoves in the Cedar Mesa, Entrada, and Navajo sandstones on the Colorado Plateau, and in the Redwall and Muav Limestone in Grand Canyon. There are 76 plant species that are mostly or entirely restricted to hanging gardens. The most characteristic species is maidenhair fern, which is a tropical-subtropical plant. A study of 60 hanging gardens on the

Colorado Plateau found that 75 percent of their more than 20 endemic plant species are derived from boreal-temperate, higher-latitude ancestors (Spence 2008). It may be that such species became established during colder periods of the Pleistocene, and that their disjunct modern populations are relicts of that time. Many of them do favor cooler, shadier sites. With this isolation has come a great deal of evolution. At least four new species of hanging garden columbines have been described in recent years. Other endemic species include sedge, monkey flower, and Clausen's violet. These hanging garden endemics make up about 15 percent of all endemic plants in this part of the Colorado Plateau.

## Plants and Animals in the Water

Vannote et al. (1980) developed the river continuum concept to make sense of how rivers function ecologically from their headwaters to their mouths. In general, biological complexity is predicted to increase downstream from headwaters. This concept is supported by many, though not all, studies of North American rivers. According to Vannote et al. (1980), where rivers originate in forested mountains, their ecology is relatively simple, characterized by abundant overhanging terrestrial vegetation falling into cold, clear water. Shredding insects break down this organic material. Despite this upstream herbivory, considerable plant material makes it downstream, and as organic particles accumulate, more and different types of insects feed on them; these insects are, in turn, fed upon by other insects and by fish. This influx of vegetation is important along western rivers since terrestrial vegetation diminishes as rivers descend into arid and semiarid landscapes. There is less shading and less input of vegetation

from the shoreline. Because of this, populations of aquatic plants such as algae increase downstream. Since there is more sunlight to enable photosynthesis, aquatic algae are far more abundant in western than eastern rivers.

Downstream from the headwaters, shredding insects are replaced by collectors, which use smaller bits of organic material, and by grazers, which feed on algae and other organic materials. Microbes such as bacteria and fungi help break down organic material into a more edible form. Fish communities in headwater streams tend to be less diverse and, generally, feed on insects, while farther down a river's course, in warmer waters, fish become more diverse and more variable in diet, and include fish-eating and plankton-eating species.

Characteristics of western rivers that challenge the river continuum concept include the many dams that decrease water temperatures and disrupt the movement of water, sediment, nutrients, and species, and the presence of extensive dark, narrow canyons that limit productivity.

Algae, as aquatic plants, form an important base of the aquatic food web. They are the main producers of leafy green plant material in water. Sunlight is especially important in determining their success. Historically, heavy loads of sediment reduced the diversity of the photosynthesizing algae in western rivers, but as dams now hold sediment in reservoirs, the Colorado River below them runs clear and cold, and algae have flourished. Today, diatoms, filamentous green algae, cyanobacteria, and aquatic macrophytes make up nearly 90 percent of the aquatic plant community in Grand Canyon (Blinn and Poff 2005). Many of these are cold-adapted algae since the water in Grand Canyon comes from the base of Glen

Canyon Dam and is frigid compared with pre-dam water. *Cladophora glomerata* is most abundant directly below Glen Canyon Dam and becomes less common as the water gets murky or turbid downstream with muddy tributary input (Stevens, Shannon, and Blinn 1997). Unlike plankton or floating forms of algae, diatoms occur as biofilm on rock surfaces and also grow on other species of algae and other aquatic plants, where they are the preferred food of chironomid midges, snails, and even fish.

Aquatic insects are quite diverse in the headwaters of the Colorado River basin (Blinn and Poff 2005). Ward and Kondratieff (1992) reported 63 species of stoneflies, 57 species of caddis flies, and 48 species of mayflies in the upper reaches of the Colorado drainage, making up 97 percent of all invertebrates in the headwaters. The diversity of aquatic insects declines as the Colorado River becomes siltier and murkier across the Colorado Plateau and farther downstream. Forty species of stoneflies have been found in the rivers of the Great Basin (Nelson 1994). Though a great diversity of leaf-shredding insects lives in the cold, clear Colorado River headwaters, they are absent from the cold, clear water in the Colorado River in Grand Canyon due to a lack of streamside vegetation (Stevens, Shannon, and Blinn 1997).

Amphibian diversity generally declines and amphibians become more desert-adapted farther downstream in the Colorado River basin. Arizona hosts more than fifteen amphibian species, including frogs, toads, and the tiger salamander.

## NATIVE FISHES IN THE COLORADO RIVER AND GREAT BASIN DRAINAGE SYSTEMS

Native fishes, even more than other creatures, have been placed in great peril since the arrival of Euro-American settlers in the West. Most of the river, spring, and lake habitats of western native fishes have been altered or destroyed by dams, water diversions, and nonnative fish. Dams and water diversions reduce water temperatures and limit flows, nutrient cycling, and migrational corridors in rivers and streams. Where native fishes have managed to survive river regulation, nonnative fishes pose a significant threat. Incredibly, native fishes in some rivers have been poisoned to eliminate what managers call *trash fish* and thus expedite the introduction of nonnative sport fishes such as trout and bass; this occurred in the Green River in Utah in 1962. Another problem is the introduction of species by people who can't bring themselves to destroy their aquarium creatures and instead dump them into rivers or springs. This has led to the introduction of devastating predatory fish such as cichlids, mollies, swordtails, and guppies. Other species, such as crayfish, bullfrogs, and bait fishes, are released by fishermen.

The near ubiquitous stocking of nonnative trout in mountain lakes and streams throughout the West has led to the loss of native trout lines through hybridization. By mating with rainbow trout, native trout are hybridized right out of existence. According to Wendell Minckley (1991), "native fishes of the American West will not remain on earth without active management." He contends that control of nonnative, warm-water species is the single most important requirement for achieving that goal. Currently, 83 percent of fish species in the Colorado River through Grand Canyon National Park are nonnatives (Minckley 1991, Stevens et al. 2001).

That said, the natural history of native fish in the arid West is truly amazing: they have managed to spread through even the most

**2.16.** Native fishes of the upper Colorado River basin: *top to bottom*, the bonytail chub (*Gila elegans*), the razorback sucker (*Xyrauchen texanus*), the Colorado pikeminnow (*Ptychocheilus lucius*), and the humpback chub (*Gila cypha*). These fish range in size from a maximum length of 20 inches for the boneytail chub, 2 feet for the humpback chub, 3 feet for the razorback sucker, and 6 feet for the Colorado pikeminnow. These species are thought to have originated in the upper Colorado River basin, and then spread throughout the system as upper and lower basins became connected some 5 Ma. Courtesy of John Rinne.

remote and tiniest streams. Many endemic species are confined to small western drainages and occur nowhere else on earth. Other species dispersed through the length of the Colorado River before it was dammed. In those days the mighty Colorado pikeminnow would have been able to swim hundreds and hundreds of miles.

Early in the Miocene, much of the West was largely an extensive flat plain (Minckley

et al. 1986, Spencer et al. 2008). Fish populations thus had broad, continuous distributions. But with extensive mountain building in the West, many populations became isolated; consequently, new species such as squawfish and chubs emerged. In the western fossil record extending from the Miocene into the Pleistocene there are minnows, suckers, bullhead catfish, sunfishes, char, trout, salmon, muskellunge, killifishes, sculpins, and sticklebacks.

The following section describes native fishes in the Colorado River drainage basin and the central and southern Great Basin, and relates some of their history (Table 2.1; Figs. 2.16, 2.17). Most western freshwater fishes are suckers and minnows. The suckers may have arisen from the minnow family, which is the largest freshwater fish family with more than 1,500 species. In the western United States, there are 52 species of minnow, including pikeminnow, dace, and western chub.

Although the western United States has less than a quarter as many native fish species as the East, the Colorado River basin and the Great Basin have the highest *proportions* of endemic fishes in the country (66 percent and 59 percent, respectively [Table 2.1]) (Miller 1959; Smith et al. 2000; Smith et al. 2002). This is so despite the fact that the aridity of the West has resulted in high extinction rates that have led to lower overall numbers of fish species. The geographic complexity of these western drainage basins and the alternating periods of high flows and aridity have contributed to this diversity of endemic species. Extinction and extirpation have also contributed to endemism by narrowing and isolating the ranges of surviving species. By contrast, the mighty and mesic Mississippi River drainage basin has about 265 species of

**TABLE 2.1.** NATIVE FISH SPECIES OF THE COLORADO RIVER, SOUTHERN GREAT BASIN, AND ASSOCIATED DRAINAGES, ILLUSTRATING PART OF THE HISTORY AND CONNECTIONS OF THE REGION.

| SPECIES | | Colorado River Faunas[a] | | | Great Basin Faunas[b] | | | | | | |
|---|---|---|---|---|---|---|---|---|---|---|---|
| | | Upper | Lower | Pluvial White River | Owens River | Bonneville Basin | Lahontan Basin | Death Valley System | Railroad Valley | Steptoe and Franklin Valleys[c] | Clover Valley |
| **SALMONIDAE** | | | | | | | | | | | |
| Cutthroat trout | *Oncorhynchus clarkii* | x | | | | x | x | | | | |
| Apache trout | *O. apache* | | xx | | | | | | | | |
| Gila trout | *O. gilae* | | xx | | | | | | | | |
| Mountain whitefish | *Prosopium williamsoni* | x | | | | x | x | | | | |
| Bear Lake whitefish | *P. abyssicola* | | | | | xx | | | | | |
| Bonneville whitefish | *P. spilonotus* | | | | | xx | | | | | |
| Bonneville cisco | *P. gemmiferum* | | | | | xx | | | | | |
| **CYPRINIDAE** | | | | | | | | | | | |
| Desert dace | *Eremichthys acros* | | | | | | xx | | | | |
| Utah chub | *Gila atraria* | | | | | x | | | | | |
| Virgin River chub | *G. seminuda* | | xx | | | | | | | | |
| White River chub | *G. jordani* | | | xx | | | | | | | |
| Roundtail chub | *G. robusta* | x | x | | | | | | | | |
| Bonytail chub | *G. elegans* | xx | xx | | | | | | | | |
| Humpback chub | *G. cypha* | xx | xx | | | | | | | | |
| Tui chub | *Siphateles bicolor* | | | | x | | x | | x | | x |
| Leatherside chub | *Snyderichthys copei* | | | | | x | | | | | |
| Least chub | *Iotichthys phlegethontis* | | | | | xx | | | | | |
| Lahontan redside | *Richardsonius egregius* | | | | | | xx | | | | |
| Redside shiner | *R. balteatus* | | | | | x | | | | | |
| Colorado pikeminnow | *Ptychocheilus lucius* | xx | xx | | | | | | | | |

**TABLE 2.1.** CONTINUED

| SPECIES | | Colorado River Faunas[a] | | | | Great Basin Faunas[b] | | | | | |
| --- | --- | --- | --- | --- | --- | --- | --- | --- | --- | --- | --- |
| | | Upper | Lower | Pluvial White River | Owens River | Bonneville Basin | Lahontan Basin | Death Valley System | Railroad Valley | Steptoe and Franklin Valleys[c] | Clover Valley |
| Longnose dace | Rhinichthys cataractae | | | | | x | | | | | |
| Longfin dace | Agosia chrysogaster | | x | | | | | | | | |
| Speckled dace | Rhinichthys osculus | x | x | x | | x | x | x | | | x |
| Relict dace | Relictus solitarius | | | | x | | | | | xx | |
| Moapa dace | Moapa coriacea | | xx | | | | | | | | |
| White River spinedace | Lepidomeda albivallis | | | xx | | | | | | | |
| Pahranagat spinedace | L. altivelis | | | xx | | | | | | | |
| Virgin spinedace | L. mollispinis | | xx | | | | | | | | |
| Little Colo. spinedace[d] | L. vittata | | xx | | | | | | | | |
| Spikedace | Meda fulgida | | xx | | | | | | | | |
| Woundfin | Plagopterus argentissimus | | xx | | | | | | | | |
| Loach minnow | Tiaroga cobitus | | xx | | | | | | | | |
| CATOSTOMIDAE | | | | | | | | | | | |
| Utah sucker | Catostomus ardens | | | | | x | | | | | |
| Tahoe sucker | C. tahoensis | | | | | | xx | | | | |
| Owens sucker | C. fumeiventris | | | | xx | | | | | | |
| Sonora sucker | C. insignis | | xx | | | | | | | | |
| Flannelmouth sucker | C. latipinnis | xx | xx | | | | | | | | |
| Bluehead sucker[e] | C. discobolus | x | | | | x | | | | | |
| Desert sucker | C. clarki | x | | | | x | | | | | |
| Mountain sucker | C. platyrhynchus | | xx | xx | | x | | | | | |
| Razorback sucker | Xyrauchen texanus | x | | | | x | x | | | | |
| June sucker | Chasmistes liorus | | xx | | | xx | | | | | |
| Cui-ui | C. cujus | | | | | | xx | | | | |

**TABLE 2.1.** CONTINUED

| SPECIES | | Colorado River Faunas[a] | | | Great Basin Faunas[b] | | | | | | |
|---|---|---|---|---|---|---|---|---|---|---|---|
| | | Upper | Lower | Pluvial White River | Owens River | Bonneville Basin | Lahontan Basin | Death Valley System | Railroad Valley | Steptoe and Franklin Valleys[c] | Clover Valley |
| GOODEIDAE | | | | | | | | | | | |
| Ash Meadows killifish | *Empetrichthys merriami* | | | | | | | xx | | | |
| Pahrump killifish | *E. latos* | | | xx | | | | | | | |
| White River springfish | *Crenichthys baileyi* | | | xx | | | | | | | |
| Railroad Valley springfish | *C. nevadae* | | | | | | | | xx | | |
| CYPRINODONTIDAE | | | | | | | | | | | |
| Salt Creek pupfish | *Cyprinodon salinus* | | | | | | | xx | | | |
| Amargosa pupfish | *C. nevadensis* | | | | | | | xx | | | |
| Devils Hole pupfish | *C. diabolis* | | | | | | | xx | | | |
| Owens pupfish[f] | *C. radiosus* | | | | xx | | | | | | |
| Desert pupfish | *C. macularius* | | x | | | | | | | | |
| POECILIIDAE | | | | | | | | | | | |
| Gila topminnow | *Poeciliopsis occidentalis* | | x | | | | | | | | |
| COTTIDAE | | | | | | | | | | | |
| Mottled sculpin | *Cottus bairdi* | x | | | | | | | | | |
| Bear Lake sculpin | *C. extensus* | | | | | xx | | | | | |
| Utah Lake sculpin | *C. echinatus* | | | | | xx | | | | | |
| Paiute sculpin | *C. beldingi* | x | | | | x | x | | | | |
| *Total species* | | | 32 | | | | | 32 | | | |
| *Endemics* | | | 21 (66%) | | | | | 19 (59%) | | | |

*Notes:* x = native presence; xx = endemic (occurring in only one region).

[a] The Grand Canyon is here considered to separate the upper and lower Colorado River basins.

[b] The hydrographic Great Basin includes many isolated units not considered here; many are in the north, with former connections to the Columbia and Snake rivers.

[c] Steptoe and Franklin valleys are part of a complex that includes Waring and Gale valleys.

[d] The Little Colorado spinedace is found in the Little Colorado River, which flows north into Grand Canyon. Faunistically, the fish is related to the Lower Colorado River fauna.

[e] The bluehead sucker lives in the Colorado River from the headwaters through Grand Canyon, as well as in the northern Bonneville Basin and upper Snake River.

[f] The Owens River had a connection to the Lower Colorado River, perhaps through the Death Valley region, in the Pliocene, and to the Lahontan Basin in the Pleistocene.

native fishes, about 41 percent (108) of them endemic.

Several recent studies have revealed a great deal about the evolutionary history of the fishes in these two western drainage basins and a great deal about the evolution of the basins themselves (Smith et al. 2002; Spencer et al. 2008). These studies combined information from the fish fossil record, DNA or genetic analyses of modern fishes, and geology to understand the history of these fish from the Miocene to the present. The studies suggest that the Colorado River and Great Basin river basins and their faunas were assembled from preexisting drainages and faunas, and that the subsequent subdivision of these drainages by mountain building and aridity led to the evolution of new species.

There are many closely related fish species in the Great Basin and Colorado River drainages, although the fish and the basins are entirely separated from one another today. Many of these species occur in the upper parts of each basin, including their mountainous headwaters. Upper Colorado River basin fish—including headwater types such as native cutthroat trout, mountain whitefish, sculpins, suckers, and the speckled dace—have their closest relatives in the headwaters of the Pleistocene Lake Bonneville: the Bear River and the upper Snake River (Columbia) drainages (Miller 1959; Smith et al. 2002). These montane species probably attained their broad distributions by means of headwater transfer across low divides during major floods. Consequently, none of the thirteen fish species in the upper Colorado basin are endemic.

There are also interesting relationships between fish in the Great Basin and the lower Colorado River. While the pluvial White River drainage is a part of the

**2.17.** Native fishes of the lower Colorado River basin: *top to bottom*, the desert pupfish (*Cyprinodon macularius*), ~2.5 inches long; the woundfin (*Plagopterus argentissimus*), ~3 inches long; the Virgin spinedace (*Lepidomeda mollispinis*), ~4 inches long; and the spikedace (*Meda fulgida*), ~3 inches long. These species originated in the lower Colorado River basin and never dispersed through the upper basin because they could not ascend the steep and turbulent Grand Canyon. Courtesy of John Rinne.

hydrographic Great Basin, its fish are genetically related to those of the Colorado River (Table 2.1; Hubbs and Miller 1948, Williams and Wilde 1981, Smith et al. 2002, Spencer et al. 2008). These rivers were connected during the wet Pleistocene, which allowed fish to move between them. The White River's channel has dried out since then and eliminated contact. Today, 10,000 years later, six endemic fish species and a number of subspecies live in isolated springs along its dry course (Table 2.1). Railroad Valley is also a part of the hydrographic Great Basin and has a species from the Colorado fauna, as well as one from the Lahontan Basin fauna. The evolutionary history of these fish has also shed light on the formation of the Colorado River.

*Evolution of Upper and Lower Colorado River Fishes*

The Colorado River is the largest desert river and one of the most regulated rivers in North America. The former led to an impressive diversity of native fishes, but the latter threatens their survival. The Colorado River basin has the greatest percentage of endemic fishes of any river basin in North America: 21 of its 32 native fish species (66 percent) are endemic (Table 2.1).

It appears that the upper and lower basins of the Colorado River formed separately and remained separated until about 5 Ma (Spencer et al. 2008). The upper Colorado River basin occurs above the Grand Canyon and the lower basin occurs below, and as a result, different species developed in each (Table 2.1). Fossils of upper basin fish have been found in the ancient beds of Hopi Lake (Bidahochi Formation), which once occupied much of northeastern Arizona. Fish fossils found in the Bidahochi Formation date back to the Miocene and include the enormous Colorado pikeminnow (reaching up to 6 feet long), the roundtail chub, the bonytail chub, and the humpback chub, all of which are still with us today (Table 2.1, Fig. 2.16).

A diverse group of small stream species originated in the lower basin (Table 2.1, Fig. 2.17). Few of them exceed 2.5 inches in length. Smaller lower basin species include a variety of dace and spinedace, including the White River and Virgin spinedace (Table 2.1, Fig. 2.17). Once the upper and lower Colorado River basins became connected, most upper basin species extended their ranges

down through the lower basin; however, few of the lower basin species have been able to migrate up through the turbulent Grand Canyon into the upper basin (Spencer et al. 2008).

The distribution of different species of suckers in the upper and lower Colorado basins also reveals a great deal about the river's history. The desert sucker occurs only in the lower basin, while the bluehead sucker occurs only through Grand Canyon and the upper basin. The flannelmouth sucker, however, occurs throughout the Colorado basin. The mountain sucker occurs in a number of western drainages that are separated from one another today, including the Bonneville Basin, the Lahontan Basin, and the Colorado River basin (Smith et al. 2002).

The larger fish of the upper Colorado River basin have attributes that allow them to swim in powerful, turbulent and silty rivers: large, streamlined bodies and fins, small eyes, and thick, leathery skin with small scales. Collectively, these traits reduce friction and sediment abrasion, and help in navigation. They are all streamlined, with small, depressed skulls, large predorsal humps or keels, or both, and elongated and thin caudal peduncles, or tails, for maintaining position and maneuvering in the swift, turbulent currents of the Colorado River (Fig. 2.16; Minckley 1991). The humpback chub epitomizes the general shape of large Colorado fishes—a large, humped back made of muscle (Fig. 2.16). And they can be long-lived: up to seventy-five years for the pikeminnow and more than twenty for the humpback sucker, which may see species through stressful times (Minckley 1991).

Before the Colorado River was dammed, the bonytail chub and the razorback sucker, along with the Colorado pikeminnow, ranged hundreds of miles through its mainstem and tributaries. They were found from the mountains of Colorado to brackish estuaries in Mexico.

The pikeminnow has been present in the upper Colorado drainage for at least the last 6 million years (Spencer et al. 2008). Its remains have turned up in prehistoric Indian ruins dating back more than a thousand years (Aton and McPherson 2000). It is a lie-and-wait predator and may feed on chubs (Minckley 1991). The largest of the minnows, it can weigh up to 80 pounds. This species helped to feed early explorers and settlers, and it was on the table of the Stanton party for Christmas dinner at Lees Ferry during their exploration of the Colorado River in 1889 (Adler 2007). The Colorado pikeminnow now lives only in the upper Colorado River basin; it had disappeared downstream of Grand Canyon by the 1970s. Pikeminnows are still able to migrate up to about 150 miles in the upper basin, and they are known to revisit the same spawning sites for many years, perhaps locating them by smell. There are related species of pikeminnows in the Sacramento–San Joaquin, Columbia, and Umpqua river drainages.

*Evolution of Great Basin Fishes*

After the Colorado River basin, the central and southern Great Basin has the greatest proportion of endemic fish in North America (59 percent). Within the central and southern Great Basin lakes and streams, nineteen of thirty-two native fish species are endemic (Table 2.1) (Smith et al. 2002). There are many subspecies, especially among the salmonids, cyprinodonts, and cyprinids. According to Hubbs and Miller (1948), the Great Basin's complex landscape is ideal for extensive genetic divergence and speciation. This, combined with Pleistocene floods, resulted in the spread and then isolation of populations of these fish, which led to the evolution of so many endemic species. Most of the small, isolated populations went extinct, as evidenced by the declining diversity of fish through the Cenozoic fossil record and depauperate local faunas today. The Great Basin fossil record and contemporary data show that periods of dryness and isolation eliminated many species, perhaps because the arid cycles were so extreme. Clearly, the dry and unpredictable climatic conditions of the Great Basin challenge the survival of fish there. An exception to this trend is Bear Lake in Utah, which is a deep lake refuge for four endemic fish species native to ancient Lake Bonneville. This is the highest number of endemic fish in any lake in North America.

Smaller basins within the Great Basin tend to support the fewest fish species. The Bonneville system is the largest and supports the most species (nineteen); 37 percent of them are considered endemic (Table 2.1). The Bonneville drainage system includes the Snake River above Shoshone Falls, since Lake Bonneville spilled into that river 15,000 years ago. The isolated Lahontan Basin is smaller and has just ten species of fish; its three endemic species are the desert dace, Lahontan redside shiner, and Cui-ui sucker. It shares whitefish, trout, and sculpin with the Bonneville and Columbia systems due to ancient headwater exchanges.

Minnows (Cyprinidae) are the most widespread and diverse fishes in the Great Basin. Of these, the speckled dace is the most widespread freshwater fish west of the Rocky Mountains (Minckley 1991). This little fish's range extends from northern Mexico to southern Canada, and from desert springs to mountain headwaters. There are many subspecies of speckled dace (Smith and Dowling 2008). Its two basic forms—adapted to slow- versus fast-water rivers—are also highly variable.

Gila chubs occur in the Bonneville, Snake, Los Angeles, Colorado River, and Rio Grande basins, as well as several in northern Mexico. In the western Great Basin, the Tui chub is particularly diverse in the Lahontan Basin, with more than eight subspecies. Catostomidae, or suckers, are among the hardiest and largest aquatic survivors of the Great Basin's harsh and variable climates (Smith et al. 2002). There are twenty-five species of western suckers in the basin's lakes and rivers, and in the headwaters of mountain streams.

Trout and whitefish also live in mountain streams and the deep, cool lakes of the northern Great Basin. The cutthroat trout has been in the Great Basin at least since the Pliocene Epoch, ~5 million years ago.

The pupfishes are the showpiece species of Great Basin ichthyology. R. R. Miller's studies of these fish revealed the relationship between isolation and differentiation in the Great Basin (Miller 1948, 1959, 1961, 1981; Smith et al. 2002; Echelle 2007). These little fishes rarely exceed 3 inches in length (Fig. 2.17). There are about fifteen different pupfishes (*Cyprinodon* spp.) in the Southwest and Mexico today. There are nine species and subspecies in the saline and sometimes warm waters of the Death Valley system at the southwestern edge of the Great Basin. The pupfish with the smallest range, the endangered Devil's Hole pupfish, lives in a warm-water cave spring hole of about 24 square yards in Death Valley National Monument. It may have diverged from *C. nevadensis*, which lived in nearby springs between 200,000 and 600,000 years ago, perhaps when its unique habitat formed. Pupfish often live in habitats that present severe salinity and thermal challenges. Being

more tolerant of such conditions than are most other fish, they often occupy their habitats alone. Species such as the Devil's Hole pupfish may produce more than one generation per year due to warm waters.

The Owen's pupfish, of the Owen's River, is the sister species of the desert pupfish of the lower Colorado River. Other sister species live in the Amargosa River, Devil's Hole, and Ash Meadows in Nevada, suggesting that these areas were once connected during the Pliocene and Pleistocene. Pupfish abounded in the enormous lower Colorado delta that formed above the Gulf of California when the Colorado River still ran that far.

*Western Trout*

It seems utterly improbable that trout could find their way into so many small and remote mountain streams in the West. Most trout populations were present in the headwaters of western North American rivers long before the Pleistocene. All native western trout came from cutthroat or rainbow trout, both of which came from the sea. The ancestral cutthroats still migrate from the sea, where they feed, to freshwater, where they spawn.

Western trout, unlike ancestral trout or salmon, have mostly given up migration to the sea. Perhaps because of this, they reproduce up to seven times in their lifetime, unlike their migrating salmon relatives, which reproduce only once. Since the migration routes of seafaring salmon may cover thousands of miles, it's easy to understand this trade-off.

The history of trout in the headwaters of western mountain streams and rivers dates back to the end of the Miocene (5 Ma), when the major groups of the trout and salmon subfamily, including Pacific salmon and trout, were in place (Behnke 2002). During the Pliocene and throughout Pleistocene times, the salmonids were influenced by dramatic climate changes. During glacial periods, the rainbow trout group occurred as far south as central Mexico; this pattern of southern expansion was seen in other parts of the world with the Masu salmon in Taiwan, the North African brown trout, and the taimen of the Yangtze River in China. The present distribution of the Apache, Gila, and Mexican trout indicates that basins of the lower Colorado River and northern Mexico were once accessible to these cold-water fishes.

Although rainbow trout are the most famous in the world, cutthroat trout once had an even greater distribution. Cutthroats dispersed eastward across the continental divide and established subspecies in the South Saskatchewan, Missouri, South Platte, Arkansas, and Rio Grande River basins. It may be that the cutthroat trout's ancestors dispersed inland into the Columbia River basin and blocked greater inland access for the later-invading rainbow trout.

Behnke (2002) lists fourteen subspecies of cutthroat trout in western North America, but two of those have recently gone extinct. Their collective range extends from headwaters in the Snake River basin, Lahontan Basin, Bonneville Basin, and the upper Colorado River basin through the Rockies to the Missouri River headwaters, the Rio Grande, and into Mexico. Western rainbow trout species and subspecies number about eight, with additional, as yet unnamed, groups occurring in Mexico. The range of rainbow trout in western North America includes the headwaters of the Snake River in the northern Great Basin and the Kern River basin, as well as the northern Sacramento River basin and the Gila and Salt rivers, tributaries to the Colorado River in southern Arizona and

Mexico. All native western trout, including rainbow and cutthroat, can interbreed and produce viable offspring.

These inland fish face great challenges as the West becomes increasingly arid. An example of how precarious their survival is involves the southern Gila and Apache trout that live in the headwaters of the Salt and Gila rivers in central Arizona. During low precipitation years, when streamflows decline, dense numbers of small trout (less than 8 inches) crowd into small pools sustained mainly by groundwater seeps. Their populations may fluctuate tenfold over the course of a few years. They are slow growing and do not reproduce until the age of three, at which time females may spawn only seventy eggs.

On the Colorado Plateau ephemeral pools in sandstone potholes support communities of amphibians, insects, crustaceans, and algae (Van Haverbeke 1990). These small, shallow pools and their communities form during summer monsoon storms and are quickly gone as the storms end and the land dries out. As they form, there are intense dynamics in pools occupied by the predaceous crustacean tadpole shrimp, which devour fairy shrimp, tadpoles, fly larvae, and one another when they co-occur. It's a lucky fairy shrimp that manages to occupy a pothole without tadpole shrimp. As the water dries out, survivors go dormant until the next rainy season.

Dams, diversions, nonnative animals and plants, and pollution are wreaking havoc with water throughout the world, but some conservation efforts are also making a difference. Restoring natural flow regimes to rivers has been shown to restore native biodiversity (Minckley and Meffe 1987, Fahlund 2000, Marchetti and Moyle 2001, Valdez et al. 2001). Removal of a dam from the

Milwaukee River in Wisconsin resulted in a switch from a fish community dominated by pollution-tolerant nonnative species that are common in urban environments across North America to a fish assemblage characterized by native darters and suckers (Kanehl et al. 1997).

It is my hope that this crash course in water in the West shows how important and fragile water is, along with the diverse life-forms it supports. I once saw a documentary about an indigenous tribe in the Himalayas that considered putting anything into streams and rivers to be a sin. Most of us are far from that perspective, but perhaps having a better understanding of western water systems will make it easier to recognize their value.

# CHAPTER 3

# Cool, Dark, Western Mountains

As I sit in an alpine meadow high up in the San Francisco Peaks in northern Arizona, I look down below the mountain forests and see only low, dry landscapes (Fig. 3.1). How did these high-elevation plants colonize this montane island through these surrounding, uninhabitable deserts? This question goes to the heart of my interest in the ecosystems explored in this book. These plants have all "gotten around" over many millennia, providing further evidence that the world around us is more dynamic than most of us can grasp.

This chapter describes many aspects of the mountain habitats of the Southern Rockies and the Intermountain West. Alpine tundra occurs above treeline from about 10,000 feet to more than 14,000 feet. Below it are dense coniferous forests with mainly Engelmann spruce and subalpine fir at the top. Below them is a more diverse coniferous forest that includes lodgepole pine, Douglas fir, blue spruce, white fir, and beautiful stands of aspen. At still lower, drier elevations are

ponderosa pine forests and pinyon-juniper woodlands, which are described in the next chapters.

Most western forests are in some stage of recovery from prior disturbance by fire, wind, insects, disease, grazing, avalanches, landslides, extreme weather, volcanism, and humans (Peet 1989). Such phenomena make these forests, like other ecosystems, highly dynamic. Disturbances such as fire can open

**3.1.** The San Francisco Peaks in northern Arizona. Cold desert habitat to the east separates its tundra from that of the Southern Rockies.

up closed forests and allow less shade-tolerant plants to become established, whether by seed or from underground stems, as do aspen. Most often, the previous trees will return, shading out the light-dependent species, making for an endless, successional cycle of life-forms.

## Alpine Tundra: The World Above Treeline

Tundra refers to vegetation occurring above treeline in cold climates with short growing seasons (Barbour et al. 1980; Billings 1988, 2000; Peet 2000). Inhabiting a world of intense radiation, wind, cold, snow, and ice, alpine tundra consists mainly of perennial herbaceous plants such as forbs, grasses, sedges, mosses and lichens, and dwarf shrubs less than a foot tall. Most are mat-forming, or spreading, plants (Plate 14). Annual plants are extremely rare in the tundra.

Alpine ecosystems are extensions of arctic ecosystems, which lie at the upper latitudes of the world. At lower latitudes, alpine ecosystems occur at higher elevations where cold conditions exist. At the northern end of the Rockies, in the southern Yukon, treeline occurs at about 4,500 feet. With decreasing latitude, treeline rises at a rate of about 325 feet per degree of latitude to an elevation of over 11,700 feet in northern New Mexico. Alpine ecosystems, therefore, face harsher conditions—including stronger winds, higher levels of radiation, higher surface temperatures, and greater desiccation—than do arctic ecosystems.

In the United States, nearly all alpine tundra occurs in the West. This is because its youngest, tallest mountains—the Rockies, the mountains of the Great Basin, and the coastal and Alaskan mountains—occur there (Figs. 1.1, 3.2). Alpine communities are

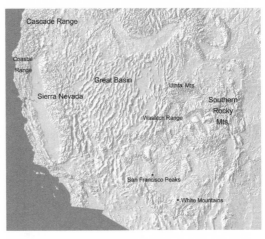

3.2. The Southern Rockies and other mountain ranges of the Intermountain West.

found in the Coastal Cordillera from the Alaska Range to the Sierra Nevada, and in the Rocky Mountain Cordillera from the Brooks Range of northern Alaska to northern New Mexico and Arizona. Limited alpine tundra occurs on the highest peaks of the Intermountain region. In the East, alpine vegetation occurs only on isolated mountaintops in the northern Appalachians, including Mount Washington, New Hampshire, and mountains in Newfoundland and Labrador. The peaks of these older ranges are lower in elevation. Alpine communities in Mexico and Guatemala contain some species that also occur in the Southern Rockies, while alpine communities farther south, in Panama and Costa Rica, are more closely related to vegetation of the Andes. Not surprisingly, the alpine habitat type is one of the smallest in North America, perched as it is on mountaintops.

Tundra plants can live high above treeline. In the Himalayas, plants have been found living above 19,000 feet. Some of them also occur at more temperate elevations but are also able to tolerate profoundly cold temperatures and short growing seasons (Webster 1961).

*Evolutionary History of Western Alpine Floras*

The evolutionary history of alpine floras of North America is complicated (Campbell 1997). Today these floras contain endemic species as well as a mix of plants from the Arctic, from alpine habitats in the Northern Hemisphere (including Asia and Europe), and from surrounding low-lying areas. Although many alpine species may have originated by the end of the Cretaceous (~65 Ma), others originated more recently when the North American plate moved northward to the cooler high latitudes where it sits today. That, combined with extensive mountain building, led to the evolution of many modern alpine genera by the Mid-Miocene (~15 Ma).

The numerous islands of alpine tundra through the Rockies and the Intermountain West were connected by cold conditions during the Pleistocene, making it a little easier to imagine how plants migrated from the Arctic. At that time, alpine communities were larger and more interconnected than they are today (Carrara et al. 1984).

North-south-oriented migrational corridors have been crucial to the survival of mountain species as climates have changed. Many arctic plant species migrated or shifted their ranges southward and downslope during the Pleistocene, avoiding extinction due to glaciation.

There are only about 63 alpine plant species on Mount Washington in the northern Appalachians, and as many as 70 percent of them are also found in the Arctic. There are nearly 200 alpine species in the Rocky Mountains, about 50 percent of which are arctic species (Billings 2000). The Rocky Mountains are the longest, most massive of all North American ranges and provide many habitats for alpine tundra. The flora of the Sierra Nevada is the least studied of western ranges, but Billings (2000) has speculated that it has a more diverse alpine flora than other ranges, with only about 20 percent of its alpine plants being found in the Arctic.

The greater proportions of arctic species in the Rockies and northern Appalachians versus the Sierra Nevada relate directly to their different climates. The Sierra Nevada receives abundant winter snowfall, but very little summer precipitation; the Rockies have strong winters and summer monsoon rains; and the northern Appalachians receive rain and snow throughout the year. Perhaps similar numbers of arctic plant species migrated down through all of these ranges during the Pleistocene, but the wetter weather in the East and the Rockies enabled more of them to persist there, whereas species were lost in the Sierra Nevada due to its dry summers.

The origin of the alpine flora in the young Sierra Nevada, with so few arctic species, shows how some alpine communities can form. While some of its alpine plants are from the Rocky Mountains, a larger number migrated up from neighboring deserts to become alpine plants. The few plant genera there—including buckwheat, penstemon, cinquefoil, lupine, and vetch—have diverged into many species (Zwinger and Willard 1972).

Annual plants are more common in deserts and rarer in alpine habitats—except in the Sierra Nevada. Nearly 15 percent (ninety-one) of the alpine species there are annuals, and they are mostly related to surrounding desert species. One of the few annual alpine plants in the Rockies is a tiny buckwheat. It occurs at only a few meadow sites in the Rockies, but as far north as Alaska's North Slope and into Siberia (Walker et al. 2001, Axelrod and Raven 1985).

Plants of western deserts have traits that preadapt them to alpine ecosystems, including a tolerance of freezing nighttime temperatures and short growing seasons, and, of course, being able to reproduce at low temperatures (Chabot and Billings 1972, Packer 1974, Campbell 1997). Alpine species of bluegrasses, sedges, cinquefoils, and buttercups are not very different from their lowland counterparts. This upward migration of lowland species has been especially important in the Sierra Nevada and Great Basin ranges, where a lack of closed forests allows easier dispersal between desert and alpine habitats.

Many alpine plants have extensive elevational ranges. An *occasional* alpine species is sneezeweed. It was reported by Schaack (1983) as a recent arrival in the alpine system in the San Francisco Peaks, having migrated up several thousand feet from the foothills, where it is abundant. At lower elevations it blooms early each year and bears large, beautiful orange flowers, but in the alpine zone it never blooms. It is as though it has reached its limit of tolerance there and is unable to muster the energy during the short growing season to reproduce by seed. Muttongrass often occurs above treeline through the Rockies and Great Basin mountains, but it also occurs as low as 3,000 feet (McDougall 1973).

Within the Great Basin, most alpine-arctic communities occur in mountains near the Rocky Mountains, and most of their alpine plants migrated from there. Fewer alpine communities occur in mountains in the central and western Great Basin (Billings 1988).

Even though many alpine plants in North America also occur in the Arctic, it is not absolutely clear that they originated there. During the Early Tertiary, when much of the world was warm and wet, flowering plants ranged from the tropics to the Arctic. Perhaps some of these plants originated in the continental United States, migrated north during the Tertiary, and returned from the Arctic to the alpine habitats of North America during the Pleistocene. Regardless, it is hard to imagine that these plants, many of which do not disperse their seeds very far, could migrate thousands and thousands of miles. It may be that with global warming some are migrating to northern refugia—and right under our noses. It is a delightfully complicated history.

The tiny patch of alpine tundra in the San Francisco Peaks covers only about 2 square miles, and yet it provides many insights about how alpine plants have dispersed. The Peaks are an isolated mountain island surrounded by hundreds of square miles of low, dry deserts, and they are the southern end of the line for alpine communities extending southward from the Arctic. Moisture comes from winter snow and summer rains, and it is this nearly year-round moisture regime that allows these plants to persist in such a dry, warm region.

There are eighty plant species found above treeline in the San Francisco Peaks, and most of them (60 percent) also occur in the Rocky Mountains (Schaack 1983). Nearly a quarter (24 percent) of these species also live in the Arctic, thousands of miles away. While the following chapters recount migrations of many other plants in the West, few have migrated as far as arctic plants. It is hard to imagine the desert floor between the San Francisco Peaks and the Rocky Mountains being covered by populations of alpine plants, but that is how these plants extended their range to the Peaks.

The current distributions of alpine plants provide clues about how such migrations occurred. A snapdragon known as foothills kittentails ranges from Wyoming along the eastern side of the Rockies to New Mexico, and into the White Mountains and San Francisco Peaks in Arizona. It does not occur in either the Great Basin or the coastal ranges, leading taxonomist Clark Schaack to believe that its current distribution reflects its route south during the Pleistocene, when prolonged cold temperatures dropped the elevational ranges of most plant species by thousands of feet. Kittentails seed does not disperse far from the parent plant; therefore, getting from the Rockies to northern Arizona was a long-term and, frankly, improbable proposition. Given that the volcanic San Francisco Peaks erupted about 600,000 years ago, this whole process occurred fairly recently.

*Living Above Treeline*

William Dwight Billings (2000), an authority on alpine environments, referred to mountaintops as high-elevation deserts. He studied both alpine and desert habitats, and found many similarities, including intense radiation, limited water availability, and short growing seasons (Billings 1988). Of all the features of alpine ecosystems, the persistent ice and snow are what determine where plants live and how successful they will be. While snowbanks can protect plants in winter from severe winds and temperatures, during the growing season snow can keep temperatures cold, making an already short growing season even shorter. In some years, snow may not melt completely, leaving plants unable to reproduce.

*Alpine Habitats*

Alpine habitats typically include relatively protected wet and dry meadows at the base of snowmelt areas, and exposed, harsh, rocky areas such as fellfields (Fig. 3.4). Although most plants favor wet meadows, which are the most productive alpine environments, others occur most commonly in fellfields. Many species live in both habitats.

Alpine temperatures stay low throughout the year. At Niwot Ridge, in alpine tundra in the Colorado Rockies, the mean annual temperature is below freezing. Average daily temperatures range between about 0°F in winter to about 45°F in summer, and yet the small plants that live in alpine zones stay warm because they are close to the ground, which absorbs the intense solar radiation at these higher elevations. Temperatures are much higher at the soil surface compared to just 3 feet up, where the wind cools things down (Billings 1988). Fellfields are snow free most the year because snow is simply blown away by the most ferocious winds on earth: the highest wind speed on record—231 miles per hour—was recorded at the summit of Mt. Washington, New Hampshire, in the northern Appalachians in 1934. In the Rockies, winds in the tundra can exceed 100 mph between October and February.

At Niwot, annual snow depths range from only 6 inches or so in fellfields, where the growing season is about 109 days, to some 50 inches in meadows, where growing season is just 52 days (Walker et al. 2001). Plants there have just two options: bitter, dessicating winds with a long growing season, or protection and moisture with a short growing season.

Alpine meadows are typically occupied by a great diversity of species common to western mountain ranges and have dense plant cover (Campbell 1997). Wet meadows downslope of melting snowbanks may stay wet throughout the growing season. Alpine avens, a mat-forming plant (Fig. 3.3), grows in both sheltered and fully exposed

**3.4.** Protected alpine habitats support lush meadows, while more exposed sites are sparsely vegetated: *top*, a meadow full of summer wildflowers; *bottom*, bristlecone pines at treeline, San Francisco Peaks, northern Arizona. Courtesy of the Ecological Restoration Institute, Northern Arizona University.

**3.3.** Common Rocky Mountain tundra species: *top to bottom,* alpine avens (*Geum rossii*), tufted hairgrass (*Deschampsia caespitosa*), and a puffy form of alpine campion (*Silene acaulis*). Courtesy of William Bowman.

areas, and often dominates alpine meadows in the Great Basin and the Rockies. It also has an enormous circumpolar range through Asia, the Arctic, and much of North America. Other meadow plants include species of actinea, saxifrage, Jacob's ladder, phlox, buckwheat, bluebell, goldenrod, sage, mustard, avens or cinquefoil, and buttercup.

Some meadows are dominated by grasses. One of the most common is tufted hairgrass, a spreading grass that often covers large areas of wet meadows in alpine tundra throughout the Northern Hemisphere (Fig. 3.3). Bluegrasses and fescues are also

common. As many as seventeen species of bluegrass have been found in Rocky Mountain National Park. Sedges are also extremely common and diverse in alpine zones. It is thought that these grassy communities may be late successional communities, often outcompeting forbs over long periods of time. This process may be accelerated by the effects of increasing air pollution (see the discussion of human impacts below).

Fellfields, or rock gardens, are considered alpine deserts (Fig. 3.4) because they occur on windblown slopes and ridge crests, locations that do not support the diversity or productivity of plants in more protected areas. Plant cover is usually sparse and dominated by mat-forming and cushion plants.

Cushion plants are puffier than the flatter, mat-forming species, and this form protects them from the wind. Temperatures and moisture levels are more favorable inside their little canopies than outside. In drier and windier places, alpine campion assumes a cushion shape (Fig. 3.3), whereas in milder sites it grows in a flatter form.

Alpine plants can photosynthesize and grow at remarkably low temperatures. In nine years of growth studies in the Rockies (Bowman and Fisk 2001), no relationship was found between plant growth and air temperature during the growing season, suggesting that growth may be related more to soil temperatures. Alpine sedge stores carbohydrates in the form of oligosaccharides in leaves. These sugars probably contribute to the frost hardiness of the alpine sedge's evergreen leaves, as well as making carbohydrates more available during the winter (Walker et al. 1995).

When alpine plants do flower, they may do so within days of snowmelt. Many form flower buds at the end of the previous growing season so they are closer to reproducing by spring. Alpine bistort produces "bulblets" that have the first leaf already in place. These fall off the plant ready to take root and grow without having to go through the step of seed germination.

It was thought for some time that most alpine plants reproduce asexually or vegetatively rather than sexually due to the short growing season, lack of nutrients, cold that inhibits pollination, and damage to seedlings from frost and needle ice. The pervasive mat-forming habit in the tundra was thought to be a reflection of this. However, sexual reproduction and seed production are not uncommon in alpine habitats. Forbis (2003) found high numbers of seedlings in alpine populations at Niwot in the Rocky Mountains. It turns out, though, that it may be many years before alpine plants even

begin to reproduce. Seedlings often colonize areas disturbed by gophers, rockfall, and damaging storms.

The few tundra annuals in the Rockies get through the short growing season by living in wet meadows or areas where spring snowmelt provides a large initial water supply (Reynolds 1984). With their small, shallow root systems, they cannot survive on exposed slopes where snow is blown away. Annuals flower early after producing only one or two leaves, which allows them to produce seeds during the very short growing season.

When water is limited, plants cannot photosynthesize at maximum capacity. Common alpine species—including tufted hairgrass, alpine avens, and alpine sedge—all photosynthesize less, and consequently grow less, when water availability declines, but they are remarkably tolerant of drought conditions—and more so than arctic plants (Johnson et al. 1974, Johnson and Caldwell 1975).

Alpine soils are much less fertile than those of other ecosystems, and not surprisingly, plant growth is slower (Bowman and Fisk 2001). Infertile soils and cold temperatures slow the rate at which plant litter decomposes, releasing key minerals such as nitrogen and phosphorus that plants can absorb through their roots.

In a way, slow growth is an adaptation. Perennial herbaceous plants live longer in the tundra than they do elsewhere, with alpine campion estimated to live more than 300 years, Rydberg's sandwort more than 200 years, and cushion paronychia possibly more than 325 years (Forbis and Doak 2004). Clonal species, such as alpine sedge, may live for thousands years (Steinger et al. 1996).

Alpine plants can have over 90 percent of their biomass in their root systems. At Niwot

Ridge, root to shoot ratios ranged from 4:1 to 25:1 (Monson et al. 2001). These are among the highest such ratios known, with the exception of some plants in the Arctic and harsh deserts. Growth naturally focuses on root production because that is where the limited nutrients are absorbed.

Most plants in more temperate and productive ecosystems take up nitrogen that has been broken down to an inorganic level and is devoid of carbon, usually occurring as $NO_3$ or as $NH_4$. By contrast, alpine plants can absorb nitrogen in an organic form, as an amino acid or protein, through their roots. The alpine sedge does this, absorbing the amino acid glycine and growing more quickly than plants that rely on inorganic forms of nitrogen (Monson et al. 2001).

Many species have fungal or mycorrhizal associations that help their roots absorb water and nutrients more efficiently (Walker et al. 2001). One Rocky Mountain buttercup that has a variety of fungi associated with its roots is abundant in snowbed communities, which have the shortest growing season of all.

Because high mountains rise into thin, clear air, solar radiation is more intense than at lower elevations. Some alpine plants are able to minimize ultraviolet radiation (UV) damage to tissues that are responsible for photosynthesis by absorbing radiation in outer, or epidermal, leaf layers. Other plants contain compounds such as phenols and alkaloids that are quite effective at absorbing UV radiation while remaining transparent in the visible portion of the solar spectrum. This means that they don't block the process of photosynthesis. Some plant features, such as hairy surfaces, help to reflect radiation.

Competition among alpine plants, such as alpine avens and tufted hairgrass, is often fierce. Alpine avens, which often dominates

wet meadows, has a slow growth rate. It produces high levels of phenolic compounds that stimulate soil microbes to take up nitrogen, generally rendering the area around the plant low in critical nitrogen. This process makes it hard for fast-growing, nitrogen-demanding plants such as tufted hairgrass to establish and grow vigorously anywhere near it. In experiments, the growth rate of tufted hairgrass in pots with alpine avens litter was much lower than in pots with tufted hairgrass litter (Monson et al. 2001). This trait has enabled avens to persist and dominate alpine habitats; however, this dynamic may be changing in the Rockies due to the effects of air pollution from the Denver area.

## Human Impacts on Alpine Habitat

Although mining, grazing, and recreation have had negative effects on some of the Rocky Mountain alpine tundra, more important today are factors such as climate change and air pollution (Bowman 2000). Temperatures are remaining fairly constant in the Rockies, but precipitation has increased significantly over the last fifty years. The connection of increased precipitation to global warming is not a given; however, it is consistent with the prediction of increasing evapotranspiration at lower elevations and its subsequent transport to nearby mountains. In an experiment designed to study the effects of increased precipitation on alpine tundra, researchers at Niwot set up a fence to catch more snow in dry alpine meadows. The fence increased snow levels by up to 200 percent, which delayed the short growing season by up to two weeks. The dominant alpine sedge of dry meadows responded to increased snowpack with decreased growth and seed production, and greater mortality. At the same time, the cover of a common legume, Parry's clover, increased because this and other alpine clovers derive most of their nitrogen from the atmosphere.

Although alpine ecosystems may be nitrogen limited, Niwot Ridge and possibly much of the Colorado Front Range have experienced significant increases in nitrogen deposition over the past several decades (Welker et al. 2001). Sources for this nitrogen include car and industrial emissions within the urban corridor at the base of the Rockies, between Fort Collins and Colorado Springs, where 4 million people live, and power plant emissions in western Colorado. Another source may be the dust created by several centuries of overgrazing through much of the West (Neff et al. 2008). Much of this nitrogen is deposited along with snowfall. Because moist meadows receive the most snowmelt, they are likely to be most affected by increased nitrogen. Nitrogen-sensitive grasses such as tufted hairgrass may ultimately replace forb species that are insensitive to nitrogen fluxes, such as alpine avens (Welker et al. 2001). Alpine avens is at a competitive disadvantage when nitrogen levels increase and the balance of the system changes. Fertilization experiments have already demonstrated this outcome, whereby with increased nitrogen, tufted hairgrass increases in size, but alpine avens does not (Bowman 2000).

## Treeline

At the edge of the alpine tundra, at about 11,500 feet, is treeline, where trees from the subalpine zone make a last stand in the face of fierce winds, cold, and snow. Tree densities are low here, and tree height declines to a spreading, shrublike form. Any stems that do stand up look like flag poles, with branches occurring only on the lee side of their trunks (Fig. 3.4). Very often alpine

drought and wind cause them to fail, and it is thought that they rarely reproduce. It's hard not to think "Why bother?" but, of course, plant seeds don't get to decide precisely where they will live.

Plant "migrations" occur when plant populations establish themselves elsewhere by seed in response to changing climates. While these are termed *migrations* in a figurative sense, in the *krummholtz*, or "crooked tree," treeline zone, individual plants quite literally migrate! At treeline, Engelmann spruce and subalpine fir form tree islands that are essentially one individual that tends to migrate away from harsher to more favorable conditions. In the Rockies, they typically move in an easterly direction, away from prevailing westerly winds. Branches on the harsher windward side die off, while lower branches on the lee side develop adventitious roots; they then spread, leaving a prostrate stem and dead branches behind them. Stems sprout roots when in snow, a process referred to as layering. Rates of annual migration are slow (~1 inch per year), yet with some treeline species living more than 500 years, they can relocate at least a short distance (Benedict 1984).

## Mountain Forests

In the West, extensive coniferous forests dominate the mountains from the foothills to treeline. Subalpine forests grade downslope into transitional mixed conifer forests. Below these lie ponderosa pine forests that grade into pinyon-juniper woodlands. At the base of western mountains, woodlands give way to grasslands and deserts.

Conifers originated long before flowering plants and disperse their pollen on the wind, which is an ancient trait, especially compared to more modern flowering plants that

**3.5.** Extensive spruce-fir forests (*top*) cover much of Colorado: *lower left,* subalpine fir (*Abies lasiocarpa*); *lower right,* a tall, narrow Engelmann spruce (*Picea engelmannii*).

be the most pristine of all regional forests because they tend to grow on steep slopes that are hard for loggers to access.

Canada's boreal forests are dominated by white spruce, black spruce, balsam fir, and several pines. Boreal forests are less diverse than other forests, perhaps because they have only re-formed in the last several thousand years after being scoured by Pleistocene glaciers. Engelmann spruce, a dominant species in western subalpine forests, is actually a subspecies of white spruce. The two trees hybridize where they meet in the northern United States and Canada. Subalpine fir is very closely related to the boreal balsam fir and hybridizes with it. In the Appalachians, red spruce and Frasier fir are closely related to white spruce and balsam fir, respectively. The basic elements of the subarctic and subalpine forests of the western United States are very similar. This is also true of understory species.

In the United States, these dense, dark subalpine forests extend down through the many north-south-trending mountain ranges, including the Pacific coastal ranges and the taller peaks in the Great Basin, the Rocky Mountains, and the Appalachians. In the Rockies, subalpine forests occur between about 9,000 feet and treeline.

Engelmann spruce and subalpine fir are by far the most common trees in Rocky Mountain subalpine forests. In the northern and central Rockies, they are joined or

attract insects, birds, and bats to do the job for them. Conifer seeds are often wind dispersed as well, although several species have coevolved with birds for dispersal purposes. Conifers are among the longest-lived trees on earth, with species such as bristlecone pines persisting for more than 5,000 years (Beasley and Klemmedson 1980). Walking through coniferous forests, you can sense how ancient they are.

Subalpine forests in the United States are really extensions of the enormous boreal forests of Alaska and Canada. Boreal forests occur throughout the Northern Hemisphere below the Arctic Circle and account for about a third of the world's forests. Subalpine forests are easily recognized by the dark green and very narrow canopies of both spruce and fir trees (Fig. 3.5). They may replaced by whitebark pine and sometimes lodgepole pine. In the Southern Rockies, limber pine and bristlecone pine are often present. Aspens often grow in areas opened up by fire, avalanche, or other disturbances. Unlike the vast tracts of boreal spruce-fir forests, the extent of subalpine forest in the mountain peaks is small, especially farther south. Subalpine forests of Arizona and New Mexico cover less than 2 percent of the land (Moir and Ludwig 1979).

Farther down the mountain are mixed conifer forests. In the Rockies, this zone occurs between about 8,000 and 9,500 feet. Mixed conifer forests are not well represented in the north, where it is too cold for most of its characteristic species, so these forests are more typical of the western mountains of the United States. While some conifers are very prominent in mixed conifer forests, this zone is in many ways a transitional one between cool, moist subalpine forests above and low, dry ponderosa pine forests below. In the northern and central Rockies, Douglas fir and lodgepole pine are very common, along with grand fir and western larch. Farther south are forests of Douglas fir, white fir, blue spruce, and southwestern white pine. Ponderosa pine, subalpine spruce, fir, and limber pine sometimes extend their ranges into mixed conifer forests. Aspen, the dominant deciduous tree of the Rockies—and the world, for that matter—has a strong presence in these forests, although often a transitional one.

Subalpine trees, like most conifers, originated in the Northern Hemisphere. According to Axelrod (1990), the trees of western North America's subalpine forests arose before the tall mountains that they would ultimately come to inhabit. The oldest records of western subalpine forests are from fossil remains in northern Nevada and central Idaho. By the Mid-Eocene (~45 Ma), fir, larch, spruce, pine, hemlock, Douglas fir, red cedar, and false-cypress were present in Idaho, Nevada, Wyoming, Montana, Colorado, and British Columbia. Understory species in the fossil record include currants, serviceberry, Oregon grape, chokecherry, and blueberries. A single aspen leaf was found (Axelrod 1990).

At least three spruce species occurred in the Canadian Arctic by the Mid-Eocene, indicating that this genus had already diversified. Spruce probably originated in boreal North America and then spread southward as well as westward to Asia and Europe (Ledig et al. 2004).

With the uplifting of the Rocky Mountains and the subsequent development of the coastal ranges within the last 22 million years, the mountain forests formed (Plate 15). Indeed, the formation of these ranges, with their very different climates and numerous peaks, led to considerable evolution and divergence of these trees. As with ponderosa pine, there are different varieties of bristlecone pine, white fir, Douglas fir, lodgepole pine, spruce, and fir in the Rockies, the Great Basin, and the coastal ranges. Typically, the Rocky Mountain varieties are slower growing and more drought tolerant. In the northern Pacific coastal mountains, which house some of the most productive forests on earth, Douglas fir can reach heights of over 300 feet and diameters exceeding 16 feet!

While Douglas fir's Pacific and Rocky Mountain varieties existed by the Miocene (~13 Ma), they have diversified even further, possibly during the Pleistocene (Li and Adams 1989). Through the ebb and flow of glacial periods, their populations may have expanded and contracted, becoming isolated at times. Today there are numerous disjunct populations of Douglas fir throughout the Southern Rockies, many of them quite different from one another.

During the Pleistocene, between about 1.6 million and 10,000 years ago, the distributions and genetics of mountain trees were totally rearranged. During the last glacial period, between about 20,000 and 11,000 years ago, glaciers scoured most of the boreal forests and Northern Rockies, and species such as white spruce shifted their distributions into the Great Plains and as far south as North Carolina. The boreal forests of Canada and Alaska reestablished only within the last several thousand years.

The western mountains owe much of their rugged terrain to the effects of ice sheet and alpine glaciation during this time (Plate 16; Barnosky et al. 1987). Large ice fields formed in the Cascades, Colorado's Front Range, the Wind River Range, the Yellowstone Plateau, and the San Juan Mountains. In the Southern Rockies, ice sheets extended over thousands of square miles and were over half a mile thick. Many ecosystems were displaced by glaciation and bitter cold. Surprisingly, these full glacial periods were drier than today's climate because moisture was simply bound up in ice. Many high-elevation sites not covered with glaciers were colonized by drought-tolerant species such as woody sages and grasses. Good fossil records of species that occurred during and after glaciation have been found in the Teton Mountains and Yellowstone National Park (Whitlock 1993). These plants were the first to colonize newly exposed soils that had been covered by ice.

During the last glacial phase, the elevational ranges of most plants shifted downward by thousands of feet (Van Devender et al. 1987, Betancourt 1990). As the southwestern deserts and the cold desert became

home to pinyon and juniper woodlands, areas between 4,000 and 6,000 feet, their former range, became dominated by Engelmann spruce, subalpine fir, blue spruce, Douglas fir, and limber pine escaping cold and ice. Today Engelmann spruce and subalpine fir occur between about 9,000 and 11,500 feet.

The migration of forest species down and horizontally from their narrow mountain zones during the Pleistocene made it a time of great range expansion. Many plants had broader elevational and latitudinal ranges during that time than they do today (Barnosky et al. 1987), and many of the subalpine trees that now occur in isolated stands on peaks in the Great Basin, on the San Francisco Peaks, and in many other ranges in the southwestern deserts probably colonized those areas during these cold times. Spruce-fir forests replaced the extensive ponderosa pine forests on the Mogollon Rim in northern Arizona (Anderson 1989, Van Devender et al. 1987), and spruce, white fir, and Douglas fir established themselves as far south as Mexico. Today most species of spruce in North America also occur in Mexico, with many probably arriving during this event. Douglas fir has been found in Baja, Mexico, where it occurs on cooler, north-facing slopes.

Limber pine, white spruce, blue spruce, aspen, and even mountain-dwelling land snails also made their way into Great Plains refugia during the Pleistocene. The presence of other mountain forest plants and animals such as marmots, red squirrels, and various voles indicate that this region was heavily forested during the last glacial maximum, a mere 18,000 to 14,000 years ago; it has only recently assumed its semiarid grassland character (Wells and Stewart 1987). Small, relict populations of these mountain trees and animals still survive in the Great Plains.

As the glaciers receded between 14,000 and 11,000 years ago, early colonizing sages, grasses, and alpine plants were quickly replaced at high-elevation sites by common juniper. As moisture levels increased, Engelmann spruce returned from protected refugia near the edge of the region's glaciers. It was soon followed by its contemporary associates, subalpine fir, lodgepole pine, and whitebark pine.

The migration of spruce populations back to mountain and boreal habitats following the Pleistocene is documented in the fossil record. Engelmann spruce migrated from the southern ice margin in the Teton Mountains to the previously glacier-covered Yellowstone National Park at a rate of about 650 feet per year (Whitlock 1993). This compares well to the northward spread of white spruce to Canada from refugia in the Great Plains at rates of between 650 and 2,600 feet per year as glaciers receded 12,000 years ago (Ritchie and MacDonald 1986). The rapid migration rates may have been due to favorable wind patterns and the fact that the land had been laid open by glacial scouring. White spruce seeds are light and winged, and are easily moved great distances by wind. In the process of migrating back north, white spruce did not necessarily stay very long in any one place. In parts of Canada, white spruce was locally outcompeted by black spruce within several thousand years as soil conditions improved.

*Subalpine Forests Today*

The subalpine forest climate is one of heavy snowfall, extreme temperatures (-50°F to 90°F), average annual temperatures at near freezing, and fierce winds that exceed 100 mph in winter (Tomback 1988). Today's subalpine spruce-fir forests are cool, dark havens that seem to stretch endlessly

through western mountains (Fig. 3.5). They extend from the Yukon Territory in Alaska into Mexico. Engelmann spruce and subalpine fir are found on a number of peaks in the Great Basin and northern Cascades, although their dominance in forests is most pronounced in the Rockies. They are well adapted to the continental climate of the Rockies, where some of the largest, oldest trees of these species are found, often reaching more than 3 feet in diameter and 120 feet in height (Mutel and Emerick 1984). Engelmann spruce often exceed 500 years in age, with some individuals living more than 800 years; subalpine fir rarely live longer than 300 years, although 400-year-old trees are occasionally found.

*Spruce-Fir Dynamics*

The Engelmann spruce and subalpine fir that dominate Rocky Mountain forests have a very dynamic and somewhat enigmatic relationship (Peet 2000). When the two species co-occur, which they often do, the most common pattern is for Engelmann spruce to be represented by a greater number of large trees and greater area of overstory cover, while subalpine fir is represented by a larger number of trees overall, although they tend to be smaller understory saplings and seedlings. Engelmann spruce produces many seeds that are readily wind dispersed, allowing it to aggressively colonize canopy openings caused by disturbance. Its seeds can disperse up to 800 feet in a good wind, and it is tolerant of a broad range of site conditions, including wet or boggy sites and dry ones. Intolerant of shady conditions, Engelmann spruce tend to colonize more-exposed sites, including areas with mineral soils following fire. By contrast, subalpine fir establishes more successfully in shade and in more organic soils.

The development of subalpine forests has a fairly predictable cycle. Disturbance—or, more specifically, stand destruction—is eventually followed by massive recolonization by spruce, fir, whitebark pine, lodgepole pine, limber pine, and/or aspen. Competition for light occurs among the trees, and shade-intolerant species such as whitebark pine, lodgepole pine, limber pine, and aspen are phased out or marginalized. Openings in Engelmann spruce–dominated forests allow subalpine fir to gain a foothold, although they may never replace Engelmann spruce. In stands dominated by subalpine fir, spruce may also increase in importance without becoming dominant. Early colonizers such as limber pine are overtopped and outcompeted by the taller and more shade tolerant spruce and fir on more desirable sites, and so persist only on dry and rocky microsites (Donnegan and Rebertus 1999). Eventually some trees die, opening space for limited colonization by new trees. If tree mortality and new tree recruitment both occur, it is possible for the forest to reach a steady state, although this rarely happens in the Rockies due to the frequency of natural disturbances (Peet 2000).

A variety of disturbances—including fire, insect outbreaks, avalanches, and windthrow—make subalpine forests dynamic places over long periods of time (Peet 2000, Veblen et al. 1994). These forces interact to affect forest succession, nutrient cycling, forest composition, and species diversity (McCullough et al. 1998), creating mosaics of species and conditions. Although these overgrown, high-elevation forests seem frozen in time, gothic with lichens and strands of bryophytes hanging down, disturbance may be just around the corner. Such disturbance in subalpine forests can occur on an enormous scale and change everything.

### Fire

Fire has historically been the most important form of natural disturbance in subalpine forests, although fires are infrequent in the subalpine zone, typically occurring at intervals of 300 years or more (Fischer and Bradley 1987). Cooler temperatures and greater moisture naturally limit fire in subalpine forests. These conditions also lead to the accumulation of enormous amounts of needles, branches, and dead trees, and ultimately catastrophic fires in which whole stands of spruce and fir can be killed. Such fires are in sharp contrast to the frequent, low-intensity surface fires that historically occurred in lower-elevation ponderosa pine forests (Tables 3.1, 3.2).

Fire cycles in subalpine forests vary with elevation and aridity. In western Montana, fire frequencies in subalpine forests range from about every 100 years to more than 350 years, with the shorter frequency occurring in forests near the lower edge of the subalpine zone, and the longer interval occurring in cooler, wetter forests at higher elevations.

Most subalpine trees cannot tolerate fire because of their very thin and resinous bark, branches that reach to the ground, and their tendency to grow in dense forests. Subalpine fir is the least fire tolerant fir in the Northern Rockies. It's as though these forests are designed to burn. While the fire histories of fire-tolerant ponderosa pine forests have been determined using fire scars, such scars are rare in Engelmann spruce and subalpine fir since they are typically destroyed by fire. Instead, the estimates of 300-year fire frequencies in these forests have been developed by studying the age structures of the stands themselves (Veblen et al. 1994).

**TABLE 3.1.** PRESETTLEMENT FIRE REGIMES IN WESTERN FORESTS OF NORTH AMERICA

| Vegetation Type | Region | Fire Frequency (years) | Reference |
|---|---|---|---|
| Gambel oak | AZ, CO, NM | 20 to 30 | Arno 1985 |
| Ponderosa pine | | | |
|   parklike stands | AZ, NM | 2 to 5 | Swetnam 1990 |
|   and savannas | Region-wide | 5 to 25 | Arno 1985 |
| | OR | 3 to 38 | Agee 1993 |
| Douglas fir | | | |
|   open canopy | CO, MT, WY | 25 to 60 | Arno 1985 |
|   and/or young forest | OR, WA | 20 to 30 | Arno 1985 |
| Mixed conifer | | | |
|   parklike ponderosa pine | AZ, NM, TX | 6 to 10 | Swetnam 1990 |
|   open canopy mixed conifer | AZ, NM, TX | 7 to 9 | Swetnam 1990 |
|   Douglas fir, larch, grand fir | ID, WA, OR, MT | to 150 | Kilgore 1981 |
|   dry site Douglas fir | Northern Rocky Mts. | 7 to 20 | Kilgore 1981 |
|   wet site Douglas fir | MT | 117 to 146 | Kilgore 1981 |
| Lodgepole pine | Region-wide | 25 to 150 | Kilgore 1981 |
| | Region-wide | 60 to 500 | Arno 1985 |
| Spruce and/or subalpine fir | | | |
|   young, open | Region-wide | 50 to 300 | Arno 1985 |
|   spruce-fir | Region-wide | >150 to 350 | Kilgore 1981 |
|   lodgepole pine | Region-wide | >150 to 350 | Kilgore 1981 |
|   spruce-fir | MT, WA | 25 to 300 | Agee 1993 |

**TABLE 3.2.** RELATIVE FIRE RESISTANCE OF COMMON WESTERN CONIFERS

| Species | Bark Thickness | Stand Habit | Fire Resistance |
|---|---|---|---|
| Ponderosa pine | very thick | open | very resistant |
| Douglas fir | very thick | moderate | very resistant |
| Lodgepole pine | very thin | open | medium resistance |
| Engelmann spruce | thin | dense | low resistance |
| Subalpine fir | very thin | dense | very low resistance |

*Source*: Flint 1925.

*Natural Enemies of Subalpine Forests*

The spruce beetle is the most damaging insect in the subalpine zone of the Southern Rockies. Some of its outbreaks are so extensive that this beetle is considered as ecologically significant as fire. It attacks Engelmann spruce rather than subalpine fir and so also plays a major role in their interactions. Spruce beetle populations persist in scattered live large trees and fallen dead trees, and periodically erupt into enormous populations that kill most spruce over extensive areas (Veblen et al. 1994). Spruce beetles typically attack trees larger than 4 inches in diameter. Beetle outbreaks have been associated with mild winters, drought, blowdowns, and logging.

Not surprisingly, there are important interactions between fire and the spruce beetle in the subalpine zone. In northwestern Colorado, Bebi et al. (2003) found that spruce-fir stands in a subalpine forest that had burned in the late 1880s were less susceptible to attacks by the spruce beetle because the colonizing trees were too young and small to be attractive/susceptible to the beetles. They predicted that these young forests would remain somewhat immune to beetle attack for 150–200 years. And while conventional wisdom predicted that beetle-killed stands of spruce would be more susceptible to fire due to the heavy fuel load created by beetle-killed trees, this has not been the case. They concluded that beetle-killed trees and debris in wetter subalpine forests break down quickly enough in normal years that they are less vulnerable to fire. Weather is a critical factor, however, and this might not be the case in drought years. Ultimately, both fire and beetle destruction set the stage for colonization by new spruce and fir seedlings, and enhanced growth of surviving seedlings and saplings.

While subalpine fir may escape being attacked by the voracious spruce beetle, it has its own significant natural enemy: balsam wooly adelges, an aphidlike, sap-sucking insect that was introduced from Europe into the northeastern United States around 1900. This insect deforms and kills subalpine fir and poses a significant threat to the species throughout its western range. Discovered in Idaho in 1983, the insects now affect subalpine fir in a third of the state (14,000 square miles). It is another classic case of an herbivore becoming extremely successful after being removed from its suite of natural enemies. In 2002 more than 800,000 trees on 350,000 acres died due to the western balsam bark beetle and disease pathogens. Once subalpine fir reach about 150 years old, they are also susceptible to some deadly fungal pathogens. Fungi such as wood rots and broom rusts cause most disease losses.

Neither Engelmann spruce nor subalpine fir is particularly stout trunked or deep rooted, and both are susceptible to blowdowns in which whole stands may be knocked over by intense wind storms. Typically, older stands with a high incidence of trunk rot are most susceptible to such wind damage. Stands that are damaged by wind may become susceptible to insect outbreaks.

In a study of one subalpine forest in Colorado, Veblen et al. (1994) compared effects of different disturbance factors and found that 9 percent of the area had been affected by avalanches, 38 percent by spruce beetle outbreak, and 59 percent by fire. The time required for these habitats to recover following disturbance was 521 years following fire and 259 years following spruce beetle outbreaks. These data suggest that such forests are always in a state of flux, but changing too slowly to perceive.

*White Pines*

On the dry ridges and exposed southern slopes of the subalpine zone, spruce and fir are replaced by white pines (Peet 2000), including whitebark pine, limber pine (Fig. 3.6), and bristlecone pine (Fig. 3.4). These shorter, round-crowned pines form more open forests in the subalpine zone. They are often the first to colonize disturbed sites, only to be replaced by more mesic, shade-loving species. However, they are often able to persist on exposed slopes and at treeline.

In the Northern Rockies, down through Wyoming, whitebark pine is the dominant white pine. It forms pure stands on well-drained soils at high elevations in parts of Idaho, Montana, and northern Wyoming and California, but is less prominent everywhere else. It is not particularly tolerant of either competition or shade, and so it functions as a transitional species that is eventually replaced by more shade tolerant species such as Engelmann spruce and subalpine fir. Whitebark pine's lower limit within the subalpine zone is determined by competition for light, water, or nutrients (Weaver 2001). Neither spruce nor fir is as tolerant of wind-induced drought, so whitebark pine can dominate exposed slopes and ridges.

Whitebark pine is one of the stone pines, a small group whose seeds are adapted to be dispersed by animals and birds such as Clark's nutcracker (Fig. 3.7), a member of the jay family (Corvidae). Unlike ponderosa pine cones, whitebark pine cones do not open wide enough to release seeds when they are fully developed. Instead they open only enough to reveal their delectable, wingless seeds, which are seated deeply in the cone and do not readily fall out. The seeds attract birds, bears, and squirrels, which rip into the brittle cones and disperse and cache the seeds at a distance from the parent tree.

**3.6.** Limber pine (*Pinus flexilis*) with abundant, large cones, San Francisco Peaks, northern Arizona.

The phenomenon of bird-dispersed pine forests has been speculated about for hundreds of years, but it has only been in the last thirty years that wingless pine seeds have been shown to be dispersed by birds, leading to the establishment of whole forests (Lanner 1996). One of these seed dispersers is Clark's nutcracker, named after Captain William Clark, of the Lewis and Clark expedition, who in 1805 first described it feeding on pine seeds. Hutchins and Lanner (1982) have shown that Clark's nutcrackers are the only birds in whitebark pine forests that consistently feed on its seeds. These jays harvest seeds from August through November, both eating and caching them.

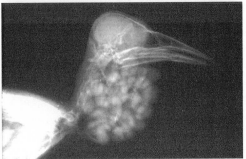

**3.7.** A Clark's nutcracker on the branch of a white-bark pine (*Pinus albicaulis*); *below,* radiograph of Clark's nutcracker with twenty-eight seeds from a singleleaf pinyon (*Pinus monophylla*) in its sublingual pouch. The bird weighed 141 grams, and the seeds 31 grams. Courtesy of Diana Tomback, Steve Vander Wall, and Oxford University Press.

By winter, each nutcracker has harvested about 130,000 seeds, storing about 75 percent of them. Seeds are cached at a depth of about an inch, which is ideal for germination. There is also a deliberateness to the caching done by Clark's nutcrackers compared to other dispersers, such as robins, which simply defecate leftover seeds during flight. Hutchins and Lanner (1982) observed groups of ten to fifteen nutcrackers collecting seeds without aggressive behavior, and their role as dispersers became clear when they cached seeds in communal areas more than 2 miles away (Hutchins and Lanner 1982, Lanner 1996). The Clark's nutcrackers' aggressive harvesting and long-distance dispersal and caching of seeds can lead to forest regeneration following disturbances such as fire (Hutchins and Lanner 1982, Lanner 1996,

Tomback 1978, Lanner and Vander Wall 1980). Since learning this, I look at burn sites that are being recolonized by bird pines in a different way, knowing that recolonization probably would be impossible otherwise.

Whitebark pine is in trouble these days, as are the forests it occupies (Kendall and Keane 2001, McDonald and Hoff 2001). This species plays a crucial role in colonizing disturbed sites and paving the way for later successional trees, and it also provides animals with a key source of unparalleled rich food. Hibernating bears need its seeds to survive through the winter. Like many forest trees, whitebark pine is threatened by a lack of fire, which has limited its establishment opportunities since it needs exposure to sunlight. Fire suppression has led to dense whitebark pine forests, which are vulnerable to attack by deadly mountain pine bark beetles. Perhaps even more important, its populations are being laid to waste by a fungus, white pine blister rust, which was inadvertently introduced into North America in the early 1900s along with pines from Europe. Despite control efforts, the rust has spread throughout the northwestern United States and much of the Rockies. In parts of the Columbia River basin and the Bob Marshall Wilderness complex in Montana, cover of whitebark pine has declined by more than 45 percent. In the Bitterroot Range in Montana, whitebark pine has declined by more than 98 percent! The highest mortality from blister rust in the Rocky Mountains has occurred in northern Idaho, northern Montana, and Canada, where up to half of all whitebark pines are dead, and nearly all of the remaining trees are infected—truly an ecological crisis. The last hope for the survival of the whitebark pine is that some trees will prove to be resistant to this disease, and, in fact, some canker-free trees have been found, demonstrating natural selection in action. Other white pines—including limber pine, bristlecone pine, white pine, eastern white pine, sugar pine, and foxtail pine—are also at risk. This pathogen requires currants (*Ribes* spp.) as alternate hosts to help it to spread.

*Limber Pine*

At lower, drier latitudes, whitebark pine is replaced by the more drought tolerant limber pine (Fig. 3.6). Like other white pines, it has five needles. Its distinctive characteristic is having branches flexible enough to be tied into a loose knot—hence, the name "limber" pine. Its seeds are also adapted to be dispersed by birds. Limber pine occurs throughout the Rocky Mountains and on some peaks in the Intermountain region. Like whitebark pine, limber pine establishes early following disturbance and is often replaced by more shade tolerant and taller spruce and fir on moist sites. Young trees are fairly intolerant of fire, but older trees often survive. They are thought to be best protected from fire on rocky sites, where they may live more than 1,000 years (Donnegan and Rebertus 1999). Like whitebark pine and bristlecone pine, limber pine often persists on exposed sites that few other species tolerate. These three species often take on the same gnarly look in areas where they become climax species.

According to Lanner (1996), limber pine is the most recent descendent of a Mexican and Central American white pine that is actually a wind-dispersed species. He contends that wind-dispersed seeds are able to establish successfully without the benefit of caching in wetter (e.g., tropical) climates, but in drier regions north of Mexico, seeds are more likely to germinate when cached. Jays migrated north with this pine into the dry southwestern United States, caching its seeds along the way. There is a northward gradient of pine divergence from acahuit pine to southwestern white pine to limber pine. Some regard southwestern white pine as a subspecies of limber pine.

Limber pine seeds are wingless (Fig. 3.8), large, and nutritious, and their cones are highly visible and erect in the canopy, where birds find them and remove their seeds efficiently. Occasionally, limber pines produce seeds with vestigial wings—tiny remnants of their winged origin. As with whitebark pine, Clark's nutcracker may be the single most important disperser of limber pine seeds, carrying up to 125 of them in its unique sublingual pouch in one trip (Fig. 3.7; Lanner

**3.8.** Cones with bird- and wind-dispersed seeds: *left to right*, seeds of Colorado pinyon (*Pinus edulis*), ponderosa pine (*Pinus ponderosa*), and limber pine (*Pinus flexilis*). Note the winged seed and the spines on the cone of the wind-dispersed ponderosa pine, and the lack of wings and spines associated with the bird-dispersed pinyon and limber pine.

1996). Lanner and Vander Wall (1980) found that Clark's nutcrackers cached approximately 12,000 seeds—mainly limber pine—within a 1-acre site.

In one study in Colorado, limber pine was found to have been the first species to colonize twenty-five burned sites, thanks to Clark's nutcracker (Lanner and Vander Wall 1980). Wind-dispersed Engelmann spruce followed, although only after 94 years, and subalpine fir after 116 years.

### Bristlecone Pine

Farther south and west, limber pine is replaced on dry, exposed ridges by the even more drought tolerant bristlecone pine (Fig. 3.4). It is also a white pine and occurs in the Southern Rockies, while the closely related Great Basin bristlecone pine is only found on peaks in that region. After limber pine, bristlecone pine is the most widely distributed pine in Nevada. Bristlecone pines are known for their longevity and drought tolerance, and individuals in the Great Basin can live to be more than 5,000 years old (Beasley and Klemmedson 1980). Like the other shade-intolerant white pines, they persist longest on rocky and exposed sites, where they are slow growing. Needles can stay photosynthetically active for more than fifteen years, and occasionally up to forty-five years (Richardson and Rundel 1998). "Seedlings" that are forty years old may be less than 6 inches tall. Bristlecone pine seeds are winged and smaller than those of limber pine. Even though they are not adapted for bird dispersal, the seeds are occasionally dispersed by Clark's nutcrackers (Keeley and Zedler 1998).

### MIXED CONIFER FORESTS

Mixed conifer forests in Arizona and New Mexico cover only about 4 percent of the land (Moir and Ludwig 1979). These forests are more dynamic than those of the subalpine zone because they are warmer and drier, and as a result experience shorter fire cycles (Tables 3.1, 3.2). In mixed conifer forests, there is less moisture to decompose plant material or to slow fires. Species such as lodgepole pine, ponderosa pine, southwestern white pine, and aspen behave as early successional species by rapidly colonizing burned sites, only to be replaced eventually by species such as Douglas fir, white fir, and blue spruce. In southwestern mountains, Douglas fir and white fir forests are widespread. In the Great Basin, white fir, Douglas fir, and a number of pines mix with whitebark pine, bristlecone pine, limber pine, subalpine fir, and Engelmann spruce in the subalpine zone. Mixed conifer forests have been exploited far more intensively than subalpine forests for timber harvesting, recreation, and other activities because of their greater accessibility.

### Douglas Fir

Douglas fir occurs from British Columbia deep into Mexico. Not a true fir, it is mainly found on south-facing slopes in the northern part of its range, and north-facing slopes in the southern part of its range. It forms large, pure stands in the cooler coastal ranges and the Northern Rockies. In the Front Range of the Southern Rockies in Colorado, it is the dominant tree on north-facing slopes and in deep ravines, and occurs in more exposed areas at higher elevations. Douglas fir codominates mixed conifer forests in the Southern Rockies along with white fir and blue spruce. Its populations become smaller and more fragmented at lower latitudes in Arizona and Mexico.

Douglas fir plays different ecological roles. Sometimes it is an early successional species, and sometimes a climax species.

In general, the Rocky Mountain variety of Douglas fir occurs as a climax or persistent species in warmer, drier areas, and as a seral or transitional species in more moist areas. Its fire resistance helps it gradually form large stands in some areas (Tables 3.1, 3.2). The thick, corky bark of the Douglas fir's lower trunk and roots, and its adventitious roots make it more fire resistant than many mixed conifer species, and so it remains a dominant species in western forests.

In the Rockies, Douglas fir rarely lives longer than 400 years; it grows to 160 feet on the best sites. In the coastal mountains, a different variety (*P. menziesii* var. *menziesii*) grows to enormous heights, often reaching more than 250 feet; trees there commonly live longer than 500 years and occasionally more than 1,000 years. The tallest Douglas fir on record (330 feet) was found in Washington (Lotan and Critchfield 1990).

Douglas fir's wind-dispersed seeds typically do not reach more than 300 feet from the parent tree. While seedlings do best in partial shade initially, older plants require more sun. Douglas fir is, however, more tolerant of shade than ponderosa pine, lodgepole pine, or western larch. It also grows well in a range of soils. In Montana it is able to colonize highly calcareous soils, while Engelmann spruce, subalpine fir, and lodgepole pine cannot. Douglas fir is one of the most valued timber species in the western United States, particularly in the Northwest and the Northern Rockies.

## Lodgepole Pine

Lodgepole pine dominates post-fire areas in much of the mountainous west. Following fire, its heavy-duty, fire-resistant cones release large numbers of seeds, producing dense, even-aged stands. Its seedlings grow quickly in these sunny landscapes.

Lodgepole pine needs an open landscape because it is a poor competitor, even with grasses, and is strongly intolerant of shade. It is gradually replaced by shade-tolerant conifers such as subalpine trees, Douglas fir, and white fir.

Lodgepole pine occurs from the Yukon Territory of Canada to the Sangre de Cristo Mountains in southern Colorado. It also occurs in Baja California and probably arrived there during the Pleistocene. Like ponderosa pine, white fir, and Douglas fir, it has diverged into different varieties in the coastal ranges and in the Rocky Mountains. It is thought that this differentiation occurred during the Pleistocene (Thompson 1990). Lodgepole pine is most closely related to jack pine, a dominant species in the boreal forests of Canada and Alaska.

Lodgepole pine's ability to colonize infertile soils made it well suited for colonizing soils that were scoured by glaciers at the end of the Pleistocene. It is more tolerant of infertile soils than many conifers, and it is also unique in its tolerance of acidic, rhyolitic soils, which are derived from volcanoes. In Yellowstone National Park, infertile rhyolitic plateaus are covered almost exclusively by lodgepole pine forests (MacDonald et al. 1998). It colonized these plateaus 10,000 years ago and has persisted ever since. Other climax forests of lodgepole pine occur in Colorado's Front Range and across southern Oregon (Agee 1998, Moir 1969).

Lodgepole pine's serotinous, fire-adapted cones stay closed for one or more years after maturation and then open rapidly following fire as high temperatures melt the resins that seal the cone scales. These pines actually invest more energy in their thick cones than in the seeds themselves. With this protection, seeds can survive temperatures of more than 390°F (Keeley and Zedler 1998). This is a different strategy for dealing with fire. In the subalpine zone, whitebark pine seeds get flown into burned sites by Clark's nutcrackers, while spruce and fir take their time and blow in. But lodgepole pine seeds are already there, and once they are established, they grow quickly in open, burned sites. They don't grow particularly large (typically less than 100 feet), and they are not particularly long lived, rarely living more than 350 years (Agee 1998), indicating that they are adapted for a relatively rapid turnover (Tables 3.1, 3.2).

Not all lodgepole pine cones are serotinous, however. They are where the species is most common—in low-gradient, drier, warmer sites where fuel can accumulate and fires can spread with little interruption—but not in the subalpine zone where fires are less frequent, or on rocky sites where fires stay small. Apparently, this trait in lodgepole pine involves relatively few genes: it takes only one gene to determine the melting temperature of cone resin (Keeley and Zedler 1998).

Lodgepole pines have their own disturbance story, involving fire, the mountain pine beetle, and disease. Although it is fed on by more than 450 species of insects (de Groot and Turgeon 1998), the coevolutionary relationship between lodgepole pine and the mountain beetle is particularly ancient and refined. Periodic outbreaks of the mountain pine beetle, a bark beetle, can destroy large numbers of trees, causing an enormous buildup of fuel, which leads to fire and lodgepole pine regeneration. What is interesting about this cycling is that the beetle favors trees that are at least seventy years old, which is precisely when lodgepole pine begin to produce the most seeds. Thus a large, even-aged stand of lodgepole pine reaching seventy years of age is set

for a major recycling of the whole system (Amman 1977, Stark 1982).

Typically lodgepole pine stands are low in productivity because they tend to grow in nutrient-poor soils; the mountain pine beetle therefore plays an essential role in revitalizing this system. Disease also influences this interaction. The beetle preferentially attacks trees weakened by fungi. These trees become reservoirs for fungi and for beetles for future outbreaks as the stand population ages. This is why the mountain pine beetle is regarded as the ultimate forest manager in most lodgepole pine populations (Preisler and Mitchell 1993).

Studies of the multitude of animal species associated with this wide-ranging tree have revealed complicated relationships (Benkman 1999, Siepielski and Benkman 2004). Destructive moths, pine squirrels, and a seed-eating bird, the red crossbill, all favor different cone/seed dynamics and exert strong and different selective pressures on lodgepole pine. Where only crossbills and lodgepoles occur, there is strong selection for larger, more protective cones since crossbills can get into smaller, thinner cones more readily. Where cone moths and lodgepoles occur together, there is strong selection for smaller cones since moths favor larger cones with more seeds. Where squirrels are present, they are so destructive that they override the effects of other species. It's interesting to think of such an imposing tree being so strongly affected by these small creatures and essentially pulled in so many ecological and evolutionary directions.

In the Central and Southern Rockies, white fir and a sprinkling of blue spruce become more common in mixed conifer forests, along with Douglas fir, creating mesic, soft forests (Moir and Ludwig 1979, Fechner 1990). Neither white fir nor blue spruce is strongly shade tolerant, although they are able to establish under the canopies of other conifers and persist for long periods. Like so many mountain trees, these trees can act as either pioneering or climax species, partly because they can persist on soils that are not tolerated by most other trees. Blue spruce can successfully colonize streamside soils, and soils derived from limestones or calcareous sandstones.

The soft wood and heart rot susceptibility of white fir makes it, along with Douglas fir, a common nesting tree for woodpeckers and many other birds, including the Mexican spotted owl. Growth of white fir can be retarded by spruce budworm outbreaks, which are reflected in smaller growth rings (Swetnam and Lynch 1993). Both species are often cultivated for landscaping and for Christmas trees since their forms are so classic and symmetrical. Blue spruce is grown in Europe as well as the United States.

### Aspen

What a miracle of a tree the aspen is! After tromping through a dry, dusty pine forest, entering an aspen grove is a welcome change. Aspen is the softest, lushest tree in the West, and for many people it defines the Rocky Mountains; it is even considered an aesthetic resource (DeByle 1985). Unlike the conifers with which it occurs, aspen is a modern flowering plant. It is dioecious, producing separate female and male plants. It is a strong photosynthesizer, better than conifers, and even photosynthesizes through its bark.

Aspen is the most widely distributed deciduous tree species in North America (Fig. 3.9). Only the Eurasian *Populus tremula*, with which the North American aspen hybridizes, has a larger distribution. *Populus tremula* occurs throughout Europe,

**3.9.** An aspen stand with a lush understory (*top*) and another with severe elk browsing/antler rubbing damage, San Francisco Peaks, northern Arizona.

northern Asia, and northern Africa. Combined, these two species have an extensive circumboreal distribution, the largest range of any tree in the world. It may be that their classification as separate species is more a matter of taxonomic convenience than reality. According to Harper et al. (1985), a case could be made for lumping our aspen and the Eurasian aspen into one circumboreal superspecies, except for the fact that the extensive genetic variation that exists within each of them already stretches the concept of a species.

In North America, aspen occur from the Arctic to Mexico, and from coast to coast. In the eastern United States, aspen form large, continuous stands at lower elevations, while in the West it is a mountain species with separate stands scattered among the many peaks. Aspen extends to lower elevations in north-facing canyons and ravines (Jones 1985), and many of these populations are isolated Pleistocene relicts. In the Rockies, aspen range from about 6,000 feet to treeline in some places. The largest populations occur in Utah and Colorado, where stands cover more than a million acres.

Aspen's evolutionary history is similar to that of many other mountain species in the West. Its ancestors have flourished in the West since the Miocene (Axelrod 1990), and it may have originated in Asia (Newsholme 1992). One of aspen's most remarkable characteristics is its habit of cloning, or spreading vegetatively by underground stems or ramets. This spreading habit helps create its habitats and prolong its life. Most aspen regeneration is by root sprouting rather than by seed. Like all species in the willow family (Salicaceae), aspen seeds are very short lived and extremely particular about the conditions in which they can germinate. The clonal nature of aspen is obvious in the fall, when whole sections of trees on a mountain hillside turn the same hue of yellow or orange at the same time (Larson 1944, Cottam 1954, Barnes 1966).

The degree to which an aspen clone can dominate a landscape is staggering, with a single clone—or individual plant—often exceeding an acre in size (Mitton and Grant 1996, Kay 1997). Mature clones can produce 400,000 to a million shoots per acre, and the sprouts may grow 3 feet per growing season initially. Aspen's productivity far outpaces that of colonizing coniferous species establishing by seed, which may be one reason why it is so successful at colonizing sites after fire—it is already there. A large clone in Utah known to encompass more than 100 acres has more than 47 million stems, making it the largest known living organism (Mitton and Grant 1996)!

People often marvel at the longevity of species such as bristlecone pines or creosote bush, but it is very likely that aspen clones live much longer. While it is impossible to absolutely date such large clones, their enormous size combined with the rarity of their establishment by seed has led some to believe that clones became established during much wetter climates, perhaps as far back as the end of the Pleistocene, more than 10,000 years ago. Some clones may be more than a million years old, making these ancient beings the longest-lived organisms on earth (Mitton and Grant 1996).

Like so many trees, aspen plays different ecological roles in the western mountains. Sometimes it persists as a climax forest; sometimes it establishes quickly from root sprouts following fire and persists until it is replaced by shade-tolerant conifers. In some areas, new sprouts are chewed to pieces by burgeoning elk populations that reduce clones or groves to a few stems (Fig. 3.9). Aspen is most likely to persist as a climax or stable stand when it occurs next to lower-elevation coniferous forests, such as ponderosa pine forests, that burn frequently. These fires may prevent pines from colonizing aspen stands. Aspen, unlike conifers, may also occur in stable stands on substrates such as Colorado Plateau shales (Romme et al. 2001).

Aspen clones benefit from fire. Though their stems can be killed by even very light fires due to their thin bark, they need the light provided by newly burned spaces and are able to reestablish quickly and vigorously. It's a daunting image, that of this subterranean biological mass rearing up again after fire reopens the landscape. It reestablishes quickly after fire and can develop an extensive canopy in only three to five years (Brown and DeByle 1987). Most even-aged aspen groves sprouted following fire. In the San Francisco Peaks in northern Arizona, I have seen abundant aspen sprouts in burn sites that were less than a week old.

Fires often stop when they reach aspen stands, which have been referred to as "asbestos type" and "firebreak" trees because they are so moist (DeByle 1985, Kay 1997). Even crown fires in nearby conifers drop to the ground and spread only short distances into aspen stands. This is important because aspen roots are not especially fire tolerant, and when stands do burn, it is usually during drier times of the year, with invading conifers typically carrying the fire. Overall, lightning fire ignition rates for aspens are the lowest of any western forest type, less than half that of all other cover types.

Aspen stands are moist compared with surrounding conifer stands. They typically support a dense understory of mesophytic shrubs, forbs, and grasses, in sharp contrast to most conifer stands (DeByle 1985, Peet 2000). The understory of conifer stands consists of dense layers of pine needles and considerable woody debris, but only sparse vegetation. While the dense undergrowth of aspen stands is partly due to the fine-textured and more fertile soils that it colonizes, it is also often a function of more basic differences between aspens and conifers. The aspen's soft, rapidly decomposing wood and relatively nutrient rich deciduous leaves result in rapid nutrient cycling, with little woody fuel accumulation, which encourages growth of mesophytic understory species (Vitousek et al. 1982). Thus, aspen has greater root-sprouting potential by supporting a forest understory that experiences only low-intensity fires.

The shade cast by aspen canopies makes it hard for conifers to establish and succeed or replace them. Still, individual aspen stems, or trunks, are relatively short

lived—typically less than 150 years—so eventually openings occur in the canopy where conifer seedlings are able to establish and may eventually succeed them; however, conifer seedlings are just as often buried under piles of aspen leaves.

Aspen forests support a greater diversity of plants and animals than any other ecosystem in the West except for riparian ecosystems (Mitton and Grant 1996, Chong et al. 2001). As a keystone species, aspen has a critical influence on the ecosystem that builds up around it, with many animals feeding on both aspen and their many diverse understory plants. Stohlgren et al. (1997) found that 43 percent of the vascular plants in the Beaver Meadows area in the Rocky Mountains were associated with aspen stands that covered only 1.2 percent of the land. A related study found 188 plant species occurred in aspen stands, and, not surprisingly, that most butterflies in the area were also associated with aspen (Plate 17; see Chong et al. 2001 for a list of plant and butterfly species in aspen groves). Aspen understory plants are wonderfully diverse, among them columbine, aster, lupine, paintbrush, larkspur, vetch, geranium, fleabane, cinquefoil, penstemon, goldenrod, groundsel, coneflower, violet, sedge, muhly, fescue, bluegrass, alumroot, spirea, rose—just to name a few.

Like all members of the willow family, aspen is fast growing, rather short lived, and produces copious lush foliage. Young vigorous growth is what most herbivores are attracted to. As with other deciduous trees, aspen photosynthesizes far more than conifers, which means that it produces more carbohydrates for growth and reproduction. As a result, aspen and other members of the willow family are among the most heavily fed-upon plant groups in the world (Southwood 1961). Not surprisingly, many of the mammals that browse on aspen also feed on willow and cottonwood.

While aspen produces an array of chemicals—including phenolic glycosides and tannins, which are thought to deter herbivores—many animals remain undeterred. More than a hundred kinds of insects feed on aspen, including nine species whose populations can erupt into major outbreaks, some involving millions of acres of trees. Aspens are fairly tolerant of extreme herbivory by defoliating lepidopterous insects such as tent caterpillars, gypsy moths, and the large aspen tortrex (Lindroth 2001). While some clones may experience reduced growth following defoliation, others can entirely compensate for such damage.

More than 130 species of birds are associated with aspen and aspen-conifer forests (DeByle 1985, Bartos 2001), a greater diversity and number than found in stands of conifers. And because so many insects are associated with aspens and their understory plants, many of these birds are insectivorous. Cavity-nesting birds account for 30 to 60 percent of all birds encountered in aspen forests. Cavity-bearing trunks are common in aspen forests due to the naturally short lives of individual trunks, their soft wood, and their susceptibility to decay fungi that provide hollow centers in living trees. Primary cavity nesters, such as sapsuckers and hairy and downy woodpeckers, prefer aspen. And of course, as they move out, a large array of secondary cavity nesters move in. Many of the birds associated with aspen rely on leaves and catkins (flowers) for food. During the winter, species such as the ruffed grouse, which mostly occurs in aspen forests, can persist on male flower buds. Black bear also

feed on aspen buds and catkins, so the next time you see what appear to be bear tracks up an aspen trunk, they may be just that.

More than fifty species of mammals rely on aspen habitats, including dwarf shrew, pocket gopher, porcupine, beaver, hare, rabbit, deer, bear, moose, bison, and elk (DeByle 1985). Many feed on aspen leaves, shoots, leaf and flower buds, catkins, roots, and bark. The herbivory of subterranean pocket gophers on new, spreading shoots can be fierce, successfully preventing aspen from expanding outward through suckering. It has been estimated that the gophers can consume more than 20 percent of the belowground growth in aspen stands. Beaver are largely dependent on the willow family for dam-building materials, but the ponds created by their dams can kill nearby aspen.

All kinds of animals eat aspen bark. Mice, voles, porcupines, rabbits, and hares may eat large patches of bark from the base of trees, sometimes girdling and killing them, but it is the big grazing/browsing mammals—elk, moose, cattle, and deer—that are creating the biggest threat to aspen today. Elk may be the worst offenders. They are browsing aspen to death in parts of the West. Often they feed on other plants such as understory forbs and grasses—only to shift to browsing on aspen later in the growing season and into the winter (Fig. 3.9). Then they gnaw at aspen bark, strip it off, leave deep gouges in the bark from rubbing their antlers, and break tree trunks to browse new shoots, buds and leaves that is so harmful to aspen—relentless behaviors that are exceeding the tolerance of aspens to herbivory (Keigley and Frisina 2008).

Although one might tend to think that because aspen stems can be part of enormous clones, the loss of several or even many trunks to herbivory ultimately won't matter, such is not the case. In northern Arizona, it has been estimated that a burned aspen stand has about three to five years of root reserves to establish a new stand (Rolf 2001). In areas with heavy ungulate browsing, newly spouted aspen forests must be protected by tall fences or aspen will be removed from the forest system. This is happening in localized areas throughout much of the tree's western range. Protective fences have been constructed in many states to promote aspen regeneration, but fencing is costly, and the number of aspens lost is outpacing the small acreages that have been fenced.

Historical records indicate that elk and other wild ungulates were rare in the 1800s. Explorers in Yellowstone reported seeing elk only about once every eighteen days, while today there are nearly 100,000 elk there (Kay 1997). Records from the Canadian Rockies, Utah, Arizona, New Mexico, and Colorado tell essentially the same story: elk were rare. There is some debate as to why this may have been so. Some scientists believe that Native Americans were very effective hunters of elk and other large ungulates, while others hypothesize that animals such as coyotes, wolves, and mountain lions, which are far less common today, kept elk numbers down. Perhaps some combination of human and animal predation was responsible.

Aspen are now threatened throughout the western United States, with populations having decreased by 50 to 96 percent (Bartos 2001). It is thought that overbrowsing and fire suppression are the main causes. Suppression of fire over the last 150 years has enabled conifers to overtake and stress aspen stands, which then become susceptible to pathogens that can help to kill them.

Certainly elk, in their unprecedented numbers, are an enormous part of the problem. In Arizona, where 96 percent of aspen cover is gone, the state Game and Fish Department increased elk hunting permits by 400 percent following astronomical elk population growth in the 1980s and early 1990s (Rolf 2001).

## Plants and Animals in Mountain Forests

Although coniferous forests provide great structural habitat for birds and small mammals, as well as insects, seeds, and root fungi to eat, it is the forest openings, with a greater diversity of fruit-bearing woody shrubs and herbaceous plants, that are the busiest places. Abundant grasses, flowers, and shrubs occur in meadows and more open forests in western mountains. Many of these species grow throughout the mixed conifer, subalpine, and tundra habitats.

Flowers have a particularly broad elevational range in the mountains. Common understory species include lupine, iris (Plate 18), geranium, Solomon seal, goldenrod, valerian, vetch, violet, bluebell, strawberry, fleabane, sage, columbine, pussytoes, penstemon, mountain parsley, gentian, and meadowrue. Cool-season mountain grasses are diverse and lush, and include poa or bluegrass, fescue, nodding brome, muhly, and sedge.

A large variety of shrubs and small trees occur throughout western forests, offering food resources for animals and an aesthetic resource for humans in the form of fall color. Bigtooth maple, which grows in wet side canyons throughout the Intermountain West, turns hot pink in the fall, giving eastern trees a run for their money. So do wild rose, sumac, and oak, which turn deep red at the end of the season.

Many of these species are fruit bearing and provide fall food for birds and mammals. These include wax currant, golden currant, gooseberry, whitestem gooseberry, elderberry, snowberry, mahonia, serviceberry, chokecherry, raspberry, honeysuckles, twinberry, ninebark, spirea, and oaks. Huckleberry and cranberry are found farther north. Around Flagstaff, Arizona, I have noticed that nearly all fruit-bearing shrubs are distributed under the canopies of ponderosa pine and along fence lines—evidence of their dispersal by birds.

Even the shallowest drainages in western mountains host willows. Many of these are circumboreal, or at least also occur in the Arctic, and probably migrated south ahead of the glaciers during the Pleistocene.

The most conspicuous insects in mountain forests are those whose populations periodically erupt into major outbreaks. Most forest trees have outbreak insect species associated with them. Such insects include foliage-feeding moths and bark beetles. Many outbreaks are remarkably cyclic, and these cycles are sometimes intertwined with fire and encouraged by drought. And these insects have been around for as long as their forest hosts: fossils of many modern-day wood-boring and bark beetles from the Florissant shale beds in Colorado date back 35 million years, when many of these forests were forming (Furniss and Carolin 1977).

The western spruce budworm feeds on nearly all western conifers and is the most destructive defoliating insect in North America (Furniss and Carolin 1977). Although budworms do not kill the trees outright, outbreaks may last for decades and significantly reduce plant growth, affecting forest structure (Swetnam and Lynch 1993). In New Mexico, three major outbreaks per century have occurred over the last 300 years, as indicated by reduced tree-ring growth in Douglas fir and white fir. Spruce budworm outbreaks in New Mexico forests were by far the worst in the twentieth century, possibly due to the advent of Euro-American land practices such as heavy logging, overgrazing, and fire suppression. The density of forest tree stands has increased dramatically during the twentieth century, which has stressed forests, so budworm outbreaks can help to correct such unhealthy forest conditions.

Most vertebrates range throughout the different mountain zones. None are restricted to the alpine zone, and in fact most reach their limits of tolerance there, just as the plants do. In contrast to the herbivory of other ecosystems, it has been suggested that most herbivory in alpine zones is by warm-blooded animals rather than insects (Dearing 2001). The same is true for the Arctic. And yet there are reports of amphibians such as the tiger salamander, western chorus frog, and boreal toad occurring above treeline in Colorado (Armstrong et al. 2001).

Birds are especially diverse in aspen stands, but they nest throughout mountain forests. Above treeline there are dozens of visitors during warmer months, but only about five species breed in the tundra (Conry 1978, Armstrong et al. 2001). The classic tundra bird species is the white-tailed ptarmigan, which changes color between seasons to blend in with snow in winter and bare ground in summer. The horned lark, water pipit, and white-crowned sparrow also breed in the tundra or at treeline, as well as in lower elevations, while mountain bluebird and American robin have been reported foraging in tundra during winter months in Colorado.

The mammals of the high mountains range through the Western Cordillera and, in some cases, extend up into the boreal forests and southern Alaska. Many high-elevation species in the Southern Rockies are marooned on these relatively small mountain islands surrounded by deserts (Armstrong et al. 2001). Few mammals overwinter in the tundra, but one exception is the deer mouse, which has been proposed on several occasions to be designated the "national mouse." Another is the nearly equally ubiquitous pocket gopher, which doesn't bother to hibernate but instead burrows under deep snow that insulates the ground, keeping it warmer (Dearing 2001). Pocket gophers feed on both cached and live roots during the winter. Porcupines eat the bark of an array of pine species. Pika (Plate 32) do not hibernate either and also cache plants, storing as much as 50 pounds of plant material for winter use. They are generalist vegetarians during summer, but in winter their diet consists largely of cached stores of the common alpine avens. Although the plant's abundant tannins limit the pikas' digestion of proteins and fiber; they also inhibit bacterial growth, so caches of it actually make it through the winter. Other small mountain mammals include voles, marmots, mice, and ground and tree squirrels.

Larger ungulate mammals in western mountains include elk, deer, and pronghorn, which occur throughout the central and Southern Rockies and in some Great Basin ranges. With a decline in significant predators, elk populations may be higher than ever before, while deer and pronghorn are declining, perhaps due to competition with elk. The reintroduction of gray wolves in Yellowstone and parts of Idaho, New Mexico, and Arizona offers some hope for restoring balance in mountain ecosystems, but wolves continue to be persecuted throughout the West, as they have been historically.

In summary, the mountains of western North America are havens of diversity, and because they are mainly north-south oriented, plants and animals have migrated through them and diversified as climates have changed over millennia.

**1.** Vishnu Schist, the Precambrian basement of the Southwest, exposed at the bottom of the Grand Canyon. Photo courtesy of Wayne Ranney.

**2.** Pennsylvanian marine limestone exposed along the San Juan River in Utah. Photo courtesy of Wayne Ranney.

**3.** The Honaker Trail Formation along the San Juan River, composed of rocks that were deposited alternatively in marine and continental environments. Photo courtesy of Wayne Ranney.

**4.** Red beds exposed in Coyote Gulch, Utah. These were deposited in continental environments and include windblown Navajo Sandstone (rounded upper cliff) and the fluvial Kayenta Formation (lower terraces). Photo courtesy of Wayne Ranney.

**5.** Chinle Shale beds laid down by continental processes, including rivers, northern Arizona. Photo by author.

**6.** Bryce Canyon National Park, Utah. The pink rocks were deposited by continental processes early in the Cenozoic. Photo courtesy of Jeffrey Eaton.

**7.** Abundant shoreline vegetation occurs where the San Juan River passes through the cold desert of southwestern Utah. Photo by author.

**8.** Vasey's Paradise, Grand Canyon, Arizona. Lush vegetation surrounds a gushet spring issuing from the 350-million-year-old Mississippian Redwall limestone. Photo courtesy of Larry Stevens.

**9.** Tufa (calcium carbonate) sculptures in Pyramid Lake, Nevada, a modern remnant of ancient Lake Lahontan. Photo courtesy of Frank DeCourten.

**10.** Bonneville salt flats, Utah, the extensive remnants of Pleistocene Lake Bonneville. Photo courtesy of Frank DeCourten.

**11.** Pleistocene Lake Bonneville sediment, Utah. Photo courtesy of Frank DeCourten.

**12.** Infrared aerial photo of vegetated deltas created from Grand Canyon sediments deposited in the slack water of Lake Mead. Photo courtesy of U.S. Geological Survey, Flagstaff, Arizona.

**13.** Hanging garden in Ribbon Canyon at the interface of the Navajo and Kayenta formations along the upper Colorado River, Utah. Photo courtesy of John Spence and the National Park Service.

**14.** Alpine campion (*Silene acaulis*) in its puffy form. Note the alpine avens growing up through its canopy. Photo courtesy of William Bowman, University of Colorado.

**15.** Great Basin forest near Fandango Pass, Cedar Mountains, California. Photo courtesy of Frank DeCourten.

**16.** Alpine forests below glacier-sculpted peaks in Colorado's Rocky Mountains. Photo by author.

17. Two-tailed swallowtail (*Papilio multicaudata*). This butterfly feeds on many western plants. Photo courtesy of Paul Beier, Northern Arizona University.

18. Rocky Mountain iris (*Iris missouriensis*). This species is widespread in wet meadows in the western and central regions of the United States. Photo by author.

19. Surface fire in ponderosa pine. Natural surface fires are beneficial and are no longer suppressed in many forests. Photo courtesy of the Ecological Research Institute, Northern Arizona University.

**20.** Historical photo of an open Hart Prairie surrounded by aspen groves, northern Arizona, 1909. Photo courtesy of the Ecological Research Institute, Northern Arizona University.

**21.** Hart Prairie's modern ponderosa pine forest, northern Arizona, 1992. Photo courtesy of the Ecological Research Institute, Northern Arizona University.

**22.** The Rodeo-Chediski wildfire, 2002. Nearly half a million acres in east-central Arizona were burned. Photo courtesy of the Ecological Research Institute, Northern Arizona University.

**23.** An open ponderosa pine forest on the Powell Plateau in northern Arizona that has a relatively intact fire regime and diverse herbaceous cover. Photo courtesy of the Ecological Research Institute, Northern Arizona University.

**24.** Adult Pandora moth male with a 3-inch wingspan. Photo courtesy of Michael Wagner, Northern Arizona University.

**25.** Like many outbreak forest insects, Pandora moths often succumb to nuclear polyhedrosis virus when their populations become too large, resulting in the "inverted V" form. Photo courtesy of Michael Wagner, Northern Arizona University.

**26.** Pupae of Pandora moth (*Coloradia pandora*). The pupae feed on ponderosa pine needles and are harvested by Paiute Indians as a traditional food source in the Southwest. Photo courtesy of Michael Wagner, Northern Arizona University.

**27.** Beetle-killed ponderosa pine forest in central Arizona, 2002. Photo courtesy of Michael Wagner, Northern Arizona University.

**28.** Resin output in ponderosa pine in response to a bark beetle infestation that probably killed this tree in northern Arizona. Photo courtesy of Michael Wagner, Northern Arizona University.

**29.** Pine siskin (*Spinus pinus*). These birds overwinter in western coniferous forests. Photo courtesy of Nathan Renn.

**30.** Great horned owl (*Bubo virginianus*), an important American predator. Photo courtesy of Nathan Renn.

**31.** Mountain lions (*Felis concolor*), important predators throughout the Americas. Photo courtesy of Donna Krucki.

**32.** Pika (*Ochotona princeps*). These talus-dwelling creatures store plants such as bluebells to eat during winter in the Rockies. Photo courtesy of Chris Ray, University of Colorado.

**33.** Salt cedar and rabbitbrush in saline Hamblin Wash. These plants are typical in the cold desert of northern Arizona. Photo by author.

34. Rocky Mountain columbine (*Aquilegia caerulea*). This species is pollinated by both hawkmoths and large bees in Rocky Mountain meadows. Photo by author.

35. Western columbine (*Aquilegia formosa*). Note the nodding habit of this hummingbird-pollinated flower. Photo courtesy of Scott Hodges.

36. Rocky Mountain blue columbine (*Aquilegia saximontana*) near Pikes Peak, Colorado. This species is often pollinated by bees. Photo courtesy of Justen Whittall.

37. Hawkmoth-pollinated long-spurred columbine (*Aquilegia pinetorum*) at Hualapai Park, near Flagstaff, Arizona. Photo courtesy of Justen Whittall.

**38.** Yellow columbine (*Aquilegia chrysantha*), northern Arizona. This endemic species of the Four Corners region is pollinated by hawkmoths. Photo courtesy of Mark Daniels, Northern Arizona University.

**39.** Rocky Mountain penstemon (*Penstemon strictus*), a species that is pollinated by an array of insects. Photo by author.

**41.** Scarlet bugler (*Penstemon barbatus*), a species that is pollinated by hummingbirds. Photo by author.

**40.** Broad-tailed hummingbird (*Archilochus platycercus*), common in the Rockies and an important pollinator in the West. Photo by author.

**43.** Indian paint-brush (*Castilleja integra*), a hemi-parasite of neighboring plants such as lupines and grasses in the West. Photo by author.

**42.** Dayflower (*Commelina dianthifolia*). This southwestern endemic offers no nectar to pollinating flies and bees, but instead attracts them with the appearance of lots of pollen. Photo by author.

**45.** Blue butterflies (*Euphilotes ancilla*) feeding and mating on sulfur flower buckwheat (*Eriogonum umbellatum*). The two species co-occur throughout much of the West. Photo courtesy of Gordon Pratt, University of California, Riverside.

**44.** Scarlet gilia (*Ipomopsis aggregata*), a species that is hummingbird pollinated. Photo courtesy of Lisa Machina.

# CHAPTER 4

# Fast-Moving Ponderosa Pine Forests

When I first moved to Flagstaff, Arizona, nearly thirty years ago, I never imagined that I would find the endless expanses of ponderosa pine forests interesting, and yet, of course, they are.

*Pinus* is the most ecologically and economically important tree genus in the world (Richardson and Rundel 1998). Pines are ancient plants, dating back about 130 million years in the fossil record. They are the more modern elements of the ancient gymnosperm ("naked seed") lineage, which dates back more than 300 million years. Pines are the dominant vegetation type over much of the Northern Hemisphere, where they originated. Their economic value to humans cannot be overstated; their wood, pulp, nuts, and resins are used worldwide. Ecologically, they exert a strong influence on the world's climates. The northern boreal forests create warmer winter temperatures than would occur in their absence. More than a thousand species of insects feed on them, as well as numerous vertebrates.

Ponderosa pine, which occurs only in western North America, is the most widely distributed pine in the West. It is the principal pine species on more than 30 million acres there. Both its pollen and seeds are wind dispersed; it is somewhat tolerant of fire; and it is one of the more drought-tolerant western pines. The origins of pine are mysterious, and its history in North America is dramatic. Ponderosa pine's recolonization of much of the West in the last 10,000 years shows how quickly complex forests can become established.

## THE HISTORY OF PINES

The oldest pine fossil discovered so far is from Belgium and dates to 130 Ma, during the Early Cretaceous (Millar 1998). Pollen from an Early Cretaceous pine was also found in amber deposits in Alaska, but all other pine fossils have been found in Mid- to Late Cretaceous deposits. Fossils of a great diversity of Cretaceous pines and a predecessor genus, *Pityostrobus*, are known from

Japan. Pines may have originated in western Europe, northeastern North America, or Asia. All of these continents were connected during this time in the supercontinent of Laurasia. Pines spread throughout the middle latitudes (31° to 50°) of Laurasia before it broke up into the modern-day continents of North America, Asia, and Europe. Not surprisingly, today the natural ranges of pines are almost exclusively in these Northern Hemisphere continents, although they are cultivated worldwide.

It is noteworthy that flowering plants, or angiosperms, as well as pines were evolving and speciating profusely by the end of the Cretaceous (~66 Ma). The fossil record shows that during this time, flowering plants exploded. The stage was set for the evolution and distribution of flowering plants and pines to ebb and flow on a global scale. During warmer, wetter periods, flowering plants dominated western North America, whereas pines became more abundant when climates cooled.

With further warming in the Late Paleocene and Early Eocene, tropical and subtropical flowering plants spread widely throughout the middle latitudes in both the Northern and Southern hemispheres. This "boreotropical" flora extended as far as 70° north in Alaska. The few pine fossils known from this time occurred at high and low latitudes in the Northern Hemisphere, indicating they existed only at the edges of the boreotropical expansion (Millar 1998). The ancestors of lodgepole pine and jack pine, species that make up much of Canada's enormous boreal forests, were probably established in these northern refugia during this time.

It appears that pines were either outcompeted by flowering plants or could

not tolerate the warm, humid conditions that were so pervasive. Pines are generally regarded as intolerant of warm, humid conditions, and they are particularly poor competitors with flowering plants under such conditions (Millar 1998, Bond 1989). Flowering plants have become far more diverse than pines, even though the former originated fairly recently. Today there are between 250,000 and 300,000 species of flowering plants, but only about 111 species of pines among only 560 species of conifers.

Toward the end of the Eocene, the fluctuations between warm and cold gave way to a long period of consistently colder conditions. Temperatures dropped by more than 20°F within a million years, precipitation declined, and seasonality increased. Loss of boreotropical flora occurred worldwide as a result of this long period of cooling. These extinctions at the end of the Eocene were mirrored by a great expansion of pines and other cold-tolerant species. Sites that had contained boreotropical plants became dominated by cool-temperature pines. In some places this change took place within as little as a million years (Axelrod 1965). Pines recolonized regions where they had occurred more than 100 million years before and extended their range as far south as Chiapas, Mexico. They flourished throughout the middle latitudes of North America, Asia, and Europe into the warmer Miocene. Mountain building isolated many populations, and their capacity for selfing, or inbreeding, may have led to the formation of new races and species of pines (Richardson and Rundel 1998). The ancestors of many modern pine species are found among Miocene fossils. Pines remained in their expanded range and many new species arose over the course of the Tertiary period.

PONDEROSA PINE'S HISTORY

The oldest recorded ponderosa pine is from British Columbia and dates to ~50 Ma (Bonnicksen 2000). Ponderosa pine fossils have also been found in the Rocky Mountains dating back to 25 Ma, and in Nevada dating to the Miocene and Pliocene (Axelrod 1988, Moir et al. 1997).

Ponderosa pine's ancestors and closest relatives (subsection Ponderosae) may have originated in both northern and southern refugia during the warm part of the Eocene. Ten to seventeen species in this group are endemic to Mexico and Central America, while the wide-ranging ponderosa pine has a northern distribution and northern ecological affinities in its habitat preference and vegetation associates. Early Tertiary pines most closely associated with ponderosa pine have been found in British Columbia, Washington, and Montana.

*Disappearance of Pine during the Pleistocene*

Although ponderosa pine was widespread before the Pleistocene and, of course, is today, it was largely absent from much of the West during the Late Pleistocene (Anderson 1989, Betancourt et al. 1990, Norris et al. 2006). The contents of many packrat middens found in the West indicate that during the Late Pleistocene ponderosa pine occurred only in low-elevation refugia in southern Arizona, New Mexico, and, perhaps, Mexico.

The absence of ponderosa pine from much of the Rockies and Intermountain West during the Late Pleistocene is curious because so many of the plants it occurred with previously and today, such as Douglas fir and Rocky Mountain juniper, did persist there; they are well represented in the Pleistocene fossil record, and their responses to

this change in climate are well documented. During the Pleistocene many plant species in western North America migrated more than 3,000 feet lower in elevation from their present distributions as the region cooled, and glaciers and ice sheets moved down from the Arctic. However, unlike ponderosa pine, they still occurred through the West, and often in large populations.

So why did ponderosa pine disappear through so much of the West during the Pleistocene? One can only speculate, but Norris et al. (2006) modeled the current distribution of ponderosa pine along with the climatic regimes it occurs in to find out about its past as well as its future prospects. Today, ponderosa pine typically occurs throughout the West in a low montane zone between pinyon-juniper woodlands and grassland habitat at lower elevations and mixed conifer forests at higher elevations. Ponderosa pine's upper elevational range is limited through much of the West, possibly because it may be outcompeted by more mesic mixed conifers. Ponderosa pine typically lives in dry, lower-elevation sites with poor soils and strong southern exposures, a zone that surrounding species may not be able to colonize due to its poor quality. Perhaps because it does live in such marginal places, ponderosa pine requires significant precipitation during the summer growing season (Jackson et al. 2005, Holmgren et al. 2006, Norris et al. 2006). Summer monsoon storms are now common in the Southern Rockies and the Southwest, but during the last glacial period these summer rains were restricted to southern Arizona and New Mexico. It is thought that a combination of little or no summer precipitation and colder temperatures may have eliminated the ponderosa pine's lower montane niche in northern Arizona, Colorado, Utah, Wyoming, and Montana during the Late Pleistocene. This idea is corroborated today by the absence of ponderosa pine in parts of the Great Basin that receive little summer rain. It is also absent from the Teton and Yellowstone regions, which have adequate summer moisture but cold temperatures.

Packrat middens and pollen cores extracted from old lakes show that by the end of the Pleistocene, some 10,000 years ago, ponderosa pine had reestablished itself in the West. In a time sequence study in northern Arizona, which lies in the heart of the largest modern stand of ponderosa pine, Anderson (1989) found that vegetation at Potato Lake (~7,300 feet) was dominated by spruce, Douglas fir, white fir, sagebrush, and grasses between 35,000 to 25,000 years ago, and ponderosa pine was absent. The last glacial phase of the Pleistocene was in full swing during this time. Ponderosa pine was still absent between 25,000 and 10,600 years ago; however, by 10,600 years ago, most of the cold-tolerant species, such as Douglas fir and spruce, were gone, and ponderosa pine had reappeared along with grasses, oaks, and sunflowers. It has been expanding its range ever since.

In an ongoing analysis of packrat middens throughout the western United States, ponderosa pine remains are turning up at progressively later times in middens from increasingly northern latitudes, indicating a northward migration since the end of the Pleistocene. Middens from northern Arizona and New Mexico show that ponderosa pine was present about 10,000 to 14,000 years ago, while farther north in Utah and Colorado, the earliest date at which ponderosa pine appears in middens is about 6,000 years ago (Anderson 1989; Betancourt et al. 1991; Betancourt, Lyford, and Jackson,

unpublished data). Finally, ponderosa pine reached northern Wyoming and central Montana within the last 3,000 years (Norris, unpublished data). The return of monsoon storms and the fires that their lightning ignite on the Colorado Plateau may have helped ponderosa pine to migrate so quickly (R. Scott Anderson, personal communication). We may never know for sure, but the questions and the research are fascinating. As I look out on this massive forest of ponderosa pine on the southern edge of the Colorado Plateau, it is hard to imagine that it and its plant and animal associates have been here for only 10,000 years—a very short time, relatively speaking, for an enormous and complex ecosystem with very large, slow-growing trees to become established.

Paleoecologist Daniel Axelrod (1979) refers to the time since the Pleistocene, the Holocene period, as a time of expanding deserts. Occurring on the heels of the ice ages, the warming climate has affected the ranges of western plants and animals, including ponderosa pine, which are shifting again toward higher elevations and latitudes. It is hard to predict precisely how far ponderosa pines will extend their range, but many pines are expanding their ranges globally (Richardson and Rundel 1998).

As ponderosa pine established or reestablished itself through the mountain ranges of the western United States in the last 10,000 years, it became the West's most widespread pine (Fig. 4.1), spreading from northern Mexico through the Rocky Mountains and into Canada. It also occurs in Utah and, less commonly, Nevada. Its distribution through the Pacific coastal mountains during the Pleistocene is not well understood, but ponderosa pine now occurs throughout the Sierra Nevada and Cascades and into British

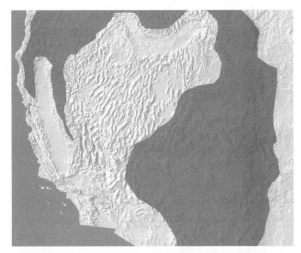

**4.1.** Approximate distribution of ponderosa pine (*Pinus ponderosa*) (shaded area) in the United States.

Columbia. Its wide distribution encompasses at least two varieties, several possible races, and many populations that exhibit genetic differences (Norris et al. 2006).

*Formation of Different Varieties of Ponderosa Pine*

Major genetic and ecological differences have arisen between populations of ponderosa pine in coastal ranges and the Rocky Mountains (Conkle and Critchfield 1988). These vastly different climates have provided strong natural selection, shaping their respective pine populations accordingly. *Pinus ponderosa* var. *ponderosa,* the coastal variety, occurs throughout the coastal mountains. The Rocky Mountain variety, *Pinus ponderosa* var. *scopulorum,* extends from the northern Plains states, including Montana and Wyoming, through the Southwest and down into northern Mexico. The Rocky Mountain variety is strongly dependent on summer precipitation, which is a feature of the Rockies, the Colorado Plateau, and the Laramie Range, while the coastal variety depends on winter precipitation (Norris et al. 2006). Some of their

differences may have arisen before the Pleistocene.

Essentially, the Rocky Mountain variety of ponderosa pine is far more drought adapted and slower growing than the coastal variety. These differences have been shown to be genetically based through growth trials in which seeds from the different populations were grown in common gardens and still expressed the same traits. The coastal variety of ponderosa pine is less drought adapted and faster growing; nearly all of its populations have three needles per fascicle, or needle bundle. The Rocky Mountain variety varies in needle number. Of all ponderosa populations, only the plants in the Northern Rockies typically have two needles per bundle. Despite the emerging differences among ponderosa pine populations, they still interbreed, which implies that they are, technically speaking, still a single species.

The two different varieties of ponderosa pine also occur in very different kinds of forests. In the Sierra Nevada and Cascades, the coastal variety typically occurs with white fir, Douglas fir, and oak, rarely forming pure stands. In contrast, the Rocky Mountain variety occurs in pure stands through much of its range on the Colorado Plateau, in the Rockies, and in the high plains of Montana, Wyoming, North and South Dakota, and Nebraska.

There are also differences *within* each of the varieties in the chemical makeup of their resins and their growth rates, and differences between northern and southern populations within the Rockies. Even within the southwestern populations of ponderosa pine there is a great deal of variation in growth rates, much of it relating directly to the number of frost-free days in the different regions (Mitton 1995).

The Rocky Mountain variety of ponderosa pine meets the coastal variety near the Continental Divide in Montana—the only point of contact between them (Kelley and Mitton 1999, Latta and Mitton 1999). It is thought that these populations came into contact only within the last 1,000 years, after having been separated through at least the Late Pleistocene. The two varieties hybridize here, but most of the gene flow is by pollen moving west to east with prevailing winds. The western pine beetle, a bark beetle associated with ponderosa pine, feeds on both the coastal and Rocky Mountain varieties, and at the genetic level it appears to have diverged into different species on each variety.

## HEALTHY PONDEROSA PINE FORESTS BEFORE EURO-AMERICAN SETTLEMENT

After the Pleistocene, ponderosa pine stands often developed into open forests with enormous trees. The forests occurred as small clusters of multiple-aged trees surrounded by extensive grasslands (Fig. 4.2). These pre-Euro-American settlement—or presettlement—forests were described as beautiful open parklands. A combination of historical observations and creative studies have described the nature of these forests, often with an eye toward better managing today's populations (e.g., Pearson 1923, Cooper 1960, White 1985, Covington and Moore 1994a, 1994b). Both Amiel Whipple in 1856 and Edward Beale in 1858, on expeditions through

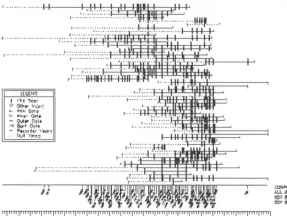

4.2. Changes in ponderosa pine forests in northern Arizona over the last 120 years: *top to bottom*, open, old-growth parkland forest typical of presettlement times; intense sheep grazing; the fire record at Camp Navajo, in northern Arizona: the numerous vertical bars indicate frequent fires between the early 1600s and late 1800s, but only a few after fire suppression began. Courtesy of the Ecological Restoration Institute, Northern Arizona University; Camp Navajo fire record graph courtesy of Fule et al. (1997) and the Ecological Society of America.

the West, described ponderosa pine stands as open and parklike, with stands of trees surrounded by dense grass cover (Covington 2003, Beale 1858). Beale reported forests of tall pines in northern Arizona surrounded by extensive grassy meadows as far as the eye could see, making travel easy. In 1904, Vernon Bailey reported that ponderosa pine stands in the Jemez Mountains of New Mexico were also open and parklike with well-spaced trees and grama grass meadows (Allen 2002). The trees were large, often 5 feet in diameter and 80 to 100 feet high, with beautifully smooth trunks. Forester Gus Pearson (1923), who would be influential in increasing our understanding of how to manage these forests, noted that the canopies of ponderosa pine rarely covered more than 30 percent of the land in southwestern forests.

Studies of early ponderosa pine forest structure began in northern Arizona in the 1960s with Charles Cooper (1960), followed by Alan White (1985), and Wallace Covington and Margaret Moore (1994a, 1994b). In a study of a protected experimental forest near Flagstaff, Cooper confirmed earlier oral accounts that presettlement stands of trees often occurred in clusters surrounded by grasslands. In the same forest, Alan White showed that these tree clusters, or cohorts, were made up of multiple-aged trees from multiple colonization events, and numbered between three and forty-four trees per group. To determine presettlement forest structure, he studied only trees that were established before 1875, a date after which the natural fire cycle in these regional forests ended and extensive fire suppression began. The clusters of older trees covered only 22 percent of the 17-acre study site. Some trees in this forest are more than 600 years old (Mast et al. 1998). The same clustering

pattern has been found in old-growth ponderosa pine stands in the Rockies (Huckaby et al. 2003).

The large, older trees referred to as "old growth" were a major feature of presettlement forests (Huckaby et al. 2003). These trees typically exceeded 200 years in age and were characterized by spiky dead tops, smooth orange bark, and fire scars at their bases. Old bark lacks the deep fissures, large flakes, and black color of younger ponderosa pines. Given the wide spacing between the trees, competition among them was probably minor. Among the oldest ponderosa pines today are an 843-year-old tree in central Utah, one at 780 years in Mt. Rosa, Colorado, and a 742-year-old tree in northwestern Arizona. Old-growth trees and stands are rare today due to intensive logging, but their value is incalculable to wildlife, especially cavity nesters such as owls.

Ponderosa pine forests were kept open and healthy by frequent fires and by competition from surrounding grasslands (Covington 2003). Ponderosa pine's ability to tolerate frequent, low-intensity fires indicates a long evolutionary history with fire, reflected in its protected buds, very thick bark, resinous needles, flammable litter, prolific seed production, and fast-growing seedlings (Agee 1998). Ponderosa pine bark is thick enough to tolerate fire, as reflected by living trees whose scars are evidence of frequent fires (Fig. 4.3). Before Euro-American settlement of the West, fires in ponderosa pine forests were frequent, occurring every 2 to 25 years (Covington and Moore 1994a, 1994b; Mast 2003). These fires typically were started by summer monsoon lightning and were generally low-intensity surface fires that burned away plant debris and pine seedlings (Plate 19). In a study near Flagstaff, fire scars on trees were dated, revealing that fires

occurred there every
2 to 5 years (Dieterich
1980). In some parts of
the Southwest, fires may
have occurred almost
annually during the
eighteenth and nine-
teenth centuries (Peet
1989). In the Rocky
Mountains, ponder-
osa pine forests burned
every 5 to 12 years for at
least 8,000 years due to
a combination of light-
ning- and aboriginal-
set fires (Tables 3.1, 3.2;
Mast et al. 1998). From
this and other studies, a
picture has emerged of
a forest system that was
kept healthy by fire.

**4.3.** Trunk of a ponderosa pine (*Pinus ponderosa*) with a fire scar, often referred to as a "cat face" (*left*), and a cross section from a pine with dated fire scars. Courtesy of the Ecological Restoration Institute, Northern Arizona University.

Lightning causes most forest fires worldwide, even in boreal forests (Agee 1998,
Stocks and Street 1983), and lightning strikes
cause more than 90 percent of fires on the
Mogollon Rim, along the southern edge of
the Colorado Plateau. Not surprisingly, ponderosa pine forests here are strongly fire
adapted. Low-intensity fires in ponderosa
pine stands were considered the norm, historically, and larger ponderosa pines, with
their thick bark cortex, could survive such
fires with only scarring. Often these fires
burned large areas and moved quickly, with
residence times of less than a minute, stop-
ping only at river banks or edges of areas
previously burned.

Helping to keep the pine forests open
were high densities of highly competitive
grasses. It is hard to imagine grasses outcompeting pine trees, but they did, and still do
(Covington 2003). Dense expanses of grasses
physically make it hard for pine seedlings

to become established. Grasses also provide
critical fine fuel for carrying the frequent
fires that killed many pine seedlings. The
grasses also benefited from the fast-moving
fires as they burned dead leaves and recy-
cled nitrogen into the soil. This combination of conditions kept pine forests open and
healthy by helping to limit the establishment
and survival of ponderosa pine seedlings.
In fact, seedling germination in ponderosa pine was originally regarded as an infrequent event (Pearson 1923, Heidmann et al.
1982, White 1985). White (1985) suggested
that pine seedlings could only become established where many trees within a cluster
burned, and burned hotter than the typical ground fires. These hotter, localized fires
would have cleared debris and grasses, creating safe establishment sites for seedlings.

## MODERN PONDEROSA PINE FORESTS

Today's ponderosa pine forests are vastly
different from those of only a hundred years

**4.4.** Dense ponderosa pine seedling establishment in the early 1900s resulted in so-called dog-hair thickets of pines: *top*, pine seedlings; *below*, a dog-hair thicket near Flagstaff, Arizona. Courtesy of the Ecological Restoration Institute, Northern Arizona University.

including Utah, Montana, Idaho, Oregon, Washington, California, Arizona, and New Mexico.

Three major factors caused these rapid and enormous changes in western ponderosa pine forests: the intense overgrazing of associated grasslands, the suppression of natural periodic fires, and chance—in the form of a climatic event that, combined with the first two factors, would change the shape of ponderosa pine forests for centuries (Savage et al. 1996).

During the late 1800s livestock grazing and overgrazing became a major feature of forested ecosystems. Overgrazing continued well into the twentieth century, with cattle and sheep stocked on grasslands in numbers that were ecologically destructive (Fig. 4.2; Covington 2003). Overgrazing resulted in the loss of grasses, the loss of grassland habitats through erosion of topsoils, and even lowering of groundwater tables. The loss of fine fuels from grasses that carried the cooler, faster fires was a critical change because it set the stage for the explosion of ponderosa pine forests and, ultimately, an entirely different kind of fire regime. Grazing as a form of disturbance also improved conditions for pine germination (Savage 1991). Ironically, overgrazing was regarded as a means of fire suppression, but instead the opposite has proven to be the case.

Early foresters regarded the relatively cool surface fires as detrimental to ponderosa

ago: since that time, the number of trees has increased exponentially, by forty to fifty times, through much of the West (Plates 20 and 21, Fig. 4.4) (Covington and Moore 1994a, 1994b). This transformation has been attributed, in large part, to Euro-American intervention. It is estimated that 100 years ago ponderosa pine forests contained 20 to 60 trees per acre, in contrast to the up to 200 to 600 trees per acre common today. And whereas presettlement clusters of trees were surrounded by extensive grasslands, modern ponderosa pine forests occur in dense, continuous "doghair" thickets (Fig. 4.4). Typically, the trees are stunted and unproductive, with few grasses or other plants associated with them, so diversity is diminished. Similar changes in ponderosa pine forests have been reported throughout the West, pine forests and began an effective campaign of fire suppression starting in the late 1800s (Fig. 4.2; Pyne 1982, Covington 2003). This policy continued through much of the twentieth century, despite the fact that consequences of fire suppression in pine forests were apparent early on. Foresters Gus Pearson, Aldo Leopold, and Harold Weaver all saw the forests expanding rapidly in the early 1900s and understood many of the causes. Unlike fires in public land forests, fires on Native American lands in Arizona and Mexico were still allowed to burn. Leopold (1920, 1937) observed firsthand the contribution of fire to maintaining healthy, open ponderosa pine forests. By contrast, tree densities were increasing rapidly in fire-suppressed forests.

Although these changes were already leading to increased pine numbers, a climatic event in 1919 led to unprecedented pine seedling establishment over millions of acres of the Colorado Plateau (Pearson 1923, Arnold 1950, Cooper 1960, Savage et al. 1996). In 1918, ponderosa pine produced exceptionally large numbers of cones and seeds, with larger trees bearing up to 3,500 cones. The following year, 1919, was one of the wettest and warmest on record, and one of only two years (1919, 1992) to have a moist and warm May. Normally, May and June are extremely dry months on the Colorado Plateau, strongly limiting seedling survival. Gus Pearson referred to the 1919 ponderosa pine regeneration event as "epoch-making" and destined to shape forest structure for many years. High establishment rates of ponderosa pine were reported in other years around that time, but scientists think that the 1919 cohort of pines resulted in the greatest forest density increase in the Southwest. Photos taken in 1909 at the Gus Pearson Experimental Forest in northern Arizona show an open forest with no visible seedlings and

saplings. By 1920 an average of 60,000 seedlings per acre were recorded, and by 1921, 7,600 seedlings per acre still remained.

The warm, wet weather of 1919 was the primary factor in increasing densities from 23 trees per acre in 1876 to 1,254 trees per acre by 1992 at the experimental site (Mast et al. 1998). With these high densities, the forests became less healthy, as though they had exceeded the region's available resources, such as water and nutrients. The older, larger ponderosa pines began experiencing increased mortality due to competition with high densities of younger trees.

This recent history of overgrazing, fire suppression, and increasingly dense pine populations has created dangerous conditions in modern ponderosa pine forests. High densities of trees and a massive buildup of plant debris have changed the nature of fire in these forests throughout the West, with fires becoming larger and more destructive, burning the crowns of trees rather than remaining on the forest floor. In pre- and early settlement times, fires of several thousand acres in size were considered large, but fires today are substantially larger and more deadly. One of the most recent, the Rodeo-Chediski fire in 2002, was the largest fire on record in Arizona (Plate 22). It burned nearly half a million acres of ponderosa pine forest and many buildings in several towns in east-central Arizona. In Colorado, the fire season of 2002 burned more acreage than in the preceding ten years combined (Huckaby et al. 2003).

In addition to being larger than presettlement fires, modern crown fires have become stand-replacing fires. Without fire for up to 100 years, the accumulation of branches, cones, needles, and bark on the forest floor is often many feet thick and extremely flammable. Anyone living in a ponderosa pine stand knows how many needles and cones are dropped each year—filling bags and bags in even the average yard. Such a debris layer also prevents grasses, flowers, and even shrubs from persisting, much less establishing. They are literally buried under duff.

Today's ponderosa pine forests, with too many trees and enormous accumulations of fuel, are increasingly vulnerable to massive wildfires that destroy ecosystems rather than keeping them healthy. Crown fires kill trees and spread quickly, leaving few survivors. These hot fires also sterilize soils, which limits colonization by plants and makes them highly prone to erosion.

These conditions have been further exacerbated by drought, which has persisted since the 1990s (Breshears et al. 2005). Drought, higher temperatures, and high densities have stressed the trees and made them susceptible to deadly bark beetles. All of these conditions make forests more flammable.

*Re-Creating Healthy Forests*

Managing the large expanses of unhealthy forests while trying to avert disaster is a daunting task. Fortunately, attitudes about fire have changed, and in 1974 the first prescribed fire research program in the Southwest was established by John Dieterich and Stephen Sackett of the Forest Service's Rocky Mountain Research Station, along with Wallace Covington of Northern Arizona University (Covington 2003). They began to study current forest fuel conditions and natural fire regimes, and conducted experiments to determine how to successfully reintroduce fire into ponderosa pine forests. Early burning experiments revealed that the deep layers of duff that have accumulated at the base of old-growth trees must be removed before prescribed burning because they burn so hot

that they kill the trees. Removing the debris prior to burning allows such trees to survive.

These and other studies have shown that forest restoration is more complicated than simply reintroducing fire, and they have laid the groundwork for ongoing studies in northern Arizona focused on restoring ponderosa pine forests to healthier presettlement conditions (Plate 23). Restoration efforts involve a variety of techniques, including thinning or removal of trees and different burning regimes. The degree of thinning and burning is determined by the presettlement condition of each site. Research is also being conducted on how to restore understory species to the more open pine forests. The Ecological Restoration Institute (ERI) at Northern Arizona University, directed by forest ecologist Wallace Covington, has been researching and developing forest restoration techniques throughout the Southwest since 1996. The program's findings are being used to help local and federal land managers, and the program is growing. Research centers have also been established at universities in Colorado and New Mexico.

Forest management has always been complicated and controversial, and ERI's goal of returning ponderosa pine stands to presettlement conditions is certainly no exception. Nevertheless, this applied science, based on both a long history of research and tremendous vision, is exciting. When all is said and done, fires will continue to rage in the West, but scientists are now studying ways to use them to create healthier and less dangerous forests.

## Basic Ponderosa Pine Biology

The major source of genetic diversity in pines involves mutations at the gene level rather than at the chromosome level, as is the case with flowering plants or

**4.5.** *Left,* developing male cones of a ponderosa pine (*Pinus ponderosa*); *right,* male cone of a Colorado pinyon (*Pinus edulis*) ready to release pollen. Actual length of these cones is less than 1 inch.

angiosperms (Mirov 1967). This may be why there are far fewer species of pines than of flowering plants, although pines have been around longer. Flowering plants have speciated quickly and dramatically due to polyploidy, which involves increases in chromosome numbers (e.g., doubling), but it is rare in pines.

Like all pines, ponderosa pine is monoecious, which means "one house," a name referring to the fact that individual trees produce both female and male cones (Fig. 4.5). The seed-bearing female cones are 3 to 6 inches long and take up to three years to develop. They are heavily fortified with spines to keep out seed-eating animals, and the seeds are wind dispersed with the help of thin wings (Fig. 3.8). Male cones are small, typically less than an inch long. They develop in the spring, produce pollen, and then fall from the tree during the summer. Pollination occurs in May or June, and cones are developed by fall of the next year. Their pollen is wind dispersed, an ancient trait and characteristic of all conifers. There is a

point during the summer in Flagstaff when everything is covered with a thick layer of heavy yellow pollen from ponderosa pines. It seems like an inefficient form of reproduction, compared to the insect pollination of many flowering plants, and yet pine trees are widespread throughout much of the Northern Hemisphere.

Ponderosa pine seedlings require full sun and mineral soil to become established and grow vigorously (Huckaby et al. 2003). These conditions are often created by disturbances such as fire and logging. Adults also depend on full sun for vigorous growth. The habitat of ponderosa pine has been described as the most xeric, or dry, of the true forest types of the western United States (Holechek et al. 1998), excluding pinyon woodlands. Established populations receive an average of 20 inches of precipitation annually, although levels range from 10 to nearly 30 inches depending on aspect, local conditions, and elevation. Coastal populations receive much more rain, with those in northern California, Oregon, and Washington receiving up to

95 inches per year. This difference makes it easy to understand why the Rocky Mountain variety is more drought tolerant.

Ponderosa pines are able to tolerate drought due to a number of adaptations, including sunken stomates, or leaf pores, that are very sensitive to changes in water availability; thick bark, or cortex; the ability to store water in the heartwood; and mycorrhizal fungi associated with their roots. They are also able to absorb atmospheric moisture or dew through their needles. The needles quickly detect a decline in water availability and can close their stomates to conserve moisture. When the stomates in pine needles open to take in $CO_2$, they inadvertently lose water to the drier atmosphere, but they are able to continue photosynthesizing during water shortages better than Douglas fir. It is interesting that ponderosa pine's ability to store water in the heartwood is not shared by Douglas fir, which occurs with it only in wetter sites. Water storage in the heartwood surely contributes to the ability of ponderosa pine to occur in drier sites. Seedlings are able to grow 20-inch roots in the first year, which helps increase water availability and survival through the first, dry months of summer.

## PLANTS, ANIMALS, AND FUNGI ASSOCIATED WITH PONDEROSA PINE

Many species of plants, animals, fungi, and other life forms depend on ponderosa pine, and these associated species have helped to shape its natural history.

Mycorrhizal fungi associated with ponderosa pine roots are essential to this species' ability to inhabit dry, low-nutrient soils. The fungi form a mantle over the tree's roots and assist it by extending outward and increasing the area from which the roots can draw

water and nutrients (Read 1998). Mycorrhizae are even able to absorb nitrogen and phosphorus from decomposing litter layers on the ground surface, something that plants are typically not thought to be able to do. The relationship between ponderosa pine and mycorrhizae is strongest in poorer sites, and experiments have shown that trees with mycorrhizae have higher growth and survival rates. Mycorrhizae also help to exclude pathogenic fungi and prevent the uptake of toxic metal ions. In return for their services, the mycorrhizae receive enormous amounts of carbohydrates produced by trees through photosynthesis.

There are many diseases and pathogens associated with ponderosa pine (Harrington and Wingfield 1998), including stem, root, and butt rots, and canker, needle, rust, and nematode diseases. Between all of these and ponderosa pine's other natural enemies, it's a wonder that the species has survived at all, and yet its populations continue expanding (Richardson and Higgins 1998).

Ponderosa pine is often the dominant tree in the lower, drier elevations of the Southwest and the Rocky Mountains. It forms what are described as "climax" communities in which it persists and is not replaced by other species of trees. At lower and higher elevations, it co-occurs with other tree species, and these associations increase the complexity of habitat and food resources, which, in turn, increases the diversity of forest animals.

Many shrub species are associated with ponderosa pine, and their densities can become quite high, adding considerable resources for animals. Shrubs associated with ponderosa pines include manzanita, mountain mahogany, and fruit-bearing shrubs such as currants, skunkbush, blue elderberry, roses, and serviceberry, as well as buckbrush and rabbitbrush. Around Flagstaff, the fruit-bearing shrubs typically occur under the canopies of ponderosa pines, since birds perch on their lower branches to eat the fruits. Because of this, ponderosa pines have a large impact on the distribution of fruit-bearing shrubs through its range. In Arizona and New Mexico, it is common to see yuccas and agaves in ponderosa pine stands on south-facing rock outcrops.

A dominant grass species throughout much of the ponderosa pine's range is blue grama. Other grasses include bunchgrasses such as mountain muhly, little muhly, pine dropseed, nodding brome, Arizona fescue, Junegrass, muttongrass, Kentucky bluegrass, sideoats grama, and squirreltail. These grasses are common in Arizona, New Mexico, Colorado, and Utah and also occur in Wyoming and Montana. Common understory wildflowers include scarlet gilia, penstemon, paintbrush, buckwheat, lupine, and geranium.

In higher-elevation mesic sites, ponderosa pine encounters more tree species, including Douglas fir, white fir, spruce, limber pine, sometimes bristlecone pine, and occasionally aspen. Ponderosa pine does not extend very far into these wetter forests due to its shade intolerance. Shrubs in such sites include currants, rock spirea, roundleaf snowberry, and maples.

### Dwarf Mistletoe

The disease that most afflicts ponderosa pine is dwarf mistletoe. This parasitic flowering plant ultimately taps into a tree's xylem, or vascular system, to derive most of what it needs to live and reproduce. In the course of the mistletoe's improbable life history, a seed lands and germinates on a pine branch; however, only after several years of growth on the stem surface does it penetrate the bark and sink a root into the pine's vascular system. Unlike the human vascular system—which is made up of arteries, veins, and capillaries that deliver water, oxygen, and nutrients to and remove waste from cells throughout our bodies—the tree's vascular system is mainly a layer surrounding the woody layer just under the bark. It is made up of the xylem and the phloem, which collectively transport water and nutrients, including minerals, from the roots through the tree, and also carbohydrates, the products of photosynthesis, from the needles through the plant. All kinds of vertebrate and invertebrate herbivores, as well as dwarf mistletoe, favor this nutritious living layer in trees. Within several years, mistletoe sends branches out through the host's bark and reproduces there.

Mistletoe can reduce growth in ponderosa pine hosts by as much as half and cause considerable mortality. In the Northern Rockies, more than 3 million acres of forest are infested, with enormous losses of trees occurring each year (Monnig and Byler 1992). Dwarf mistletoe parasitizes trees in over 36 percent of the ponderosa pine's range through the Southwest (Hawksworth and Shaw 1988), while a different species has infested ponderosa pine in the Sierra Nevada and Cascade ranges.

Dwarf mistletoe pulls water from its host's xylem by transpiring or sweating water to the atmosphere through its own leaves, which creates lower water potential in its tissue than in that of its host. Consequently, it draws the water from the tree by osmosis (Fischer 1983). As mistletoe grows, it turns the shape of the branch it lives in into a "witch's broom"—a thickened, grossly distorted branch.

Modern, denser ponderosa pine forests have contributed to dwarf mistletoe infestations. It spreads most successfully from the upper canopies of trees, where it sends out seeds as projectiles that can travel up to 30 feet. These infestations directly compromise ponderosa pine survival and also make them more susceptible, or perhaps more attractive, to attacks by other natural enemies such as bark beetles and defoliating butterflies and moths. This leads to some wonderfully complicated interactions among ponderosa pine, dwarf mistletoe, the insects that feed on the mistletoe, and the birds that feed on the insects. In a study of a mistletoe-infested ponderosa pine stand in northern Arizona in 2002, most dead pines were infested with *both* dwarf mistletoe and bark beetles (Kenaley 2004). The same relationship has been reported in pinyon pine. In the Rockies, Johnson et al. (1976) found that trees with greater infestation of mistletoe were also more heavily attacked by the mountain pine beetle.

Fortunately for ponderosa pine, many animals feed heavily on mistletoe. A variety of butterfly and moth caterpillars feed on seeds and mine in stems, and some even mimic mistletoe. Herbivores can remove up to 75 percent of mistletoe stems, reducing its impact on its ponderosa pine host (Mooney 2006). Many kinds of true bugs, or sap-sucking insects (including mirids, spittlebugs, and thrips), are harmful to mistletoe and yet pollinate its flowers. In turn, many of those insects are fed upon by birds. The mountain chickadee may devote up to 25 percent of its feeding time to eating insects attracted to dwarf mistletoe shoots (Parker 2001).

*Insects*

More than 350 species of insects feed on ponderosa pine (de Groot and Turgeon

1998). Collectively they feed on all plant parts, including the seeds, seedlings, needles, bark, phloem and xylem, wood, roots, and cones. Butterflies, moths, and beetles account for more than 75 percent of the insects that feed on ponderosa pine. Moths and butterflies feed on or mine stem tips, needles, and cones, while many beetles mine in bark and wood.

The Pandora moth, a saturniid moth, is one of the largest pine-defoliating insects (Plate 24). The caterpillar is about the size of an adult finger and feeds voraciously on ponderosa pine needles. In outbreak phases, its populations can defoliate large stands of ponderosa pine throughout its range. Although defoliation can reduce a tree's growth rate for several years, the Pandora moth rarely causes mortality (Wagner and Mathiasen 1985); however, when moths defoliate trees that are already heavily infested with dwarf mistletoe, mortality is likely. Following a Pandora moth outbreak on the Kaibab Plateau between 1979 and 1981, when moths defoliated more than 20,000 acres of pines, tree mortality was high in areas attacked by both mistletoe and moths. Ironically, the Pandora moth can help to limit mistletoe infestations in some stands because when the tree host dies, the mistletoe does too. As with other forest insect outbreaks, when moth populations explode, they are ultimately controlled by a virus that spreads quickly through their populations and causes them to collapse. The caterpillars themselves literally collapse into the classic "inverted v" shape as the virus renders them liquid (Plate 25).

Pandora moths in the pupae, or preadult, stage are still harvested, roasted, and eaten by Paiute Indians in the Owen's Valley and Mono Lake areas in California (Plate 26; Blake and Wagner 1987). During the 1920s,

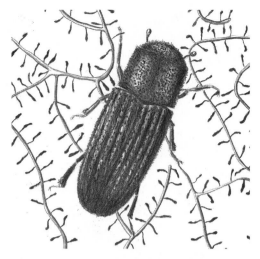

**4.6.** Drawing of an adult western pine beetle (*Dendroctonus brevicomis*) and its larval mining galleries. The actual length of this bark beetle is less than a quarter inch.

up to 1.5 tons were collected in one season, so perhaps this is a good resource to keep in mind.

Of all forest insects, bark beetles are the most destructive to ponderosa pine, killing them outright (Plate 27). It's fair to say, however, that population explosions of bark beetles are most often symptomatic of poor forest health. Bark beetles are smaller, often much smaller, than a grain of rice, and five species of *Ips* and *Dendroctonus* beetles are particularly destructive to ponderosa pine throughout much of its range: the western pine beetle (Fig. 4.6), the mountain pine beetle, the roundheaded pine beetle, the pine engraver, and the Arizona fivespined ips. In the southwestern United States the western pine beetle and the pine engraver beetle are causing most of the mortality in ponderosa pine stands. The western pine beetle typically attacks just the lower portions of larger trees, but the pine engraver attacks all sections of smaller trees and the tops of larger ones. Bark beetles may have two to six generations a year, so populations can expand quickly.

Bark beetles are remarkably efficient at killing ponderosa pine. They are always present in low numbers in most pine populations, and when densities are low, the beetles act as a selective force that removes unhealthy old or young trees from the forest, or serve as thinning agents in much the same way that fire does. In outbreak phases, such as during recent drought years throughout much of the West, exploding beetle populations can kill whole stands of trees. Under such conditions, the relationship between insect and tree changes, and even healthy trees can be destroyed. Beetles can kill enormous trees by mass attacking them in response to a pheromone, or scent, of male beetles that attracts others to a particular tree. A fatal mass attack can involve as many as fifteen beetles per square foot of trunk. Bark beetles lay eggs that hatch, mine, and feed in a tree's phloem and xylem, and it is by disrupting this nutrient transport system that bark beetles kill trees.

Bark beetles also inoculate pine trees with spores of bluestain fungus and other fungi while mining and create a whole new set of complex interactions (Paine and Stephen 1987, Hofstetter et al. 2006). Once considered deadly to trees, the bluestain fungus is no longer regarded as the primary cause of pine mortality (Bridges et al. 1985, Klepzig et al. 2005).

The standard defense of ponderosa pine against bark beetles is straightforward: resin flow (Cates and Alexander 1982). Pine resin is highly viscous and oozes out of wound sites, trapping attacking insects (Plate 28). Have you ever seen insects in amber? In a study in southern Colorado, Cates and Alexander (1982) found that the level of resin flow determined which trees were successfully attacked by bark beetles. Resin canals carry resin or sap through branches, bark, and even pine needles. When plant tissues are damaged, the resin begins to flow. Resins contain chemical compounds called terpenes that deter some animals, but it's the flow of the viscous sap that deters beetles. Resin flow is dependent on high water pressure within the plant. During dry periods water pressure is lower and pines release less resin, making them less resistant to bark beetles. Although western pine beetles in California favor ponderosa pine with low levels of a particular terpene, populations in the Rockies exhibit no such preferences (Sturgeon and Mitton 1986).

The current drought in western North America is rendering ponderosa pine populations more vulnerable to bark beetles. Drought stress combined with greater densities of trees predisposes pine stands to enormous bark beetle outbreaks (Kolb et al. 1998). In Arizona in 2003, more than 600,000 acres of ponderosa pine were killed by the western pine beetle, the pine engraver, and other bark beetles. A key means of controlling these outbreaks involves thinning stands of ponderosa pines. Either humans will thin them, or the bark beetles will.

In contrast to the destructive bark beetles is another genus, *Pityophthorus,* which is regarded as harmless or even beneficial to ponderosa and other pines. This largest genus of bark beetles includes twenty-four species associated with ponderosa pine, but these mine only in shaded, lower branches and help to prune the trees (Furniss and Carolin 1977, de Groot and Turgeon 1998). This natural pruning reduces a tree's susceptibility to fire. The next time you find a small-diameter branch on the ground with beetle mining galleries in it—and they are everywhere—you'll know it was probably fed on by a twig beetle, a "good" bark beetle.

Other pine-feeding insects include enormous aphids (*Cinara* sp.) that suck sap from ponderosa pine branches. When their populations increase, the ground beneath them is shiny with honeydew—their excrement. Like all aphids, ponderosa pine aphids tap their beaklike mouthpart into the phloem and suck a large volume of sap to get nutrients such as amino acids.

One study in Colorado showed that ponderosa pine aphids fed so heavily that they reduced tree growth (Mooney 2006); however, insectivorous birds such as chickadees, nuthatches, and warblers can reduce aphid populations and limit their negative effects on tree growth. Accordingly, birds effectively increased pine growth by 21 percent in 2002 and 35 percent in 2003 by aggressively feeding on aphids. Like most insects associated with ponderosa pine, however, these aphids rarely cause mortality in established plants.

### Vertebrates

More than 180 species of vertebrates, or creatures with backbones, live in the ponderosa pine forests of the Southwest. These include reptiles, birds, and mammals.

Among the reptiles associated with ponderosa pine are several lizards, snakes (including the black rattlesnake), and skinks. They feed on insects, other reptiles, and small mammals, and many of them nest and forage in downed trees.

### Birds

More than 60 species of birds are associated with ponderosa pine forests (Szaro and Balda 1979, Rosenstock 1998, Parker 2001), and more than 40 of those breed in them. Of these, 25 species are year-round residents, while 17 species are neotropical migrants that come from Central and South America for the warmer months and migrate south in the fall.

Some birds, including the pine siskin and several grosbeaks, feed on pine seeds (Plate 29). A variety of woodpeckers feed on sap, and other species such as Virginia's warbler feed on insects feeding on ponderosa pine or dwarf mistletoe. Some birds, such as owls and raptors, feed on other birds and small mammals (Plate 30). When forest birds are breeding and need extra resources, most of them eat insects that feed on ponderosa pine.

Birds that commonly winter in pine forests include the pygmy nuthatch, white-breasted nuthatch, the mountain chickadee, and the dark-eyed junco. All of these birds pick and dig in ponderosa pine bark for insects. Other common birds of ponderosa pine forests include violet-green swallows, robins, and western bluebirds. Two species thought to be good indicators of healthy bird populations in northern Arizona forests are the pygmy nuthatch and violet-green swallow. When these two species are present in high numbers, there tend to be higher numbers of most other ponderosa pine forest birds.

The well-developed spines on ponderosa pine cones have been shown to deter seed-eating birds (Fig. 3.8; Coffey et al. 1999). They do not, however, deter tassle-eared squirrels, which simply bite the whole scale off in search of a seed. Most animals take longer to extract seeds when they have to contend with a spine. Coffey et al. showed experimentally that red crossbills took 20 percent longer to get seeds from cones with spines versus cones with spines removed. Ponderosa pine cones open while still in the tree, and their winged seeds are dispersed from the cones by wind (Fig. 3.8). The seeds are favored by junco, Cassin's finch, pine

siskin, evening grosbeak, Clark's nutcracker, red crossbill, chickadee, sparrow, pinyon jay, and Steller's jay. In the Southwest, pinyon jay and Steller's jay cache more ponderosa pine seeds than other birds do (Russell Balda, personal communication). The inner bark of pines is used by birds such as Williamson's sapsucker.

Many birds nest in cavities in dead or partially dead ponderosa pines. These include owl, chickadee, titmice, woodpecker, flycatcher, swallow, nuthatch, wren, bluebird, and brown creeper. Cavity-nesting birds are common in stands infested with mistletoe as there tend to be more snags (dead trees) present. Woodpeckers are primary cavity nesters, meaning they excavate the cavities themselves, while most other species are secondary cavity nesters that make use of woodpeckers' cavities when they abandon them. Snags are key ecological features in forests and are now included in most habitat management plans. It has been suggested that four to seven snags or large-diameter trees per 2.5 acres are necessary to provide an adequate number of cavities for birds. Some birds favor stands of large, old-growth ponderosa pine. These include the hermit thrush (with its haunting ventriloquial call), red-faced warbler, Cordilleran flycatcher, Mexican spotted owl, northern goshawk, Grace's warbler, and pygmy nuthatch.

The diversity of birds in ponderosa pine stands is much higher when Gambel oak is present (Rosenstock 1998). Gambel oak offers additional resources for birds, including cavities, high numbers of insects, and, of course, acorns. The Mexican spotted owl, listed as an endangered species, nests almost exclusively in pine-oak habitats, steep canyons, and riparian forests.

Wild turkey live in ponderosa pine forests as well as many other types of forests

4.7. An Abert's squirrel (*Sciurus aberti*), a ponderosa pine specialist, in northern Arizona. Courtesy of Sylvester Allred.

throughout the United States. In our western forests, turkeys forage in more open areas during the day; they are diurnal and have great day vision but poor night vision. At night they roost in ponderosa pine canopies, which protect them from predators. They are fast runners, having been clocked at 25 mph, and decent fliers. Turkeys flock together in winter months. Adults and young feed on a great variety of foods, including acorns, berries, insects, new shoots on pines and oaks, and small reptiles. Their numbers became quite low in the early twentieth century, but with better management, there are now more than 6 million turkeys in North America. This is another animal that benefits from both dense and open stands of ponderosa pine.

*Mammals*

Abert's squirrel (*Sciurus aberti*) is a tree squirrel that is nearly completely dependent on ponderosa pine for food and housing, and it co-occurs with ponderosa pine throughout its southwestern range (Colorado, Utah, Arizona, and New Mexico) (Fig. 4.7; Keith 2003, Allred 2010). Abert's squirrel does not inhabit northern stands of ponderosa pine due to their longer winters and deeper

snows. Other squirrels, such as the red tree squirrel, also feed on ponderosa pine, but Abert's squirrel is the most common through its southern range. Abert's squirrel populations can vary wildly between years, with their numbers declining during particularly severe winters when snow persists for long periods and resources are patchy.

Abert's squirrel has a complicated diet and feeds on different parts of ponderosa pine. It doesn't cache much food, so it feeds aggressively on plants and mushrooms through the seasons. It feeds mainly on the inner bark of pines in winter, on cones and new shoots through late summer, and on mushrooms through the fall. During the winter it feeds on the inner bark, which is low in protein and just about everything else. When fed a steady diet of inner bark, squirrels lose weight, become stressed, and experience greater mortality. Protein deficiency may be the main cause of winter mortality, when deep snow persists, covering up other resources such as mushrooms and fallen cones. When feeding on inner bark or phloem, squirrels select the outer 3 to 5 inches of a branch, clip the terminal pine needles, and then peel back the bark on the remaining twig so they can chew off the thin, moist layer of inner bark. Needle bundles and peeled twigs litter the ground under some trees. Squirrels can clip hundreds of twigs from a single tree over the course of a year. At the end of a very cold winter in Flagstaff, their extensive thinning of ponderosa pine canopies is highly evident. It is thought that the squirrels may be important agents of natural selection for ponderosa pines as they differentially feed on particular trees, leading to reduced cone production or even mortality (Snyder 1998).

Fortunately, the Abert's squirrel's diet changes in the spring from inner bark to developing cones, seeds, and new shoots (Linhart et al. 1989, States 1990). They can, however, reduce a tree's cone crop by 75 percent. From late summer through fall, squirrels feed intensively on several of the thirty mushroom species associated with ponderosa pine forests. They dig in the loose soil and debris under pine canopies to find and feed on mycorrhizal fruiting mushrooms that grow in association with pine roots. These subterranean mushrooms depend on squirrels for dispersing their spores. Abert's squirrel also feeds on Gambel oak acorns at this time. Squirrels also cache pine cones and then spend much time digging to relocate them. Not surprisingly, pine seeds provide the most energy per gram of their diet, but they also feed on mistletoe.

Abert's squirrel typically nests in ponderosa pine. They build their nests in branch clusters or in witch's brooms formed by mistletoe, and consistently place them on the southeast side of trees to catch morning sun. Nests are composed of needles and other debris. In my own backyard, squirrels tore apart a cushion and hauled the cotton stuffing up to their nests. They also hauled off my daughter's small plastic Pooh Bear doll, to what end I know not.

There are six subspecies of Abert's squirrel, all of which are associated with ponderosa pine (Hoffmeister and Diersing 1978, Lamb et al. 1997). Collectively their range extends from Wyoming into Mexico, but they differ in size and coloration. Each subspecies is associated with geographically isolated stands of ponderosa pine, including those on the Kaibab Plateau in northern Arizona, in the Chuska and Tunicha mountains in northeastern Arizona and New Mexico, in the eastern Rockies, and in several mountain ranges in Chihuahua, Mexico.

Genetic analyses have determined that Abert's squirrels may have migrated back through the West quickly, perhaps following the rapid expansion of ponderosa pine at the end of the Pleistocene (Lamb et al. 1997). This study also determined, however, that this species group diversified earlier in the Pleistocene, and perhaps repeatedly, in response to the many climatic changes that occurred during that time.

Porcupine also feed on ponderosa pine's phloem or inner bark, but they occur throughout North America and feed on a variety of other plants as well. Ponderosa pine phloem is, however, a major winter food source for porcupine in the western United States. Mistletoe appears to be another favorite porcupine food. In some instances, porcupine may feed only on mistletoe rather than a tree's inner bark, which ultimately benefits the infested tree (Linhart et al. 1989).

Among the hundreds of plants and animals that depend on ponderosa pine, Abert's squirrel, porcupine, bark beetles, and mistletoe have all been shown to favor different biochemical and physical characteristics (Mitton 1995, Snyder 1998). For example, in a study of Abert's squirrel and porcupine living in the same ponderosa pine stand, of 655 trees attacked by either species, only 18 were used by both, showing their different tastes in inner bark phloem (Linhart et al. 1989).

Although ponderosa pine seeds are primarily wind dispersed (Fig. 3.8), many small rodents, including mice, ground squirrels, and chipmunks, have been shown to disperse seeds twice as far as those dispersed by wind. One study in northern Arizona found that field mice and chipmunks collected enormous numbers of ponderosa pine seeds and cached or buried them in sites that encouraged germination (Compton 2004).

While rodent populations can be quite low in dense ponderosa pine forests, thinning treatments that leave slash behind can lead to increases of 200 to 1,000 percent in species such as deer mice, chipmunks, brush mice, and woodrats (Goodwin and Hungerford 1979).

Elk, deer, antelope, rabbit and hare, black bear, red and grey fox, skunk, coyote, raccoon, mountain lion (Plate 31), bobcat, weasel, marmot, and pika (Plate 32) interact with ponderosa pine and often feed on it. Mule deer can completely defoliate lower branches (Linhart 1988). Although fire is

regarded as the primary means of natural population control of ponderosa pine forests, mammals—including pocket gophers, deer, elk, hares, rabbits, and small rodents— feed heartily on small pines, killing many of them. Many bats, which are important insectivores, roost in large dead pines, either under the bark or in cavities.

Ponderosa pine forests are currently expanding their ranges north and into higher elevations in the Rockies and Intermountain West. The pinyon-juniper woodlands—which normally occur below ponderosa pine forests but are already moving in to take their place around Flagstaff— are the subject of the next chapter.

# CHAPTER 5

# The Pinyon-Juniper Woodlands

Western pinyon-juniper woodlands are unique to North America. While juniper occurs throughout the Northern Hemisphere, pinyon pine occurs only in western Northern America. The pinyon-juniper woodland is comprised of overlapping bands of pinyon and juniper that live at the base of many mountain ranges throughout the West. Pinyon typically adjoin ponderosa pine stands at higher elevations, with juniper butting up against pinyon at its upper limit and downward into grasslands or shrub steppe. This lower-elevation ecosystem receives still less water than neighboring ponderosa pine, and pinyon and juniper compete fiercely for it, yet also serve as nurse plants for one another.

Like so many other plants, pinyon and juniper have an incredibly dynamic history involving a major northward migration at the end of the Pleistocene. They have been on the move ever since, migrating up and down through their more recent range. Their story is all the more amazing since

they are both dependent on birds and mammals to disperse their seeds. Today, pinyon and juniper live together in some of the driest pine habitats in the world (Rundel and Yoder 1998). There are about 47 million acres of pinyon-juniper woodlands in the western United States (Lanner 1996). They also cover large areas in Mexico (Figs. 5.1, 5.2). At lower elevations pinyon-juniper woodlands are readily burned by fire and are especially susceptible to drought. Both characteristics have contributed to their very dynamic history in the West.

The most common pinyon species in the United States are Colorado pinyon (*Pinus edulis*) and singleleaf pinyon (*P. monophylla*) (Fig. 5.2). Although their ranges overlap in many places, Colorado pinyon generally occurs at higher elevations than singleleaf pinyon, and its range extends from Mexico into northeastern Utah and northwestern Colorado, while singleleaf pinyon occurs from Baja California through the Great Basin (where there are at least four varieties) and

**5.1.** Shaded area shows the approximate distribution of pinyon-juniper woodlands in the western United States.

**5.2.** Common species found in pinyon-juniper woodlands: *top*, a one-seed juniper (*Juniperus monosperma*) and to its right, a Colorado pinyon (*Pinus edulis*), northern Arizona; *bottom*, close-up of foliage of Colorado pinyon (*left*) and one-seed juniper.

as far north as southern Idaho. At its southern limits in Baja, singleleaf pinyon typically occurs on north-facing slopes, while at its northern limits in Utah and Idaho it lives on south-facing slopes (Lanner 1981). Colorado pinyon and singleleaf pinyon often hybridize where their ranges overlap.

Five species of juniper form part of the pinyon-juniper ecosystem in the Rockies and Intermountain West: one-seed juniper (*Juniperus monosperma*), Utah juniper (*J. osteosperma*), Rocky Mountain juniper (*J. scopulorum*), alligator juniper (*J. deppeana*), and western juniper (*J. occidentalis*). Generally speaking, one-seed juniper occurs from Mexico northward along both sides of the Rockies as far north as Utah and Colorado, while Utah juniper occurs only west of the Rockies, from northern Arizona through the Great Basin into Montana and Wyoming. Alligator juniper and Rocky Mountain juniper are never as abundant as the other species, but Rocky Mountain juniper has the largest range, extending into Canada. Western juniper occurs in the northwestern portion of the Great Basin, extending into Oregon, Washington, and Idaho. Pinyon-juniper woodland communities typically consist of singleleaf juniper and Colorado pinyon in the eastern and southern foothills of the Rockies, while Utah juniper and singleleaf pinyon occur together throughout much of the Great Basin.

## EVOLUTIONARY HISTORY OF THE PINYON-JUNIPER WOODLAND

Pinyons are a recently evolved plant group—or at least their first appearance in the fossil record is fairly recent, dating back to the Eocene, ~50 Ma (Lanner 1981, 1996). This was a time of great pine expansion and diversification in western North America. Pinyons are thought to have diversified in Mexico or Central America, with their ancestors being more mesic species. Tropical pines are unique in producing "summer shoots" that elongate soon after buds have developed in spring rather than waiting until the next year. Summer shoots become less common in drier and colder climates. Northern pinyons also have this trait, suggesting a tropical origin. The pinyon group may have originated in Eurasia and, eventually, made its way from Asia to North America, carried by a Eurasian nutcracker species.

Eleven pinyon species are listed in Ronald Lanner's 1996 book *Made for Each Other: A Symbiosis of Birds and Pines*. The taxonomy of pinyons is challenging, partly because so many species have only recently been recognized, and the pinyon group has lots of variation.

Singleleaf pinyon is an offshoot of the two-needled Colorado pinyon. Fossils of singleleaf pinyon found in the Mohave Desert indicate that this speciation event had occurred by 25 Ma. With a strong drying trend in the West beginning in the Late Miocene, the stage was set for pinyon to expand its range, leaving its mesic ancestry behind and becoming more drought tolerant.

By contrast, the evolutionary history of the juniper family, Cupressaceae, is obscure, although it is thought to have originated by the Cretaceous. Various fossils of wood and foliage are known from that period from New Jersey and Alaska (Miller 1988). Like pine, juniper occurs almost exclusively in the Northern Hemisphere, suggesting that they also originated there prior to the breakup of the supercontinent Laurasia. Juniper occurs south of the equator only in East Africa (Cronquist et al. 1972). There are sixty to seventy species and forty varieties of juniper worldwide. Common juniper (*Juniperus communis*) occurs throughout the Northern Hemisphere at higher elevations and latitudes. In the San Francisco Peaks of northern Arizona, it occurs in its prostrate form at treeline. It is also widely cultivated,

partly because its berries are used in making gin.

The greatest numbers of juniper species occur in the southwestern United States, Mexico, the Mediterranean, and western China. *Juniperus* is the second largest conifer genus and remarkably diverse, which makes it difficult to describe succinctly. The feature binding the genus together is the morphology of the female cone with its fruitlike bract, a trait that is distinct to juniper and a few other conifers. There are at least thirteen juniper species in the United States and Canada.

## The Pleistocene Record of Pinyon-Juniper Woodlands

The Pleistocene record for pinyon and juniper reflects a very dynamic history. Both groups are well represented in packrat middens and pollen samples from the last 40,000 years. During this time, pinyon and juniper migrated to elevations lower than 4,500 feet. These Ice Age woodlands covered the lowlands of the Chihuahuan, Sonoran, and Mohave deserts during the peak of the Wisconsin glacial advances (Betancourt et al. 1990). Much of the Chihuahuan Desert was dominated by Texas pinyon (*Pinus remota*) during the Late Pleistocene, though today it has only a relict distribution in the mountains of northeastern Mexico and southern Texas.

According to the packrat midden record, these desert woodlands were stable during the Late Pleistocene, but the northward migration of pinyon and juniper at the end of that period mirrored that of ponderosa pine. Singleleaf pinyon had replaced limber pine in the Elena Range in the southern Great Basin by about 11,500 years ago and had reached the central Great Basin by about 6,000 years ago (Betancourt et al. 1990).

At least one pinyon population was established farther north, possibly due to human dispersal of seeds. Pinyon shells found in Danger Cave in northern Utah date to 7,920 and 7,410 years ago (Lanner and Van Devender 1998). While bird versus human dispersal patterns may complicate the picture of these migrations, the general trend has been a northward migration from refugia in the southern deserts up along the Rockies and through the Intermountain West.

In the northwest part of the Great Basin, where the ranges of both western juniper and singleleaf pinyon were expanding, a severe drought settled in between 8,000 and 4,500 years ago, and pollen samples suggest that they were replaced by desert plant species (Miller and Wigand 1994). By 4,500 years ago, temperatures cooled, precipitation increased, and juniper pollen levels began to rise again, remaining high until 1,900 years ago. High pollen levels indicate a time of population expansion, and in this case juniper were also migrating downslope by as much as 450 feet in elevation. Between 1,900 and 1,000 years ago, a drier climate set in, and again juniper pollen levels declined. About 1,000 years ago, the climate became wetter, and both juniper and pinyon pollen levels increased.

## The Modern Pinyon-Juniper Woodland

Pinyon-juniper woodlands have continued to expand to the present day, and populations have moved downward into adjacent grasslands or shrub steppe, upward into receding forests, and into existing woodlands. In southwestern Utah alone, pinyon-juniper woodland increased to five times its former area and six to twenty times its former density between 1864 and 1940 (Chambers et al. 1999).

Euro-American settlement in the West may have influenced the expansion of pinyon-juniper woodlands (Tausch et al. 1981, Peet 1989, West 1999). Tausch et al. suggest that the expansion of pinyon-juniper woodlands in the Great Basin coincided with the introduction 150 years ago of heavy livestock grazing and fire suppression, both of which were ongoing into the 1970s. Domestic cattle reduced the cover and vigor of associated grasses, eliminating the fine fuels that carried the cool surface fires that regulated juniper establishment. As with ponderosa pine today, fires in pinyon-juniper woodlands are shifting from cooler surface fires that recycle litter and limit seedling establishment to deadly, stand-replacing fires.

A study of 486 pinyon-juniper woodland populations in 66 mountain ranges in the Great Basin showed that over 50 percent of the stands had no trees older that 120 years in age (West 1999). The oldest trees were found on steep, rocky sites, suggesting that expanding populations were migrating down from these sites onto finer-grained soils, such as on gently sloping bajadas (Burkhardt and Tisdale 1976, West 1999). According to West, the pinyon-juniper woodland may historically have been confined to steep and rocky sites and only recently migrated into flatter areas such as western grasslands. While individual junipers are known to reach ages of thousands of years, few such trees are found today.

Aboriginal exploitation of the pinyon-juniper woodland for fuel over several thousand years may have significantly reduced its presence in some areas, in which case today's expansion would represent a recovery to earlier densities (Samuels and Betancourt 1982). Alternatively, pinyon-juniper woodland populations may have been restricted historically to rocky outcrops by competing grasslands and by the high frequency of lightning-caused fires, which regularly occurred through much of their range.

A study in northern Arizona found that nineteenth-century pinyon-juniper woodland expansion was strongly influenced by the substrate on which the populations grew (Landis and Bailey 2005). Stands growing on basalt- or sandstone-derived soils had large increases in tree densities, while populations on limestone-derived soils experienced a slow, steady increase.

Allen and Breshears (1998) described a rapid expansion, or migration, of pinyon-juniper woodland upslope in the Jemez Mountains in northern New Mexico following a drought that lasted from the late 1940s into the late 1950s—the worst since the 1500s. It caused massive vegetation die-off from the deserts up into coniferous woodlands. The pinyon-juniper woodland quickly migrated up into a ponderosa pine stand that had died back by as much as 50 percent, shifting the ponderosa pine/pinyon-juniper ecotone. Pinyons and junipers migrated over a mile into this higher-elevation site in less than five years. Such a large-scale die-off opened up the site to more readily available resources such as sunlight, water, and nutrients. Despite increased precipitation following this period, these vegetation changes have persisted. This rapid response to drought shows that even a brief climate change can have profound and persistent ecosystem effects. Such population shifts may occur globally since semiarid forests and woodlands are widespread and thought to be the most sensitive to changes in climate.

Today's ongoing western drought, which began in 1995, is again redefining the range of the pinyon-juniper woodland. Pinyon mortality has exceeded 90 percent at Mesa Verde, Colorado, and near Flagstaff, Arizona (Breshears et al. 2005). Recent drought conditions have been more extreme and destructive than those of the 1950s due to warmer maximum annual temperatures. While pinyon mortality following the 1950s drought was patchy and typically involved trees more than 100 years old, recent mortality has been nearly complete across size and age classes due to drought and insect attacks. Ironically, it is thought that anomalously high precipitation in the Southwest from 1978 to 1995 ultimately exacerbated the effects of this drought because it allowed rapid tree growth and increased densities, which led to greater competition for limited water and greater susceptibility to drought and bark beetle infestations. One-seed juniper, though far more drought tolerant than pinyon, also experienced drought-related mortality between 1999 and 2003, ranging from 2 percent to 26 percent at various sites. Blue grama grass, a dominant grass associated with the pinyon-juniper woodland, also underwent more than a 50 percent reduction in cover during this time.

Within the Great Basin, expansion of the pinyon-juniper woodland has slowed over the last two to three decades after more than 100 years of expansion (Robin Tausch, personal communication, 2006). Some mortality of singleleaf pinyon has occurred due to the recent drought, with juniper sustaining less mortality. Unlike the Southwest, the Great Basin had above-average precipitation in 2005 and 2006. Today, scientists can only speculate about whether this is the beginning of a significant and long-term drying trend or only one more drought event in the West's cycling of dry and wet periods.

As I look out on the seemingly endless stands of dead pinyon now surrounding Flagstaff, I imagine that this is how things have always looked—many dead trees of one species or another standing in place, while their young are establishing in areas with more conducive conditions. There are many, many junipers and a few pinyons scattered through the ponderosa pine forests here, showing that theirs is a migration in progress.

*Pinyon and Juniper Interactions*

The co-occurrence of pinyon and juniper throughout the semiarid West is a result of their having very similar ecological needs—which also makes them intense competitors for precious water and nutrients. Junipers typically live at lower elevations in the pinyon-juniper woodland because they are more drought tolerant than pinyon (Rundel and Yoder 1998, Linton et al. 1998). In pinyon-juniper woodlands in Utah and northern Arizona, Linton et al. found that Utah juniper could absorb water from drier soils than Colorado pinyon could. Plant roots must have lower water levels than the soil itself in order to draw water from it through osmosis. The water transport system of these plants, the xylem, is comprised of tiny, tubelike cells called tracheids. Transport through the xylem can fail under severe water stress due to an event called *xylem cavitation*, when outside air drawn into a tracheid forms a gas bubble, blocking movement of water. Juniper roots are more resistant to cavitation than pinyon roots are, and this contributes to juniper's greater tolerance of drought. When soil water levels dropped during a drought in 1996, pinyons stopped conducting water through their roots or branches. At the same time, water conductance in junipers declined only 25 to 50 percent. The other part of this story is that even under drought conditions, Utah juniper can continue to absorb essential $CO_2$

for photosynthesis, whereas pinyon has to stop in order to avoid water loss through leaf pores. The more a plant photosynthesizes, the more it can grow and reproduce. Linton et al. (1998) suggest that juniper could live in far more stressful sites than those where they're found now, and that they have the ability to expand their range into the lower, drier grasslands.

Up to half of the Southwest's annual precipitation falls as rain in summer months, when most of it evaporates before soaking very deeply into soil. Both pinyon and juniper have extensive, shallow root systems that allow them to capitalize on this ephemeral water. Dense, fine roots occur in the upper 12 inches of soil and extend well beyond the plant's canopy to absorb water and nutrients. In the pinyon-juniper woodland in northern Arizona and northern New Mexico, oneseed juniper is able to extract more moisture from soil beyond its canopy edge than Colorado pinyon (Breshears et al. 1997).

Kristin Haskins (2003) studied root-level interactions between pinyon and juniper north of Flagstaff, where the soils are of volcanic origin and low in nutrients and water. She found 1.5 times more juniper root mass than pinyon root mass where the trees co-occurred, suggesting that juniper captures more water and nutrients. To study their interactions, she dug 12-inch-deep trenches around a series of pinyons, thereby isolating them from juniper roots. Freed from competition, the trenched pinyons doubled their fine root mass, leading Haskins to conclude that during periods of drought, pinyon is competitively inferior to juniper in acquiring water and nutrients.

The fact that pinyon manages to coexist with the hardy juniper at all is surprising. In northern Arizona today, the ponderosa pine forests above the pinyon zone have been colonized by junipers. So why hasn't juniper fully replaced pinyon throughout its range? This is best understood by examining the shift from juniper dominance to pinyon dominance along the elevational gradient that generally separates them. At the upper elevations of the pinyon-juniper woodland, where more water is available, pinyon has a greater maximum net photosynthesis rate than juniper, which leads to greater carbon gains and ultimately larger trees that can tower over and shade juniper (Martens et al. 2001).

Another important interaction between pinyon and juniper involves their reliance on each other as nurse plants. In stressful environments nurse plants provide seedlings with shade, lower temperatures, increased nutrients (such as phosphorus, potassium, and total nitrogen), greater soil water, slower summer drying, protection from herbivores, and protection from wind (Chambers 2001, Chambers et al. 1999, Haskins 2003). Juniper and pinyon have been shown to have greater establishment levels in the shade of tree canopies in Nevada, Oregon, and northern Arizona, even though they are less shade tolerant when older. Chambers (2001) found that pinyon seedlings may require nurse plants until they are more than forty years old. In the Southwest, where strong summer monsoon rains usually occur in July and August, the need for a nurse plant may lessen, allowing juniper, in particular, to establish in open spaces. Pinyons growing under recently drought-killed nurse trees can have even greater growth rates than those growing under living trees, perhaps due to increased light as pine needles fall from the dead tree (Haskins 2003). One northern Arizona study of a pinyon-juniper woodland site found that more than 85 percent of seedlings were under tree canopies,

particularly their north-facing portions (Sampson 1988), and that there were nearly equal numbers of pinyon and juniper seedlings under the canopies.

### Fire in Pinyon-Juniper Woodlands

The fire history of pinyon-juniper woodlands is unclear, but it is being intensively studied (Chambers et al. 1999; Romme, Floyd-Hanna, and Hanna 2003; Floyd et al. 2004). It appears that fire cycles may vary according to whether the pinyon-juniper woodland occurs in grasslands and plains versus rugged slopes, canyons, and mesa tops. In rugged habitats or canyon bottoms, intense, 400-year fires can occur, replacing entire stands of trees.

Fire records are lacking for many pinyon-juniper woodlands because they rarely bear fire scars such as those on ponderosa pines, which are so useful in constructing fire histories. The lack of fire scars suggests that fires in the pinyon-juniper woodland are typically of the severe, stand-replacing type. One study that did find trees with fire scars and considerable amounts of charcoal in juniper stands in Idaho also found evidence of frequent fires, with some portion of the region burning every year up until Euro-American settlement (Burkhart and Tisdale 1976). Chambers et al. (1999) suggest that there were fires in the pinyon-juniper woodland every 50 to 100 years prior to Euro-American settlement. Floyd et al. (2003) report stand-replacing fires with a rotation of 400 years or longer in Mesa Verde National Park in southern Colorado. And this is despite the fact that the number of lightning-caused fires there has averaged eight per year. Most fires extinguish naturally after burning an individual tree or a small patch of ground. Only 2 percent of these fires were very large, but they accounted for over 95 percent of the area burned at Mesa Verde over the course of the twentieth century.

All of the large twentieth-century fires at Mesa Verde occurred during periods of prolonged drought and high winds that carried fires into tree canopies (Floyd et al. 2004). Since 1976 some of these conditions have been caused by the El Niño—Southern Oscillation system (ENSO). This ENSO climate pattern has strongly affected fire frequency in the southwestern United States (Floyd et al. 2004, Swetnam and Betancourt 1998).

Colorado pinyon, Utah juniper, and Rocky Mountain juniper are easily killed by even low-intensity fires (Romme, Oliva, and Floyd 2003). Their thin bark provides little insulation or protection for the delicate vascular tissues just below it, and pinyon and juniper both have low-hanging foliage that helps fires to spread into their canopies. The susceptibility of pinyon-juniper woodland to fire probably contributes to pronounced turnovers in many of its populations, which are strongly skewed toward younger individuals.

The commitment to grazing cattle in the western United States has led to efforts to reduce the extent of the pinyon-juniper woodland and convert it to grasslands. Beginning in the 1950s and 1960s, land managers began altering pinyon-juniper woodlands and savanna using a method called *chaining*. This clearing method involves dragging an anchor chain or cable between two tractors over the trees and then raking them into piles. Grass seeds, often Asian grasses, are then sowed to establish grasslands. Such "conversions" have declined but, remarkably, still occur today (West 1989). According to Ronald Lanner (personal communication), cutting and

chaining of old trees in these conversion areas has destroyed pinyon's fire history. Given that the pinyon-juniper woodland has less value as a commodity to humans than taller trees do, there is less incentive to manage populations in a sound way. According to West, the best way to manage pinyon-juniper woodland is through a combination of prescribed burning, thinning, and limited grazing.

## BASIC BIOLOGY OF PINYON-JUNIPER WOODLANDS

As ancient cone-bearing plants, pinyon and juniper are dependent on wind to disperse their pollen, which is often an inefficient process (Lanner 1980, Fuentes and Schupp 1998, Chambers et al. 1999). The proportion of fertilized, developed seeds in cones can be variable. In Colorado pinyon, nearly half of the seeds in mature cones can be empty, and in singleleaf pinyon, 18 percent and then 21 percent of seeds were found empty during two successive years (Chambers et al. 1999). The number of filled seeds per cone averaged four in the former and sixteen in the latter. Filled seed rates can be even lower in junipers, ranging from 0 to 33 percent. Seed failure in pinyon is typically the result of self-pollination or inbreeding.

Pinyon seeds take up to three growing seasons to develop. Like ponderosa pine, pinyon are monoecious. Male cones are small and typically located in the lower portions of the tree, while the female cones are larger and typically located in the upper portion of the canopy (Figs. 3.8, 4.5). Pollination occurs in early summer, after which developing seeds first fill with water and then are infused with large amounts of carbohydrates, proteins, and lipids. When fully developed, the seed coats harden, and the cones dry out and begin opening in September (Fig. 3.8; Chambers et al. 1999).

Many junipers are dioecious, whereby each sex is housed in separate plants, such as in one-seed juniper. By contrast, Utah juniper is typically monoecious, like pinyon. Male cones occur at the tips of branches as tiny yellow-orange bulbs containing pollen sacs. Female cones also develop in the outer canopy, and their fleshy scales fuse to form their cones, which are referred to as berries. Generally, male cones dump pollen in the early spring. Juniper may produce one seed per cone, as in one-seed and Utah juniper, or up to five seeds per cone, as in alligator juniper (Chambers et al. 1999). Juniper seeds may take one (one-seed juniper), two (Utah juniper), or even three (common juniper) growing seasons to mature following pollination, and they tend to be quite long lived. Utah juniper seeds can germinate even after forty-five years, and 50 percent germination was found in one-seed juniper seeds after twenty-one years. By contrast, pinyon seeds rarely remain viable for more than a year.

Despite large losses from natural abortion and predation, both pinyon and juniper produce enormous cone crops at intervals of two to seven years, depending on the species. Production of a bumper seed crop, or *masting*, often appears synchronized within populations and sometimes across regions. Such synchronization probably reflects a similar response to favorable weather conditions (Chambers et al. 1999). Colorado pinyon produces large cone crops about every five years, while single-leaf pinyon produces bumper crops every two to three years. The size of cone crops in the intervening years ranges from moderate to nil. Barger and Ffolliott (1972) reported mast years for Colorado pinyon

in the Southwest in 1936, 1943, 1948, 1954, 1959, and 1965. Vander Wall (1997) found that singleleaf pinyons in Nevada produced an average of 5,936 viable seeds in a heavy cone production year, and 1,873 seeds per tree in a moderate year. Masting patterns in juniper are also variable; western juniper can produce heavy seed crops annually, but most other species produce heavy seed crops every two to five years (Chambers et al. 1999).

At Mesa Verde, the oldest pinyons are between 300 and 400 years old, but they are rare; most trees are less than 190 years old. Likewise, the oldest junipers at Mesa Verde are between 500 and 700 years old, but most are younger than 400 years. In both groups today the vast majority of trees are less than 100 years old (Floyd et al. 2003). An 860-year-old pinyon was discovered near Mesa Verde along with a 1,350-year-old Utah juniper.

## PLANT, ANIMALS, AND FUNGI OF PINYON-JUNIPER WOODLANDS

At least a thousand species of plants, animals, and fungi are associated with Colorado pinyon, making this rich system a world unto itself (Whitham et al. 2003).

Like 90 percent of all plants, pinyon and juniper have symbiotic fungi, called mycorrhizae, associated with their fine roots. These symbionts help the trees survive in the semiarid West. Mycorrhizae tend to be most abundant on the roots of plants growing in stressful substrates, such as cinders, as opposed to sites with finer-grained soils such as loams. These fungi improve a plant's ability to absorb water and nutrients, but they uptake as much as 60 percent of all the carbohydrates that the host plant produces through photosynthesis. That's a lot—and leads to tight energy budgets and a tug-of-war with the various herbivores that extract pinyon resources for themselves.

Pinyon and juniper have different species of fungi associated with their roots, and if a pinyon seed happens to land in a pure stand of junipers, it may not find the appropriate fungus to help its roots acquire adequate nutrients and water. By contrast, juniper shares many of its mycorrhizal fungi with common native grasses, such as blue grama grass, making it easier for juniper to establish in a pinyon-blue grama grass microsite (Haskins 2003).

Both pinyon and juniper are parasitized by mistletoe, which extracts its share of the host plant's carbon products to support its own growth. It does this by tapping into its host plant's vascular system. Pinyon is parasitized by pinyon mistletoe, which is among the most damaging pathogens of southwestern conifers (Adams 1967, Hawksworth and Shaw 1984). This relationship becomes more damaging during periods of drought. In northern Arizona, the percentage of pinyon infected with dwarf mistletoe can be four-fold higher at sites that are particularly stressful, such as those with poor soils (Mueller 2004). Ultimately, mistletoe attack leads to increased water stress and branch dieback. Mueller also found that higher levels of mistletoe infection were associated with higher levels of mycorrhizal root fungi, and the types of root fungi were different from those associated with parasite-free pinyon.

The mistletoe associated with one-seed juniper also most often attacks trees that occur in stressful habitats (Gehring and Whitham 1992), and in such areas it attacks three times as many female as male junipers. This may result from female trees investing so much in producing thousands of seeds. Another intriguing explanation

for greater mistletoe infestation on female plants involves associated birds that feed on *both* juniper berries and mistletoe seeds. At sites that were less stressful (e.g., with better soil), female and male trees were attacked to a comparable degree. Unlike pinyon, juniper trees that were attacked by mistletoe had lower levels of mycorrhizal fungi associated with their roots, sometimes nearly 40 percent less. This could mean that the mistletoe suppresses mycorrhizal formation on roots, or that junipers with high levels of mycorrhizae are able to resist mistletoe attack.

### Pinyon Insects

Many of the insects associated with pinyon are well studied, and their complex interactions are fascinating. Nearly 300 arthropod species have been collected from pinyons in northern Arizona, and the number of species and individuals on pinyons was found to be up to six times higher during wet periods than during drought (Scudder 2005). Leatherman and Kondratieff (2003) list more than 55 insect species thought to be associated with pinyon pine at Mesa Verde.

Collectively, these species feed on just about every plant part that pinyon has to offer. They include scale insects that feed on needles, cone beetles, an enormous sap-sucking aphid, defoliating moths and sawflies, flies, and several types of insects that form galls in needles. The bark beetle associated with pinyon, the pinyon ips, is deadly and can erupt into outbreaks that kill whole stands of trees. As with ponderosa pine, drought and high tree densities can set the stage for bark beetle outbreaks.

In northern Arizona, volcanic eruptions about 800 years ago sent lava sheets flowing over deep, sandy-loam soils, creating a mosaic of poor and good quality sites,

**5.3.** A susceptible Colorado pinyon (*left*) with its architecture altered by the stem-boring moth *Dioryctria albovittellia*, and next to it, a resistant pinyon, northern Arizona. Courtesy of Thomas Whitham.

both of which have been colonized by pinyon. Pinyons growing on lava or cinder soils are chronically stressed by lack of water and nutrients, and heavily attacked by a stem-boring moth larva (*Dioryctria albovittella*), whose mining can reduce female cone production by more than 90 percent (Mueller et al. 2005). On stressful sites, 70 percent of pinyon pines are susceptible to moth attacks (Cobb 1997). The resulting damage can reduce trunk growth by nearly 50 percent and dramatically alter morphology from that of a tall tree to a flattened shrub (Fig. 5.3; Whitham and Mopper 1985, Mopper et al. 1991). Moth damage can also reduce the presence of symbiotic mycorrhizal root fungi by more than 30 percent; making things even worse, the few seeds that are produced are smaller and less viable than those of resistant trees (Mueller et al. 2005). When moth larvae were experimentally removed from susceptible trees, cone and seed production and levels of mycorrhizal root fungi all increased.

Perhaps in response to the severity of damage, which constitutes strong natural selection, some pinyons are genetically resistant to the stem moth (Mopper et al. 1991). This is especially evident at stressful cinder sites, where resistant varieties of pinyon maintain normal tree morphology, and moth attacks are less successful. As with other pines, resin or sap output is key in reducing moth damage. Genetically resistant pinyons have been found to produce twice the amount of resin in response to wounding as susceptible trees, and Mopper et al. (1991) found that trees growing in the stressful cinder sites differ genetically from trees growing on less stressful sites. In this case, poor site conditions themselves serve as a form of natural selection, favoring forms that can tolerate harsher conditions. A particularly intriguing aspect of this relationship is that the cinder fields colonized by pinyon are geologically young. Sunset Crater, their source, stopped erupting only 800 years ago, so the evolution of resistance to stem moths and tolerance of poor soils may be quite recent.

Severe and recent long-term drought in northern Arizona has altered pinyon-juniper woodland ecology in dramatic ways. Contrary to predictions, moth-resistant trees have experienced mortality levels three times greater than moth-susceptible trees, making them equally common on cinder sites (Sthultz et al. 2009). Other insects that were more abundant on stressed trees, such as aphids, scale insects, sawflies, moths, and flies, have declined in numbers with drought, as have most pinyon insects, showing that even a preference for stressed plants has its limits (Cobb 1993, Trotter et al. 2008, Scudder 2005).

## Birds Associated with Pinyon-Juniper Woodlands

Both pinyon and juniper seeds are dispersed by birds. San Miguel and Colyer (2003) list more than 100 bird species that occur in old-growth pinyon-juniper woodland at Mesa Verde. Members of this well-rounded avian community include ground foragers, nectar sippers (associated with flowers), foliage gleaners, bark gleaners, wood borers, flycatchers, raptors, rock gleaners, generalists, and of course, nut and berry feeders.

Its nutritious seeds are what attract birds to pinyon, whereas it is the fruit coat of juniper that herbivores cache and devour. Compared with the cones of many other conifers, pinyon cones are rather flimsy and easily broken into by birds. Colorado pinyon seeds have high fat and protein levels (63 percent and 11 percent, respectively [Chambers et al. 1999]). Pinyon seeds have thinner coats than many other large-seeded pines, making them accessible to large corvids (such as jays), smaller birds, and rodents.

The animal-friendly pinyon cones and seeds have given up their ancestral wind-dispersal traits. Their seeds are too heavy to be dispersed very far by wind, and they lack the thin, membranous wings that help ponderosa pine seeds disperse on the wind (Fig. 3.8). Each pinyon seed is contained within a deep chamber that keeps it in the cone until some creature collects and disperses it. A wind of about 100 mph can only move a pinyon seed 30 feet as it falls from a height of 30 feet (Lanner 1996). Most unharvested seeds fall under the parent plant canopy.

## Pinyon Pine and Jays

Two of the most important dispersers of pinyon seeds are Clark's nutcracker (Fig. 3.7) and the pinyon jay, both in the family Corvidae, which also includes crows, ravens, magpies, and other jays. Clark's nutcracker and the pinyon jay are highly evolved seed specialists and, like all corvids, incredibly smart. Among the many corvids that feed on pinyon seeds, these two are noteworthy for their ability to open green cones, disperse seeds long distances, and cache them.

At least ten subspecies of nutcracker are associated with pinyon ancestors in Eurasia, each of which has an enormous range, from the Arctic Circle to the Tropic of Cancer. In contrast, there are no subspecies or even varieties of Clark's nutcracker, which is relatively new to North America (Lanner 1996). Eurasian nutcrackers, however, have differentiated over a much longer period of time. Lanner suggests that pinyon pine was brought by the Eurasian nutcracker to North America, where both then differentiated into new species. The soft pines, with wingless seeds (there are about twenty-two species in the Old and New worlds), may have evolved through the selective action of corvids (Lanner 1996). Unlike Old World jays, the pinyon jay and Clark's nutcracker have a jaw structure, shared with other New World jays, that aids in opening acorns. This similarity between these two pinyon seed feeders is the result of *convergent evolution*, shaped by natural selection due to their shared seed-feeding habit (Lanner 1996).

Pinyon pines are regarded as fully evolved bird pines (Lanner 1996), and all species from Mexico to southern Idaho have wingless seeds. Evidence of a jaylike corvid associated with pinyon has been found in the Miocene fossil record in Colorado, so their relationship may be at least that old.

In northern Arizona, Clark's nutcrackers form harvesting flocks of up to 150 birds, and in a good cone year they will harvest and cache as many as 5 million pinyon seeds during the fall (Vander Wall and Balda 1977). It is no coincidence that the nutcracker breeds earlier in the year than any other passerine bird in North America because of this cached food source. (Passerines, in the order Passeriformes, include perching birds and songbirds.) Vander Wall and Balda concluded that the nutcracker caches far more seeds than it ever eats, up to two to three times its caloric needs. Unclaimed caches lead to germination and the establishment of new trees. It is this overcompensation that renders the pinyon-nutcracker relationship a mutualistic one. In Vander Wall and Balda's (1977) study, the nutcrackers favored green, closed cones, which they easily open with their strong bills, something few other jays are able to do. Four to six times a day, the nutcrackers carried pinyon seeds to caching sites quite high up in a mixed conifer stand in the nearby San Francisco Peaks, thousands of feet higher than the pinyon collection site and up to 15 miles away. Nutcrackers carried an average of 55 pinyon seeds per trip in their sublingual pouches,

with some carrying as many as 95 (Fig. 3.7). Unique to nutcrackers, the sublingual pouch is clearly essential to their collection and caching of seeds. In poor cone crop years, nutcrackers also feed on seeds of limber and ponderosa pine. In years when no pines produce good cone crops, they do not breed.

The many journeys between harvesting and caching sites cost nutcrackers an enormous amount of energy. Vander Wall and Balda (1977) showed that they make the most of this effort by being adept at identifying viable seeds, whose coats have a distinctive dark color. Nutcrackers also distinguish the odd nonviable seed with a dark coat by rattling, or "bill clicking," the seed in its bill. Few nonviable seeds are transported.

Nutcrackers place five to ten seeds in each cache, all of them located on steep, south-facing slopes for better access during the winter. Such caches are accessible one to two months earlier than they would be in shaded sites. Vander Wall and Balda (1977) have found pinyon seedlings germinating from abandoned caches at high-elevation mountain sites where they would not otherwise occur, so the next time you see a pinyon that seems to be out of place, you'll know its seed was probably cached there by a jay.

This seed dispersal and caching system is strongly affected by several stem moth species that can decimate the cone crop of individual trees and stands. According to Christensen and Whitham (1993), nutcrackers sometimes avoid harvesting seeds from trees and stands attacked by stem moths. Consequently, individual plants that are resistant to the moth damage and do produce large cone crops can be passed over if they occur within a stand that produces few cones as a whole.

Christensen and Whitham (1993) also found that when they excluded birds from trees, seed-harvesting rodent populations increased, showing that competition can be keen for pinyon seeds among a large group of species. Conversely, when they excluded small mammals, the numbers of seed-harvesting birds increased, including nutcrackers, pinyon jays, and scrub jays.

*Pinyon Jays*

Although the nutcracker uses the seeds of many western pines, the pinyon jay is a specialist, caching an enormous amount of pinyon seeds by working in flocks that number into the thousands (Balda and Bateman 1971). In northern Arizona these tight, integrated flocks establish home ranges of up to 8 square miles that can encompass ponderosa pines, pinyon-juniper woodland, and grasslands. In poor crop years, pinyon jays may range hundreds of miles in search of seeds. From August until early winter, working dawn to dusk, pinyon jays collect seeds, their throats bulging with up to thirty at a time, and cache them on steep, south-facing hills. These cache sites become noisy several months later as the flocks return and begin retrieving seeds (San Miguel and Colyer 2003). As dispersers, pinyon jays don't carry seeds very far, in some cases less than a mile from the harvest trees (Balda and Bateman 1971).

The pinyon jay is also an early breeder, and this is because of its stores of pinyon seeds, which are fed along with insects to nestlings, fledglings, and nesting and brooding females. In good cone crop years, pinyon jays are able to breed twice, in late winter and also in the summer (Balda and Bateman 1972, Ligon 1978).

Pinyon jay flocks are highly organized and may include fifty or more extended families, forming the largest known avian social groups. Their societies are strongly hierarchical, with an alpha male dominating a group of subdominant males (Marzluff and Balda 1992). Their variable and graded call repertoire includes warning calls, after which they may mob potential predators such as raptors. Pairs mate for life.

*Pinyon Rodents*

Rodents also help with dispersal, caching, and germination of pinyon seeds. It was once thought that their caching of uneaten seeds in deep burrows would prevent germination. However, in the Great Basin in western Nevada, Vander Wall (1997) found that rodents established many scattered, shallow caches under the canopies of shrubs, including big sagebrush, bitterbrush, rabbitbrush, and Mormon tea. He also found that most germination of pinyon seedlings occurred under the same types of shrubs, suggesting that some germination may have occurred in shallow rodent caches. Four species of seed-caching rodents collected and cached more than 50 percent of singleleaf pinyon seeds that fell to the ground in a heavy cone production year; about a third of them were cached under shrubs. Vander Wall concluded that in such a year, seed production far exceeded the needs of both birds and rodents.

The relatively short distance of seed dispersal by rodents (125 feet versus several miles) is important for maintaining local pinyon populations, but the great distance that jays disperse pinyon seeds has been key in its expansion into new habitats—perhaps especially following the major climatic changes that have influenced the elevational range of pinyon in the West. Rodents may also play an important role in filling in pinyon distributions within those new habitats.

*Animals and Insects Associated with Juniper*

The animals associated with juniper are less well studied than those associated with pinyon. Still, some intimate associations have been noted, despite the fact that juniper foliage is low in nutrients and high in chemicals that reduce digestibility. Juniper associates include insects, the foliage-feeding Stephen's woodrat, and an array of birds and mammals that feed heartily on its copious berries.

Leatherman and Kondratieff (2003) list fifteen species of insects that may be associated with Utah juniper around Mesa Verde in southern Colorado. Several defoliating moths form tents in junipers, as well as in pinyons, and feed through the winter.

Many insects, including moths and wasps, attack juniper berries, while gall-forming flies (Cecidomyiidae) destroy seeds (Chambers et al. 1999). Another gall former, the juniper tip midge, produces colorful "artichoke" galls at the tips of foliage. Several species of juniper berry mites are known to destroy entire fruit crops of some trees (Morgan and Hedlin 1960). A beetle studied on one-seed juniper in Arizona was present in 25 percent of the fruits sampled on trees and in 65 percent of the fruits that had fallen to the ground. The beetles had high mortality rates in fallen or abscised seeds, which may have benefited the tree (Fernandes and Whitham 1989).

The fleshy cones or berries of all junipers are fairly high in energy and are geared to attract fruit-eating vertebrates. Berries occur on the outer layers of foliage and turn either red or blue to attract birds. Available for up to three years, juniper berries provide an important food source for birds and mammals during the winter. The seeds are hard and difficult to damage, but there is an account of a white-tailed antelope ground squirrel destroying nearly the entire cone crop of a single Utah juniper over a several month period while ignoring nearby

trees (Chambers et al. 1999)—one of the few records of vertebrates acting as predators of developing juniper seeds.

Of the many bird species associated with juniper berries—both as herbivores and potential dispersers—the bluebird, Townsend's solitaire, robin, and waxwing may be the most important (Salomonson and Balda 1977, Chambers et al. 1999). In northern Arizona, the winter feeding territories of Townsend's solitaire contained 27 million one-seed juniper cones per 2.5 acres in a good year, and 1 million cones the following year. Townsend's solitaires guard these territories against other foraging birds, so many berries are not dispersed. An interesting twist to this juniper-bird relationship involves the influence of juniper mistletoe. Van Ommeren and Whitham (2002) found that while seed production in one-seed juniper in northern Arizona varied ten- to fifteen-fold over three years, mistletoe berry production in junipers did not vary appreciably, and stands with high levels of mistletoe infestations had greater visitation by seed-dispersing birds. Because Townsend's solitaire favors juniper fruits in bumper crop years, but mistletoe fruits otherwise, there were more seedlings in juniper stands that had higher mistletoe infestations. The mistletoe thus acts as kind of a mutualist with respect to the junipers that they parasitize. Other birds that feed on both one-seed juniper berries and mistletoe fruits include the cedar waxwing, western bluebird, and American robin.

Robins and waxwings also feed heavily on Ashe's juniper (*J. ashei*), a native of eastern New Mexico and western Texas. Like so many birds, they are dependent on juniper fruits during winter. During one study (Chavez-Ramirez and Slack 1994), individuals of both species collected more than 500

**5.4.** A Stephen's woodrat (*Neotoma stephensi*) feeding on the foliage of a one-seed juniper (*Juniperus monosperma*), northern Arizona. Courtesy of Ken Dial, the American Society of Mammologists, and Allen Press, Inc.

juniper seeds per day, with population-level seed collection exceeding more than 35,000 seeds for waxwings and nearly 6,000 for robins.

While a variety of mammals are known to disperse large numbers of juniper seeds some distance (see below), one appears content to feed only on juniper's foliage. Stephen's woodrat (*Neotoma stephensi*) specializes on one-seed juniper foliage in northern Arizona, southwest Utah, and western New Mexico, and on California juniper to the west (Fig. 5.4; Vaughn 1982, Vaughn and Czaplewski 1985). Stephen's woodrat is one of only two North American mammals that feed on conifer foliage, and the only mammal known to specialize on juniper foliage. Low in nutritional value to begin with, juniper foliage contains secondary compounds such as tannins, flavinoids, and terpenes that reduce digestibility by acting on flora within the stomach. It is also quite low in nitrogen, potassium, phosphorus, iron, and manganese. What juniper foliage does have is a high water content (~50 percent), and it

provides most of the woodrat's water. The woodrats feed heavily on certain junipers while avoiding others, and in some instances up to 99 percent of the branches of preferred trees may be clipped and fed upon.

The poor nutritional quality of juniper has strongly shaped the life history of Stephen's woodrat, which seems as if it has been slowed down and scaled back to use this poor yet abundant food source. Females reproduce late in life (at ten months) and typically have only one baby. Mothers suffer severe weight loss during lactation, the young grow slowly, and there is broad overlap between nursing and beginning to feed on juniper. Only 15 percent of females survive to produce a second litter, a remarkably low reproductive rate among woodrats. The red tree mouse, the only other mammal that feeds on conifer foliage (in this case, Douglas fir), has a similar life history (Hamilton 1962).

Coyotes may be the single most important dispersers of juniper seeds (Schupp et al. 1997, Chambers et al. 1999). While rabbits, elk, and deer disperse small numbers of seeds, coyotes leave feces that sometimes contain hundreds of juniper seeds and little else.

In summary, the pinyon-juniper woodland, as the third largest habitat type in North America, has as complex a history and as complicated an ecology as other ecosystems. Climate change and modern land use practices are causing the pinyon-juniper woodland to impinge on another fascinating ecosystem that typically lies just downslope, western grasslands, the subject of the next chapter.

# CHAPTER 6

# Western Grasslands

Grasses are everywhere. Even though they are relatively young in origin, grasslands are the world's dominant vegetation type. They typically occur in arid and semiarid regions with harsh and variable climates characterized by extreme heat, cold, and distinct wet and dry seasons. In fact, the climatic range of grassland habitats is greater than that of any other North American biome (Sims 1989). In the West, grasslands occur from deserts to mountains (Fig. 6.1). Grasses undoubtedly evolved and spread due to their ability to adapt to seasonally dry habitats, and yet some grasses, such as rice, occur in shallow aquatic habitats.

Grasses are essential to human survival, providing corn, wheat, rice, sorghum, sugar cane, millet, barley, oats, and rye, as well as pasture and forage grasses for livestock. The first record of grass cultivation is at least 10,000 years old, from Jericho, where cultivated forms of barley and wheat were found a considerable distance from their wild relatives (Chapman 1996). Rice was among the

first of the cultivated grasses, having been cultivated by the Chinese more than 7,000 years ago. As the climate dried out during the Miocene (22–5 Ma), grasslands became widespread through much of the world, and a great diversity of animals evolved with adaptations for feeding or grazing on grasses. The first humans evolved in Africa during this time, becoming bipedal as forests gave way to grasslands. This transition was a major coevolutionary event between plants and the animals that feed on them. The diversity of grazing mammals in western North America and the Great Plains peaked during this time and rivaled the contemporary fauna of the Serengeti Plain of Tanzania, which today supports the most diverse and dense ungulate fauna on earth (Van Devender 1995). Today's grasslands, including savannas (grasslands with interspersed woodlands), are also highly productive ecosystems (Lauenroth 1979). And not surprisingly, levels of mammalian grazing in African grasslands today are greater than in

**6.1.** Western grasslands occur from the mountains to the deserts: *top to bottom*, subalpine grassland, San Francisco Peaks, northern Arizona; Government Prairie, northern Arizona; cold desert grassland, southern Utah.

24 percent of the earth's vegetation. Grasslands and savannas combined cover more than a third of the world's land surface (Jacobs et al. 1999). Among the larger grasslands are the Russian steppes, South African velds, South American pampas, the Hungarian *puszta*, and the North American Great Plains.

## THE EVOLUTIONARY HISTORY OF GRASSES

Grasses arose during a warm and humid time. From the end of the Cretaceous and extending into the Eocene, rain forests with tree ferns and cycads were widespread, and temperatures and rainfall were constant through the year (Wolfe and Upchurch 1986, Van Devender 1995, Kellogg 2000). Broad-leaved evergreen forests extended across North America, and there were even deciduous rain forests in southeastern Colorado. It was a very productive climate for life on earth.

Early grasses lived in the understory of these tropical forests and were broad-leaved to better capture light (Van Devender 1995). Broad-leaved grasses are still found in the understory of tropical deciduous forests, such as in Sonora, Mexico. Early grasses were ancestors of bamboo and were probably $C_3$ photosynthesizers (discussed further below).

The earliest records of grass microfossils such as pollen are from South America and Africa and date to 55–60 Ma, during the Early Eocene. The earliest macrofossil found in North America—a grass flower, or

any other vegetation type (Jacobs et al. 1999). During the last 130 years, western grasslands have been subjected to another mammalian grazing onslaught in the form of domesticated cattle and sheep, to such a degree that there may be no western regions that have been unaffected.

Grasses, in the plant family Poaceae, occur on all continents. There are approximately 10,000 species, making them the fourth largest plant family behind orchids, sunflowers, and legumes. Certainly in terms of the number of individual plants, grasses are more abundant than any other kind of plant. Grasslands cover more area than any other vegetation type, accounting for about spikelet— also dates to about this time. The fossil record for grasses is spotty until the Miocene, when extensive grasslands were forming through much of the world for the first time. Given their herbaceous makeup, it's not surprising that grasses have not left much of a fossil record. Because of this, a good understanding of their evolutionary history has required study of the mammals that came to graze in expanding grasslands. Their abundant fossil remains have been incredibly informative and tell a remarkable story.

By the beginning of the Miocene (~22 Ma), the earth began to dry out, and the endless forests opened up, setting the stage for the explosion of the world's first grasslands. The fossil record from this time shows a shift from woodlands to grasslands in North America, Eurasia, and Australia, but grasslands in South America and Africa may have formed even earlier (Jacobs et al. 1999). It is a testament to the power of climate that the same pattern repeated itself over and over again on all of these continents.

According to Van Devender (1995), the evolution and formation of North American grasslands was complete by the end of the Miocene (~5 Ma). The fossil record is rich with grasses by then, and includes species from all five modern grass subfamilies (Pooidae, Panicoideae, Eragrostoideae, Oryzoideae, and Arundinoideae). In North America, Miocene grasslands probably extended from the northern Great Plains south onto the Mexican Plateau, and plant assemblages were dominated by grasses, ragweed, and other sunflowers, with chenopods appearing for the first time. There is some debate as to the degree of grassland dominance during this time, and some scholars have suggested that many areas were more savanna-like than strictly grasslands

(Webb 1977). In any event, forests did open up and give rise to unprecedented expanses of grasses.

The feathergrasses (*Stipa* spp.), thought to come from Eurasia, were very common during the Miocene. Fossil beds rich with stipoid seeds have been found in Miocene deposits extending from central North America to Colorado and New Mexico. By the Pliocene (~5 Ma), ricegrass (*Oryzopsis spp.),* a close relative to stipa and an important western grass, was also found. In the Great Plains today, stipa has been replaced by species of bluestem and grama grasses (Stebbins 1981).

### Grasslands and the Evolution of Grazing Mammals

Just as the aridity of the Miocene led to the establishment of the world's first grasslands, their rapid spread led to the evolution of an open-country mammalian fauna adapted to graze grasses (Webb 1977). In fact, the diversity of land mammals in North America reached its zenith during the middle of the Miocene, with an array of species comparable to that of African savannas today. In North America, where the record is clearest, most early mammals were small to medium-sized arboreal and climbing forms that were mainly frugivorous, omnivorous, or insectivorous. Hooved (ungulate) mammals came next, during the Paleocene and Eocene epochs (65 to 35 Ma); they browsed foliage and fruits in vast, lush forests. As browsers, they typically had low-crowned, or brachydont, teeth, somewhat like human teeth. In fact, at the beginning of the Miocene, there was a phenomenal diversity of browsing mammals, suggesting that plant productivity was very high (Janis et al. 2000).

As forests gave way to grasslands, grazing mammals came to outnumber browsers

(Webb and Opdyke 1995). Fossils of 16 families of mammals with 60 genera and at least 141 species are known from grassland sites in North America that date to this explosive time in mammalian and grassland evolution. At one site fossil evidence of up to 20 genera of ungulates has been found. A key find in the fossil record is the remains of three extinct grasses (*Berriochloa* spp.) preserved in the enamel infolding of the teeth of a North American rhinoceros (*Teleoceras major*). These Late Miocene deposits in Nebraska, dating from 9 Ma, provided the first direct evidence of large herbivores eating grasses (Van Devender 1995).

During the Miocene, a great diversity of camel, pronghorn, rhinoceros, ruminant, peccary, and rodent species arose, and they increased both in numbers and size. The rhino *Teleoceras* is thought to have weighed more than 2,200 pounds, and some horses may have exceeded 1,000 pounds, though their ancestors probably weighed less than 50 pounds (Webb 1982). Grazing camels also arose, even though they had largely been represented by browsers previously (Webb 1982). Grazers tended to have square, broad muzzles and larger chewing musculature than browsers. Even small rodents such as kangaroo rats, rabbits, and beavers evolved special grassland attributes such as high-crowned teeth and the ability to burrow. These attributes would be critical for small animals in an open landscape. At several Pleistocene sites in southern Arizona, fossils of a diverse fauna including mammoth, bison, camel, horse, rhinoceros, llama, and mastodon were found (Van Devender 1995). These herbivores, in turn, were fed upon by sabertooth tigers, American lion, American cheetah, giant short-faced bear (which were 30 percent larger than modern grizzlies!), and dire wolf (Grayson 1994).

A major adaptation for feeding on grasses was large, high-crowned (hypsodont), continuously growing teeth, which enabled sustained grazing of silica-rich grasses. The high concentration of silica in grass tissue played a very important role in the coevolution of grasses and their herbivores since silica wears down tooth enamel. There were few mammal groups with high-crowned teeth during the Early Cenozoic, and the greatest diversification of mammals with high-crowned teeth occurred during the Miocene (Webb 1977, 1982). There must have been very strong natural selection for this trait to become so widespread so quickly. Their teeth became indeterminate, like beaver's teeth, so that they continued to grow as the surfaces of their teeth were ground down. The age of domestic horses today is determined by tooth length, which with a soft diet will continue to grow, giving rise to the expression "long in the tooth" as a euphemism for old age (Benson 1979).

### The Case of the Horse

The horse provides a classic example of grazing mammal evolution during this time. Its fossils are well represented in Miocene deposits, and the number of grazing horse species increased from one to as many as sixteen contemporaneous species in North America within 4 million years, between 16 and 12 Ma (MacFadden 1997, Jacobs et al. 1999). The oldest known horse, eohippus (*Hyracotherium*), was a small animal that lived in forests throughout North America ~60 Ma (Fig. 6.2). A short creature standing only 10 to 20 inches at the shoulder, eohippus looked more like a dog than a modern horse. It browsed on fruit and soft foliage with low-crowned teeth and had spreading toes, rather than hooves, for walking on soft ground or mud.

As the forces receded and grasslands expanded, horses adapted to living in these open, more exposed habitats through the evolution of one strong toe (or hoof), by becoming very large and fast running, and by developing large, high-crowned teeth (Fig. 6.3). With few trees and places to hide, the ability to run fast was essential. The modern horse still runs and walks on this single toe per foot but has small bones on either side that are vestiges of multiple toes of the ancestral horse of 15 Ma. Several lines (*Anchitherium, Hypohippus*) increased considerably in size and retained teeth equipped for browsing, while others evolved different teeth for cutting off and chewing tough, silica-rich grasses. Beginning with *Merychippus*, horse species with high-crowned teeth radiated and diversified rapidly. Their teeth had complex patterns of enamel accompanied by cement (Stebbins 1981).

It is noteworthy that the horse originated in North America, dispersed to South America, and to Asia across the Bering land bridge, and thereafter spread through and diversified in the Old World. The horse subsequently died out in North and South America but was reintroduced by Spanish explorers thousands of years later. Bison, one of the last large herbivorous mammal species of North America,

**6.2.** Early four-toed horses (*Hyacotherium*) depicted as small, browsing, forest-dwelling creatures in the Eocene. Courtesy of the American Museum of Natural History.

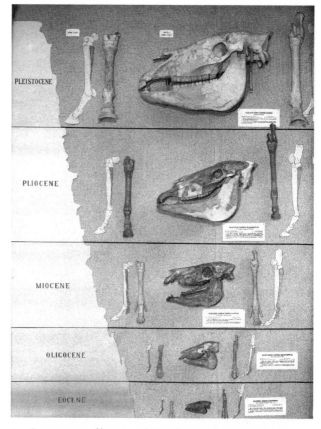

**6.3.** Progression of horse evolution from browsing to grazing ungulates, as represented in the fossil record from the Eocene to the Pleistocene. Note the increasing size and the loss of lateral toes. Courtesy of the American Museum of Natural History.

are believed to have replaced horses there as important grazing mammals. They arrived in North America some 150,000 years ago from Eurasia and occurred throughout much of the continent (Van Devender 1995).

## The Demise of Grazing Mammals

All of North America's large grazing animals, except for bison, were extinct by the end of the Pleistocene (Martin 1973, MacFadden and Hurlbert 1988, Webb and Opdyke 1995, Jacobs et al. 1999). Aridity increased during the Miocene, and by 5 Ma the extensive North American savanna had been replaced by grasslands or steppe, which lacked trees and shrubs. Diversity of the large grassland mammals began to decline, with browsers affected first, as early as 12 Ma. Quarries in Idaho have yielded only one or two species of horses for this time period, where previously there had been many more. Horse diversity declined precipitously between about 7 and 5 Ma, with most species, including the modern genus *Equus,* not surviving into the Pliocene. It may be that the grazing and browsing pressure of vast herds of ungulates accelerated the decline of savanna and the expansion of the steppe, a transition that can be seen today in Africa during extended drought. By 11,000 years ago, nearly two-thirds of the large mammals of North America had become extinct, bringing to an end this remarkable evolutionary experiment. The cause for the end of this era of large mammals is unclear and controversial, and may have resulted from multiple factors including climate change and possibly overhunting by humans, at least in the case of the mammoth and mastodon. In the last 10,000 years, desert grasslands have had the fewest large herbivores of any time in the last 20 million years (Van Devender 1995).

It has also been suggested that an increase in more drought tolerant warm-season grasses ($C_4$) over the lush and more palatable grasses ($C_3$) during the Late Miocene (6–7 Ma) may have contributed to the demise of the large grazing mammals (Jacobs et al. 1999). Macrofossil evidence indicates that by the end of the Miocene, the distribution of $C_4$ grasslands had expanded at the expense of $C_3$ grasses, a distribution that is similar to what it is today. A decrease in atmospheric $CO_2$ near the end of the Miocene may have resulted in a shift toward $C_4$ grasses and thus contributed to the demise of the large grazing mammals. The increase in $C_4$ grasslands may also have resulted from increasing aridity and possibly overgrazing of $C_3$ grasses.

## MODERN GRAZING

Today, a combination of drying conditions and the relentless onslaught of domesticated grazing mammals is transforming western grasslands. In fact, livestock grazing may be the most important and widespread influence on native ecosystems in the western United States (Fleischner 1994).

Dramatic examples of overgrazing by domestic livestock are all too common in the West. I have seen a herd of cattle beat down a small riparian area in the Sawtooth Mountains in Idaho, and cold desert grasslands in northern Arizona that appeared grazed beyond redemption, replaced by communities of noxious weeds or bare ground. I have also seen cattle left to die in the Sonoran Desert in Arizona, lying on the ground with their mouths covered with cactus pads. But I have also spent time in an Arizona fescue prairie that was well managed with limited grazing. Several photographs of the impacts of grazing on western lands are included in George Wuerthner and Mollie Matteson's book *Welfare Ranching: The Subsidized Destruction of the American West* (2002).

Even though as much as 90 percent of western public lands are grazed by livestock (Armour et al. 1991), supporting an industry that is heavily subsidized through leases on state and federal land, only a tiny fraction of the cattle in the United States are produced there. Most cattle production occurs on more mesic lands in the central and eastern states. Grazing also impacts wildlife: nearly 100,000 natural predators—including badgers, wolves, coyotes, bears, foxes, bobcats, and mountain lions—were killed in 1999 alone to support western grazing (Wuerthner and Matteson 2002).

Given that western grasslands have been subjected to intense grazing pressure for more than 120 years, few ungrazed or benchmark areas are left (Hastings and Turner 1965, Chambers and Holthausen 2000, Floyd et al. 2003). Although domestic cattle and sheep were introduced into North America hundreds of years ago by the Spanish, their greatest numbers, and greatest impact on western grasslands, occurred in the late 1800s (Wildeman and Brock 2000). In 1888, 8.9 million cattle were brought into New Mexico from Texas, and in 1891, 4.5 million Texas cattle were brought into Arizona. Between 1940 and 1990, the number of cattle in the West exceeded 50 million (Fleischner 1994, Belsky et al. 1999).

One of the clearest historical accounts of grazing impacts in the late 1800s describes the Little Colorado River basin in northern Arizona. William Abruzzi (1995) quotes an early pioneer who in 1876 described the region as covered with tall grasses so abundant that they were harvested for hay over miles and miles in all directions. The Aztec Cattle Company of Texas grazed as many as

60,000 cattle over this cold desert region, which was two to three times more than the land could support. Following this overstocking, many grasses were eliminated, and subsequent flooding resulted in the cutting of ravines and gullies that are still seen today. Overgrazing, combined with severe drought in the 1890s, further damaged the grasslands and killed most of the livestock (more than 75 percent by some accounts). Overgrazing continues to be a problem today, as evidenced by sparse vegetation cover and the dominance of unpalatable grasses, shrubs, and junipers. The degraded ranges of the Little Colorado River basin have yet to recover from overgrazing, which continued from the late nineteenth century well into the twentieth, and today the basin supports only a third to half the number of livestock that it did prior to the 1880s.

The grasslands of the Great Basin were also subjected to overgrazing, with disastrous results for both the land and livestock. The Great Basin's short growing season, sandwiched between a cold spring and a hot summer, "would eventually haunt the domestic livestock industry" (Young 1994). The combination of low productivity and an open, or commons, grazing tradition transformed many of the region's plant communities from grasslands hosting shrubs to pure shrubland, and ultimately led to ecosystems dominated by nonnative plants. At higher elevations, in particular, the removal of grasses increased the cover of big sagebrush. Already dealing with limited water and food resources, the cattle industry in the Great Basin was dealt a severe blow by the harsh winter of 1889–1890. The range sheep industry quickly stepped in, growing rapidly and further degrading Great Basin rangelands.

Scientists had begun documenting the negative effects of grazing in the Great Basin by the 1880s, and as the public became increasingly aware of the problem, editorials began appearing in regional newspapers (Young 1994). The outcry over such extensive environmental degradation finally led Congress to enact the Taylor Grazing Act (48 Statute 1269) on June 28, 1934, to "stop injury to the public grazing lands by preventing overgrazing and soil deterioration, to provide for their orderly use, improvement and development, to stabilize the livestock industry dependent on the public range, and for other purposes."

Grazing's long and widespread history in the West has limited our ability to know very much about what it looked like before. This situation has forced researchers to reformulate the questions that are being asked—that can be asked—about western grazing. The lack of critical information has also led to controversy about identifying the causes of current grassland conditions and what ecological goals are appropriate for these ecosystems (Chambers and Holthausen 2000, Valone et al. 2002). Several studies suggest that western ecosystems, as arid and semiarid lands, exhibit long-term responses to disturbances such as grazing and climate change (Valone et al. 2002, Floyd et al. 2003). These ecosystems are surprisingly fragile, and their dynamics can change quickly following even brief disturbances, often taking decades to recover (Wiegand and Milton 1996).

At Chaco Canyon in north-central New Mexico, Floyd et al. (2003) compared plant communities at sites that had excluded cattle for more than fifty years, for two to five years, and that were currently being grazed. Areas in the West that have been protected

from grazing for forty to fifty years are very rare and valuable reference sites (Valone et al. 2002, Floyd et al. 2003). As one would expect, the diversity of plant species, including native grasses, was greatest at those protected sites. Native bunchgrasses, including Indian ricegrass and feathergrass, were found there, whereas blue grama grass was the most common in the recently protected and currently grazed sites. In a study in southern Arizona, Valone et al. (2002) found that perennial grass cover was greater at sites that had been ungrazed for thirty-nine years, but not in those that had been ungrazed for twenty years, suggesting that recovery of grasses is indeed a very slow process. Biological crusts, which can provide critical nitrogen and preserve soils in the West, were also best developed at long-term protection sites. Beyond these patterns, there was considerable variation among the sites, showing how extensive studies must be. Colonizing woody species and nonnative plants were found in both protected and grazed sites.

One measure of restoration on overgrazed western grasslands is the return of native bunchgrasses, which can take decades (e.g., Floyd et al. 2003, Valone et al. 2002). Intense grazing often results in a loss of grasses such as Arizona fescue, mountain muhly, and little bluestem, all favored by cattle in southwestern mountains (Chambers and Holthausen 2000, Arnold 1950). In western forest grasslands and in the shortgrass steppe in eastern Colorado, blue grama grass, squirreltail, and weedy plants such as snakeweed and Colorado rubberweed often increase with grazing (e.g., Hanks et al. 1983, Milchunas et al. 1989).

Plant diversity often, though not always, decreases with grazing. In mesic tallgrass prairie in Kansas, grazing increases diversity by allowing more mesic ($C_3$) grasses and forb species to be present (Collins et al. 1998). This positive effect of grazing on diversity is greater in more productive ecosystems. In drier western grasslands, the patterns are more variable. Although Floyd et al. (2003) found greater plant species richness on protected versus grazed sites, Loeser et al. (2007) noted little difference in plant diversity in moderately grazed versus protected sites. Valone et al. (2002) also saw little difference in the number of plant species in long-term protected versus currently grazed sites. Milchunas et al. (1989) did, however, observe a greater diversity of plants in ungrazed shortgrass steppe. Local topography within sites—for example, swales versus ridgetops—greatly influences how many plant species might be present. Ungrazed swales tend to have the greatest plant diversity and productivity, and also tend to receive more water and have better soils (Milchunas et al. 1989).

In the context of global warming, a serious concern in arid and semiarid lands is loss of plant cover, which can lead to loss of soil and, ultimately, desertification, whereby a landscape loses even the potential to be productive (Valone et al. 2002). This condition can be caused by drought or overgrazing and is exacerbated by their combination (Warner 2004). Recovery of arid and semiarid grasslands from overgrazing may not be possible even after fifty years of cattle exclusion if soils are seriously damaged or eroded, as in the Jornada Experimental Range in southern New Mexico (Hennessy et al. 1983).

Plant cover often declines in response to grazing. Allison Jones (2000) reviewed several grazing studies and determined that a significant number of them showed decreases in plant cover on grazed versus ungrazed sites. In northern New Mexico, Floyd et al. (2003) found increased native grass cover on four of six protected sites relative to nearby grazed sites. In southern Arizona, Valone et al. (2002) found greater or increased perennial grass cover only on sites protected for nearly forty years, with no difference in grass cover on grazed sites versus those protected for twenty years, showing how difficult it can be to discern impacts. They suggested that time lags of twenty years or more are required for such recovery. On a heavily grazed shortgrass steppe site in eastern Colorado, more bare ground was found on grazed versus ungrazed sites, with bare ground indicating a loss of plant cover (Milchunas et al. 1989). Despite an overall loss of plant cover, cover of blue grama grass can increase with grazing. It is noteworthy that blue grama may be the most grazing tolerant grass in the western United States (Bock and Bock 2000). While grazing, and especially overgrazing, often results in a loss of plant cover, important changes in these plant communities may occur without a change in cover.

A critical aspect of assessing changes in plant diversity and plant cover in response to grazing involves considering the actual plant species involved. In a quantitative review of grazing studies in the West, Allison Jones (2000) notes that many studies provide information only on broad categories of vegetation, such as grasses, forbs, or shrubs, with little regard for the particular species involved. In such cases, the extent of plant cover may not change, but it may be that native palatable forbs and grasses have been replaced by species that are neither native nor palatable. A consideration of which species are involved, including whether or not they are native, is essential to the validity of grazing impact studies.

Because different types of native grasses may predominate in grasslands with different grazing histories, an understanding of the ecological behavior of grasses and each area's history is important in assessing responses to grazing. In an area with a long grazing history, native grasses may have been replaced by other native grasses that are more tolerant of heavy grazing, such as blue grama grass, and species such as western wheatgrass and squirreltail, which have been widely seeded by public land agencies. It is possible that some grasslands show little response even to intense grazing because these tougher species have become predominant following a long history of overgrazing. It is surely no coincidence that grazing-tolerant species are more and more pervasive in western grasslands. Perhaps they do make for more durable rangelands, but at the expense of many native species and the integrity of grassland ecosystems.

Blue grama grass is the most grazing tolerant grass in North America, and not surprisingly it is the dominant grass in the shortgrass prairie of the Great Plains and throughout much of the western United States (Larson 1940, Laycock 1994). This is partly because of its low-to-the-ground, spreading form, which makes it tolerant of trampling.

Encroachment of woody plants into western grasslands has been noted for many decades (e.g., Hastings and Turner 1965, Loftin et al. 2000). While overgrazing is thought to have contributed to the spread of shrubs and trees into grasslands, it may be that grasslands are simply a subclimax or earlier successional phase to woody plants, and overgrazing may just be hastening a natural progression (Brown 1950, Van Auken 2000, Rowlands and Brian 2001). It is also likely that livestock help to spread some woody shrubs and trees by directly dispersing their seed (Schlesinger et al. 1990, Loftin et al. 2000). Schlesinger et al. (1990) note that when grazing causes loss of plant cover, water moves less uniformly across the land, and shrubs can increase where water accumulates in erosional channels and along intermittent streams.

The relationship between grazing and nonnative plant invasions is another complicated aspect of western grazing impacts. Some studies have found greater nonnative plant densities in grazed sites (e.g., Loeser et al. 2007, Valone et al. 2002), but others note that nonnative plants establish well across both grazed and ungrazed sites (e.g., Floyd et al. 2003). At one northern Arizona site, cheatgrass cover increased from 5 percent to 100 percent on heavily grazed sites in just eight years; however, moderate grazing was strongly correlated with lower numbers of exotic plant species, suggesting that it may help to control nonnatives (Loeser et al. 2007). Another study (Milchunas et al. 1989) supports this, having found three times more nonnative and opportunistic species on ungrazed than grazed sites in the shortgrass steppe community in eastern Colorado. It appears that a lack of grazing becomes problematic in a plant community such as shortgrass steppe that has evolved with heavy grazing.

One justification for livestock grazing has been the phenomenon of *overcompensation* as a response by grasses and other plants to herbivory. Overcompensation occurs when plants grow more and/or reproduce more after being grazed upon than they would otherwise. The basis for this fascinating response may indeed represent an evolutionarily honed response to being eaten. Even in a semiarid grassland in northern Arizona, a single grazing event resulted in a 27 percent increase in the aboveground growth of squirreltail (*Elymus elymoides*) (Loeser et al. 2004). However, this study also showed that previously grazed plants compensated less, so there are limits to the ability of plants to overcompensate, or even compensate, for grazing. In mesic tallgrass prairie, repeated mowing over three years nearly eliminated overcompensation effects, although drought also limited this response (Turner et al. 1993).

Grasses have surprisingly few reserve resources for regrowth following defoliation. The crown, or grass base, has been shown to house only enough carbohydrates to support grass survival and growth for three days (McClaran 1995). There is no large store of carbohydrates in the base of a grass for regrowing plant tissue following grazing, as was once thought. Despite the fact that up to 90 percent of a grass's biomass might be underground in roots, this biomass is not available for regrowth. Most of the regrowth that occurs in grazed grasses is created by photosynthesis in remaining, ungrazed plant tissue; up to 99 percent of the carbohydrates used for regrowth are produced by unde-foliated tissue. So the more heavily grazed a grass is, the less regrowth potential it has. The length of the growing season and water and nutrient availability following graz-ing ultimately determine how well grasses recover from grazing damage. In this regard, grasslands in the semiarid and arid West are particularly susceptible to overgrazing.

But what actually constitutes overgraz-ing? There is considerable disagreement, but ultimately, it may be defined as when grazed perennial grasses cannot sustain themselves in a long-term context under current man-agement, as when there are too many live-stock to allow sustained forage availability. Overgrazing can also occur when plants severely grazed in the growing season are grazed again while attempting to regrow leaf biomass (Savory 1988).

A lack of disturbance, or overrest, can also be detrimental to the health of grass-lands. If they go for too long without fire or grazing by either wild or cultivated ungu-lates, they can lose productivity and diver-sity. Grasses and other plants requiring full sunlight become shaded by old foliage, and vigorous growth, seed production, and regeneration decline (Moir and Block 2001). This is the condition in my own backyard, where a beautiful stand of native mutton-grass needs either grazing or burning. The lovely clumps are dying out, literally, as their new growth is choked out by their accumu-lated dead leaves. The native flowers that grow in the interspaces are also disappearing due to lack of space and light. The grasses and forbs in my yard would probably benefit from being grazed about every three to four years now that this area no longer burns at that interval, as it did in presettlement times.

Drought can severely exacerbate the dam-aging effects of heavy grazing in the arid and semiarid West (e.g., Fuhlendorf and Smeins 1997). One study in northern Ari-zona (Loeser et al. 2007), found that drought led to large losses of plant cover at rested sites that had previously been heavily grazed, showing that grazing can have significant long-term effects. This pattern of increased sensitivity to grazing with increased aridity has been found on a global scale (Milchunas and Lauenroth 1993). If aridity increases as some are predicting, grazed arid and semi-arid grasslands are at risk, but the strategies required for protecting them are extremely complicated.

Despite the fact that the grazing lobby is very powerful, and grazing is surely here to stay, many people are trying to make a dif-ference. Grazing practices are gradually changing in some parts of the West, and there seems to be a growing consensus that grazing has no place in riparian areas and desert lowlands. Within Coconino National Forest in northern Arizona, fewer grazing leases are being granted, and most of those are for summer only rather than year-round. Some ranchers are also responding to the West's long-term drought by removing cattle from grasslands that can no longer support them (e.g., Loeser et al. 2007).

In Arizona and across the West, scientists, environmentalists, land managers, and ranchers are beginning to work together to figure out how to graze western grasslands while also restoring and protecting them as native habitats. Ranchers have even agreed to participate in scientific studies, some of which are considering how to include western grazing in the trend toward local, sustainable agriculture (e.g., Loeser et al. 2001, Sisk et al. 1999, Sisk 2007, Grand Canyon Trust website).

## Fire in Grasslands

The relationship between grasslands and fire is complicated, but to put it simply, fire keeps trees and shrubs from encroaching into grasslands. A study of the upland desert grasslands of Arizona and New Mexico found that fires every three to four years keep trees at bay while sustaining native perennial grasses and wildflowers (Bock and Bock 2000). In northern Arizona today, where fires have been and continue to be suppressed, ponderosa pines and junipers are quickly moving into prairies of Arizona fescue and of blue grama grass, while mesquite and creosote bush are moving into warm desert grasslands. In the absence of fire in the tallgrass and shortgrass prairies and abandoned farmlands of the Great Plains, oak, ash, and elm are taking over

ancestral grasslands. In the tallgrass prairie, the relationship between total plant species richness and the number of times a site is burned is positive (Samson et al. 1998). Recently burned tallgrass prairie also provides stopover habitat for many migrant birds such as the lesser golden plover and the endangered Eskimo curlew.

There is evidence that forested grasslands or savannas were historically maintained by repeated ground fires carried by continuous herbaceous fuels and fine litter from conifers (Moir and Block 2001). When forest canopies are thinned, grasses often reappear, but in the current era of fire suppression, forest expansion into grasslands is outpacing the rate of thinning and canopy opening. These conditions often set the stage for catastrophic fires that destroy everything, even the capacity of the soil to nourish new plants. Grasslands generally recover from burning if fires occur while grasses are dormant, as in spring or fall, but recovery is more prolonged during periods of drought (Bragg 1995).

## North American Grasslands

Contemporary North American grasslands are thought by some (e.g., Benson 1979) to have been hastily reconstructed during the last 10,000 years, since the end of the Pleistocene. Many grasslands were replaced by forests during glacial phases, as, for example, a site in Kansas that was covered with boreal forest 25,000 years ago but was recolonized by tallgrass prairie during the last 10,000 years (Van Devender 1995).

There is very little endemism among North American grass species, which means the same species occur throughout central and western North America from Canada to northern Mexico. Some species are more prevalent in the Great Plains or the West, but most, like blue grama grass, occur throughout. Effective seed dispersal contributes to this lack of endemism: the seeds of many grasses support bristles or beards that help them disperse by wind, water, or attachment to animal fur, which surely contributes to the global distribution of grasses despite their relatively young age.

Of the endemic, or narrowly distributed, species in the West, even Arizona fescue, a regional endemic, still occurs throughout the Four Corners states and Texas. Black dropseed occurs only in Arizona, yet occupies much of the state. Sometimes grass species simply grade into one another across a larger range. Arizona fescue is closely related to and replaced by Idaho fescue north of Arizona.

Grasslands once covered nearly 3 million square miles of the United States, whereas today they total only about 500,000 square miles (Sims 1989). In the Great Plains, grasslands now cover less than 5 percent of their former area, due to extensive habitat loss and loss of groundwater.

*Great Plains Grasslands*

The prairies of the Great Plains are the classic grasslands of North America. They are also the best studied (Whiles and Charlton 2006), and therefore worth mentioning here. Grasslands once covered the central United States, with its lush soils shaped by Pleistocene glaciers, and formed in the floodplains of the Missouri and Mississippi rivers. Three grassland types are found in the Great Plains, each increasing in stature with increasing precipitation farther east. Western-most is the shortgrass prairie, which lies in the rain shadow of the Rocky Mountains from Wyoming through Colorado, then wraps around west to the Colorado Plateau. To the east, the shortgrass prairie grades into the mixed grass prairie, which grades into the tallgrass prairie farther east.

The Great Plains grasslands receive as much as 20 to 40 inches of precipitation per year, enabling an acre of tallgrass prairie to host between 200 and 400 plant species; 75 percent of these are flowers or forbs, though grasses are most common, and warm-season ($C_4$) grasses predominate (Whiles and Charlton 2006). The bearded grasses, big and little bluestem, are dominant in the tallgrass prairie, constituting more than 70 percent of vegetation on ungrazed sites (Knopf et al. 1988). Big bluestem grows up to 6 feet in height, making it the tallest of the tallgrass prairie species. Other commonly occurring species include switchgrass and Indian grass, which occur less commonly in the West. The mixed grass prairie supports grasses from both the short- and tallgrass prairies.

The shortgrass prairie east and southwest of the Rocky Mountains is the driest of the plains grasslands, and the one most similar to western grasslands. Its grasses, including the dominant blue grama grass and buffalograss, are short in stature (12 to 18 inches), and nearly all are warm-season species. Their roots may penetrate a foot deep in soil. Precipitation levels here range from 10 to 30 inches of rain per year. Today these grasslands are commonly used for grazing since they are more tolerant than other Great Plains grasses. Unlike the more eastern species, shortgrass prairie species provide highly nutritious foliage that remains high in protein and digestibility over the winter. When overgrazed, however, shortgrass prairie is susceptible to invasion by species such as prickly pear, Russian thistle, and yucca.

The Great Plains prairies evolved with a diverse community of modern grazing mammals, including ground squirrels, prairie dogs, deer, pronghorn, and bison, and their life histories have influenced the science of range management (Knopf et al. 1988). Endemic birds such as the mountain plover and chestnut-collared longspur favor grasslands that have been grazed by mammals such as bison (Samson et al. 1998).

Restoring native grasslands in the Great Plains is a long-term process. An agricultural field in north-central Colorado that had been abandoned for forty years was found to share only half of the grass species that occurred in unploughed fields (Feinsinger et al. 1981). Another abandoned farm site was initially dominated by weedy plants such as Russian thistle, followed by short-lived perennial grasses such as squirreltail and sand dropseed. These grasses were replaced within twenty years by three-awn and then by blue grama grass and buffalograss. The three-awn stage may last for as much as fifty years (Lauenroth and Milchunas 1992).

## Intermountain Grasslands

The grasslands of the Intermountain West are rarely discussed other than as a subset of the Great Plains or the southern desert grasslands. Cold desert grasslands occur in northern Arizona, New Mexico, and northward into the Great Basin, and consist of blue grama grass, black grama grass, sideoats grama, galleta grass, stipas, and dropseeds. More cold-temperate grasslands include blue grama grass, sideoats grama, muttongrass, Junegrass, black dropseed, and squirreltail, with a sprinkling of other species such as little bluestem and some of the many muhlenbergias that are so diverse in the West. Nearly 116,000 square miles of grasslands are associated with ponderosa pine forests through the Rocky Mountains (Sims 1989). At still higher, more montane elevations, muhlenbergias and bluegrasses are present

along with Arizona fescue. Near Flagstaff, there are very large prairies dominated by Arizona fescue. Farther north it grades into Idaho fescue, which also occurs in extensive prairies. At higher elevations, fescues, bromes, bluegrasses, and muhlenbergias form lovely meadows.

Western grasslands can be quite diverse. In northern Arizona's Coconino County alone, there are more than 200 species of grasses (Graybosch 1981) occurring over an elevational range of 4,000 to over 12,000 feet. At Camp Navajo, a 40-square-mile military facility in the Coconino National Forest, there are more than 40 species of grasses in open meadows, although at least 10 of them are nonnative.

## Common Grass Species

*Bouteloua* is a New World genus with about forty species. Seventeen species of grama grass occur in North America, with most occurring in the West. The others occur in Central and South America. Blue grama grass (Fig. 6.4) is a dominant species of the western Great Plains, the Rockies, and upland elevations in the West. Its wide distribution may be due in part to its tolerance of grazing (Bock and Bock 2000). Blue grama is a beautiful grass found in prairies between about 5,000 and 7,000 feet. A classic warm-season ($C_4$) grass, it grows and reproduces during the summer rainy season (Sala and Lauenroth 1982). Around Flagstaff, blue grama grass typically remains dormant until summer monsoon season in July, when it quickly grows soft green foliage.

Blue grama grass has a characteristic flower head for which it was named by early Spanish explorers. *Grama* means "flag," which is what the inflorescence looks like until it curls in preparation for dispersing its seeds. Blue grama grass is one of the most drought-tolerant North American grasses. Many factors contribute to this, including its dormancy until summer rains begin, and a curling of leaves that reduces water transpiration. During the dust bowl era of the 1930s, even blue grama grass cover declined, though less than other native grasses (Albertson et al. 1966). In drought experiments with seedlings of fourteen Great Plains grasses, Mueller and Weaver (1942) found that blue grama grass seedlings were the most drought resistant, with three times as many blue grama seedlings surviving. It is replaced by black grama grass at lower elevations in the cold desert. Sideoats grama is also widespread throughout the Great Plains and the West.

The bearded grasses, including little and big bluestem, occur throughout much of the world. They are also warm-season (C$_4$) grasses. Big bluestem's stature of 6 feet or more inspired the label "tallgrass prairie." Although big bluestem's range includes the Great Plains and much of the western United States, its populations are largest in the tallgrass prairie, where its roots extend 9 feet deep. Little bluestem is also widely distributed throughout the Plains and the West. In the southwestern portion of its range, it is most common in rock outcrops. Its foliage turns salmon-pink in the fall.

Approximately 160 species of the genus *Muhlenbergia* occur throughout the New World and eastern Asia. It is common in western North America and especially Arizona, where there are 30 species. Mountain muhly dominates large upland meadows in northern Arizona, while the annual little muhly forms a dense patch of tiny pink plants during summer monsoon season. Little muhly is noteworthy in that its whole structure is a seed head, with only a few tiny basal leaves. Deer muhly is a large

**6.4.** Two common western grasses: *top*, warm-season blue grama grass (*Bouteloua gracilis*), one of the most drought tolerant, grazing tolerant, and widespread grasses of the Southern Rockies and the Intermountain region (courtesy of Mark Daniels); *below*, muttongrass (*Poa fendleriana*), a cool-season grass whose range extends from British Columbia to Arizona.

bunchgrass that favors drainages and is widely used in cultivated landscapes. All of the *Muhlenbergia* are warm-season grasses.

The stipas, or needlegrasses, are cool-season (C$_3$) grasses that occur from the tropics into Canada. There are nearly 100 species, with most occurring in the western United States, particularly in more arid regions. While many stipas are widespread, they rarely form extensive communities, though they may have been far more common during the Miocene. Stipas are important components of cold desert grass communities and provide good forage for herbivores. Some species, however, such as needle-and-thread grass and feathergrass have needlelike

**6.5.** Stand of cheatgrass (*Bromus tectorum*) in a northern Arizona forest. Courtesy of the Ecological Restoration Institute, Northern Arizona University.

seeds that harm herbivores so they cannot be grazed after flowering. The stipas commonly hybridize with one another and also with closely related ricegrass.

Ricegrasses are common C$_3$ perennial bunchgrasses that occur in cool, temperate regions of both hemispheres. In western North America, Indian ricegrass is common in cold deserts and pinyon-juniper woodlands. Its leaves stay nutritious in winter, providing forage for cattle and pronghorn antelope. Its beautiful large seeds were once harvested by Native Americans (Cronquist et al. 1977). Its large seeds (3–4 mg) withstand abrasion, and seedlings are able to emerge from great depths of sand. High in carbohydrate content, the seeds are favored by desert granivores (Veech and Jenkins 2005), and desert rodents are important in dispersing and caching its seeds. Indian ricegrass hybridizes with grasses in the genus *Stipa*.

There are 150 to 200 species of *Poas*, or bluegrasses, most of them in temperate and arctic regions. They are lush, cool-season grasses. Many, including muttongrass (Fig. 6.4), Sandberg bluegrass, Nevada bluegrass, and Kentucky bluegrass, are favored

by livestock in western grasslands. The poas are known to hybridize readily with one another. More-spreading versions of the native bunchgrass muttongrass may be the product of hybridization with Kentucky bluegrass (Cronquist et al. 1977).

Kentucky bluegrass is a curious species. It is native to temperate and arctic Eurasia, and also occurs in temperate regions throughout the world. It is represented by many varieties, often as a result of hybridization with other *Poa* species, and it may have the most extensive series of polyploidy chromosome numbers of any species in the world (Barkworth et al. 2007).

Bromes are cool-season grasses that occur in temperate regions worldwide and include annuals, biennials, and perennials. Of the approximately 100 species, some are beautiful native montane bromes, but several species from central Asia are transforming the grasslands and shrubsteppe of western North America—and not for the better. Ripgut brome produces seeds that can pierce the intestines of grazers, but the real scourge of the West is an annual brome called cheatgrass (Fig. 6.5; Young and Clements 2009). Its native range extends from western Europe through the Trans-Caspian cold deserts and into Asia Minor (Billings 1994). It arrived in the more mesic regions of eastern North America in the seventeenth and eighteenth centuries but has remained rare there, probably because of abundant moisture and competition from taller plants and trees (Billings 1994). It is now found throughout the United States, and it has spread rapidly and widely in the West over the last century.

Cheatgrass was not noted in western North America until the late 1800s, and then suddenly it was everywhere: British Columbia (1890), Washington (1893), Utah (1884),

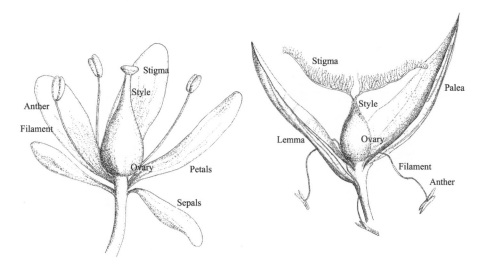

**6.6.** Basic structure of a perfect, insect-pollinated flower (*left*) and a wind-pollinated grass flower.

Nevada (1906). As Aldo Leopold put it, "One simply woke up one fine spring to find the range dominated by a new weed…cheatgrass (*Bromus tectorum*)" (Billings 1994). Apparently it was introduced into the drier regions east of the Cascades and Sierra Nevada as a contaminant in grain seed, and it is still expanding its western range. It is also the dominant species on more than 100 million acres of the Intermountain West (Whisenant 1990), where it reached its current distribution by the 1930s. By then it had replaced sagebrush as a dominant plant in the Great Salt Lake District and quickly covered recently burned sites (Billings 1994). Although no more tolerant of fire than other western plants, it is better able to rapidly colonize burn sites due to its high densities, annual cycle, and enormous seed banks (Billings 1994).

Cheatgrass's habit as a cool-season annual has made it very successful in the arid West. Seeds germinate in the fall, establish a good root mass, and are ready to capitalize on late winter and early spring moisture to reproduce. It sets seed in late spring and completes its cycle just as available moisture

disappears. Cheatgrass leaves and stems become tinder dry by summer, helping to fuel enormous western fires.

Cheatgrass seeds are designed to hitch a ride on the wind or in animal fur with their long awns, or hairs, and needle-sharp points, which can work their way down between shafts of fur and pierce skin. After my shaggy dog walked through a cheatgrass patch that was ready to drop seed, it took me three days to pull the seeds from her fur and skin, which she was gnawing at as she tried to remove them herself. A wild fur-bearing animal would have no such helper, and it's easy to imagine the painful wounds it would have to endure.

## Basic Biology

Grasses are part of the flowering plant revolution that has been underway since the beginning of the Cretaceous, ~145 Ma. Grasses originated late in the Cretaceous and took a different ecological path than most other flowering plants. While a major aspect of the flowering plant revolution was the evolution of flowers to attract insect pollinators, grass flowers returned to wind pollination, which has contributed to their success throughout the world over the last 20 million years. Nearly all grasses are wind pollinated, and they are far more efficient at it than are older wind-pollinated, pre-flowering plants such as pines, ferns, and mosses. Among the few grasses with insect-pollinated flowers are herbaceous bamboos, found in the understory of South American tropical forests. There, where there is little wind to move pollen, species of flies consistently attend their flowers, even between widely separated localities (Chapman 1996).

Accompanying the shift to wind polli-nation was a reduction in the showiness of grass flowers. They lack the petals, sepals, and fragrances that characterize flowers such as roses and orchids, and instead have small and inconspicuous florets. They have a series of spiky bracts designed not to attract insects or birds, but to protect the florets and to make sure that they open to disperse and receive pollen on the wind (Fig. 6.6). Grasses have much lighter pollen than do wind-pol-linated pines, and each flower has three large stamens, or pollen-bearing structures, that are flexible and easily shaken by the wind. The two female stigmas bear featherlike tri-chomes that readily catch wind-borne pol-len, which may travel as little as 15 feet from the parent plant, as in the case of corn, or more than 650 feet in the case of perennial rye grass (Chapman 1996).

The streamlined grass flowers have defi-nite advantages over more conventional flow-ers. Their seed heads photosynthesize and can produce up to 60 percent of the energy that goes into creating seeds (McClaran 1995). Most other types of flowers, by con-trast, do not photosynthesize at all.

While many grasses have seeds that are adapted to attach to animals, others, such as needlegrasses, have long awns that disperse the seeds and drill them into the ground, beyond the reach of seed herbivores such as ants (Schöning et al. 2004). The long awn itself proves cumbersome or unworkable to small seed-eating ants. It can also help seeds germinate by placing them more deeply in the soil. This seed-drilling phenomenon is also reported in the grasses *Avena, Aristida,* and *Stipagrostis.*

More than 70 percent of grass species originated through a process called poly-ploidy, which involves doubling, qua-drupling, and so on of the basic parental chromosome number—a process that allowed many flowering plants to rapidly diversify. Polyploidy can occur within a spe-cies or through hybridization—that is, mat-ing with another grass species. The latter is how western wheatgrass arose, and today it is an extremely widespread, hearty grass of the Great Plains and western United States (Chapman 1996).

Grass growth forms include bunchgrasses or clump grasses such as little bluestem and spreading, sod-forming grasses such as Ken-tucky bluegrass and blue grama grass, and annual forms. Spreading grasses grow later-ally along the ground with tillers from the base or with underground stems called rhi-zomes.

Silica is absorbed as monosilicic acid $[Si(OH_4)]$ by plant roots. Grasses absorb more silica than most other plants and deposit it in epidermal or outer cell walls where it forms phytoliths, or opals. These are tougher than mammalian enamel, which may have influenced the evolution of inde-terminant teeth in grazing mammals dur-ing the Miocene. High silica content may make some grasses less attractive to graz-ers (McNaughton et al. 1985, Gali-Muhta-sib and Smith 1992). Its deleterious effects include increased tooth wear, reduced palatability and digestibility of grasses, abrasion of mouth tissues, esophageal cancer, and silica urolithiasis, which can be fatal to calves (Gali-Muhtasib and Smith 1992). Grasses with a heavy grazing history often produce higher levels of silica (McNaughton et al. 1985). Grasses also naturally accumulate higher silica through the growing season and with age.

## C3 and C4 Grasses

Grasses are classified as either $C_3$ or $C_4$ according to how they take carbon dioxide ($CO_2$) from the atmosphere and use the process of photosynthesis to convert it into sugars for growth. The differences between the two types are what allow grasses to occur throughout much of the world. Cool-season ($C_3$) grasses dominate at higher elevations and latitudes with lower temperatures and lower evaporative stress, while warm-season ($C_4$) grasses favor lower elevations and warmer latitudes and do especially well in areas with summer monsoon rains, such as those that occur through much of the western United States (Teeri and Stowe 1976). The $C_3$ photosynthetic pathway is the ancestral type, with the $C_4$ pathway arising later. It is thought that $C_3$ grasses originated in temperate and arctic regions, while $C_4$ grasses originated in warmer subtropical and tropical latitudes. Today $C_4$ photosynthesis occurs in nearly half of all grasses (about 4,600 species), while it is found in only about 3 percent of other flowering plants (Kellogg 2000, Sage et al. 1999). It is a trait that has evolved independently at least five times in different groups of grasses.

$C_4$ grasses are named for their unique production of four-carbon molecules used in photosynthesis. This process enables $C_4$ plants to concentrate more $CO_2$ molecules

within cells (Thompson 2004). The $CO_2$ concentrations in $C_4$ plants can be ten times greater than those found in $C_3$ plants. This "stockpiling" of $CO_2$ allows $C_4$ plants to continue to produce sugars at relatively high rates even when their stomates or leaf pores are closed, which reduces water loss. Unable to store so much $CO_2$, $C_3$ grasses must open their stomates wider or longer, or have more stomates on the surfaces of their leaves, in order to take in atmospheric $CO_2$, and so risk high rates of water loss or transpiration. The differences in water loss between $C_3$ and $C_4$ grasses are greatest in warm climates.

Higher $CO_2$ levels in $C_4$ plants also reduce the impact of photorespiration, a metabolic process in which oxygen from the atmosphere is assimilated by the primary photosynthesis enzyme, ribulose biphosphate carboxylase (RubisCO) (McClaran 1995). Ultimately, $O_2$ competes with $CO_2$ for space on the RubisCO enzyme, especially at higher temperatures, but the higher concentrations of $CO_2$ in $C_4$ plants reduce that competition. When $CO_2$ rather than $O_2$ molecules attach to RubisCO, photosynthesis can proceed, which means the plant can continue to produce sugars for growth and reproduction.

The greater efficiency of $C_4$ grasses over $C_3$ grasses in the production of carbohydrates is significant: $C_4$ plants produce 1 gram of biomass for every 9 to 12 ounces (250 to 350 grams) of water transpired, whereas $C_3$ grasses produce 1 gram of biomass for every 23 to 28 ounces (650 to 800 grams) of water transpired (Ehleringer and Monson 1993). Ecosystems dominated by $C_4$ plants can produce 2.5 times more foliage annually than $C_3$ dominated grasslands (Heckathorn et al. 1999).

In a classic study, Teeri and Stowe (1976) gained great insight into the distribution of $C_3$ and $C_4$ grasses in North America. They found that the daily minimum temperature in July was the single greatest determinant of $C_4$ grass distributions. In other words, areas with higher temperatures and a longer frost-free growing season support more $C_4$ grasses. Not surprisingly, more than 95 percent of all grasses in the southern deserts are $C_4$ species. In the mountains of northern Arizona, where temperatures are cooler and precipitation greater, $C_3$ grasses (*Agrostis, Bromus, Elymus, Festuca, Koeleria, Panicum, Poa*) are dominant. $C_4$ grasses such as blue grama grass dominate drier meadows. At the higher latitudes in North America, a mix of $C_3$ and $C_4$ grasses occurs, at least at lower elevations. In the tallgrass prairie of the Great Plains, a mix of $C_4$ grasses, including bluestems and panic grasses, and $C_3$ grasses such as western wheatgrass and feathergrass occur together. The transition from $C_3$ to $C_4$ grasses occurs in the temperate latitudes between 45° and 30° in both hemispheres (Sage et al. 1999).

Where $C_3$ and $C_4$ grasses overlap, the cool-season ($C_3$) grasses green up and bloom early in the year, whereas warm-season ($C_4$) grasses lie dormant until temperatures rise and summer rains arrive. They then green up, grow, and bloom into the fall months. In Flagstaff, the $C_3$ muttongrass begins to bloom in February (with its red flower stalks often coming up through snow), while $C_4$ blue grama grass looks dead until monsoon rains start in July.

Although $C_4$ grasses now dominate modern tropical savannas and temperate grasslands, their dominance has fluctuated considerably since the Mid-Miocene (Jacobs et al. 1999). The earliest macrofossil of a $C_4$ grass was found in California and dates to ~12.5 Ma. A major shift from $C_3$ to $C_4$ grasslands occurred between 5 and 8 Ma both in North America and throughout the world.

The fossil record shows that $C_4$ grasses increased throughout the Pliocene and most of the Pleistocene. It is thought that $C_4$ grasses became more abundant as levels of atmospheric $CO_2$ declined, as occurred throughout the Pleistocene, perhaps because low $CO_2$ levels put $C_3$ grasses at a disadvantage (Polley et al. 1993). Following the last ice age, $CO_2$ levels increased, and there is evidence that $C_3$ plants increased in dominance in some ecosystems (Cole and Monger 1994). An increase in atmospheric $CO_2$ levels from ~180 ppmv (parts per million/volume) ~18,000 years ago to ~275 ppmv (~10,000 years ago) coincided with a shift from $C_4$ to $C_3$ grasses in New Mexico (Cole and Monger 1994). Experiments by Polley et al. (1993) showed that aboveground biomass in $C_3$ plants increased with $CO_2$ levels. Increased $CO_2$ levels are also thought to have contributed to increased $C_3$ wheat yields in the United States in recent decades (Mayeaux et al. 1997).

The ability of $C_4$ grasses to photosynthesize and produce sugars with little water loss may explain why they are also more tolerant of saline soils. Their use of less water may reduce the amount of salt with which they must contend (Sage et al. 1999). $C_4$ salt lovers, or halophytes, such as saltgrass and alkali sacaton, and the $C_4$ chenopods dominate the salty basins of the Great Basin.

Despite predictions that herbivores would favor $C_3$ grasses over $C_4$ grasses because they are more nutritious, responses to these two grass types are highly variable, with some herbivores preferring one type or the other, while others do not discriminate between them (Ehleringer and Monson 1993, Heckathorn et al. 1999,). The nutritious photosynthesizing cells in $C_4$ plants are less available and harder to digest because they are tightly wrapped around vascular bundles rather than occurring throughout leaf tissue, as in $C_3$ grasses. Many insects do favor $C_3$ grasses. The vascular bundles of $C_4$ plants pass undigested through an insect's gut. There is a general pattern of smaller mammals showing a preference for $C_3$ forbs and grasses over $C_4$ grasses, though many larger ungulate mammals do not discriminate. Grazing mammals such as the wildebeest (*Connochaetes taurinus*) and buffalo (*Syncerus caffer*) feed only on $C_4$ grasses. Mammals that both browse and graze, such as elephants and impalas, may feed on $C_4$ grasses during the rainy season and then shift to $C_3$ grasses during the dry season.

Most cultivated tropical $C_4$ grasses are able to fix nitrogen due to microbial associations in their roots, and they are preferred by sucking insects such as spittlebugs (Thompson 2004). Of course, sucking insects do not have to chew through tough fibers to feed on grass leaves. This nitrogen-fixing habit may occur because the high photosynthetic efficiency of $C_4$ plants can more easily bear the metabolic cost of feeding such associates. In North America, little bluestem exhibits weak nitrogen fixation and hosts several species of spittlebugs. It has been predicted that $C_3$ grasses will benefit from increased $CO_2$ levels tied to global warming, and possibly regain dominance in regions that gave way to $C_4$ grasses since the historic decreases in atmospheric $CO_2$ concentrations. Levels are now at about 350 ppmv, up from 280 ppmv at the beginning of the industrial revolution. However, the increased temperatures and potential for increased summer rains in some regions, which are also associated with global warming, may benefit $C_4$ grasses.

## PLANTS AND ANIMALS IN MODERN GRASSLANDS

Grasslands typically support more species of forbs or flowers than grasses, although grasses are always more abundant. An acre of intact tallgrass prairie may support 200 to 400 plant species, 75 percent of which are forbs (Whiles and Charlton 2006). Typical flowers include sunflowers such as sage, thistle, and goldenrod, and legumes such as lupine, locoweed, vetch, lily, and flax. A great diversity of buckwheat (*Eriogonum* spp.) is common in western grasslands.

More than 3,000 species of animals live in grasslands (Sims and Risser 2000). Worldwide, large native herbivores and cattle remove 30 to 40 percent of aboveground grass tissue, while insects remove 5 to 15 percent (Joern and Keeler 1995). Burrowing herbivores may remove 6 to 40 percent of belowground production.

### Grassland Insects

Despite much research on grassland insects, there is still a great deal to be learned about their diversity, numbers, and impacts on grasses (Whiles and Charlton 2006). Generally speaking, insect diversity declines with aridity, so shortgrass prairie supports many fewer insects than either the mixed grass or tallgrass prairie (Lauenroth and Milchunas 1992, Collinge et al. 2003). More than 3,000 species were collected from a tallgrass prairie in northeastern Oklahoma, while about 1,600 insect species were counted in a shortgrass prairie in Colorado (Samson and Knopf 1994). In the shortgrass prairie, beetles and sucking insects such as leafhoppers make up 60 percent of all plant-feeding insects (Lauenroth and Milchunas 1992). Leafhoppers, which are among the most diverse terrestrial insects in grasslands (Whitcomb et al. 1990), have sucking mouthparts and feed on plant sap. Up to 20 species of leafhoppers are associated with blue grama grass, and their presence is a good indicator of healthy grasslands. Some are widely distributed across grasslands, while others have very limited ranges or are endemic.

One of the most common insects of grasslands is the grasshopper, and it is often the most abundant, in terms of both numbers and biomass. Bock and Bock (2000) found more than twelve grasshopper species to be common in ungrazed desert grasslands, with different species occurring in adjacent grazed grasslands.

### Grassland Reptiles and Amphibians

Most grassland reptiles and amphibians are widely distributed, with half of the species found in Alberta, Canada, also occurring in northern Mexico. More than forty species are associated with prairies, and the number occurring locally is strongly enhanced by the presence of water, such as temporary ponds. Of course, amphibians reproduce only in water. Prairie dog burrows provide important hibernation and breeding habitat for reptiles and amphibians, and declines in the former may be responsible for declines in the latter (Slobodchikoff et al. 2009).

### Grassland Birds

There are twelve species of birds considered to be endemic to grasslands in the United States, which is fewer than occur in other types of ecosystems (Mengel 1970, Knopf 1994). And yet 330 of the 435 bird species breeding in this country have been documented to breed in the Great Plains (Samson and Knopf 1994). Many grassland

birds, including a number of sparrows, feed on seeds and insects. According to Bock and Bock (2000), the grasshopper sparrow (*Ammodramus savannarum*) is also a voracious predator of grass-feeding grasshoppers in desert grasslands and can significantly reduce their numbers.

Birds that are endemic to grasslands typically occur in low numbers in any one area—much lower than those of visiting birds. These species may migrate to different grassland regions in western North America with the seasons. Endemic grassland birds nest mostly in northern portions of the central grasslands, and especially in Montana. Some species may overwinter in southern grasslands extending into Mexico. The long-billed curlew and the ferruginous hawk may nest as far west as the northwestern Palouse Prairie and surrounding shrublands in Oregon. Populations of these species and the mountain plover winter in Great Basin grasslands and shrublands. Some of these species also migrate as far south as Argentina during the winter, making for some of the longest migrations known. More research is needed on the wintering habits of grassland birds (Knopf 1994).

In cold-temperate grasslands in northern Arizona, encroachment of one-seed juniper is causing a loss of habitat for the few grassland birds that occur there (Rosenstock and Van Riper 2001). Ground-nesting grassland species, including horned larks and western meadowlarks, predominate in uninvaded grasslands and decline as tree densities increase. Overall bird diversity increases, although comprised of different species, as juniper invasions increase.

Grassland birds have shown more consistent, steeper, and more geographically widespread declines than birds associated with other ecosystems, largely as a result of habitat degradation and loss (Knopf 1994). Between 1980 and 1989, losses of 25 to 65 percent were measured (Knopf 1992). The fragmentation of grasslands in the midst of staggering losses—exceeding 80 percent in many areas throughout the Great Plains— has been a major cause of declines in grassland bird populations (Knopf 1994). Many birds are intolerant of smaller patches (Vickery et al. 1999, Brennan and Kuvlesky 2005).

### Grassland Mammals

Bison came to North America from Asia during the Pleistocene, when sea levels were lower and the Bering land bridge was exposed. They grazed heavily on grasses throughout most of North America, and historical records tell of enormous herds, estimated at 4 million individuals, which were 20 to 50 miles wide (Lauenroth and Milchunas 1992). Presumably such a herd would deplete local grasses quickly, requiring constant migration. They so thoroughly consumed the grasses of the plains that U.S. soldiers found little forage for their mules and horses. By 1890, bison numbers had declined from many million to several million due to severe overhunting. Only 80,000 or so are left, mainly in national parks and preserves. In dietary studies, bison have been found to be less selective than either pronghorn or cattle about which plants they feed on and are thus thought to exert a more uniform pressure across the landscape.

The pronghorn, an antelope-like mammal, is the fastest mammal in North America, and second fastest in the world after the African cheetah. In the mid-1800s, members of the Lewis and Clark expedition compared the sight of pronghorn running to that of birds in flight, moving so quickly as to barely be discernable (Ambrose 1996).

In the Great Plains, pronghorn prefer forbs through much of the season, and cool-season grasses when forbs are not available. During the Miocene, there were as many as twelve species of pronghorn in North America, and pronghorn once numbered in the millions in grasslands from the Great Plains through much of the West. Populations are smaller today, and some are at great risk of local extinction or extirpation. One population near Flagstaff numbered 2,200 in the 1940s but had declined to 280 by 2000 (Loeser et al. 2004).

Prairie dogs may have numbered as many as 5 billion in North American grasslands at an earlier time (Hartnett and Keeler 1995), but their numbers have declined by 98 percent as people in the West, particularly ranchers, have sought to eradicate them. Prairie dogs feed on a variety of plants, including grasses and, especially, roots. They have strong, positive effects on nutrient cycling, soil formation, and the composition of grassland plants and animals. Dietary studies (e.g., Hartnett and Keeler 1995) have shown that during the growing season, prairie dogs in shortgrass steppe preferentially feed on the aboveground portions of sedges, blue grama grass, sand dropseed, sage, and globemallow. In the winter they feed on the roots of blue grama grass and shrubs.

Prairie dogs are a keystone species (*cynomys* spp.) that 200 other grassland species depend upon, including insects, reptiles, birds, and mammals (Slobodchikoff et al. 2009). Their burrowing activities affect vegetation structure directly, and perhaps also indirectly by altering hydrology and nutrient cycling. Prairie dog activities create habitats and resources for other animals, and consequently, the abundance of reptiles, lagomorphs, rodents, insects, and ants is often higher on prairie dog colonies (Weltzin et al. 1997). It has been shown experimentally that prairie dogs can help to maintain grasslands by feeding on and generally removing encroaching woody plants (Weltzin et al. 1997). Their abandoned tunnel systems provide habitat for burrowing owls. Even ungulates such as bison, pronghorn, and livestock preferentially graze colonies because prairie dog browsing and digging influence plant composition and often lead to higher plant nitrogen levels (Krueger 1986). With a decline in prairie dogs, associated species such as the black-footed ferret and the mountain plover have been put at risk.

Prairie dogs are social creatures and use a variety of calls to warn one another of approaching predators, issuing different sounds for hawks, owls, eagles, coyotes, badgers, ferrets, and snakes (Slobodchidoff et al. 2009). Their extensive burrow systems include listening rooms near the surface, false tunnels to confuse predators, and even passages below the living rooms for absorbing floodwaters (Hartnett and Keeler 1995).

Grasslands have had a wild evolutionary history, and they are fascinating because of the many large grazing mammals that coevolved with them. Perhaps more than any other ecosystem, the evolution of grasslands and grazing mammals throughout the world clearly shows how evolution, coevolution, and climate shape the world as we know it. The fact that grasslands occupy arid and semiarid climates makes them especially vulnerable to human disturbances such as grazing and to changing climates, but some efforts are being made to better protect them. At the edge of the grasslands is the cold desert. This vast, arid corridor that extends through much of the Intermountain West is described in the next chapter.

# CHAPTER 7

# The Spare and Beautiful Cold Desert

The cold desert is a wide, dry corridor that extends from northern Arizona into southern British Columbia (Fig. 7.1). It typically receives less than 10 inches of precipitation annually, and its evaporation rates are very high, often far exceeding 10 inches, which also helps create and define desert conditions (Warner 2004). Because it lies north of 30° latitude, winters are cold.

The cold desert spans the Colorado Plateau in the south and the Great Basin to the northwest, and while there are many differences between these regions, they are both arid and cold in the winter. Cold deserts typically occur at higher latitudes and therefore have greater seasonality than warm deserts do (Warner 2004). Most of the North American cold desert is above 4,500 feet, which means it gets bitterly cold in winter, yet summer daytime temperatures often exceed 100°F. It's difficult for plants and animals to survive in such a tough environment, and consequently, there is a spareness to it (Fig. 7.2).

While this region is described by Shelford (1963) as the cold desert biome, Neil West (1989) makes the point that it is cold only in winter, and the region also encompasses semidesert scrub and shrub steppe landscapes. For simplicity's sake, I refer to the entire region as the cold desert, while also discussing these other ecosystems.

The cold desert is a land of shrubs, most of them endemic to western North America.

7.1. Approximate distribution of cold desert in the Colorado Plateau and Great Basin regions.

**7.3.** Cold desert shrublands: *top to bottom*, big sagebrush (*Artemisia tridentata*), southern Utah; stand of shadscale (*Atriplex confertifolia*), Nevada; black greasewood (*Sarcobatus vermiculatus*) in salt pan, Nevada. Courtesy of James A. Young.

**7.2.** Typical cold desert landscapes: *top to bottom*, Basin and Range mountains and valleys, southern Nevada; sedimentary bluffs on the Colorado Plateau, southern Utah; eroded remnants of sedimentary layers dominate the surrounding shrublands, Monument Valley, northern Arizona.

In some places, stands of woody sagebrush, chenopods, or blackbrush go on as far as the eye can see (Figs. 7.3, 7.4). Shrubs dominate landscapes where water and nutrients are too limited to support larger growth forms (McArthur 1989). As you drop down in elevation below pinyon-juniper woodlands into the cold desert, you encounter woody sagebrush and then salt-tolerant chenopods—including saltbush, shadscale, greasewood, and winterfat. Few plants occur below the saltshrubs in Pleistocene lakebeds or shale pans; the soil is just too saline. Cold-desert grasses grow among these shrubs, especially at higher elevations. Blackbrush is found only on the southern edge of the cold desert. To the southwest, it grades into creosote

**7.4.** Stand of blackbrush (*Coleogyne ramosissima*) in Nevada. Courtesy of James A. Young.

bush where the cold desert meets the warm Mohave Desert. Creosote bush's northern distribution ends where freezing winter temperatures turn the land into cold desert.

Ecosystems in the cold desert have been adversely affected by human disturbance perhaps more obviously than any others. This is partly because this region is so dry, and because it has been invaded by truly nasty weed species from very similar habitats in Asia.

## EVOLUTIONARY HISTORY OF THE COLD DESERT

The geologic changes that have shaped the cold desert's natural history are discussed in chapter 1 but merit a brief review here. The cold desert formed after the coastal mountains—the Sierra Nevada and the Cascades—arose during the Miocene and Pliocene, creating a massive rain shadow and reducing precipitation levels by as much as a third. To the east are the Rocky Mountains, which keep storms in the Great Plains from making their way into the cold desert (West and Young 2000).

The Colorado Plateau, as an undeformed block of sedimentary layers, was lifted up and has been weathered and dissected by the Colorado River basin ever since, revealing an array of rock surfaces to which different plant species respond quite differently. Colorado Plateau rocks include sandstone, shale, mudstone and limestone, and igneous and metamorphic strata. The ongoing stretching and block faulting of the Great Basin has resulted in the formation of more than 100 landlocked basins, setting the stage for the evolution of diverse and extensive shrub communities. Sloping alluvial fans occupy up to 75 percent of these basins (Smith and Nowak 1990). In the Great Basin, cliff-forming limestone and dolomite are common

in the southern and eastern regions, while igneous and metamorphic rocks dominate the central and northern sections and some eastern sections (Thompson 1991).

During the Pleistocene, the rivers and streams of the Colorado River basin carried glacial melt to the sea during warmer phases; they ran big and continued to weather and dissect the sedimentary rocks of the Colorado Plateau. This process isolated plant populations and in some places created very saline conditions (30,000 ppm salt in Mancos Shale is not uncommon [Welsh 1978]).

Because the Great Basin is a hydrologically closed system, glacial melt formed enormous lakes in its many basins, and when these dried, they left behind saline landscapes with numerous challenges but also evolutionary opportunities for colonizing plants (Antevs 1948, Benson and Thompson 1987, Thompson 1991). These lakes reached their largest size between 16,000 and 12,000 years ago. Lake Bonneville, the largest, was more than 1,000 feet deep and covered 20,000 square miles—most of western Utah (Fig. 2.3). Great Salt Lake, the remnant of Lake Bonneville, is approximately eighty times saltier than the world's oceans (DeCourten 2003). Farther west was Lake Lahontan, which covered more than 8,000 square miles with up to 125 feet of water some 13,000 years ago; Pyramid Lake, in Nevada, is a remnant of this lake. Morrison (1968) refers to these as *pluvial lakes* and notes that they contain some of the best records of climate change during the Pleistocene.

### Evolution of Cold Desert Shrubs

By sampling pollen from wells in Great Salt Lake, Davis and Moutoux (1998) have chronicled the development of much of the cold desert. Greasewood, a chenopod, and joint-fir dominated the uplands of the cold desert from the Late Miocene onward. Greasewood persisted in the cold desert in Washington, Idaho, Wyoming, Nevada, California, and northern Arizona during the full glacial periods of the Pleistocene, while other plants were migrating down to elevations 3,000 feet lower. According to Betancourt (1990), accumulated salt in the halophytic, or salt-loving, chenopods acts as an antifreeze in colder climates. During the Pliocene and Early Pleistocene, other species of chenopods and sagebrush began to gain dominance. High levels of sagebrush pollen in the West during the cold Wisconsin glacial phase were coming from its abundant populations above treeline and its expanding steppe populations. Sagebrush easily colonized landscapes disturbed by glaciers and became especially widespread (Axelrod 1972, Davis and Moutoux 1998). By the end of the Pleistocene, cold desert plant communities became more diverse as more species of sagebrush and chenopods appeared in the expanding desert niches.

The fossil record shows that blackbrush did not occur in the cold desert until the end of the Pleistocene. Instead, it was found in the southern deserts along with other Great Basin species at elevations as low as 600 feet near Yuma, Arizona (Wells and Berger 1967, Van Devender 1990, Trimble 1999). Even during the relatively recent "Little Ice Age," between 1,000 and 1,700 years ago, blackbrush occurred 150 to 300 feet lower in the Mohave Desert than it does today (Cole and Webb 1985, Hunter and McAuliffe 1994).

Sagebrush, rabbitbrush, winterfat, greasewood, shadscale, and saltbush have all evolved into complex groups of closely related species, subspecies, varieties, and races that occur only in the West. Some scientists suggest that the evolutionary

explosions of many of these groups, particularly in the Great Basin, may have occurred in response to climatic upheavals during the Pleistocene (Axelrod 1950, 1977; McArthur and Plummer 1978; Reveal 1979), though their parental forms are known from the Eocene. The Pleistocene was a chaotic time, with plants migrating from mountains into valleys and then back, again and again, in response to oscillating climates. Species of both sagebrush and *Atriplex* are also found in Asia, so they may have migrated to North America from there.

*Polyploidy*

The diversity of cold desert sagebrush, rabbitbrush, and salt-loving chenopod has been strongly influenced by polyploidy and hybridization. Polyploidy—an increase in the number of chromosomes an individual has—arises commonly in nature and has helped produce many of the world's major plant and animal groups, perhaps even mammals (Ramsey and Schemske 1998). It is estimated that most or all plants have undergone one or more episodes of polyploidization, and polyploidy is largely responsible for much of the flowering plant revolution (Soltis, Soltis, and Tate 2004). It is a very powerful and immediate source of diversity that enables life forms to adapt to and exploit endlessly changing conditions, such as those of the Pleistocene.

Most species have a predictable number of chromosomes. Humans have twenty-three diploid sets, or pairs, of chromosomes containing all the genes that determine what we are and how we function. In many plants and some animals, the number of chromosome sets may increase by doubling, tripling, quadrupling, and so on. This process of polyploidy produces organisms that can be different from parents or the rest

**TABLE 7.1.** RACES OF FOUR-WING SALTBUSH (*ATRIPLEX CANESCENS*) IN THE WESTERN UNITED STATES

| Race | Habitat | Physical Features | Chromosome Ploidy # |
|------|---------|-------------------|---------------------|
| angustifolia | sandy soils | large seeds, long leaves, 3–6 ft. tall | 2x |
| aptera | badlands, grasslands | small seeds, 1–4 ft. tall | 4x |
| brevis | grasslands on basalt | narrow leaves, 1–2 ft. tall | 2x |
| diegensis | coastal dunes, canyons | wide, green leaves, 3–6 ft. tall | 6x |
| garretti | shale slopes | round, yellow-green leaves, < 1 ft. tall | 2x |
| gigantea | active dunes | long leaves, 4–8 ft. tall, often partly buried | 2x |
| grandidentatum | coastal dunes | toothed seed wings, 3–6 ft. | 20x |
| laciniata 1 | bottomlands | toothed seed wings, 6–8 ft. | 8x |
| laciniata 2 | desert dunes | toothed seed wings, 4–6 ft. | 12x |
| laciniata 3 | coastal dunes | deeply toothed seed wings, 4–6 ft. tall | 14x |
| linearis | bottomlands | small seed wings, 1–2 ft. tall | 2x |
| navajoensis | shale | 1–2 ft. tall | 4x |
| nevadensis | desert sands | deeply toothed seed wings, 1–4 feet tall | 6x |
| obtusifolia | alkaline bottomlands | small, toothed seed wings, 1–2 ft. tall | 8x |
| occidentalis | valleys, hills | toothed seed wings, 2–6 ft. tall | 4x |
| piochensis | hills with junipers | 1–6 ft. tall | 2x |
| prosopidium 1 | valleys | small, toothed wings, 1–4 ft. tall | 8x |
| prosopidium 2 | valleys | small, toothed wings, 1–4 ft. tall | 10x |
| prostrata | alkaline bottomlands | 1 to several inches tall | 6x |
| rachelensis 1 | valleys | small, toothed wings, 1–6 ft. tall | 6x |
| rachelensis 2 | alkaline bottomlands | small, toothed wings, 1–2 ft. tall | 8x |
| vallis | bottomlands | 1–3 ft. tall | 6x |

*Source*: Sanderson and McArthur 2004.

of their species. In plants, this increase in chromosome number may occur in stem tissue and transform a branch, or in the seeds of reproducing individuals. Polyploid individuals can originate within a species or through hybridization (mating between species), with either ultimately giving rise to new types.

The additional genetic information gained through polyploidy enabled cold-desert shrubs such as sagebrush and chenopods to move into harsher environments than their ancestors, and to persist or even expand in changing climates (Tables 7.1, 7.2; Sanderson et al. 1989, Ramsey and Schemske 1998). Indeed, many polyploid plant species

**TABLE 7.2.** Western woody sagebrush species and subspecies (subgenus *Tridentatae*).

| Artemisia species | Subspecies | Common name | Distribution | Site conditions | Elevation (feet) | Chromosome Numbers/ Ploidy levels |
|---|---|---|---|---|---|---|
| A. abuscula | arbuscula | Low sagebrush | western WY to CA | Dry, rocky, alkaline | 2,300–12,400 | 2x, 4x |
| | longicaulis | Lahontan low sagebrush | NV, OR, CA | Dry, rocky, alkaline | 3,445–6,560 | 6x |
| | thermophila | Hot springs low sagebrush | WY, northern UT, ID | Spring-flooded soils | 5,900–8,200 | 2x |
| A. argillosa | | Coaltown sagebrush | Jackson Co, CO | Alkaline spoil soils | 7,870–8,530 | 4x |
| A. bigelovii | | Bigelow sagebrush | Four Corners to CA | Rocky, sandy soils | 3,000–8,000 | 2x, 4x, 8x |
| A. cana | bolanderi | Bolander silver sagebrush | OR, NV, CA | Alkaline basins | 5,000–11,000 | 2x |
| | cana | Plains silver sagebrush | Canada to UT | River bottom soils | 5,000–11,000 | 4x, 8x |
| | viscidula | Mountain silver sagebrush | MT and OR to AZ and NM | Wet mountain areas | 1,000–10,000 | 2x, 4x |
| A. longiloba | | Alkali sagebrush | CO, UT, NV, MT to OR | Alkaline soils, limey soils | 5,500–8,000 | 2x, 4x |
| A. nova | nova | Black sagebrush | OR, MT, to NM | Dry, calcareous soils | 2,050–9,800 | 2x, 4x |
| | duchesnicola | Duchesne black sagebrush | northeast UT | Clay soils of the Duchesne R. Formation | 5,575–5,900 | 6x |
| A. pygmaea | | Pygmy sagebrush | NV, UT, AZ | Calcareous soils | 4,000–6,000 | 2x |
| A. rothrockii | | Rothrock sagebrush | CA, NV | Deep forest soils | 3,280–13,120 | 4x, 6x |
| A. tridentata | spiciformis | Snowbank big sagebrush | WY, ID, CO, UT | High mountain areas | 6.800–10,000 | 2x, 4x |
| | tridentata | Basin big sagebrush | B.C. to Baja California | Deep soils in valleys and foothills | 2,000–7,020 | 2x, 4x |
| | vaseyana | Mountain big sagebrush | B.C. to NM | Deep soils in mountains and foothills | 2,560–10,170 | 2x, 4x |
| | wyomingensis | Wyoming big sagebrush | ND to AZ | Well-drained, shallow soils | 2,500–7,260 | 2x, 4x |
| | xericensis | Xeric big sagebrush | west-central ID | Basaltic and granitic soils | 2,500–7,260 | 4x |
| A. tripartita | rupicola | Wyoming 3-tip sagebrush | WY | Rocky knoll | 3,390–7,085 | 2x |
| | tripartita | Tall 3-tip sagebrush | WA and MT to NV and UT | Deep, well-drained soils | 3,390–7,085 | 2x, 4x |

*Sources:* McArthur 1983, 1994; McArthur and Sanderson 1999.

are found at high elevations, in northern latitudes, and in recently glaciated
areas (Ramsey and Schemske 1998). This
is also true for the many closely related
chenopod shrub groups that live along
salt gradients, and the diverse sagebrush
found along moisture gradients in the
cold desert.

The Chenopodiaceae, or goosefoot
family, provides a good example of how
polyploidy works. Chenopods are tolerant of salty soils, so when the lakes
dried, leaving behind salty, open landscapes, the chenopods moved in. As
Howard Stutz (1978) puts it, "At the borders of every sterile, empty island in
these saline deserts, some member of
this remarkable family is at the last fron-
tier.... Every known strategy for speciation is evident...some of which have
never been reported to be nearly so significant in the evolution of other plant
groups." And speciation happened
quickly, much of it within the last 10,000
years, since the end of the Pleistocene.

The genus *Atriplex* is the most diverse of
the chenopods in the cold desert. It consists
of numerous species, ploidy races, and varieties, and many other forms are still undescribed (Table 7.1). The many isolated basins
of the Great Basin are hotbeds of *Atriplex*
evolution, with nearly every valley possessing unique forms or genotypes. Four-wing
saltbush is the most widespread *Atriplex* species in North America, extending from Mexico up into Canada (Fig. 7.5). Through both
polyploidy and hybridization, it has numerous ploidy races and additional variation
within many of those (Table 7.1; Sanderson
and McArthur 2004, Sanderson and Stutz
2001). Ancestral diploid four-wing saltbush
are found in deep sand and are taller than
their higher-ploidy offspring.

**7.5.** Four-wing saltbush (*Atriplex canescens*) in salty soils
near Tuba City, Arizona (*top*), and a close-up of the
plant's four-winged seeds.

Shadscale is another western chenopod
endemic whose genetic variation is associated with salty lakebeds (Fig. 7.3). Its diploid,
or ancestral, form occurs above the former
lakes, while races with higher chromosome
levels occur in the saltier basins. Shadscale
fossils some 27,000 years old have been
found in caves above Lake Bonneville's former shoreline (Stutz and Sanderson 1983).

Greasewood, another endemic, persisted in salty bottomlands and badlands of
the cold desert during the Pleistocene. This
group of plants has been in North America
for at least 50 million years, based on fossils
from Washington, Oregon, Idaho, Wyoming, and Colorado (Sanderson et al. 1999).
Although it was able to persist in the cold
desert during the full glacial periods, other
plants migrated to lower elevations. Greasewood is represented by 4n, 8n, and 12n

ploidy forms, with the 8n form dominating most of the Great Basin. Sanderson and others (1999) suggest that the 8n version outcompeted the more ancestral 4n form due to its greater genetic variation.

The endemic shrub winterfat is also represented by different varieties (Welsh et al. 1993). This boreal shrub was present in Nevada through much of the Pleistocene, although during the full and late glacial periods it grew only on the Colorado Plateau and in the Chihuahuan Desert (Betancourt 1990, Thompson 1990, Van Devender 1990).

A bit higher in elevation is the big sagebrush group, which is largely intolerant of salty soils. The distribution of many sagebrush species and subspecies are explained on the basis of moisture gradients rather than salt gradients (Table 7.2, Fig. 7.3; McArthur et al. 1988). The big sagebrush complex also radiated into a diverse group during the Pliocene and Pleistocene, but it did not produce as many ploidy or chromosome levels as the chenopods did. This group has eleven species, most of which contain many subspecies, and many that have several ploidy races (e.g., 2n, 4n) (Table 7.2;, McArthur 1978, 2005). Many of the different species, subspecies, and ploidy races hybridize with one another, creating still more species and varieties. Ancestral big sagebrush (2n) grows to more than 15 feet tall and lives near drainages and other mesic sites, while its tetraploid offshoot (4n) stands about 3 feet tall and grows on dry valley slopes (Sanderson et al. 1989).

Higher ploidy levels of green rabbitbrush have been found to be adapted to lower and drier sites than their diploid ancestors (Anderson 1986). Snakeweed and the chenopod hopsage also have multiple chromosome races, with each occurring in somewhat different environments (Sanderson et al. 1989).

Blackbrush has not diversified like other cold desert shrubs, and all of its populations are diploid (2n). There is, however, considerable genetic variation in seed germination traits among its populations at different elevations.

*Evolution of Cold Desert Flowers*

Diverse herbaceous flowers also occur only in the cold desert. The Colorado Plateau has the greatest number of endemic vascular plant species in North America (Welsh 1978, Kartesz and Farstad 1999, Stevens and Nabhan 2002). In 1978, Stanley Welsh, a Utah plant taxonomist, identified 340 plant species that were endemic to the Colorado Plateau. That number has increased to about 350 species today (John Spence, National Park Service ecologist, Utah, personal communication). Many of these species are restricted to exposed substrates such as shales, clays, mudstones, and sands. A number of species are endemic to the salty soils of the Bonneville Basin and to saline clays of the Mancos Formation. Some species are restricted to pockets of unusual soils such as gypsum (Shultz 1993). More than half occur below 6,500 feet (Welsh 1978). In Utah the largest groups of endemic plants include the genus *Astragalus* (42 species) in the legume family, *Cryptantha* (22 species) in the borage family, *Penstemon* (28 species) in the snapdragon family, buckwheats (*Eriogonum*, 14 species, Polygoneaceae), and sunflowers such as fleabane daisies (*Erigeron*, 13 species) (Shultz 1993). Many other species of these groups also occur in the cold desert but are not endemic.

A study of cold desert plant distributions in the Grand Staircase–Escalante National Monument in Utah showed that endemic species were found more often in dry rather than mesic habitats, and where soils had high levels of clay and low phosphorus levels (Stohlgren et al. 2005). They also found that most species, including most endemics, were rarely encountered, which appears to be a universal pattern in the biological world (Rosenzweig 1995).

Fewer flowers are endemic in the northern cold desert—the Great Basin—than on the Colorado Plateau. James Reveal determined that the Colorado Plateau had 4.2 times more endemic plants than the Great Basin (Reveal 1979, Holmgren 1972). Stanley Welsh (personal communication) attributes this difference to the formation of the Great Basin's massive lakes during the Late Pleistocene, which eliminated many plant communities. Reveal suggests that the greater stability of the Colorado Plateau during this time, as well as its greater geological diversity, also contributed to this difference. Because of this, he contends that the Colorado Plateau is a living museum for the biota of the entire Intermountain region.

*Browser/Grazer Evolution in the Cold Desert*

It is commonly thought that the prehistoric megafauna of North America occurred largely in the Great Plains from the Miocene into the Pleistocene, but these large browsing/grazing creatures were also present in the cold desert. Evidence of ground sloths, giant short-faced bears, lions, cheetahs, horses, peccarys, camels, llamas, mountain goats, shrub ox, muskox, pronghorn, and of course, mastodons and mammoths has been found there (Grayson 1994). According to Grayson, horses, camels, and mammoths were relatively common in the cold desert then, so perhaps these shrub communities, like grasslands, evolved with the large herbivores that disappeared throughout North America by about 12,000 years ago (West and Young 2000).

It is also thought that summer drought excluded the large herds of bison from grazing in the Great Basin (Weddell 1996). Bison populations numbered in the millions in the more mesic Great Plains. The impact of the large Pleistocene mammals on the cold desert shrub ecosystems is of interest to those contemplating the damaging impact of grazing mammals on cold desert plant communities today. This is a controversial topic: some argue that a possible lack of intensive prehistoric grazing hastened the degradation of cold desert grasslands by contemporary overgrazing (Fletcher and Robbie 2004), though it is more likely that arid grasslands simply cannot tolerate the high grazing levels that mesic grasslands can, regardless of grazing history.

## How Shrubs Cope in the Cold Desert

Cold desert plant communities have been shaped by the region's harsh climate, with conditions becoming progressively harsher from south to north. The entire cold desert gets winter precipitation from the Pacific Ocean, but whereas the southern part of the Colorado Plateau receives up to 50 percent of its moisture from summer monsoon storms, the Great Basin gets little summer rain (Smith and Nowak 1990). The central and northern Great Basin also have only 80 to 90 frost-free days each year. This combination of winter-only precipitation and a short growing season creates a narrow window for plant growth and reproduction.

And yet, although some parts of the Great Basin receive less precipitation than the Colorado Plateau, the fact that most of it falls in winter means that more of it infiltrates the soil. I once overheard an old rancher at the local feed store say that it's snow that feeds the soil, and so it is. Snow recharges deep water tables rather than running off, evaporating, or being transpired by plants; about half of the precipitation enters the soil in intermountain lowlands. The warmer southern deserts store less moisture in the soil per unit of precipitation than the cold desert.

Winter storms are the most predictable sources of moisture in these dry lands, and, consequently, many shrubs take up most of their moisture, grow, and reproduce on the heels of winter precipitation. The robustness of growth and reproduction is dependent on the amount of winter precipitation received. Some shrub species do not even respond to summer rains with water uptake or growth. It seems remarkable to me that even in a hot, dry summer, some plants are unable to capitalize on rainfall.

Plants that grow in response to winter precipitation include cool-season ($C_3$) species such as winterfat, some asters, snakeweed, horsebrush, rubber rabbitbrush, and grasses such as Indian ricegrass. Many of these species respond more negatively to winter drought than to summer drought because they have—physiologically speaking—put their money on winter precipitation (Schwinning et al. 2005). Interestingly, $C_4$ shadscale also grows and reproduces in early spring, although most $C_4$ plants are adapted to grow in response to summer temperatures and rains. According to Caldwell et al. (1977), natural selection has favored $C_4$ chenopods such as shadscale that have evolved the capacity to photosynthesize at low spring temperatures when water is prevalent, though this species does continue to grow to some extent in summer.

Some plants are more opportunistic and can take up moisture and grow in summer as well as late winter. Such plants must produce at least some shallow roots, since only shallow roots can collect summer moisture

that doesn't penetrate soil deeply. These species include blackbrush, big sagebrush, sand sagebrush, $C_4$ shadscale, green rabbitbrush, and resinbush.

$C_4$ species are monsoon-adapted species that grow and reproduce primarily with summer rains. A number of $C_4$ grasses, including galleta grass, blue grama, and black grama, do not start growing until summer rains start on the Colorado Plateau. Around Flagstaff, Arizona, blue grama grass appears nearly dead until monsoon storms arrive, when it grows its leaf canopy and reproduces quickly.

Both winter and summer annuals grow in the cold desert, with most $C_4$ species occurring on the Colorado Plateau, where there is adequate summer precipitation. According to Comstock and Ehleringer (1992), the lack of summer rain in parts of the Great Basin may largely eliminate an entire class of $C_4$ summer annuals that occur on the Colorado Plateau. Winter wildflower displays in the cold desert never match those of the Mohave Desert; it's simply too cold in the spring, when winter moisture is still around.

### Leaves

Many cold desert shrubs are evergreen, including big sagebrush, shadscale, blackbrush, and winterfat. The persistence of at least some leaves allows these species to continue to photosynthesize through the dry summer months. Many species do lose some leaves as conditions dry out at the end of spring. Big sagebrush drops its large (about a half inch long) spring leaves but keeps its smaller perennial leaves through the year.

Cold desert shrubs typically have small, narrow leaves that easily dissipate heat and lose less water per unit area than large leaves.

Leaves are often pale blue with bristly hairs, both of which help to regulate ultraviolet light and heat absorbance.

*Roots*

Cold desert shrubs have, proportionately speaking, some of the largest root systems on earth. Plants there may allocate up to 90 percent of their biomass to roots for capturing moisture (Dobrowolski et al. 1990), which is more than plants in the warm deserts do. It is thought that because the roots of warm desert shrubs are smaller and shallower, they are able to capitalize on a more predictable biseasonal pulse of water. Although many cold desert shrubs have thick taproots that reach 6 feet deep or more, these only account for about 5 percent of their whole root system. Most of their extensive roots are fine offshoots growing out laterally from main roots, from shallow to deep depths. In big sagebrush this network of roots may extend 5 feet or more out from the plant, depending on plant densities. The roots of shadscale, winterfat, and sagebrush follow soil moisture and develop in a wave-like pattern, drawing water from first-wetted upper soil layers and then developing at progressively deeper levels as upper soil layers dry (Dobrowolski et al. 1990). The roots die back annually, and replacing them requires a great of energy. For shadscale and winterfat, the annual cost to replace this traveling, lateral root system each year is about 75 percent of a plant's total biomass production (Dobrowolski et al. 1990).

*Mating Strategies in Cold Desert Shrublands*

The vast shrub populations in the cold desert often occur as monocultures of one species or another (Figs. 7.3, 7.4). It may be that these populations have become so widespread because nearly all of them are pollinated by wind rather than insects. The two most diverse and widespread groups— the big sagebrush complex and the chenopods—are entirely wind pollinated. Even blackbrush, with its long, skinny range along the southern edge of the cold desert, has become wind pollinated.

Wind pollination is also the dominant strategy in most other large western ecosystems, including coniferous forests, coniferous woodlands, and grasslands. Although there are more flowering than nonflowering plant species, and many flowering plants are pollinated by animals, most plants and most individual flowers depend on the wind. All you have to do is look at the plain flowers of most cold desert shrubs to see that they are not built for attracting pollinators.

Wind pollination is most common in ecosystems dominated by just a few plant species. It is also more prevalent at higher elevations and latitudes, where seasonality may limit pollinators (Pendleton et al. 1989). In the lower latitudes and elevations of the warm deserts, enormous populations of creosote bush, mesquites, acacias, paloverdes, and cacti are all insect pollinated. Although grasses, big sagebrush, and chenopods are all derived from insect-pollinated ancestors, perhaps finding pollinators for the millions or billions of flowers they produce annually might not be possible.

Wind pollination may provide large populations of shrubs with greater genetic variability for responding to the many environmental conditions that they occur in. And indeed, woody, long-lived trees and shrubs exhibit far more genetic variation than most herbaceous species (Hamrick et al. 1979, Hamrick et al. 1992, Loveless and Hamrick 1984, Pendleton et al. 1989).

Perhaps ironically, insect pollination appears to be most common in rare or endangered plant species, where localized gene flow in small populations may best support local adaptation (Harper 1979). Other shrubs that have very wide ranges but are never dominant in the cold desert—such as rabbitbrush and snakeweed, with their showy yellow flowers—are insect pollinated.

### Dioecy: The Separation of Female and Male Flowers

Most shrubs produce perfect flowers, containing both male and female parts, but many wind-pollinated cold desert shrubs are dioecious, meaning they produce only male *or* female flowers. Because dioecy is considered rare among plants, its commonness in cold desert shrubs such as the *Atriplex* group is intriguing (Pendleton et al. 1989, Freeman et al. 1980). Dioecy was traditionally regarded as a means of enhancing outcrossing, but male and female plants may sometimes occupy different microhabitats (Willson 1983). This is the case for arid land species, including shadscale, in which female shrubs occupy wetter sites than males (Freeman et al. 1976).

Some dioecious shrubs, such as saltbush, can change the sex of individual flowers or all of their flowers in response to changing environmental conditions or plant age. McArthur (1989) suggests that this ability to shift sex combined with polyploidy has allowed many of these shrubs to exploit a wider range of environments. By contrast, plants such as creosote bush that have perfect or hermaphroditic flowers tend to be insect pollinated (Fig. 6.6; Pendleton et al. 1989). Big sagebrush is an exception with its perfect *and* wind-pollinated flowers.

### COLD DESERT PLANT AND ANIMAL COMMUNITIES TODAY

#### The Salt-Loving Chenopods or Salt-Desert Scrub

The salty soils of the cold desert would be nearly barren without its twenty-eight species of chenopods in seven genera. They grow well in soils with high concentrations of calcium, potassium, and sodium salts (McArthur and Monsen 2004), and can also live in cold desert rangelands and woodlands. Chenopods live in similar continental deserts in central Asia and Australia, and occur along coastal salt marshes and alkaline plains and playas in deserts on all continents except Antarctica. The chenopods include herbaceous weeds, woody shrubs, and important cultivars such as beets and spinach.

#### Salts

The dry lakebeds in the Great Basin contain large concentrations of salts—mainly NaCl, or sodium chloride, but also phytotoxic trace elements such as boron. The salty soils of the Colorado Plateau were formed from Mancos and Chinle shales, sandstones, and limestones. Cold desert soils are also salty due to low precipitation levels and higher evaporation rates, which keep salts near the surface in root zones rather than allowing them to infiltrate more deeply (Comstock and Ehleringer 1992, Fitter and Hay 1987). Salty soils have what's called "low water potential," meaning it is harder to get water out of them. For roots to absorb water from these soils, they must create even lower water potential within their roots so that the water leaves the salty soil and migrates to the roots. Once plants achieve water uptake, they must contend with salt accumulation in their tissue, which can have toxic effects. Salts may become concentrated in leaves and dehydrate them as water evaporates through their pores, or stomates. As if that weren't bad enough, salts can also interrupt the functioning of enzymes in plant cells. Some plants, like winterfat, are able to filter salts out at the roots. Others can either dump salts or make salts work for them; some species even grow more if you add salt to their soil. Saltbush takes salt in and pumps it right on out through specialized bladderlike leaf hairs that rupture, releasing the salts. Some plants transport salts back to the roots via the phloem.

*Valley Bottoms*

Salt levels decrease and water availability increases from the valley bottoms to the uplands in the Great Basin, and different chenopod species occur along the way. In valley bottoms, where salts accumulate in brackish water, only a few species of microflora occur, including photosynthetic flagellates, cyanobacteria, and halobacteria. The halobacteria actually require high salinity for membrane stability and enzyme function. In slightly better-drained soils above the bottomlands, there are simple communities of inkweed (its old leaves are ink black), iodine bush, pickleweeds, and greasewood (Fig. 7.3). Saltgrass is the only grass there.

An endemic chenopod, greasewood occupies some of the saltiest soils of the cold desert. It grows in saline bottomlands, playa dunes, and badlands. Greasewood stands often occur in near monocultures in shallow, salty floodplains in northern Arizona badlands.

On drier, less salty sites, a great variety of chenopods, including shadscale, basin saltbush, and winterfat, thrive. Shadscale is another endemic chenopod that has become highly diverse as it has spread into the salty former lakebeds. It is similar to four-wing saltbush in many ways; it is widespread and very hearty, though it is tolerant of more finely textured soils, greater salt concentrations, and aridity. It often occurs with four-wing saltbush and winterfat.

Mat saltbush is a prostrate shrub that rarely exceeds 6 inches in height and grows in the Mancos Shale formation in Wyoming, Colorado, and Utah. It is probably the most salt-tolerant species in the genus, and is often the only plant occurring in soils with up to 13,000 ppm soluble salts (McArthur and Monsen 2004). It is also found in less salty soils with winterfat, cuneate saltbush, shadscale, four-wing saltbush, black greasewood, budsage, and gray molly.

Winterfat is highly drought tolerant, highly nutritious for both wildlife and livestock through the seasons, and it is a dominant species in fine-textured lake deposits and other calcareous soils in the cold desert (Kitchen and Jorgensen 2001). Winterfat communities are second only to those of shadscale in dominance of the 60,000 square miles of North American salt-desert scrubland found mainly in the Great Basin. Common associates include shadscale, budsage, green rabbitbrush, black sagebrush, ricegrass, galleta grass, needle-and-thread grass, and globemallow. From the standpoint of community succession following disturbance, winterfat is regarded as a late stage or climax species. Although moderately tolerant of herbivory, winterfat has declined significantly in the Great Basin due to overgrazing dating back to the 1800s. Its greatest threat today may be the exotic halophyte halogeton, which is making soils uninhabitable for it.

Spineless hopsage, a chenopod in another genus, also lives in shales that few other plants occupy. Its relative, spiny hopsage, occurs in well-drained loamy to gravelly textured soils.

Four-wing saltbush (Fig. 7.5, Table 7.1) is the most widespread and adaptable *Atriplex* shrub in North America. It grows from nearly sea level up to 8,000 feet on deep, well-drained sandy soils, sand dunes, gravelly washes, mesas, ridges, and slopes. Like so many cold desert chenopods, its range extends from Mexico, where it may have originated, into Canada. It is often found growing with greasewood, shadscale, big basin sagebrush, and occasionally black sagebrush, and also in pinyon-juniper woodlands. A number of grasses, including galleta grass and blue grama, are found with it at middle elevations, and bluebunch wheatgrass, various *Stipa* species, squirreltail, and Sandberg bluegrass occur with it at higher elevations. Four-wing saltbush is remarkably hearty and has proven valuable in habitat restoration. When appropriate strains are planted in appropriate sites, revegetation is often very successful. Through both polyploidy and hybridization, it has numerous chromosome races (Table 7.1). Today, the newer races of saltbush are more common than the ancestral group.

## Salt Scrub Animals

Most shrubby chenopods are highly nutritious, having higher protein content than most other cold desert shrubs, and are a favorite of browsing animals in winter (McArthur and Monsen 2004). Many of the mammals and birds that occur in sagebrush ecosystems also occur here, but their numbers are lower (West 1983a), and there are fewer amphibians and reptiles than in the warm southern deserts. The native fauna are dominated by rodents and lagomorphs (including rabbits, hares, and pikas), and

especially black-tailed desert jackrabbits. The chisel-tooth kangaroo rat is well adapted to feed on salt-tolerant plants due to its ability to shear off outer salty layers of shadscale leaves with its lower, chisel-shaped incisors (Kenagy 1972). Larger mammals, including pronghorn, desert bighorn sheep, and mule deer, eat these plants only when sagebrush habitat is degraded or covered in snow (West 1983a).

Insects associated with *Atriplex* are diverse. More than 100 species were collected from four-wing saltbush through sweep-netting (Haws et al. 1984), and collectively they use most parts of the plant. Several species can cause high levels of mortality, including the defoliating leaf beetle (*Monoxia elegans*) and case-bearing moths. However, mortality often occurs in restored plant populations, which may lack genetic diversity (Haws et al. 1984).

## Blackbrush

Above the salty basins and below the expanses of sagebrush, enormous stands of blackbrush extend as far as the eye can see (Fig. 7.4) Blackbrush has a narrow range along the southern edge of the cold desert through southern Utah, southern Nevada, northern Arizona, and northern New Mexico (West 1983b), one of the narrower distributions of cold desert shrubs.

Blackbrush dominates 11,000 square miles in the southwestern United States between elevations of 2,600 and 5,200 feet (Pendleton and Meyer 2004), and shrub cover can reach as high as 50 percent, which is unusual for semidesert (West 1983b). Neil West says this may be due to the great age these shrubs reach (~400 years [Christensen and Brown 1963]) and all of the debris that persists in their canopies. This little shrub in the rose family seems to favor shallow soils, or perhaps it is simply outcompeted by desert grasses where soils deepen. Although it's difficult to tell by looking out at a stand of blackbrush, many grasses and small shrubs coexist with it, including joint-fir, spiny hopsage, shadscale, galleta grass, ricegrass, sand dropseed, and blue grama.

Blackbrush's southern distribution is partly accounted for by its dependence on southerly summer rains and its intolerance of cold desert winters. In the western part of its range, it lives on the northern edge of the Mohave Desert, which is too dry for it (Hunter and McAuliffe 1994). According to Lin et al. (1996), its shallow roots allow it to take up summer moisture that only penetrates upper soil levels. The majority of its roots occur within the upper foot of soils (Lei and Walker 1997). Like many evergreen desert plants, blackbrush drops older leaves during dry periods and generally ceases to photosynthesize. A key feature of blackbrush that may contribute to its success is that it can go dormant for up to three years during drought (Pendleton and Meyer 2004).

Blackbrush has evolved into a wind-pollinated species, so it has lost the showy flowers that its ancestors produced (Pendleton and Pendleton 1998). It occasionally produces a yellow petal or two, but they are only relics from its insect-pollinated past. As thorny and tough as it is, not much feeds on blackbrush, and because it is wind- rather than insect-pollinated, it offers few resources for pollinating insects (Pendleton and Pendleton 1998). Blackbrush blooms from April to May in response to winter precipitation. This plant may be a masting species, meaning it might have low seed production for successive years but occasionally produces lots of seeds (Pendleton and Meyer 2004).

Although blackbrush does not have the chromosomal variation of many cold desert shrubs, it does exhibit adaptations to the varied conditions that occur over its elevational range of several thousand feet. While its seeds need cold in order to germinate, seeds from lower-elevation populations require only a short cold period, while those from higher elevations require longer periods of cold (Lei 1997). This requirement prevents seeds from germinating earlier than they should. In blackbrush, the cold is also critical for killing an associated fungus that otherwise kills seedlings (Lei 1997). The variation in germination requirements over blackbrush's range suggest that it will be able to adapt to predicted climatic shifts. Apparently it is migrating toward higher elevations farther north, into the southern Great Basin, presumably in response to global warming, a migration that has been ongoing through much of the Quaternary period (Lei and Walker 1997). Despite its dynamic movement, blackbrush is extremely slow growing: five-year-old seedlings studied in Arches National Monument were less than 3 inches tall (Pendleton and Meyer 2004)! This partly explains why efforts to reestablish blackbrush typically fail.

## Rabbitbrush

Rabbitbrush, another endemic western shrub, is as widespread as sagebrush, though never as abundant (Plate 33). This highly diverse group of plants includes seventeen species and forty subspecies that occur in the cold desert (McArthur and Stevens 2004). With its deep taproots, rabbitbrush is one of the cold desert's most drought tolerant plants. The most widespread species, rubber rabbitbrush, occurs from British Columbia to Baja California in plains, valleys, and foothills. It grows best in openings in sagebrush, pinyon-juniper, and ponderosa pine stands, and in sandy, gravelly, or clay soils at elevations between 500 and 9,000 feet. Green rabbitbrush is also widespread in the West, with a distribution similar to that of rubber rabbitbrush. Alkali, or white-flowered, rabbitbrush, unlike other species, is highly tolerant of salty soils and lives in salt flats with salt grass and pickleweed (Welsh et al. 1993). With its abundant, windblown seeds, rabbitbrush readily colonizes disturbed areas such as overgrazed, burned, or developed sites (Monzingo 1987). This also makes it highly useful for restoration of disturbed habitats, although it is not very competitive in undisturbed habitats.

Rabbitbrush foliage and stems support a variety of herbivores. It also supports more native pollinating bee species than other cold desert shrubs, being visited by nearly 200 species in Grand Staircase–Escalante National Monument between August and October (Griswold 2009). They must provide a lot of nectar and pollen, for the plant in my yard is aswirl with a cloud of flies, bees, and migrating painted lady butterflies each fall. Like so many cold desert shrubs, rabbitbrush has a number of gall-forming tephritid and cecidomyiid flies associated with it (McArthur and Stevens 2004). Many of them are specific to certain rabbitbrush varieties, in some cases only one. A study of plant-eating insects on low rabbitbrush in Idaho found nearly fifty species, including leaf-feeding beetles, lepidopterans, sap suckers, and flower feeders (Stafford and Johnson 1986). The chrysomelid leaf-feeding beetle can defoliate and kill rubber rabbitbrush (Dalen et al. 1986). Rabbitbrush is browsed lightly by deer and elk, primarily in the winter, and sometimes more heavily by livestock, but it is resilient in recovering from it (McArthur and Stevens 2004). Its flowers are also browsed.

*Beautiful Sagebrush*

The big sagebrush complex (*Artemisia* spp., subgenus Tridentatae) is western North America's most widespread and populous shrub group. It is considered the largest of the North American semidesert vegetation types (Fig. 7.3; West 1983c, 1983d). Sagebrush ecosystems span steppes and foothills of western mountains above the region's salty basins. Individual big sagebrush may live up to 100 years, and stands occur from northern Arizona across the Colorado Plateau and throughout the Great Basin (Smith and Nowak 1990). They occupy more than 230,000 square miles of cold desert, mostly in the northern states (West 1983c, 1983d). Sagebrush is known for its soft, blue-green color and distinctive fragrance, and when I think of it, I am reminded of a large stand of big sagebrush at the base of Black Mesa on the Navajo reservation in northern Arizona, where it is surrounded by soft pink Navajo Sandstone.

With more than 500 species, sagebrush is one of the largest genera in the sunflower family (Asteraceae). It often dominates arid and semiarid regions, such as the deserts of central Asia. The big sagebrush subgenus, Tridentatae, has a circumpolar distribution and was previously even more widespread in northern latitudes than it is today (McArthur and Plummer 1978).

Big sagebrush in the West is characterized by eleven species, most of them comprised of several to many subspecies and lower ploidy races (Table 7.2; McArthur 2005). Many of the different species, subspecies, and ploidy races hybridize with one another, creating still more variation. Big sagebrush subspecies have a broad distribution through most of the cold desert, though their abundance and productivity are strongly influenced by elevation and latitude. In the southern cold desert and at lower, drier elevations, big sagebrush plants are short, widely spaced, and less productive. Grass is sparse, but the ground, where undisturbed, is often held in place with a layer of biological soil crust (West and Young 2000). Some sagebrush occur on hummocks or little islands in which organic nutrients and sediment have accumulated. West (1983c, 1983d) describes these populations as fragile and difficult to restore following disturbances. In the southern cold desert, woody sagebrush commonly makes up more than 70 percent of plant cover and more than 90 percent of plant biomass (West 1983c). Grasses such as blue grama grass, stipa, western wheatgrass, three-awn, galleta grass, sand dropseed, and the ubiquitous Indian ricegrass occur with big sagebrush (West and Young 2000).

In the northern part of the cold desert, and at higher elevations through the Colorado Plateau, big sagebrush occurs as shrub steppe along with more grasses (West 1983d, Kuchler 1970). Shrub cover can range from 10 to 80 percent depending on the site and successional status, while herbaceous cover may reach 100 percent (West 1983d). Woody sagebrush gets quite large in these more productive habitats, often exceeding 6 feet in height. Associated grasses include cool-season species such as fescue, bluegrass, and stipa. Where grasses are grazed away, sagebrush densities often increase, showing how competitive grasses can be (West and Young 2000, Whisenant 1990). Associated grasses in the north and at higher elevations include cool-season bluebunch wheatgrass, western wheatgrass, Idaho fescue, sheep fescue, Sandberg bluegrass, Thurber needlegrass, squirreltail, and Indian ricegrass (West and Young 2000).

Flowers associated with sagebrush communities include aster, lupine, locoweed, balsamroot, mountain dandelion, buckwheat, and goldenrod. Shrubs such as rabbitbrush, joint-fir, horsebrush, bitterbrush, serviceberry, and four-wing saltbush also occur with sagebrush. In the mountains, sagebrush occurs with bitterbrush, snowberry, mountain mahogany, and chokecherry.

Different sagebrush species and subspecies grow in an array of habitats between about 750 to 13,000 feet in elevation, although most favor well-drained soils on sloping hills (Table 7.2; Mahalovich and McArthur 2004). Within the big sagebrush group, the three most common subspecies occupy different places along elevational and moisture gradients. The widespread basin big sagebrush favors deep, well-drained soils in the foothills and mountains; it is regarded as intermediate among the three in habitat preference (Table 7.2; McArthur 1978). Wyoming big sagebrush is the most drought tolerant and favors shallower soils, often underlain by caliche or silica. Mountain big sagebrush lives in foothills and high mountain areas with deep soils. Wyoming big sagebrush is a tetraploid, while the others are diploid. This diversity has enabled big sagebrush to dominate much of the cold desert. Most other species in the Tridentatae subgenus are restricted to more northern portions of the cold desert (Table 7.2). Several sagebrush species, including alkali sagebrush and budsage, are salt tolerant and live in salty basins and badlands (McArthur 2005).

Like so many species in the sunflower family (Asteraceae), sagebrush blooms in the fall and produces seeds in winter. Seed viability and germination levels are generally high (Young and Evans 1989), but their establishment may be most successful in wetter years.

Sagebrush communities have never been diverse. According to West (1983d), relict, undisturbed sites in Washington have been found to support only about twenty vascular plant species per 10,000 square feet, with up to fifty-four species found in mountain steppe populations in northern Nevada. By contrast, sagebrush ecosystems, with their great extent, provide food, cover, and breeding sites for a variety of animals. Species such as pygmy rabbit, sagebrush vole, Great Basin pocket mice, least chipmunk, sage grouse, Brewer's sparrow, and many insects are highly dependent on sagebrush. It can be particularly important to elk, mule deer, bighorn sheep, and pronghorn in winter, when grasses and forbs are dormant. Sagebrush is typically not browsed by generalist herbivores when herbaceous plants are available because its leaves contain high levels of phenolics and coumarins, which make them less palatable (West 1983c, 1983d). Of the five rabbit species that browse sagebrush, the pygmy rabbit prefers it as its primary food and may be the most reliant on it. Twenty-eight other rodents, including mice and voles, take cover and nest in sagebrush stands. Occasional surges in vole populations can lead to defoliation and mortality of sagebrush.

Of course, sage grouse are recognized for their obligate relationship with sagebrush in the cold desert. As with just about everything in the cold desert, there is more than one species of this large bird. The greater sage grouse occurs north of the Colorado River, while to the south is the Gunnison sage grouse. Sage grouse reach their greatest abundance in the sagebrush steppe. The adults have a unique gastrointestinal tract that allows them to feed on sagebrush buds and leaves while their young feed on insects in meadow areas. For their dramatic courtship and mating, adults require open "booming," or breeding, grounds.

The sage grouse was once found wherever sagebrush occurred. In pioneer times it was found in at least fourteen western states, and it was considered a leading game bird through the 1930s. Euro-American colonization of the West, with its agriculture, grazing, and hunting, diminished sage grouse populations (McAdoo and Klebenow 1978). Today their populations are much reduced due to habitat loss, fragmentation, and degradation (Beck et al. 2003). In the northern cold desert their populations have declined by nearly 40 percent in less than ten years, while in Utah up to 70 percent of their potential habitat has disappeared (Beck et al. 2003).

Songbirds commonly occurring in sagebrush communities include the horned lark, sage thrasher, mountain bluebird, loggerhead shrike, western meadowlark, green-tailed towhee, lark sparrow, black-throated sparrow, and sage sparrow (McAdoo and Klebenow 1978, Ryser 1985). Welch (1999) reported that dark-eyed juncos derive up to 70 percent of their dietary needs from big sagebrush seeds. He also observed white-crowned sparrows, horned larks, house finches, black-capped chickadees, and house sparrows feeding on sagebrush seeds.

Fautin (1946) lists five species of lizards and three snakes in sagebrush communities in western Utah. The lizards include the collared lizard, leopard lizard, brown-shouldered lizard, sagebrush lizard, and desert horned lizards. Snakes include the western rattlesnake, striped whipsnake, and Great Basin gopher snake. Amphibians are limited but include the tiger salamander (McAdoo and Klebenow 1978).

More than 300 species of insects are known from cold desert sagebrush. Nearly 30 species of cecidomyiid gall formers occur on many of the varieties (Jones et al. 1983).

*Biological Soil Crusts*

Biological soil crusts are ancient, and it is thought that they, or something like them, may have been the first life forms on land (Campbell 1979, Watanabe et al. 2000, Prave 2002). In the cold desert and other semiarid and arid regions of the world, the soil surface is often covered by a complex community of nonvascular plants including dozens of species of algae, cyanobacteria, lichens, and mosses (Comstock and Ehleringer 1992, Belnap 1993). These organisms form a crust in the upper surface of the soil, and where long-lived, they develop a rough-textured surface. The area covered by these crusts often exceeds that of vascular plants, making their contribution to ecosystem productivity considerable. The benefits that crusts afford desert ecosystems are many: they reduce soil erosion, provide nitrogen, enhance nutrient cycling, and create catchments for water (Kaltenecker et al. 1999). Within the crusts, blue-green algae, cyanobacteria, and lichens fix nitrogen and carbon, and contribute them to the soil for uptake by vascular plants, mosses, fungi, and other microbes (Comstock and Ehleringer 1992, Belnap 1993). Crusts are a major contributor of nitrogen in desert systems, which by nature are nutrient limited due to limited rainfall and few nitrogen-fixing plants. Crusts can increase soil nitrogen levels by up to 200 percent.

Crusts in the West have been damaged by livestock, fire, and development, and the process of mending them is challenging. Damaged crusts are estimated to take 40 to 250 years to recover depending on the amount of water available (Belnap 1993). They are very slow growing and require a great deal of water to heal. But there is hope: a study in Idaho has shown substantial crust recovery within 8 to 11 years in areas previously exposed to heavy cattle grazing (Kaltenecker et al. 1999). This was seen in sagebrush/grassland sites, which receive more rainfall.

## Cold Deserts at Risk

Cold desert ecosystems are at great risk today due to a convergence of factors. While all of the ecosystems described in this book have been strongly, and typically negatively, affected by Euro-American settlers and their massive herds of livestock, their impact on the cold desert has been disastrous.

*Overgrazing*

Overgrazing of the cold desert began in earnest in the late 1880s and was the first step in transforming the region's shrub communities. It eliminated native grasses and set the stage for the rapid invasion and dominance of the exotic annual cheatgrass (Fig. 6.5). Overgrazing in the shrub steppe in the Great Basin, with its low productivity, has completely transformed it, and most plants found there today are nonnative, particularly cheatgrass.

Cheatgrass began replacing native grasses in the late 1800s, and consequently, fires carried by its tinder-dry fine foliage became more widespread and more frequent (Young and Clements 2009). Cheatgrass and its fires represent the second step in the convergence of negative forces in the cold desert. By the early 1930s it had replaced sagebrush as a dominant in the Great Salt Lake District in Utah and was causing disastrous fires in the western Great Basin (Billings 1994). Through the 1940s the frequency of fires accelerated, and cheatgrass spread from the salt desert communities up through ponderosa pine forests (Billings 1994). Between 1979 and 1993, more than 4,600 square miles of cheatgrass-dominated rangeland burned in southern Idaho alone (Monsen 1994). By the 1990s, cheatgrass monocultures covered at least 7,720 square miles of the Great Basin (Bradley and Mustard 2005).

Before the cold desert shrub communities were so severely altered by man, they exhibited fire-return intervals of between 30 and 110 years (Whisenant 1990). Today the frequency of fires in lower-elevation sagebrush communities is every 3 to 5 years. The size of areas burned has also increased; over the last 5 years, more than 100,000 square miles, on average, have burned in Nevada annually (Western Great Basin Coordination Center 2004). It is estimated that over 40 percent of the area of sagebrush communities is at moderate to high risk of replacement by cheatgrass within the next 30 years (Suring et al. 2005).

Cheatgrass is the dominant species on more than 150,000 square miles of the cold desert now being managed as "annual rangelands" (Whisenant 1990). The rate of conversion from sagebrush steppe to annual grassland continues to accelerate (Whisenant 1990). Not only are larger areas burning, and more often, but the fires are more uniformly destructive, with less native vegetation remaining after the burns (Whisenant 1990). Fighting these fires and attempting to rehabilitate damaged sagebrush communities costs more that $19 million annually in Nevada alone. The extent of cheatgrass's western invasion, combined with its effects on native ecosystems through its grass-fire cycle, makes this possibly the most significant plant invasion in North America (Chambers et al. 2007, D'Antonio and Vitousek 1992).

Billings (1994) chronicled the conversion of a sagebrush steppe in northern Nevada into cheatgrass rangeland. After a fire in 1947 killed most of the sagebrush at the site,

cheatgrass invaded, and over the course of forty-five years it increased to such a degree that the land looked like it was covered with several feet of snow—an enormous amount of tinder. As the sagebrush steppe was being degraded by long-term overgrazing, livestock, especially sheep, moved in to graze salt scrub habitats. Cheatgrass has also taken over stands of salt scrub communities (Monsen 1994).

Recent experiments have proven that the removal of native perennial grasses and increased fires are a primary cause of cheatgrass success in the sagebrush steppe (Chambers et al. 2007). Both conditions increase water, nutrients, and space in upper soils, increasing cheatgrass growth and seed production 10 to 30 times. Chambers and others (2007) found that cheatgrass is more successful at lower elevations, where Wyoming big sagebrush is particularly common. They also found that healthy sagebrush communities—those with an understory of perennial grasses—were relatively resistant to cheatgrass invasions.

In the transition zone between the Great Basin and the Mohave Desert, cheatgrass gives way to red brome, which is becoming a dominant winter annual in the warm southern deserts. Like cheatgrass, red brome carries enormous fires among fire-intolerant warm desert plants. Ripgut brome, another exotic species, is actively invading habitats along the Colorado River in Grand Canyon that were previously dominated by red brome (Larry Stevens, personal communication).

In the early 1980s, as cheatgrass was continuing to spread through the West, it received a helping hand by several years of above-average precipitation. This led to large-scale die-offs of native shrubs that are intolerant of excessive water, creating even more open space for invading annuals (West 1994). In Utah up to 2,000 square miles were affected by flooding (Dobrowolski et al. 1990). The greatest mortality occurred among the most widespread cold desert shrubs, including shadscale, sagebrush, budsage, black sagebrush, winterfat, greasewood, horsebrush, spiny hopsage, bitterbrush, and low rabbitbrush.

As if cheatgrass weren't bad enough, it is being joined by a number of other exotic grasses and forbs that are further transforming the West. As a result, new ecosystems are forming that are alien, noxious, very unstable, and generally devoid of ecological value (West and Young 2000). Many of the other invaders are also annual plants. According to Stutz (1994), most weedy annuals have "given up sex" for self-pollination since finding pollen or an ovary can be unpredictable. This is certainly true of cheatgrass, which is obligately self-fertile, using its own pollen to fertilize its eggs; this is also true for other annual species of *Bromus* (Young and Clements 2009).

The rapid invasion of Intermountain rangelands by nonnative annual grasses may not be an ecological endpoint but only the beginning of dominance by an array of nonnative annuals, biennials, and perennials (West and Young 2000). Many of these, such as Russian thistle and halogeton, are adapted to a great array of habitats (Harper et al. 1996). Problem taxa include the annual medusahead wild rye (which can even replace cheatgrass), goatgrass, dyer's woad, and yellow starthistle (West and Young 2000, Vail 1994). Spotted knapweed is a short-lived perennial that now occurs on more than 11,000 square miles in the West, while Russian knapweed is very long lived and nearly impossible to eradicate. Canada thistle, leafy spurge, hoary cress, and

perennial pepper grass are also colonizing much of the West.

These invading species have distinct features that contribute to their success in displacing many native cold desert shrubs. The replacement of the once common winterfat by exotic halogeton provides an example. Winterfat, a nutritious and drought-hearty chenopod, is losing ground due to overgrazing and an invasion by this annual chenopod from Asia. Winterfat rarely recolonizes areas occupied by halogeton, which pumps salt onto the soil surface and may even change the soil microbiota, making soils uninhabitable for winterfat (Kitchen and Jorgensen 2001). Halogeton is a prolific producer of seeds that germinate nearly instantly and also persist in seed banks for up to ten years (West and Young 2000), and it is also replacing shadscale in Utah.

Is there any hope of maintaining the native plant communities of the cold desert? There is no lack of research on the topic, and many volumes of government proceedings describe the problems and restoration efforts. But the challenges to restoring native flora on such a scale are daunting, to say the least. It is possible that a trajectory of change has been set in motion that cannot easily be stopped (West and Young 2000). Land managers now realize that restoring shrublands ravaged by cheatgrass-related fires is nearly impossible because most shrubs cannot recover from it, and most of what is left behind is cheatgrass. Attempts have been made to manage the new cheatgrass rangelands with grazing, but it has not proved to be an effective tool (Vallentine and Stevens 1994). One major disadvantage of grazing is that native perennials decline even more, and further overgrazing leads to invasion by other exotic annuals and perennials such as halogeton.

There are, however, a few encouraging reports of native plants recolonizing cheatgrass stands. Bitterbrush was able to recolonize in a limited way on north-facing slopes at a site in Nevada (Billings 1994), and squirreltail has been able to reestablish in some cheatgrass and medusahead stands (Hironaka 1994). Sandburg bluegrass has also been observed invading cheatgrass stands (Monsen 1994), and in a study of cheatgrass, fire, and grazing effects on a Wyoming sagebrush stand in Utah, Hosten and West (1994) found that cheatgrass cover declined after an initial population expansion following fire. But these seem to be exceptions rather than the rule, especially in habitats that receive less than 10 inches of precipitation per year. Billings (1990) concluded that little can be done to replace cheatgrass in sagebrush ecosystems, and the only viable strategy is to prevent its spread.

The warmer temperatures, increased precipitation, and increased $CO_2$ levels associated with global warming will all affect cold desert plant communities and are predicted to benefit nonnative invaders such as cheatgrass. Increased $CO_2$ levels have already been shown to favor the success of herbaceous plants over woody shrubs (Lucash et al. 2005), as well as exotic annuals such as red brome, the lower-elevation equivalent of cheatgrass (Smith et al. 2000).

Although the movement of cheatgrass and its fellow exotics through the cold desert at this point looks like a runaway train, it's possible that native plants will assert themselves in the cold desert again, especially if we learn to protect these fragile ecosystems.

# CHAPTER 8

# A Few of the West's Gorgeous Flowers

Along with the origin of vascular and seed plants, the evolution of angiosperms, or flowering plants, represents one of the most significant events in the 475-million-year history of land plants; as William Friedman (2006) says, "flowering plants broke the mold," differing from earlier ancestral plants in many, many ways. This chapter describes the natural history of a few of the many beautiful flowers that occur in the West, including their interactions with pollinators, herbivores, weather, and the land—all of which have contributed to the explosion of flowering plants in western North America, as elsewhere.

Flowering plants arose quickly at the beginning of the Cretaceous, and by 90 Ma flowers were everywhere. The fossil record shows that they diversified quickly in terms of size, structure, and organization of flowers early in the Cretaceous (Soltis, Soltis, Chase et al. 2004; Lidgard and Crane 1988; Wing 2000). Among the earliest angiosperms were magnolias, buttercups, star anise, and water lilies (Friedman 2006). The earliest flowering plants also included a cloud forest shrub species similar to *Amborella*, found today in New Caledonia, which reveals a great deal about flowering plant origins (Friedman 2006). By one estimate, angiosperms comprised 90 percent of vascular plant species by the end of the Cretaceous (Hughes 1976). As they were expanding their ranges and becoming increasingly diverse, older, non-flowering plant groups such as cycads and ferns declined dramatically, and many gymnosperms, including many conifers, went extinct (Bond 1989).

Scientists are still looking for clear links between early flowering plants and ancient gymnosperms (Friedman 2006). Today there are more than 250,000 species of flowering plants, but fewer than 1,000 species of the gymnosperms that preceded them (Bond 1989). In the western United States, conifers are restricted to mountains and foothills, and angiosperms such as grasses and forbs compete with these forests, adding most of the plant diversity in those ecosystems.

In 1879 Charles Darwin described the origin of flowering plants as an "abominable mystery." It is still a great mystery today, although the discoveries made through morphological taxonomy, the fossil record, and DNA analysis, have greatly enhanced our understanding of this plant group. Flowering plants differ from older plants in many ways, so their rapid expansion cannot be attributed to one particular feature. The earliest angiosperms were small, tropical understory trees that produced small hermaphroditic or perfect flowers (Friedman 2006). The bundling of male and female reproductive parts into a single structure was new and helped ensure fertilization (Fig. 6.6). Early flowers lacked conspicuous petals and sepals, which evolved after angiosperms began to diversify (Friedman 2006). They have since evolved into a tremendous array of forms with complex interactions with pollinators.

Angiosperms have faster reproductive phases than gymnosperms (one year or less versus as many as three years for the production of seeds), and they are far more efficient at transporting water and nutrients due to modified phloem and xylem systems—traits that contribute to their faster growth rates. Their rapid diversification has also been strongly assisted by polyploidy.

One of the most important and distinctive traits of flowering plants, other than their flowers, involves their production of *endosperm,* an outer layer that nourishes and protects each seed. Angiosperms are the only plants to nourish their embryos with endosperm tissue, which provides nutrients to the developing embryo and contributes greatly to the success of flowering plant seeds. The endosperm layer accounts for most of the edible portion of rice, corn, and wheat, and also the meat and milk of coconuts, and it has been estimated that two-thirds of human caloric intake worldwide is from endosperm (Friedman 2006). During fertilization in flowering plants, the egg is fertilized and then additional sperm unite with additional nuclei to produce what becomes endosperm. This process constitutes double fertilization within each ovule. *Ephedra,* an older, nonflowering plant, also undergoes double fertilization but produces no endosperm (Carmichael and Friedman 1996). It's possible that double fertilization arose first, and the production of endosperm evolved later. It may be that gymnosperms gave rise to a plant such as joint-fir, or *Ephedra,* which gave rise to flowering plants (Friedman 1990).

Another distinct feature of angiosperms, the carpel, which also protects developing seeds, is a tremendously important innovation in the history of plants (Soltis, Soltis, Chase et al. 2004). A closed structure composed of modified leaves that protect the developing seed, the carpel may have been closed up by secretions in early flowering plants, and in later plants by fusion of adjacent tissues (Soltis, Soltis, Chase et al. 2004).

Of course, flowering plants coevolved with pollinating insects; many consider that relationship the basis for the rapid radiation of angiosperms. Indeed, animal-pollinated angiosperm lineages are far more diverse than their wind-pollinated relatives. Most flowering plant species are pollinated by insects, and the fossil record shows that the populations of both groups exploded during the Cretaceous, beginning an unprecedented revolution (Dodd et al. 1999). According to Eriksson and Bremer (1992), the rate of diversification of animal-pollinated flowering plant groups has been twice that of non-animal-pollinated lineages. Recent studies have found that 80 to 95 percent of flowering plant species in different ecosystems are insect pollinated, and half or more of the modern insect families appeared during the Cretaceous as both cause and effect of the angiosperm revolution (Grimaldi and Engel 2005). Characteristics of pollinating insects include the presence of a long proboscis (mouth), combs of setae or spines on mouthparts, pollen baskets on the legs of bees or beeflies, and/or specialized wings that reflect the highly maneuvered flight of many pollinators that are adapted for hovering.

Based on the fossil record and observations of extant primitive flowering plants and gymnosperms, it appears that the earliest pollinating insects were small, generalized types that quickly diversified: flies, thrips, parasitoid wasps, beetles, and primitive butterflies and moths (Grimaldi and Engel 2005). Bees, the most important pollinators, are thought to have originated about 120 Ma, becoming significant pollinators by 90 Ma (Grimaldi and Engel 2005). All of the 20,000 modern species of bees provision their nests with larval food made of nectar and pollen. Many species forage on particular plant families or genera, but the social bees, including bumblebees and honeybees, visit a greater diversity of flowers. There are more than 300 species of native bees in northern Arizona alone (Stevens et al. 2007). One mind-boggling example of how intensely bees work as pollinators involves the social honeybees, which make 8.7 million trips to gather nectar to produce a single pound of honey, producing up to 70 pounds of honey in a week (Kolbert 2007). Bees also pollinate 75 percent of major crop species, making them crucial to agriculture (Buchmann and Nabhan 1996).

Some insects were feeding on pollen as early as the Permian (~248 Ma), and gnetalans and other primitive gymnosperms were producing sticky "pollination droplets" to attract them as well as pollen, much like modern nectar does. It was during the Cretaceous that flowering plants and pollinating insects evolved mutualistic, or mutually beneficial, relationships. Some flowers offer nectar in exchange for pollination services. Others, such as pitcher-plants (Sarraceniaceae), feed on the insects they attract, but most pollinators deposit and collect pollen, collect nectar, and move on. Species such as the yucca moth (*Tegeticula* spp.) with mouthparts strongly modified to move enormous amounts of pollen, reward themselves by laying their eggs in developing yucca fruits. While it is now known that plant pollination systems range from extreme generalization to extreme specialization, we know little about the pollination systems of the vast majority of plants (Johnson and Steiner 2000).

## A Few Western Flowers

Several flower groups are conspicuous across the western landscape and particularly well studied. They are highly diverse, and their interactions with pollinators, herbivores, climates, and habitats are remarkably complex. Collectively, they provide a broad overview of the natural history of flowers in the West.

### Columbine

The beautiful western columbines (*Aquilegia* spp.) tell a great deal about the coevolution of flowering plants and their pollinators, and how specialized such relationships can become. The different shapes of their flowers, their colors, the length of their nectar spurs, and the way they hang on plant stems draw particular types of pollinators. These, in turn, disperse their pollen effectively within a population and promote their divergence from other related plant populations, thereby contributing to rapid diversification.

Twenty-five species of columbine are found in North America, including northern Mexico, and they are even more diverse than that number indicates because many species have several varieties, including the lavender Rocky Mountain columbine (*Aquilegia caerulea* [Plate 34]) and the red and yellow western columbine (*A. formosa* [Plate 35]). Many of the latter occur as endemic populations in isolated hanging gardens scattered across the Colorado Plateau (Welsh et al. 1993), and several species and groups also hybridize, giving rise to still more variation. According to John Spence, an ecologist who works at Glen Canyon National Recreation Area, new endemics are being found there all the time (personal communication). In western North America, columbine occur from alpine habitats to desert springs (Hodges et al. 2003, Chase and Raven 1975).

North American columbines have strong ties to Asian species. A spurless sister species (*Semiaquilegia adoxoides*) occurs through much of eastern Asia. The most primitive columbine, *A. ecalcarata*, occurs in the Himalayas (Grant 1994). Some have suggested that columbines arose as early as the Mid-Tertiary (~20 to 30 Ma) since the genus occurs so broadly through the Northern Hemisphere (Stebbins 1950, Grant 1994). Yet because most columbine species are interfertile and so similar genetically, they are now thought to have arisen very recently, possibly after the Mid-Pliocene (~3.5 Ma) (Hodges and Arnold 1994, Whittall and Hodges 2007). The apparently rapid rise of columbines combined with their wide distribution is still a mystery, in part because their seeds are not built to be dispersed very far from the plant.

The nectar spur in columbines, as in other flowers, is regarded as a key innovation contributing to their diversity (Hodges and Arnold 1994). In fact, spurred flower groups are often far more species-rich (Hodges et al. 2003). Floral spurs have evolved at least fifteen times in different flower genera (Hodges 1997). Of eight plant groups in which spurred and nonspurred sister groups were compared, seven of the eight spurred groups had many more species than their spurless sister taxa in the same period of time.

Floral spurs allow flowers to attract particular types of pollinators: those with tongues or beaks long enough to reach the nectar at the base of the spurs. This limits the pollinators to fewer species of insects or birds, making it more likely that the pollen will be exchanged only with plants that have the same type of flower.

Much of the divergence in *Aquilegia* is related to increases in spur length, which happened largely among North American species. Some longer-spurred flowers are more effectively pollinated than shorter-spurred flowers by hawkmoths, whose long tongues remove more pollen (Hodges et al. 2003). If spurs are too short relative to a specific pollinator's tongue, pollen is neither removed from the anthers nor deposited on the stigma. Similarly, in a study of the spurred orchids *Plantanthera* and *Disa* flowers with longer spurs had greater seed set because they received more pollen (Nilsson 1988).

According to Nilsson (1988), pollinators will extend their mouthparts only as far as needed to gather nectar. If a flower's spur is shorter than the pollinator's tongue, nectar is gathered without much or any contact with the pollen-bearing anthers or the female receptive stigma. By contrast, if a flower's nectar spur, or tubular corolla, is as long as or longer than the pollinator's tongue, the pollinator will have greater contact with the stigma and anthers. Flowers with longer spurs thus receive pollen mostly from similarly shaped flowers, which can lead to isolation and "directional selection" toward longer spurs.

The spur lengths of North American columbines vary from 0.3 to 4.8 inches (7.5–123 mm), while those of Eurasian columbines (their likely Beringial ancestors) are much shorter and less variable (0.15–0.8 inches [4.0–21.5 mm]) (Whittall and Hodges 2007). A key difference is that the ancestral Eurasian species are largely pollinated by bees (usually bumblebees), although hawkmoths also occur there (Grant 1994). Hummingbirds, important western pollinators, occur only in the New World.

Based on an analysis of the twenty-five North American species, Whittall and Hodges (2007) determined that columbines with short spurs tend to be pollinated by bees, flies, and generalist pollinators, while species with intermediate-length spurs are pollinated by hummingbirds, and those with the longest spurs are pollinated largely by hawkmoths, which have the longest tongues. (Sphingid moths, for example, such as *Sphinx vashti* and *Manduca* spp., have tongues between 2.1 and 5.4 inches [54–137 mm] long.) Flower color and orientation further enhance this pattern: bee-pollinated flowers tend to be blue or purple (Plate 36), hummingbird flowers red, and hawkmoth flowers white or lightly colored (Plate 37). Pollinators such as hummingbirds favor nodding, downturned flowers that they can hover under, whereas hawkmoths hover and probe flowers from above (Grant 1992). Among the North American columbine lineage, Whittall and Hodges (2007) discovered

two shifts from bumblebee to hummingbird pollination, and five shifts from hummingbird to hawkmoth pollination. While all of these flowers are visited by a great variety of pollinators, as well as nectar thieves, each type has some that are more effective than others.

Alcove columbine (*A. micrantha*), a smaller, pale pink or white columbine found in hanging gardens in canyons on the Colorado Plateau, is pollinated to a large degree by bumblebees (*Bombus* spp.), which feed on its pollen as well as its nectar, but it is also frequently visited by hummingbirds and hawkmoths (Miller and Willard 1983). Its spurs are short (< 0.8 inches [20 mm]), which allows access to the shorter-tongued bumblebees (Whittall and Hodges 2007). Hummingbirds have also been documented pollinating alcove columbine, attracted by its more-dilute nectar (20–25 percent sucrose versus > 30 percent sucrose in exclusively bee-pollinated columbines). Western columbine is a classic hummingbird-pollinated flower. It has short, pendant, flowers with red spurs (~0.6–0.8 inches [15–20 mm] long) and occurs through much of western North America (Hodges 1997, Whittall and Hodges 2007). Its reproductive parts, stamens and pistils, extend beyond the flower petals, making their contact with hummingbirds all the more likely.

Even within columbine species, variation in flower color and spur length can lead to pollination by different types of pollinators. One study (Miller 1981) found that in populations with white and blue flowers, the blue flowers had greater seed set in years when pollen-foraging bumblebees were abundant, and white flowers had better seed set in years when hawkmoths were plentiful.

Yellow columbine (*A. chrysantha* [Plate 38]) is one of the longest-spurred

columbines in Arizona and New Mexico (<
1.6 inches [40 mm] long), and its upright
flowers are pollinated by hawkmoths; its
nectar cannot be reached by hummingbirds
or most bees (Miller 1985). Like Colorado
columbine, its Rocky Mountain relative, this
species produces large amounts of pollen. Its
range extends from the southern edge of the
Colorado Plateau into northern Mexico.

Species such as columbine, though
strongly benefited by pollinators, are self-
compatible to a degree, meaning that they
can use their own pollen to fertilize their
eggs. Based on caging experiments in which
pollinators were excluded, Colorado columbine had 39 percent seed set (Miller 1978),
yellow columbine 31 percent (Miller 1985),
and alcove columbine 25 percent (Miller and
Willard 1983). This, in combination with
their perennial habit, may afford columbines
survival and reproduction through self-pollination if pollinators are lacking. Though
self-fertilization may not produce as many
seeds, it surely beats extinction.

*Penstemon*

While the nectar spur in columbines
determines which pollinators will be successful, in *Penstemon* spp. the entire
flower—a single, fused corolla—determines
who its pollinators will be. This New World
group, which is in the snapdragon family (Scrophulariaceae), is the largest plant
genus endemic to North America (Wolfe et
al. 2006). There are more than 270 species
of penstemon in North America, and collectively they extend from Alaska to Guatemala. Most species (85–90 percent) occur
within the Western Cordillera. They reach
their greatest diversity in the Intermountain
region (Wolfe et al. 2002, Wolfe et al. 2006).
There are nearly 70 species in Utah alone,
and many of these species are represented

by numerous varieties (Welsh et al. 1993).
Most species have a narrow distribution,
and more than 100 of them in the United
States are endemic to a single state. Much
of this diversity is attributed to evolutionary adaptations to particular pollinators, the
diverse ecological niches found in western
North America's complicated terrain (Fig.
1.1), and possibly the extreme climatic shifts
of the Pleistocene (Wolfe et al. 2006). Even
challenging habitats such as the salty lakebeds left over in the cold desert have been
colonized by penstemon. Some diversity is
also due to hybridization and polyploidy
(Wolfe et al. 2006).

According to recent DNA analyses, penstemon probably originated in the Rocky
Mountains by the end of the Tertiary (~1.6
Ma) (Wolfe et al. 2006). From there it spread
through the Cascade–Sierra Nevada cordillera, through the Intermountain region and
the Southwest, and finally over the Rocky
Mountains and into eastern North America
(Wolfe et al. 2006).

More than 80 percent of penstemon species are pollinated by bees, who are well
rewarded for their services (Wilson et al.
2006). Bee pollination is thought to be the
"pleisiomorphic," or original, condition in
penstemon (Wolfe et al. 2006). Bee-pollinated species typically have purple, blue-vio-
let, or yellow flowers, and wide floral tubes
(or corollas) that bees, wasps, and flies can
easily enter to gather nectar. Bee-pollinated
flowers produce a concentrated nectar that
bees prefer. In one study, twenty-one bee-
pollinated penstemon species were found
to offer pollinators a median sugar concentration of 36 percent in nectar; Rocky
Mountain penstemon (*P. strictus* [Plate 39])
produce even more concentrated nectar (a
sugar concentration of 42 percent) and, like
other penstemon, are able to replenish it

within a couple hours (Wilson et al. 2006, Castellanos et al. 2002). Nectar can be replenished many times in individual flowers, which leads to intense pollinator traffic, including more than 100 bumblebee visits per day (Williams and Thomson 1998).

As successful as bee pollination is, shifts in penstemon to bird pollination may have occurred as many as fifteen to twenty times across the genus (Andrea Wolfe, personal communication; Thomson and Wilson 2008). Penstemon flowers that are adapted for hummingbird pollination are radically different from bee-pollinated flowers, having a very narrow, red corolla that excludes most other pollinators. Today nearly forty penstemon species (~15 percent) are pollinated by hummingbirds (Plate 40; Wilson et al. 2006). The relative rarity of hummingbird pollination in penstemon and other North American genera may be related to a greater risk of extinction due to extreme specialization, suggesting that hummingbird pollination tends to be an evolutionary dead end (Wilson et al. 2006). As with columbines, no shifts from bird- to bee-pollinated penstemon species are known to have occurred. In one of the most widespread hummingbird penstemons, scarlet bugler (*P. barbatus* [Plate 41]), the stamens and stigma extend outside the flower, so when a hummingbird inserts its beak, its head and beak inadvertently collect and/or deposit pollen. Small bees are among the few insects that can fit into these flowers, but they have little contact with the exserted stamens and pistels and so don't help with pollination.

The effects of this specialization on bee pollination became very evident recently as I watched pollinators visit large patches of purple Rocky Mountain penstemon and red scarlet bugler at the Flagstaff Arboretum.

The penstemon patch was abuzz with many, many bees and flies, but few pollinators were visiting the hummingbird-pollinated scarlet bugler. The only insects on its flowers were larger bees that couldn't fit into the narrow corollas and so were chewing through their bases to get to the nectar. Such nectar thieves can cause significant damage, but despite this, hummingbird-pollinated penstemons such as scarlet bugler usually produce many seeds.

The nectar produced by hummingbird flowers is different than that of bee-pollinated species. One survey of fourteen hummingbird-pollinated penstemon species showed that these flowers produce a greater volume of nectar, but it is more dilute, having a median sugar concentration of 26 percent—perhaps because hummingbirds need more water (Wilson et al. 2006). Production of a greater volume of nectar may be the first step in a shift toward hummingbird pollination in penstemons (Wilson et al. 2006). It is thought that hummingbirds don't often visit Rocky Mountain penstemon, even though they can access its nectaries, because it produces less, more concentrated nectar than other species.

When hummingbirds are available, their penstemon hosts are well served. In experiments studying pollen transfer, Wilson et al. (2006) determined that hummingbirds removed an average of 9,684 pollen grains from fifteen scarlet bugler flowers, versus 3,184 from fifteen Rocky Mountain penstemons. They also deposited more pollen grains on the scarlet bugler stigmas. Hummingbirds are such effective pollinators because the scarlet bugler flower provides a better fit. They are after nectar rather than pollen, unlike many bees, which feed on both.

Some species, such as the "spectacular" penstemon (*P. pseudospectabilis*), attract both bees and hummingbirds with corollas that are the right length for hummingbird beaks but also wide enough to admit bees (Lange and Scott 1999). Rarer shifts in penstemon have been toward long-tongued fly pollination (one species), butterfly pollination (one species), and large or small bee pollination (six species) (Wilson et al. 2006).

Most western penstemons are adapted to dry conditions and a diversity of soil types, with different species found in substrates such as sand, talus, shales, and clays (Nold 1999). The endemic Sunset Crater penstemon (*P. clutei*), which originated on very young volcanic cinders (less than 1,000 years old) in northern Arizona, requires well-drained soils (Fule et al. 2001). While most penstemons are adapted to xeric habitats, some polyploid species, such as *P. digitalis* and *P. globosus,* can tolerate moist habitats (Wolfe et al. 2002).

Penstemon are also tolerant of disturbance and, as such, are often rather short-lived as they are gradually outcompeted by other plants (Nold 1999). Given their adaptability, penstemon were likely able to colonize the wide array of habitats created by the turbulent climates of the Pleistocene. Many different penstemon species are common roadside plants in the western United States, but they are unlikely to persist in gardens for long without succumbing to disease. A lack of competitiveness often goes along with the pioneering or disturbance-adapted tendency, as in the case of Sunset Crater penstemon, which was found to benefit from trenching experiments that eliminated root competition from nearby plants (Fule et al. 2001).

## Dayflower

While columbines and penstemons produce a considerable amount of nectar to attract pollinators, the dayflower (*Commelina dianthifolia* [Plate 42]) has taken a very different approach. In fact, it is a master of deception, producing no nectar but instead luring pollinators in with the false promise of a hefty pollen reward. This extraordinarily beautiful flower is my absolute favorite in the Flagstaff area.

The distribution of dayflower, which is in the spiderwort family (Commelinaceae), is strongly tied to that of the summer monsoon season in the southwestern United States, which extends into southern Utah. If the monsoon is weak, the perennial dayflower will not emerge. When it does, however, this clonal species can form large patches, with each inflorescence producing one flower each day. Flower production typically begins around 5 a.m., and by 11 a.m. the flowers are spent. This is a good strategy because monsoon storms that can impede pollinators usually occur in the afternoon. With each individual inflorescence producing up to ten flowers, and inflorescences flowering at different times, a stand may flower for over a month.

The dayflower is very striking, with three brilliant cobalt blue petals and plump, bright yellow stamenlike structures that appear loaded with pollen. These bright yellow structures are actually staminodes that produce very little pollen, and pollen that is less viable than that produced by the true stamens (30 percent versus > 90 percent viability [Hrycan and Davis 2005]). When insects visit these "fake" stamens, they unwittingly pollinate the stigma and/or collect pollen on their abdomens from the true stamens lying below. The true stamens and the stigma are somewhat cryptic, having nearly the same color as the petals. The dayflowers in my backyard appear to be pollinated primarily by flies, as has been reported for the Asiatic dayflower (*C. communis*) (Ushimaru et al. 2007).

Pollination must occur quickly in such a short-lived flower. Toward the end of a flower's life, the female stigma curls up and comes into contact with the central stamen (which produces the most pollen), so if a flower has not been pollinated, it will essentially pollinate itself (Hrycan and Davis 2005). Seed set from self-pollination can be fairly high in the dayflower. The ability of many flowers to be at least somewhat self-pollinating is a crucial survival strategy, especially if pollinator populations decrease, as is happening with bees. Nonnative bees that pollinate agricultural crops are disappearing from hives at alarming rates, and some native bees, including bumblebees, are also declining, though patterns are less clear and are currently being studied (Board of Life Sciences and Board of Agricultural and Natural Sciences 2007).

## Paintbrush

Indian paintbrush (*Castilleja* spp.) belongs to the subfamily Rhinanthoidae (Scrophulariaceae), some of whose members are partially parasitic on other plants (Plate 43). Ranging in color from nearly purple to scarlet to yellow, Indian paintbrush is commonly seen in meadows and along streams and roadways. With 200 to 250 species (Heckard 1968), this large genus presents significant taxonomic challenges. Their habitats range from alpine areas to deserts, and most species occur in western North America. Several species also occur in eastern North America and Asia, and about 15 species occur in South America (Benson 1979).

Much of Indian paintbrush's diversity and complexity can be attributed to the fact that at least half of its species are polyploid; as a result, its numbers of chromosomes range from 12 to 72 (Heckard 1968). Polyploidy, or multiplication of chromosome sets, has played a major role in the evolution of this genus, as well as most other flowering plants, probably because it can create barriers to interbreeding between different ploidy races, and because this increase in chromosomes often enables plants to tolerate different conditions (Heckard and Chuang 1977). Some individual paintbrush species are even represented by multiple ploidy numbers (Heckard 1968), which certainly challenges the notion of species being made up of populations that can interbreed (Futuyma 1986). For instance, the widespread western scarlet paintbrush (*C. miniata*) has at least four different chromosome races ($n$ = 12, 24, 48, 60), and where they overlap, a diversity in traits such as flower color and microhabitat preferences is seen. Their diversity is also increased by considerable hybridization.

In the Intermountain West, small ranges, such as the Uinta Mountains in Utah, often support four to nine species of paintbrush, with each occupying very different habitats, flowering at different times, and/or having different ploidy races. The annual *C. minor* is common in wet and alkaline valleys, while *C. chromosa* and *C. linarifolia* occur together on dry sagebrush slopes, with one flowering after the other. Western scarlet paintbrush is the most common species in moist montane settings in the Rocky Mountains.

As with penstemons, many paintbrush species (about forty-eight) in western North America are pollinated by hummingbirds (Grant 1994). Others are pollinated by bees, butterflies, and other insects (Adler 2003). The pollination and reproductive success of Indian paintbrush are much influenced by their hemiparasitic habit and the type of plants they parasitize (Matthies 1997, Adler 2003). Unlike fully parasitic plants—such as yellow mistletoes, which contain little or no chlorophyll and depend entirely on their hosts for nutrients, energy, and water—Indian paintbrush do photosynthesize. Some species can survive and even reproduce without parasitizing another plant, though many cannot. *C. integra* suffers great mortality without a host plant, while *C. miniata* and *C. chromosa* can persist and grow without hosts, though fare better with one (Matthies 1997). Paintbrush typically grow in association with meadow plants such as grasses and wildflowers, including lupine, and they grow more and produce more seeds when their haustoria (or parasitic hookups) are attached to the roots of nitrogen-fixing lupines rather than grasses. Lynn Adler (2002) found that *C. miniata* that parasitized native lupines rather than grasses produced many more flowers, which in turn attracted more pollinating bees. Ultimately, these plants produced three times more seeds than those that had parasitized grasses.

The cost of supporting Indian paintbrush and related hemiparasitic taxa can be quite high for host plants and plant communities (Matthies 1997, Adler 2002, Marvier 1998). Species such as *C. integra*, which are especially dependent on hosts for survival and growth, can reduce host plant growth by as much as 70 percent (Matthies 1997).

*Scarlet Gilia*

Scarlet gilia (*Ipomopsis aggregata* [Plate 44]), with its showy red inflorescence, is largely pollinated by hummingbirds and hawkmoths, a relationship that is thought to be mutually beneficial. Although typically hummingbird pollinated, some populations of scarlet gilia produce lighter-colored flowers late in the season that are pollinated more often by hawkmoths as hummingbirds begin to migrate south (Paige and Whitham 1985).

Scarlet gilia is a widespread biennial or short-lived perennial that occurs throughout western North America from warm desert shrub sites to alpine meadows (Welsh et al. 1993). It is a member of the phlox family (Polemoniaceae), found almost entirely in the Western Hemisphere except for several species in Eurasia (Benson 1979). Nearly all scarlet gilia species occur in western North America, with more than twenty-five in Utah alone. There are at least four varieties of scarlet gilia in the West (Welsh et al. 1993).

Scarlet gilia grows as a low rosette for one to five years, after which it produces a single flower stalk lined with red, trumpet-shaped flowers. Being semelparous, it only reproduces once, and then dies after flowering and fruit set.

Scarlet gilia sometimes has a mutualistic relationship with browsing mammals, and under certain conditions it produces more seeds when animals feed on it. This effect is entirely contrary to the long-held view that herbivory, or plant feeding, has a negative effect on plants by removing tissue and ultimately reducing a plant's fitness or reproductive success (Crawley 1983, Marquis 1992). Nonetheless, species such as scarlet gilia, wild radish, field gentian, and many grasses have all been shown to benefit from herbivory under certain conditions (Agrawal 2000).

When scarlet gilia has ample water, nutrients, and light, it can produce more seeds after it is fed upon than it would otherwise. This phenomenon is referred to as *overcompensation*, since the plant is not merely compensating for flower loss due to herbivory but sometimes doubling its seed production. When it finally reproduces, scarlet gilia produces a single flower stem. Taller stems make the flowers more visible to pollinators, but also to browsing mammals such as mule deer and elk. In Arizona, up to 90 percent of plants are browsed in some years (Gronemeyer et al. 1997), and a study at Fern Mountain, near Flagstaff, showed that browsing mammals removed up to 95 percent of each plant's aboveground biomass (Paige and Whitham 1987).

The apex of scarlet gilia's single flower stalk actually inhibits lateral branch growth (probably by hormones), and this is referred to as apical dominance. When this flower stalk is browsed, however, apical dominance is eliminated, and many lateral flower stalks are produced off of the remaining stem. These multiple inflorescences can produce more flowers and, ultimately, twice as many seeds as unbrowsed plants (Paige and Whitham 1987, Maschinski and Whitham 1989). Such a response to browsing is dependent on favorable conditions, including the herbivory occurring early enough in the season that plants can produce new stems, flowers, and seeds. The ability of scarlet gilia to overcompensate also depends on limited subsequent herbivory, and indeed most browsing does occur early on and only once (Juenger and Bergelson 2000, Levine and Paige 2004). When elk and deer at Fern Mountain do return to a previously browsed stand, they typically eat only the terminal ends of the regrown, multiple-stemmed plants and so have little effect on final reproduction (Paige 1992). This may be due to the presence of chemical defenses in regrown tissue: Juenger et al. (2005) found that seeds from browsed scarlet gilia were less susceptible to fly damage

than those of nonbrowsed flowers. This provides preliminary evidence for the defensive function of cucurbitacin B in scarlet gilia, since it occurred at higher levels in browsed plants. Thus it seems that, under favorable conditions, early browsing stimulates greater seed production *and* better protection for those seeds.

Other western populations of scarlet gilia do not exhibit overcompensation, and in fact, some populations fare worse when browsed (e.g., Juenger and Bergelson 1997, 2000). Such variation in responses may result from different site conditions or perhaps even browsing history. During drought conditions, the ability of scarlet gilia to overcompensate is lost, and unbrowsed plants produce more seeds than browsed plants. This shows how mutualism in this case is dependent on available resources such as water, pollinators, light, and nutrients. Arizona is currently experiencing its worst drought on record, and the lack of water has prevented a normally overcompensating scarlet gilia population from even compensating for herbivore damage (Levine and Paige 2004). Additionally, ungulates have been browsing scarlet gilia at unprecedented levels during this drought, which has led to decreased seed production and undercompensation. All previously browsed plants were browsed a second time, resulting in severe damage to lateral branches. In nondrought years, only 30 percent of plants were secondarily browsed.

The question raised by an adaptation like this is, why don't plants that only reproduce once reproduce maximally without having to be browsed first? It may be that because scarlet gilia is so predictably damaged by early season migratory herbivores, it holds back up to 80 percent of its reproductive energy until it is cued by the herbivory itself since there is less risk of later herbivory (Agrawal 2000). Scarlet gilia is so likely to experience early, significant herbivory that its initial production of only one flower stalk with a small number of seeds is merely a prelude to its ultimately larger reproductive output after being browsed. Add to this sometimes-mutualistic system additional factors such as limited pollination and damage by other herbivores—ranging from ground squirrels to lepidopteran fruit predators, aphids, and root-boring flies (Juenger and Bergelson 1998)—and it is hard to imagine how these plants survive to produce any seeds. But when you see a scarlet gilia with multiple stems, it may be headed for enormous reproductive success!

## Buckwheats

Buckwheat (*Eriogonum* spp.) is endemic to North America (Shields and Reveal 1988). Like penstemon it is a highly diverse genus. Most of its 250 species occur in western North America, with more than 50 species in Utah alone; most of these are also represented by numerous varieties (Welsh et al. 1993). Taxonomically, buckwheat is one of the most difficult plant groups in North America. According to James Reveal (1979), the genus probably arose during the Miocene in expanding, arid grasslands and shrub regions of North America, and successfully adapted to the drying trend that continued into the Pliocene. During the Pliocene and Pleistocene, buckwheat underwent rapid and explosive evolutionary differentiation, producing an array of new species that are mostly drought tolerant and occur mainly in arid and semiarid regions (Shields and Reveal 1988). Some species, such as *E. nummulare,* adapted to the salty lakebeds left over from the Pleistocene. The distributions of modern species were altered during and since the last glacial episode of the Pleistocene (Shields and Reveal 1988).

As with so many western plants, polyploidy is found extensively in buckwheat. Perhaps, in response to increasing aridity, all of its diploid ancestors and even early members of the genus were replaced by tetraploid offshoots by the Mid-Pliocene (Shields and Reveal 1988). Many species, such as *E. nudum,* are represented by individuals with different numbers of sets of chromosomes (Reveal, eFloras.org).

Drought tolerance in desert-dwelling buckwheat sometimes involves early spring growth as a means of avoiding dry, hot summer conditions. Desert trumpet (*E. inflatum*) lives in both the cold and warm deserts of western North America and is well adapted for tolerating summer conditions. While it was once thought that its conspicuous inflated green stems were the result of insect damage (Stone and Mason 1979), it is now known that they enable it to continue to photosynthesize and grow into the summer months, long after many other ephemeral desert plants have set seed and gone dormant or died (Price 1982, Smith and Osmond 1987). Desert trumpet's basal leaf rosette photosynthesizes through much of the spring. As its development peaks, multiple green, inflated flower stems emerge from the base and assume much of the job of photosynthesis for several more months, with those stems ultimately accounting for more than 75 percent of a plant's total photosynthetic surface. The stems are more efficient with water at warmer temperatures, in part because their vertical shape keeps them cooler than basal leaves heated by the ground (Price 1982, Smith and Osmond 1987).

Perhaps due to their rapid evolution during the turbulent Pleistocene, many buckwheat species are adapted to or at least tolerant of disturbance. Species such as *E. brandegeei* and *E. lewisii* are commonly seen along western roadways (Anderson 2006). Many other species, however, are endemics with very small ranges (Shields and Reveal 1988), and not surprisingly many of them are endangered. The entire range of steamboat buckwheat (*E. ovalifolium* v. *williamsiae*) consists of a mere 250 acres in rocklike deposits in Nevada precipitated from thermal spring flows (Archibald et al. 2001). A related variety, *E. ovalifolium* v. *vineum*, is endemic to limestone and dolomite substrates found within a 50-square-mile region of southern California (Neel et al. 2001). While there is concern about the ability of rare or endemic species to maintain genetic diversity, since they typically have greater rates of self-pollination and inbreeding, species such as *E. ovalifolium* v. *williamsiae* have greater levels of genetic diversity than many common, widespread species (Anderson 2006).

Today, buckwheat occurs throughout the western United States in habitats ranging from sea level to more than 13,000 feet (Pratt 1994). Species occur from the Pacific shoreline to the shale barrens of the Appalachian Mountains, and from Central America to Alaska (Shields and Reveal 1988). In northern Arizona, buckwheat can be found from cold desert slickrock to high-elevation meadows. Some species also grow above treeline in the Rockies and the Sierra Nevada.

Buckwheat is an annual or perennial herb or shrub (Shields and Reveal 1988) whose flowers are typically presented in flat-topped clusters (like umbels) or on stalks (also called "racemes"). Most species

have perfect (hermaphroditic) flowers, but several are dioecious. Buckwheat flowers range from requiring outcrossing to being self-pollinating (Moldenke 1976). The pollen-bearing anthers of many species begin producing pollen several days before the female stigma is ready to receive it. When the stigma does become receptive, it will either be self-fertilized or outcrossed (Anderson 2006). Steamboat buckwheat is self-compatible, but it requires a pollinator to transfer pollen from its stamen to its stigma (Archibald et al. 2001).

Buckwheat is typically pollinated by generalist pollinators such as flies and bees, and there is no clear evidence of the specialization of other species (Neel et al. 2001). It produces large amounts of nectar, especially when all the flowers of an inflorescence bloom together. Not surprisingly, Mohave buckwheat (*E. fasciculatum*) is regarded as the most important native nectar plant in California (Reveal, personal communication, 2007).

Buckwheat's entire reproductive cycle, from flowering through seed set, occurs over a brief four- to six-week period between March and November. Flowering times vary tremendously between species and even among populations within species. *E. nudum*, for example, has ten geographic varieties with different bloom times ranging from March to September (Shields and Reveal 1988). The fact that most buckwheat species have a short flowering/fruiting season and great variability in when they bloom has made for complex evolutionary interactions with a group of butterflies (*Euphilotes* spp., Lycaenidae) that use its flowers and seeds to feed their larvae.

*Euphilotes* butterflies are also called "buckwheat blues" since their larvae feed only on buckwheat (Plate 45; Brock and

Kaufman 2003). The interactions between these two species show how some plant-feeding insects may originate. These beautiful little blue butterflies (the males of which have silvery blue wings) are commonly seen in summer around water or wet soil. The five *Euphilotes* species have given rise to several dozen subspecies that have radiated within the buckwheat genus. So far they have been found on about 20 percent of all buckwheat species (Pratt 1994). Like their buckwheat hosts, they occur mainly in western North America.

Each summer *Euphilotes* emerge as winged adults just as their particular buckwheat host species starts to bloom. Adults only live for about a week, during which time they must locate a suitable host plant, find a mate, and lay eggs. Clearly, *Euphilotes* flight time must be synchronized with its host's blooming time to ensure reproductive success. Hatching larvae feed on pollen and developing seeds, and will spend their entire life feeding on the buckwheat they hatch on. Mature larvae crawl to the ground, burrow 4 inches into the soil, pupate, and overwinter; the development time from oviposition to pupation is about three weeks (Pratt 1994).

Although we do not know how most species arise, life histories suggest that some could have diverged from their parent species without experiencing geographic separation. This is referred to as *sympatric speciation,* or "the establishment of new populations of a species in different ecological niches within the cruising range of the individuals of the parental population" (Mayr 1963). The *Euphilotes* found on western buckwheat is one such group (Pratt 1994). While some species seem to have arisen in geographic isolation, very closely related sister subspecies or races of *Euphilotes* butterflies occur in the same area, or sympatrically,

and may have become isolated and diverged genetically from one another in sympatry. The key to this possibility lies in the combination of the very brief time within which adult butterflies mate *and* the differing flowering times of the buckwheats. These sympatric populations have become separated from parental populations not in space, but in time.

Gordon Pratt (1994) has studied several such complexes of sympatric *Euphilotes.* Several races of *Euphilotes enoptes* are sympatric throughout the Mohave Desert, with one colonizing *E. pusillum* while the other colonizes *E. wrightii.* Their adults emerge about 120 days apart (Pratt 1994). Such different emergence times effectively eliminate the possibility of gene flow between these populations. Several sympatric races of *E. battoides* at Westward Pass, California, colonize different buckwheat species and are separated from one another in time: race 1 adults emerge in late May to colonize blooming *E. ovalifolium,* while race 2 adults emerge in mid-July to colonize blooming *E. umbellatum* (Pratt and Emmel 1998).

Although there are clear differences in flowering times among *Eriogonum* species and in emergence times among *Euphilotes,* there is also some variation within each, which may stem from genetic variation and weather. Such variation could be highly adaptive in this system, and perhaps provide endless opportunities for *Euphilotes* to colonize new buckwheat hosts as their flowers become available. Given the very short time that *Euphilotes* adults have to find one another and reproduce, it probably would not take much of a shift in timing of flowering and emergence to effectively isolate populations. According to Gordon Pratt (1994), some host races may have formed toward the end of the Pleistocene and during the warmer, drier Holocene, when temperature changes and alternating periods of drought and abundant rain in the deserts may have caused changes in host bloom time as well as host shifts/and or seasonal shifts in *Euphilotes* activity. *E. enoptes,* in particular, is flexible about the buckwheat species it colonizes; individual races may use four to five different species—as long as they have appropriate flowering times (Pratt 1994).

Other butterfly groups have radiated similarly within the widespread and diverse buckwheat genus, including the Mormon metalmark complex (*Apodemia mormo*), which is comprised of at least five subspecies (Emmel et al. 1998, Pratt and Ballmer 1991). Three sympatric groups within this species colonize desert trumpet, Mohave buckwheat, and later-blooming buckwheat species. Among the other associated butterflies are at least six species of hairstreaks (*Callophrys* spp.), the varied blue (*Chalceria heteronea*), Gorgon copper (*Gaeides gorgon*), Edward's blue (*Hemiargus ceranus gyas*), blue copper (*Lycaena heteronea*), small blue (*Philotiella speciosa*), Boisduval's blue (*Plebeius icarioides*), acmon blue (*P. acmon*), lupine blue (*P. lupini*), veined blue (*P. neurona*), California hairstreak (*Satyrium californica*), nut-brown hairstreak (*S. saepium*), Avalon scrub-hairstreak (*Strymon avalona*), gray hairstreak (*S. melinus*), and many more as yet undescribed subspecies (Reveal, eFloras.org). Numerous other insects also feed on this significant plant resource.

\* \* \*

In summary, though they represent only a small sample, the diversity of species, subspecies, and races of western flowers mentioned here reveals the dynamic history of our western landscapes and the life forms that have evolved with them. But how will these species respond to global warming and extensive human impacts? As mentioned above, declining bee populations are resulting in a lack of incoming pollen, which could challenge the survival of many flowering plants, especially those that have become specialized in the pollinators they interact with (Buchmann and Nabhan 1996).

Given the potential loss of pollinators, it is important that many of these western plants exhibit at least a small degree of self-compatibility. While such inbreeding often has a deleterious outcome—and, in fact, self-incompatibility has arisen many times among plants, probably in response to such effects (Knight et al. 2005)—self-compatibility seems like a good alternative to extinction. There is also evidence that the selfing rate may increase in some fractured and declining plant populations (Murawski and Hamrick 1991, Franceschinelli and Bawa 2000, Ashman et al. 2004). Western flowers, however, have encountered and survived radical changes before, including extreme climate fluctuations, population declines, isolation and even losses of pollinators, eventually developing into the beautiful and diverse species that we see around us today.

# Some Common Plants and Animals of the Southern Rockies and the Intermountain Region

WESTERN RIPARIAN PLANTS
Alder (*Alnus* spp.)
Arrowweed (*Pluchea sericea*)
Arroyo willow (*Salix lasiolepis*)
Black cottonwood (*Populus trichocarpa*)
Box elder (*Acer negundo*)
Brickellbush (*Brickellia longifolia*)
Catclaw acacia (*Acacia greggii*)
Cattail (*Typha* spp.)
Common reed (*Phragmites australis*)
Coyote willow (*Salix exigua*)
Desert olive (*Forestiera pubescens*)
Fremont cottonwood (*Populus fremontii*)
Goodding willow (*Salix gooddingii*)
Maiden-hair fern (*Adiantum capillus-veneris*)
Monkey flower (*Mimulus* spp.)
Narrowleaf cottonwood (*Populus angustifolia*)
Native grape (*Vitis* spp.)
Redbud (*Cercis occidentalis*)
Rush (*Juncus* spp., *Scirpus* spp.)
Russian olive (*Elaeagnus angustifolia*)
Sedge (*Carex* spp.)
Seep willow (*Baccharis salicifolia, B. sarothroides, B. emoryi*)
Tamarisk (*Tamarix chinensis*)
Water birch (*Betula occidentalis*)
Western honey mesquite (*Prosopis glandulosa*)

COMMON RIPARIAN ANIMALS
Beaver (*Castor canadensis*)
Cinnamon teal (*Anas cyanoptera*)
Desert spiny lizard (*Sceloporus magister*)
Gadwall (*Anas strepera*)
Mallard (*A. platyrhynchos*)
Muskrat (*Ondatrazibethicus*)
Northern pintail (*A. acuta*)
Northern shoveler (*A. clypeata*)
Side-blotched lizard (*Uta stansburiana*)
Tree lizard (*Urosaurus ornatus*)
Western whiptail lizard (*Cnemidophorus tigris*)
Yellow warbler (*Dendroica pelechia*)

MOUNTAIN PLANTS

Actinea (*Hymenoxys* spp.*)*
Alpine avens (*Geum rossii*)
Alpine bistort (*Polygonum viviparum*)
Alpine campion (*Silene acaulis*)
Alpine sedge (*Kobresia myosuroides*)
Aspen (*Populus tremuloides*)
Bigtooth maple (*Acer grandidentatum*)
Blue spruce (*Picea parryana*)
Bluebell (*Mertensia* spp.*)*
Bluegrass (*Poa* spp.)
Bristlecone pine (*Pinus aristata*)
Buckwheat (*Bistorta* spp. and
    *Eriogonum* spp.*)*
Buttercup (*Ranunculus* spp.*)*
Cinquefoil (*Geum* spp.*, Potentilla* spp.*)*
Common juniper (*Juniperus communis*)
Cushion paronychia (*Paronychia pulvinata*)
Douglas fir (*Pseudotsuga menziesii*)
Fescue (*Festuca* spp.)
Foothills kittentail (*Besseya plantaginea*)
Goldenrod (*Solidago* spp.*)*
Great Basin bristlecone (*Pinus longaeva*)
Jacob's-ladder (*Polemonium* spp.*)*
Limber pine (*Pinus flexilis*)
Lodgepole pine (*P. contorta*)
Mountain sorrel (*Oxyria digyna*)
Mustard (*Draba* spp.*)*
Parry's clover (*Trifolium parryi*)
Ponderosa pine (*Pinus ponderosa*)
Pussytoes (*Antennaria* spp.*)*
Rydberg's sandwort (*Minuartia obtusiloba*)
Sage (*Artemisia* spp.*)*
Sandwort (*Arenaria* spp.)
Saxifrage (*Saxifraga* spp.*)*
Sedge (*Carex* spp.)
Southwestern white pine (*Pinus strobiformis*)
Stonecrop plants (*Sedum* spp.*)*
Tufted hairgrass (*Deschampsia caespitosa*)
White fir (*Abies concolor*)
Whitebark pine (*Pinus albicaulis*)

MOUNTAIN FOREST ANIMALS

Balsam wooly adelges (*Adelges piceae*)
Boreal toad (*Bufo boreas*)
Clark's nutcracker (*Nucifraga columbiana*)
Deer mouse (*Peromyscus maniculatus*)
Elk (*Cervus elaphus*)
Hairy and downy woodpecker (*Picoides
    villosus, P. pubescens*)
Leopard frog (*Rana pipiens*)
Mountain pine beetle (*Dendroctonus
    ponderosae*)
Pika (*Ochotona princeps*)
Pocket gopher (*Thomomys talpoides*)
Red crossbill (*Loxia curvirostra*)
Ruffed grouse (*Bonasa umbellus*)
Sapsucker (*Sphyrapicus* spp.)
Spruce beetle (*Dendroctonus rufipennis*)
Tiger salamander (*Ambystoma tigrinum*)
Western chorus frog (*Pseudacris triseriata*)
Western spruce budworm (*Archips
    fumiferana*)
White-tailed ptarmigan (*Lagopus leucura*)

PLANTS IN PONDEROSA PINE FORESTS

Arizona fescue (*Festuca arizonica*)
Blue elderberry (*Sambucus cerulea*)
Blue grama grass (*Bouteloua gracilis*)
Buckbrush (*Ceanothus* spp.)
Buckwheat (*Eriogonum* spp.)
Currants (*Ribes* spp.)
Dwarf mistletoe (*Arceuthobium vaginatum*
    ssp. *cryptopodum, A. campylopodum*)
Gambel oak (*Quercus gambelii*)
Geranium (*Geranium* spp.)
June grass (*Koeleria macrantha*)
Kentucky bluegrass (*Poa pratensis*)
Little muhly (*Muhlenbergia minutissima*)
Lupine (*Lupinus* spp.)
Manzanita (*Arctostaphylos* spp.)
Mountain mahogany (*Cercocarpus
    montanus*)
Mountain muhly (*Muhlenbergia montana*)

Muttongrass (*Poa fendleriana*)
Nodding brome (*Bromus anomalus*)
Paintbrush (*Castilleja* spp.)
Penstemon (*Penstemon* spp.)
Pine dropseed (*Blepharoneuron tricholepis*)
Rabbitbrush (*Chrysothamnus* spp.,
　Ericameria nauseosus*)
Roses (*Rosa* spp.)
Roundleaf snowberry (*Symphoricarpos
　rotundifolius*)
Scarlet gilia (*Ipomopsis aggregata*)
Serviceberry (*Amelanchier* spp.)
Skunkbush (*Rhus trilobata*)

## Animals in Ponderosa Pine Forests

Abert's squirrel (*Sciurus aberti*)
America robin (*Turdus migratorius*)
Arizona fivespined ips (*Ips lecontei*)
Black-capped and mountain chickadee
　(*Poecile atricapillus* and *P. gambeli*)
Black rattlesnake (*Crotalus viridis cerberus*)
Brown creeper (*Certhia americana*)
Cassin's finch (*Carpodacus cassinii*)
Cordilleran flycatcher (*Empidonax
　occidentalis*)
Dark-eyed junco (*Junco hyemalis*)
Evening grosbeak (*Coccothraustes
　vespertinus*)
Flycatcher (Tyrannidae)
Grace's warbler (*Dendroica graciae*)
Hermit thrush (*Catharus guttatus*)
Mexican spotted owl (*Strix occidentalis
　lucida*)
Mountain chickadee (*Poecile gambeli*)
Mountain and western bluebird (*Sialia
　currucoides* and *S. mexicana*)
Mountain pine beetle (*Dendroctonus
　ponderosae*)
Northern goshawk (*Accipiter gentilis*)
Pandora moth (*Coloradia pandora*)
Pine engraver (*Ips pini*)
Pine siskin (*Carduelis pinus*)

Pinyon jay (*Gymnorhinus cyanocephalus*)
Ponderosa pine aphid (*Cinara* spp.)
Porcupine (*Erethizon dorsatum*)
Pygmy nuthatch (*Sitta pygmaea*)
Red-breasted nuthatch (*Sitta candadensis*)
Red crossbill (*Loxia curvirostra*)
Red tree squirrel (*Tamiasciurus* spp.)
Red-faced warbler (*Cardellina rubrifrons*)
Robin (*Turdus migratorius*)
Roundheaded pine beetle (*Dendroctonus
　adjunctus*)
Skink (*Eumeces* spp.)
Sparrow (*Aimophila* spp., *Zonotrichia* spp.)
Steller's jay (*Cyanocitta stelleri*)
Swallow (Hirundinidae)
Titmice (*Baeolophus* spp.)
Twig bark beetle (*Pityophthorus* spp.)
Violet-green swallow (*Tachycineta
　thalassina*)
Western pine beetle (*Dendroctonus
　brevicomis*)
White-breasted nuthatch (*Sitta carolinensis*)
Wild turkey (*Meleagris gallopavo*)
Williamson's sapsucker (*Sphyrapicus
　thyroideus*)
Woodpecker (Picidae)
Wren (Troglodytidae)

## Pinyons, Junipers, and a Few Associated Plants

Alligator juniper (*Juniperus deppeana*)
Blue grama grass (*Bouteloua gracilis*)
Colorado pinyon (*Pinus edulis*)
Common juniper (*Juniperus communis*)
Juniper mistletoe (*Phoradendron
　juniperinum*)
One-seed juniper (*Juniperus monosperma*)
Pinyon dwarf mistletoe (*Arceuthobium
　divaricatum*)
Rocky Mountain juniper (*Juniperus
　scopulorum*)
Singleleaf pinyon (*Pinus monophylla*)

Utah juniper (*Juniperus osteosperma*)
Western juniper (*J. occidentalis*)

ANIMALS ASSOCIATED
WITH PINYONS AND JUNIPERS
Clark's nutcracker (*Nucifraga columbiana*)
Pinyon aphid (*Cinara* sp.)
Pinyon ips (*Ips confusus*)
Pinyon jay (*Gymnorhinus cyanocephalus*)
Pinyon seed-caching rodents
    Great Basin pocket mouse (*Perognathus parvus*)
    Pinyon mouse (*Peromyscus truei*)
    Deer mouse (*P. maniculatus*)
    Panamint kangaroo rat (*Dipodomys panamintinus*)
Pinyon stem-boring moth (*Dioryctria albovittella*)
Stephen's woodrat (*Neotoma stephensi*)
Townsend's solitaire (*Myadestes townsendi*)

COMMON GRASSES OF THE SOUTHERN
ROCKIES AND THE INTERMOUNTAIN REGION
Alkali sacaton (*Sporobolus airoides*)
Arizona fescue (*Festuca arizonica*)
Black dropseed (*Sporobolus interruptus*)
Black grama grass (*Bouteloua eriopoda*)
Blue grama grass (*B. gracilis*)
Cheatgrass (*Bromus tectorum*)
Deer muhly (*Muhlenbergia rigens*)
Feathergrass (*Hesperostipa [Stipa] neomexicana*)
Idaho fescue (*Festuca idahoensis*)
Indian ricegrass (*Achnatherum [Oryzopsis] hymenoides*)
Kentucky bluegrass (*Poa pratensis*)
Little bluestem (*Schizachyrium scoparium*)
Little muhly (*Muhlenbergia minutissima*)
Mountain muhly (*M. montana*)
Muttongrass (*Poa fendleriana*)

Needle-and-thread grass (*Hesperostipa [Stipa] comata*)
Nevada bluegrass (*Poa secunda*)
Ripgut brome (*Bromus rigidus*)
Saltgrass (*Distichlis* spp.)
Sand dropseed (*Sporobolus cryptandrus*)
Sandberg bluegrass (*Poa sandbergii*)
Sideoats grama (*Bouteloua curtipendula*)
Squirreltail (*Elymus elymoides*)
Three-awn (*Aristida purpurea*)
Western wheatgrass (*Pascopyrum smithii*)

ANIMALS ASSOCIATED WITH GRASSLANDS
Bison (*Bison bison*)
Chestnut-collared longspur (*Calcarius ornatus*)
Ferruginous hawk (*Buteo regalis*)
Gunnison's prairie dog (*Cynomys gunnisoni*)
Horned lark (*Eremophila alpestris*)
Long-billed curlew (*Numenius americanus*)
Mountain plover (*Charadrius montanus*)
Pronghorn (*Antilocapra americana*)
Utah prairie dog (*Cynomys parvidens*)
Western meadowlark (*Sturnella neglecta*)
White-tailed prairie dog (*Cynomys leucurus*)

SALT DESERT PLANTS
Alkali or white-flowered rabbitbrush (*Chrysothamnus albidus*)
Basin saltbush (*Atriplex tridentata*)
Blackbrush (*Coleogyne ramosissima*)
Greasewood (*Sarcobatus vermiculatus*)
Hopsage (*Grayia spinosa*)
Horsebrush (*Tetradymia* spp.)
Inkweed (*Suaeda moquinii*)
Iodinebush (*Allenrolfea occidentalis*)
Mat saltbush (*Atriplex corrugata*)
Pickleweed (*Salicornia* spp.)
Resinbush (*Vanclevea stylosa*)
Saltgrass (*Distichlis spicata*)

Sand sagebrush (*Artemisia filifolia*)

Shadscale (*Atriplex confertifolia*)

Snakeweed (*Gutierrezia sarothrae)*

Winterfat (*Krascheninnikovia [Ceratoides] lanata*)

## Plants Found Above the Salty Basins

Blackbrush (*Coleogyne ramosissima*)

Green rabbitbrush (*Chrysothamnus viscidiflorus*)

Rubber rabbitbrush (*Ericameria nauseosus*)

## Shrubs Found in Sagebrush Communities

Bitterbrush (*Purshia* spp.)

Budsage (*Picrothamnus desertorum*)

Chokecherry (*Prunus virginiana*)

Horsebrush (*Tetradymia* spp.)

Joint-fir (*Ephedra* spp.*)*

Mountain mahogany (*Cercocarpis montanus*)

Serviceberry (*Amelanchier* spp.)

Snowberry (*Symphoricarpus* spp.)

## Sagebrush Animals

Black-capped chickadee (*Poecile atricapillus*)

Black-throated sparrow (*Amphispiza bilineata*)

Side-blotched lizard (*Uta stansburiana*)

Collared lizard (*Crotaphytus* spp.)

Dark-eyed junco (*Junco hyemalis*)

Desert horned lizard (*Phrynosoma platyrhinos*)

Great Basin gopher snake (*Pituophis catenifer deserticola*)

Greater and Gunnison sage-grouse (*Centrocercus urophasianus* and *C. minimus*)

Green-tailed towhee (*Pipilo chlorurus*)

Horned lark (*Eremophila alpestris*)

House finch (*Carpodacus mexicanus*)

Lark sparrow (*Chondestes grammacus*)

Leopard lizard (*Gambelia wislizenii*)

Loggerhead shrike (*Lanius ludovicianus*)

Mountain bluebird (*Sialia currucoides*)

Pygmy rabbit (*Brachylagus idahoensis*)

Sage sparrow (*Amphispiza belli*)

Sage thrasher (*Oreoscoptes montanus*)

Sagebrush lizard (*Sceloporus graciosus*)

Striped whipsnake (*Masticophis taeniatus*)

Tiger salamander (*Ambystoma tirginum*)

Western meadowlark (*Sturnella neglecta*)

Western rattlesnake (*Crotalus viridis*)

White-crowned sparrow (*Zonotrichia leucophrys*)

## Nonnative Weeds in the West

Canada thistle (*Cirsium arvense*)

Cheatgrass (*Bromus tectorum*)

Dyer's woad (*Isatis tinctoria*)

Goatgrass (*Aegilops cylindrica*)

Halogeton (*Halogeton glomeratus*)

Hoary cress (*Cardaria draba*)

Leafy spurge (*Euphorbia esula*)

Medusahead wild rye (*Taeniatherum caput-medusae*)

Peppergrass (*Lepidium* spp.)

Red brome (*Bromus rubens*)

Russian knapweed (*Acroptilon repens*)

Spotted knapweed (*Centaurea biebersteinii*)

Tumbleweed (*Salsola tragus*)

Yellow starthistle (*Centaurea solstitialis*)

# English to Metric Conversions

Inches to centimeters:

    1 centimeter = 0.3937 inches

    1 inch = 2.54 centimeters

Feet to meters:

    1 meter = 3.281 feet

    1 foot = 0.3048 meters

    Acre = 43,500 feet$^2$

Acres to hectares:

    1 hectare = 2.47 acres

    1 acre = 0.4047 hectares

Acres to kilometers$^2$:

    1 acre = 0.004047 kilometer$^2$

    1 kilometer$^2$ = 247 acres

Miles to kilometers:

    1 mile = 5,280 feet

    1 kilometer = 3,280 feet

    1 kilometer$^2$ = 0.3861 mile$^2$

    1 mile$^2$ = 2.590 kilometers$^2$

    1 mile$^3$ = 4.168 kilometers$^3$

    1 kilometer$^3$ = 0.240 miles$^3$

Miles$^2$ to hectares:

    1 mile$^2$ = 259 hectares

Miles$^2$ to acres:

    1 mile$^2$ = 640 acres

Cubic feet per second to cubic meters per second:

    1 foot$^3$ per second = 0.028 meters$^3$ per second

    1 meter$^3$ per second = 35.315 feet$^3$ per second

Ounces to grams:

    1 gram = 0.035 ounces

    1 ounce = 28.35 grams

Ounces to milligrams (mg):

    1 ounce = 28,350 milligrams

    1 milligram = $3.527^{-05}$ ounces

Fluid ounces to microliters (μL):

    1 fluid ounce = 29,573.5 μL

    1 μL = $3.38^{-05}$ fl. oz.

Pounds to kilograms:

    1 kilogram = 2.205 pounds

    1 pound = 0.4536 kilograms

F° to C° (Celsius): °C = (5/9)( °F − 32)

# Glossary

**Angiosperms** Flowering plants, distinguished from gymnosperms by producing seeds enclosed fully by fruits. These first appear in the fossil record of the Early Cretaceous.

**Anemophily** Wind pollination.

**Anther** The male or pollen-bearing part of the stamen in flowers.

**Bajada** A broad, gently sloping depositional surface formed at the base of a mountain range in dry regions by the coalescing of individual alluvial fans.

**Boreal forest** The coniferous forest belt of the Northern Hemisphere, covering about 4.6 million square miles, which borders the tundra in the northern latitudes and mixed forests and grasslands in the southern ones.

**Browsing** Feeding on the growing tips of low tree branches and shrubs, especially by mammals such as deer and elk.

**Carbohydrate** A sugar or polymer of sugar, such as starch, glycogen, or cellulose.

**Carbon 14 dating** A radiocarbon dating technique developed in the 1940s. Willard F. Libby won a Nobel Prize in chemistry in 1960 for spearheading its discovery. This method has enabled scientists to date organic material back almost 50,000 years. Carbon has three forms, or isotopes: 12C, 13C, and 14C, with 14C being the most unstable, or radioactive. Plants and animals absorb all three carbon forms until they die; after that point, the proportion of unstable 14C can be measured to estimate the age of organic remains such as pieces of plants found in packrat middens in the western United States. The half-life of 14C is 5,730 ± 40 years.

**Chromosome** Structures containing genetic material, or DNA.

**Climax species** Plants, or communities of plants, representing either the final or an indefinitely prolonged stage of ecological succession.

**Coevolution**  Reciprocally induced evolutionary change between two or more species or populations.

**Convergent evolution**  Evolution of similar features independently in unrelated taxa, usually from different antecedent features or by different developmental pathways.

**Corolla**  Collective name for a flower's petals.

**Dioecious**  Plants having staminate (male flowers) and pistillate (female flowers) on separate plants.

**Distribution**  The geographic area within which a species lives.

**DNA**  Deoxyribonucleic acid, the molecular basis of heredity in all organisms except certain viruses. DNA encodes the amino acid sequence of enzymes and structural proteins in its sequence of four bases (thymine, adenine, cytosine and guanine).

**Ecotone**  Area of intergradation between different vegetation zones.

**Endemic**  Species whose range is restricted to a specified region or locality.

**Endophyte**  An endosymbiont, often a bacterium or fungus, that lives in a plant for at least part of its life without causing apparent disease.

**Evaporation**  Conversion of water molecules from a liquid to a gaseous form.

**Evolution**  In a broad sense, the origin of entities possessing different states of one or more characteristics, and also the sequence of changes in their proportions over time.

**Extinction**  Total loss of a species.

**Extirpation**  Loss of a species or population in some portion of its natural range.

**Fault**  A fracture in bedrock along which movement has taken place.

**Fitness**  Average contribution of one allele or genotype to succeeding generations compared with that of other alleles or genotypes.

**Flowering plants**  See *Angiosperms*.

**Forbs**  Herbaceous or nonwoody plants with flowers.

**Frugivorous**  Fruit-eating.

**Gall-forming**  A complex form of herbivory in which, typically, female insects lay eggs and possibly some virus or hormone on developing plant tissue, stimulating development of a chamber in which the insects grow and feed, later emerging as adults.

**Gene**  Functional unit of heredity.

**Genotype**  Set of genes associated with an individual.

**Grazers**  Animals, especially mammals such as cattle, that feed on grasses and low flowers.

**Gymnosperms**  Plants with naked seeds, not enclosed in an ovary.

**Hermaphroditic flower**  See *Perfect flower*.

**Hybrid**  An individual formed by the mating of genetically differentiated populations or species.

**Indehiscent**  Fruits, such as those of juniper, that do not split open at maturity.

**Invertebrates**  Animals that lack a backbone, such as insects.

**Island arc**  Curved line of islands, often formed by volcanism. Island arcs helped to build western North America.

**Keystone species**  Species whose ecological presence is key to the success of other species within its community.

**Mesic**  More moderate environmental conditions, particularly greater water availability.

**Mesophyte**  Plant growing where moisture conditions are moderate.

**Metamorphic rock**  Rock derived from any preexisting rock through changes in temperature, pressure, stress, or chemical environment.

**Migration**  Movement of populations. Traditionally applied to animals, I use the term to refer to the movement of plant populations as well. Plant migrations typically entail a range shift as plants establish by seed in a new location. During the Pleistocene, some plants migrated thousands of miles, possibly establishing a small distance at a time, over and over again, in a particular direction.

**Monoecious**  Having separate staminate (male flowers) and pistillate (female flowers) within the same plant.

**Mutualism**  Relationship in which all interacting individuals or species benefit from their mutual interaction.

**Natural selection**  Process whereby the frequency of heritable traits that better adapt a population to the environment increases from generation to generation as a result of increased reproductive success of individuals possessing these traits.

**Orogeny**  Mountain-building episode.

**Osmosis**  Movement of water across a semipermeable membrane. When the concentration of solutes is greater on one side of the membrane, the net movement of water will be from the region of lesser to the region of greater solute concentrations.

**Packrat middens**  Nests built by packrats (*Neotoma* spp.) using surrounding vegetation. Middens are found in caves and rock shelters at a range of elevations from the Arctic to Nicaragua. Packrats urinate on their nests, which crystallizes the contents and helps to protect them from weathering. Contemporary nests may contain up to 75 percent or more of surrounding plant species. These nests are abundant in the West and provide a fantastic record of western plant communities and their changes over the last 50,000 years using carbon 14 dating techniques (see *Carbon 14 dating*).

**Parallel evolution**  Evolution of similar or identical features independently in related lineages, usually based in similar modifications of the same developmental pathways.

**Passerine**  Order of songbirds.

**Perfect flower**  A flower that contains both male (stamens) and female (pistils) reproductive parts.

**Phloem**  Nutrient-conducting vascular tissue in plants.

**Photosynthesis**  Process by which plants produce carbohydrates in their leaves by absorbing atmospheric $CO_2$ through leaf pores, energy from the sun, and water from the ground. Many animals have metabolic systems that require carbohydrates for growth and energy. Another by-product of photosynthesis is atmospheric oxygen, on which most plants and animals depend.

**Pistil**  The female, ovule-bearing organ of a flower, consisting of stigma and ovary.

**Plate tectonics**  Movement of the thick plates that make up earth's outer shell and which are slowly moving and changing in size. Intense geologic activity occurs at the plate boundaries.

**Pleistocene**  The Pleistocene occurred between ~1.6 Ma and 10,000 years ago. It was a cold period in the earth's history, when glaciers expanded throughout the world in fifteen to twenty phases. Fossil records indicate massive flooding and extensive plant and animal migrations during this time.

**Pluvial** Refers to a period in the past when precipitation was greater than it is now, such as during the Pleistocene.

**Pollination** The transfer of pollen from where it was formed (the anther) to a receptive surface (usually the stigma) of plants.

**Polyploid** Possessing more than two entire chromosome complements.

**Potential evaporation** Rate of evaporation from the surface of water that has the same temperature as the adjacent atmosphere.

**Rain shadow** Areas beyond mountains that block precipitation from reaching them. Most atmospheric moisture cools, condenses, and falls to the ground as it rises up over mountains, leaving little moisture for the lee side of such barriers. As that air descends, it is warmer and drier.

**Range** Distribution of a species; where it lives.

**Riparian** Refers to streamside habitats.

**Secondary compounds** Plant-produced compounds that may function primarily to protect plants from herbivores, as does cucurbitacin B for scarlet gilia (chapter 8).

**Sedimentary rock** Rock resulting from the consolidation of loose sediments such as clay, silt, sand, or gravel that has accumulated in layers.

**Self-incompatibility** Inability to produce offspring from self-pollination.

**Semelparous, monocarpic** Perennial flowering plants that bloom only once, such as agave and scarlet gilia.

**Serotinous** Refers to pine cones covered with resins that melt at high temperatures, allowing cones to release seeds following fire.

**Sister species** Species derived from a common ancestral species shared by no other species.

**Stamen** Male organ of the flower that bears pollen.

**Stigma** Pollen-receptive portion of the female reproductive organ in plants.

**Succession** Progression of a plant community toward a climax or stable state in which species are able to withstand extremes of climate and biotic interactions, remain relatively stable in their associations, and in which the mature members of the community tend to be replaced by their own offspring.

**Synergistic** Refers to two entities that together produce a greater effect than the sum of the two acting separately.

**Tectonic forces** Forces generated from within the earth that result in uplift, movement, or deformation of part of the earth's crust.

**Vascular plants** Plants that have vascular systems made up of xylem and phloem, which transport water and nutrients.

**Vertebrate** An animal, such as an amphibian, reptile, bird, or mammal, whose spinal nerve cord is located inside a backbone, a column of bony segments called vertebrae.

**Water potential** Ability of a plant that has a low or negative water potential to draw water from surroundings with a higher (or less negative) water potential. Water typically moves from soil to plant to atmosphere along gradients from high (less negative) to low (more negative) water potential. The term also refers to the difference between the activity of water molecules in pure distilled water at atmospheric pressure and 30°C, and activity of water molecules in any other system; the addition of solutes to water decreases water potential.

**Water stress** Condition that occurs when a plant's transpiration rate, or evaporative water loss, exceeds its absorption of water.

**Western Cordillera** Mountain ranges and basins of western North America.

**Xeric** Dry.

**Xylem** Principal cells in vascular plants forming the conducting elements that carry water, dissolved salts, and sometimes previously stored food up from the roots to the leaves.

# References

Abruzzi, W.S. 1995. The social and ecological consequences of early cattle ranching in the Little Colorado River Basin. Human Ecology 23:75–98.

Adams, D.P. 1967. Late-Pleistocene and recent palynology in the central Sierra Nevada, California. *In* E.J. Cushing and A.E. Wright, eds., Quaternary Paleoecology. Yale University Press, New Haven, CT.

Adler, L. 2002. Host effects on herbivory and pollination in a hemiparasitic plant. Ecology 83:2700–2710.

———. 2003. Host species affects herbivory, pollination, and reproduction in experiments with parasitic *Castilleja*. Ecology 84:2083–2091.

Adler, R.W. 2007. Restoring Colorado River ecosystems, a troubled sense of immensity. Island Press, Washington, D.C.

Agee, J.K. 1993. Fire and weather disturbances in terrestrial ecosystems of the eastern Cascades. *In* P.F. Hessburg, coord., Eastside Forest Health Assessment, Volume III: Assessment. USDA Forest Service, Pacific Northwest Research Station, Portland, OR.

———. 1998. Fire and pine ecosystems. *In* D.M. Richardson, ed., Ecology and Biogeography of *Pinus*. Cambridge University Press, Cambridge.

Agrawal, A.A. 2000. Overcompensation of plants in response to herbivory and the by-product benefits of mutualism. Trends in Plant Science 5:309–313.

Albertson, F.W., D.A. Riegel, and G.W. Tomanek. 1966. Ecological studies of blue grama grass (*Bouteloua gracilis*). Fort Hays Studies, Science Series No. 5, Kansas State College, Hays.

Allen, C.D. 2002. Lots of lightning and plenty of people: An ecological history of fire in the upland Southwest. *In* T.R. Vale, ed., Fire, Native Peoples, and the Natural Landscape. Island Press, Washington, D.C.

Allen, C.D., and D.D. Breshears. 1998. Drought-induced shift of a forest-woodland ecotone: Rapid landscape response to climate variation. Proceedings of the National Academy of Science 95:14,839–14,842.

Allred, S. 2010. The Natural History of Tassel-eared Squirrels. University of New Mexico Press, Albuquerque.

Ambrose, S. 1996. Undaunted Courage. Simon and Schuster, New York.

Amman, G.D. 1977. Role of the mountain pine beetle in lodgepole pine ecosystems: Impact on succession. *In* W.J. Mattson, ed., The Role of Arthropods in Forest Ecosystems. Springer-Verlag, New York.

Anderson, D.G. 2006. *Eriogonum brandegeei* Rydberg (Brandegee's buckwheat): A technical conservation assessment. USDA Forest Service RMR, Species Conservation Project, Fort Collins, CO.

Anderson, L.C. 1986. An overview of the genus *Chrysothamnus* (Asteraceae). *In* E.D. McArthur and B.L. Welch, eds., Proceedings: Symposium on the Biology of *Artemisia* and *Chrysothamnus*. USDA USFS INT-200.

Anderson, R.S. 1989. Development of the southwestern ponderosa pine forests: What do we really know? *In* A. Tecle, W.W. Covington, and R.H. Hamre, eds., Multiresource Management of Ponderosa Pine Forests. USDA Forest Service GTR RM-185, 282 pp.

Andrews, E.D. 1990. Sediment transport in the Colorado River Basin. *In* Colorado River Ecology and Dam Management, Proceedings of a Symposium. National Academy Press, Washington, D.C.

Antevs, E. 1948. Climate change and pre-white man. *In* The Great Basin, with Emphasis on Glacial and Postglacial Times. Bulletin of the University of Utah 38, No. 20:167–191.

Archibald, J.K., P.G. Wolfe, V.J. Tepedino, and J. Bair. 2001. Genetic relationships and population structure of the endangered steamboat buckwheat, *Eriogonum ovalifolium* var. *williamsiae* (Polygonaceae). American Journal of Botany 88:608–615.

Armour, C.L., D.A. Duff, and W. Elmore. 1991. The effects of livestock grazing on riparian and stream ecosystems. Fisheries 16:7–11.

Armstrong, D.M., J.C. Halfpenny, and C.H. Southwick. 2001. Vertebrates. *In* W.D. Bowman and T.R. Seastedt, eds., Structure and Function of an Alpine Ecosystem: Niwot Ridge, Colorado. Oxford University Press, Oxford.

Arno, S.F. 1985. Ecological effects and management implications of Indian fires. *In* Proceedings Symposium and Workshop on Wilderness Fire, November 1983, Missoula, MT. USDA Forest Service, Intermountain Forest and Range Experiment Station. GTR INT-182.

Arnold, J.F. 1950. Changes in ponderosa pine bunchgrass ranges in northern Arizona resulting from pine regeneration and grazing. Journal of Forestry 48:118–124.

Ashman, T.L., T.M. Knight, J.A. Steets, P. Amarasekare, M. Burd, D.R. Campbell, M.R. Dudash, M.O. Johnston, S.J. Mazer, R.J. Mitchell, M.T. Morgan, and W.G. Wilson. 2004. Pollen limitation of plant reproduction: Ecological and evolutionary causes and consequences. Ecology 85:2408–2421.

Aton, J.M., and R.S. McPherson. 2000. River Flowing from the Sunrise. Utah State University Press, Logan.

Axelrod, D.I. 1950. The evolution of desert vegetation in western North America. Publication of the Carnegie Institute, Washington, D.C., 590:215–306.

———. 1965. A method for determining the altitudes of Tertiary floras. Paleobotanist 14:144–171.

———. 1972. Edaphic aridity as a factor in angiosperm evolution. American Naturalist 106:311–320.

———. 1977. Outline history of California vegetation. *In* M. Barbour and J. Major, eds., Terrestrial Vegetation of California. John Wiley Interscience, New York.

———. 1979. Age and Origin of Sonoran Desert Vegetation. Occasional Papers 132. California Academy of Sciences, San Francisco.

———. 1988. Outline history of California vegetation. *In* M.G. Barbour and J. Major, eds., Terrestrial Vegetation of California. California Native Plant Society Special Publication 9:139–194.

———. 1990. Age and origin of subalpine forest zone. Paleobiology 16:360–399.

Axelrod, D.I., and P.H. Raven. 1985. Origins of the Cordilleran flora. Journal of Biogeography 12:21–47.

Baars, D.L., and G. Stevenson. 1986. San Juan Canyons: A River Runner's Guide. Canon Publishers, Evergreen, CO.

Bailey, R.W. 1941. Climate and settlement of the arid region. *In* Climate and Man: Yearbook of Agriculture–1941. USDA, Washington, D.C., pp. 188–196.

Baker, M.B., P.F. Ffolliott, L.F. Debano, and D.G. Neary. 2004. Riparian Areas of the

Southwestern United States: Hydrology, Ecology, and Management. Lewis Publishers, Boca Raton.

Balda, R.P., and G.C. Bateman. 1971. Flocking and annual cycle of the pinyon jay, *Gymnorhinus cyanocephalus*. Condor 73:287–302.

———. 1972. The breeding biology of the pinyon jay. Living Bird 12:5–42.

Barbour, M.G., J.H. Burk, and W.D. Pitts. 1980. Terrestrial Plant Ecology. Benjamin/ Cummings Publishing Company, Menlo Park, CA.

Barger, R.L., and P.F. Ffolliott. 1972. Physical characteristics and utilization of major woodland tree species in Arizona. USDA Research Paper RM-83.

Barkworth, M.E., K.M. Capels, S. Long, L.K. Anderton, and M. B. Piep. 2007. *Poa*. Flora of North America, Vol. 24, http://herbarium.usu.edu.

Barnes, B.V. 1966. The clonal habit of American aspens. Ecology 47:439–447.

Barnosky, C.W., P.M. Anderson, and P.J. Bartlein. 1987. The northwestern U.S. during deglaciation, vegetational history and paleoclimatic implications. *In* W.F. Ruddiman and H.E. Wright, eds., North American and Adjacent Oceans During the Last Deglaciation. The Geology of North America, Vol. K-3. Geological Society of America, Boulder, CO.

Barrow, M., S. Nigam, and E.H. Berbery. 1998. Evolution of the North American monsoon system. Journal of Climate 11:2238–2257.

Bartos, D.L. 2001. Landscape dynamics of aspen and conifer forests. *In* W.D. Shepperd, D. Brinkley, D. Bartos, T.J. Stohlgren, and L.G. Eskew, Sustaining Aspen in Western Landscapes: Symposium Proceedings. USDA USFS RMRS-P-18.

Beale, E.F. 1858. Wagon road from Ft. Defiance to the Colorado River. Thirty-fifth Congress, 1st session. Senate Executive Document No. 124.

Beasley, R.S., and J.O. Klemmedson. 1980. Ecological relationships of Bristlecone pine. American Midland Naturalist 104(2):242–252.

Bebi, P., D. Kualowski, and T.T. Veblen. 2003. Interactions between fire and spruce beetles in a subalpine Rocky Mountain forest landscape. Ecology 84(2):362–371.

Beck, J.L., D.L. Mitchell, and B.D. Maxfield. 2003. Changes in the distribution and status of sage-grouse in Utah. Western North American Naturalist 63(2):203–214.

Behnke, J.R. 2002. Trout and Salmon of North America. Free Press, New York.

Belnap, J. 1993. Recovery rates of cryptobiotic crusts: Innoculant use and assessment methods. Great Basin Naturalist 53(1):89–95.

Belsky, A.J., A. Matzke, and S. Uselman. 1999. Survey of livestock influences on stream and riparian ecosystems in the western United States. Journal of Soil and Water Conservation 54:419–431.

Benedict, J.B. 1984. Rates of tree-island migration, Colorado Rocky Mountains, USA. Ecology 65(3):820–823.

Benkman, C.W. 1999. The selection mosaic and diversifying co-evolution between crossbills and lodgepole pine. American Naturalist 154 (suppl.):S75–S91.

Bennett, S.J., and A. Simon, eds. 2004 Riparian Vegetation and Fluvial Geomorphology. American Geophysical Union, Washington, D.C.

Benson, L. 1979. Plant Classification. D.C. Heath and Co., Toronto.

Benson, L., and R.S. Thompson. 1987. The physical record of the lakes in the Great Basin. *In* W.F. Ruddiman and H.E. Wright, eds., North American and Adjacent Oceans During the Last Deglaciation. The Geology of North America, Vol. K-3. Geological Society of America, Boulder, CO.

Betancourt, J.L. 1990. Late Quaternary biogeography of the Colorado Plateau. *In* J.L. Betancourt, T.R. Van Devender, and P.S. Martin, eds., Packrat Middens: The Last 40,000 Years of Biotic Change. University of Arizona Press, Tucson.

Betancourt, J.L., W.S. Schuster, J.B. Mitton, and R.S. Anderson. 1991. Fossil and genetic history of a pinyon pine (*Pinus edulis*) isolate. Ecology 72:1685–1697.

Betancourt, J.L., T.R. Van Devender, and P.S. Martin. 1990. Synthesis and prospectus. *In* J.L. Betancourt, T.R. Van Devender, and P.S. Martin, eds., Packrat Middens: The Last 40,000 Years of Biotic Change. University of Arizona Press, Tucson.

Billings, W.D. 1988. Alpine vegetation. *In* M.G. Barbour and W.D. Billings, eds., North American Terrestrial Vegetation. Cambridge University Press, Cambridge.

———. 1990. *Bromus tectorum*, a biotic cause of ecosystem impoverishment in the Great Basin. *In* G.M. Woodwell, ed., The Earth in Transition: Patterns and Processes of Biotic Impoverishment. Cambridge University Press, Cambridge.

———. 1994. Ecological impacts of cheatgrass and resultant fire on ecosystems in the western Great Basin. *In* S.B. Monsen and S.G. Kitchen, eds., Proceedings: Ecology and Management of Annual Rangelands. USFS INT-GTR-313.

———. 2000. Alpine vegetation. *In* M.G. Barbour and W.D. Billings, eds., North American Terrestrial Vegetation, 2nd ed. Cambridge University Press, Cambridge.

Birkeland, P. 1968. Mean velocities and boulder transport during Tahoe-age floods of the Truckee River, California-Nevada. Geological Society of America Bulletin 79:137–142.

Blake, E.A., and M.R. Wagner. 1987. Collection and consumption of Pandora moth, *Coloradia pandora lindseyi* (Lepidoptera: Saturniidae), larvae by Owens Valley and Mono Lake Paiutes. Bulletin of the Entomological Society of America (Spring): 23–27.

Blakey, R.C. 2003. Supai Group and Hermit Formation. *In* S.S. Beus and M. Morales, eds., Grand Canyon Geology. Oxford University Press, Oxford.

Blakey, R., and W. Ranney. 2008. Ancient Landscapes of the Colorado Plateau. Grand Canyon Association, Grand Canyon, AZ.

Blinn, D.W., and N.L. Poff. 2005. Colorado River Basin. *In* A.C. Benke and C.E. Cushing, eds., Rivers of North America. Elsevier, New York.

Board of Life Sciences and Board of Agricultural and Natural Sciences. 2007. Status of Pollinators of North America. National Academy of Sciences, Washington, D.C

Bock, C.E., and J.E. Bock. 2000. The View from Bald Hill: Thirty Years in an Arizona Grassland. University of California Press, Los Angeles.

Bond, W.J. 1989. The tortoise and the hare: Ecology of angiosperm dominance and gymnosperm persistence. Biological Journal of the Linnaean Society 36:227–249.

Bonnicksen, T.B. 2000. America's Ancient Forests: From the Ice Age to the Age of Discovery. Wiley, New York.

Bowman, W.D. 2000. Biotic controls over ecosystem response to environmental change in alpine tundra of the Rocky Mountains. Ambio 29:396–400.

Bowman, W.D., and M.C. Fisk. 2001. Primary production. *In* W.D. Bowman and T.R. Seastedt, eds., Structure and Function of an Alpine Ecosystem: Niwot Ridge, Colorado. Oxford University Press, Oxford.

Bradley, B.A., and J.F. Mustard. 2005. Identifying land cover variability distinct from land cover change: Cheatgrass in the Great Basin. Remote Sensing of Environment 94:204–213.

Bragg, T.B. 1995. The physical environment of Great Plains grasslands. *In* A. Joern and K.H. Keeler, eds., The Changing Prairie: North American Grasslands. Oxford University Press, Oxford.

Brennan, L.A., and W.P. Kuvlesky. 2005. North American grassland birds: An unfolding conservation crisis? Journal of Wildlife Management 69:1–13.

Breshears, D.D., N.S. Cobb, P.M. Rich, K.P. Price, C.D. Allen, R.G. Balice, W.H. Romme, J.H. Kastens, M.L. Floyd, J. Belnap, J.J. Anderson, O.B. Myers, and C.W. Meyer. 2005. Regional vegetation die-off in response to global-change-type drought. Proceedings of the National Academy of Science 102(42):15,144–15,148.

Breshears, D.D., O.B. Myers, S.A. Johnson, C.W. Meyer, and S.N. Martens. 1997. Differential use of spatially heterogenous soil moisture by two semiarid woody species: *Pinus edulis* and *Juniperus monosperma*. Journal of Ecology 85:289–299.

Bridges, J.R., W.A. Nettleton, and M.D. Connor. 1985. Southern pine beetle (Coleopera: Scolytidae) infestations without the bluestain fungus, *Ceratocystis minor*. Journal of Economic Entomology 78:325–327.

Broccoli, A.J., and S. Manabe. 1992. The effects of orography on midlatitude northern hemisphere dry climates. Journal of Climate 5:1181–1201.

Brock, J.P., and K. Kaufman. 2003. Butterflies of North America. Houghton Mifflin, New York.

Brown, A.L. 1950. Shrub invasion of southern Arizona desert grassland. Journal of Range Management 3:172–177.

Brown, B.T. 1989. Breeding ecology of riparian birds along the Colorado River in Grand Canyon, Arizona. Coop. National Park Resources Studies Unit Technical Report No. 25, University of Arizona, Tucson.

———. 1995. Birds of the lower Grand Canyon. *In* SWCA Environmental Consultants, Monitoring and evaluating the impacts of Glen Canyon Dam interim flows on riparian communities in lower Grand Canyon. Final report to the Hualapi Tribe, Peach Springs, AZ.

Brown, B.T., and M.W. Trossett. 1989. Nesting-habitat relationships of riparian birds along the Colorado River in Grand Canyon, Arizona. Southwestern Naturalist 34:260–270.

Brown, C.R. 1990. Avian use of native and exotic riparian habitats on the Snake River, Idaho. Master's thesis, Colorado State University, Fort Collins.

Brown, J.K., and N.V. DeByle. 1987. Fire damage, mortality, and suckering in aspen. Canadian Journal of Forestry Research 17:1100–1109.

Buchmann, S.L., and G.P. Nabhan. 1996. The Forgotten Pollinators. Island Press/Shearwater Books, Washington, D.C.

Burkhardt, J.W., and E.W. Tisdale. 1976. Causes of juniper invasion in southwestern Idaho. Ecology 57:472–484.

Bushman, M., S.T. Nelson, D. Tingey, and D. Eggett. 2010. Regional groundwater flow in structurally complex extended terranes: An evaluation of the sources of discharge at Ash Meadows, Nevada. Journal of Hydrology 386:118–129.

Caldwell, M.M., R.S. White, R.T. Moore, and L.B. Camp. 1977. Carbon balance, productivity, and water use of cold-winter desert shrub communities dominated by $C_3$ and $C_4$ species. Oecologia 29:275–300.

Campbell, J.C. 1997. North American alpine ecosystems. *In* F.E. Wielgolaski, ed., Polar and Alpine Tundra, Vol. 3 of Ecosystems of the World. Elsevier, London.

Campbell, S.E. 1979. Soil stabilization by a prokaryotic desert crust: Implications for Precambrian land biota. Origins of Life 9:335–348.

Carmichael, J.S., and W.E. Friedman. 1996. Double fertilization in *Gnetum gnemon* (Gnetaceae): Its bearing on the evolution of sexual reproduction within the Gnetales and the anthophyte clade. American Journal of Botany 83:767–780.

Carothers, S.W., S.W. Aitchison, and R.R. Johnson. 1979. Natural resources, whitewater recreation, and river management alternatives on the Colorado River, Grand Canyon National Park, Arizona. Proceedings from the First Conference on Scientific Research in the National Parks 1:253–260.

Carothers, S.W., R.R. Johnson, and S.W. Aitchison. 1974. Population structure and social organization in southwestern riparian birds. American Zoologist 14:97–108.

Carrara, P.E., W.N. Mode, M. Rubin, and S.W. Robinson. 1984. Deglaciation and postglacial timberline in the San Juan Mountains, Colorado. Quaternary Research 21:42–55.

Castellanos, M.C., P. Wilson, and J.D. Thomson. 2002. Dynamic nectar replenishment in flowers of *Penstemon* (Scrophulariaceae). American Journal of Botany 89:111–118.

Cates, R.G., and H. Alexander. 1982. Host resistance and susceptibility. *In* J.B. Mitton and K.B. Sturgeon, eds., Bark Beetles in North American Conifers: A System for the Study of Evolutionary Biology. University of Texas Press, Austin.

Chabot, B.F., and W.D. Billings. 1972. Origins and ecology of the Sierran alpine flora and vegetation. Ecological Monographs 42:163–199.

Chambers, C.L., and R.S. Holthausen. 2000. Montane ecosystems used as rangelands. *In* R. Jemison and C. Raish, eds., Livestock Management in the American Southwest: Ecology, Society, and Economics. Developments in Animal and Veterinary Sciences, 30. Elsevier, New York.

Chambers, J.C. 2001. *Pinus monophylla* establishment in an expanding *Pinus-Juniperus* woodland: Environmental conditions, facilitation and interacting factors. Journal of Vegetation Science 12:27–40.

Chambers, J.C., and J.R. Miller. 2004. Restoring and maintaining sustainable riparian ecosystems: The Great Basin ecosystem management project. *In* J.C. Chambers and J.R. Miller, eds., Great Basin Riparian Ecosystems. Island Press, Washington, D.C.

Chambers, J.C., B.A. Roundy, R.R. Bland, S.E. Meyer, and A. Whittaker. 2007. What makes Great Basin sagebrush ecosystems invasible by *Bromus tectorum?* Ecological Monographs 77:117–145.

Chambers, J.C., S.B. Vander Wall, and E.W. Schupp. 1999. Seed and seedling ecology of pinyon and juniper species in the pygmy woodlands of western North America. Botanical Review 65:1–28.

Chapman, G.P. 1996. The Biology of Grasses. Cab International, Wellington, UK.

Chase, V.C., and P.H. Raven. 1975. Evolutionary and ecological relationships between *Aquilegia formosa* and *A. pubescens* (Ranunculaceae), two perennial plants. Evolution 29:474–486.

Chavez-Ramirez, F., and R.D. Slack. 1994. Effects of avian foraging and post-foraging behavior on seed dispersal patterns of Ashe juniper. Oikos 71:40–46.

Chong, G.W., S.E. Simonson, T.J. Stohlgren, and M.A. Kalkhan. 2001. Biodiversity: Aspen stands have the lead, but will nonnative species take over? *In* W.D. Shepperd, D. Brinkley, D. Bartos, T.J. Stohlgren, and L.G. Eskew, eds., Sustaining Aspen in Western Landscapes: Symposium Proceedings. USDA USFS RMRS-P-18.

Christensen, E.M., and R.C. Brown. 1963. A blackbrush over 400 years old. Journal of Range Management 16:118.

Christensen, K.M., and T.G. Whitham. 1993. Impact of insect herbivores on competition between birds and mammals for pinyon seeds. Ecology 74:2270–2278.

Cobb, N.S. 1993. The effects of plant stress on pinyon pine (*Pinus edulis*) and pinyon herbivores. Ph.D. dissertation, Northern Arizona University, Flagstaff.

———. 1997. Increased moth herbivory associated with environmental stress of pinyon pine at local and regional levels. Oecologia 109:389–397.

Coffey, K., C.W. Benkman, and B.G. Milligan. 1999. The adaptive significance of spines on pine cones. Ecology 80:1221–1229.

Cole, D.R., and H.C. Monger. 1994. Influence of atmospheric $CO_2$ on the decline of $C_4$ plants during the last deglaciation. Nature 368:533–536.

Cole, K.L., and R.H. Webb. 1985. Late Holocene vegetation changes in Greenwater Valley, Mohave Desert, California. Quaternary Research 23:227–235.

Collinge, S.K., K.L. Prudic, and J.C. Oliver. 2003. Effects of local habitat characteristics and landscape context on grassland butterfly diversity. Conservation Biology 17:178–187.

Collins, S.L., A.K. Knapp, J.M. Briggs, J.M. Blair, and E.M. Steinauer. 1998. Modulation of diversity by grazing and mowing in native tallgrass prairie. Science 280(5364):745–747.

Compton, L.A. 2004. Ponderosa pine dispersal and recruitment: The role of seed-caching rodents. M.S. thesis. Northern Arizona University, Flagstaff.

Comstock, J.P., and J.R. Ehleringer. 1992. Plant adaptations in the Great Basin and Colorado Plateau. Great Basin Naturalist 52(3):195–215.

Conkle, M.T., and W.B. Critchfield. 1988. Genetic variation and hybridization of ponderosa pine. *In* D.M. Baumgartner and J.E. Lotan, eds., Ponderosa Pine, the Species and Its Management. Washington State University Press, Pullman, pp. 27–43.

Conry, J.A. 1978. Resource utilization, breeding biology and nestling development in an alpine tundra passerine community. Ph.D. dissertation, University of Colorado, Boulder.

Cooper, C.F. 1960. Changes in vegetation, structure, and growth of southwestern pine forests since white settlement. Ecological Monographs 30:129–164.

Cottam, W.P. 1954. Prevernal leafing of aspen in Utah mountains. Journal of Arnold Arboretum 35:239–250.

Covington, W.W. 2003. The evolutionary and historical context. *In* P. Friederici, ed., Ecological Restoration of Southwestern Ponderosa Pine Forests. Island Press, Washington, D.C.

Covington, W.W., and M.M. Moore. 1994a. Southwestern ponderosa pine forest structure: Changes since Euro-American settlement. Journal of Forestry 92:39–47.

———. 1994b. Post-settlement changes in natural fire regimes and forest structure: Ecological restoration of old-growth ponderosa pine forests. Journal of Sustainable Forestry 2:153–181.

Craig, T.P., P.W. Price, K.M. Clancy, G.L. Waring, and C.F. Sacchi. 1988. Forces preventing coevolution in three-trophic-level system: Willow, a gall-forming herbivore, and parasitoid. *In* K.C. Spencer, ed., Chemical Mediation of Coevolution. Academic Press, New York.

Crawley, M.J. 1983. Herbivory: The Dynamics of Animal-Plant Interactions. Blackwell Scientific, Oxford, UK.

Cronquist, A., A.H. Holmgren, N.H. Holmgren, J.L. Reveal, and P.K. Holmgren. 1972. Geological and Botanical History of the Region: Its Plant Geography and a Glossary; The Vascular Cryptograms and the Gymnosperms. Vol. 1 of Intermountain Flora: Vascular Plants of the Intermountain West, U.S.A. Columbia University Press, New York.

———. 1977. The Monocotyledons. Vol. 6 of Intermountain Flora: Vascular Plants of the Intermountain West, U.S.A. Columbia University Press, New York.

Dalen, R.S., R.A. Fletcher, and F.A. Winter. 1986. Rabbitbrush (*Chrysothamnus nauseosus*) mortality associated with defoliation by a leaf-feeding beetle, *Trirhabda nitidicollis*. *In* E.D. McArthur and B.L. Welch, compilers, Proceedings: Symposium on the Biology of *Artemisia* and *Chrysothamnus*. USDA USFS GTR-INT-200.

D'Antonio, C.M., and P.M. Vitousek. 1992. Biological invasions by exotic grasses, the grass/fire cycle, and global change. Annual Review of Ecology and Systematics 23:63–87.

Davis, O.K., and T.E. Moutoux. 1998. Tertiary and Quaternary vegetation history of the Great Salt Lake, Utah, USA. Journal of Paleolimnology 19:417–427.

Dearing, D. 2001. Plant-herbivore interactions. *In* W.D. Bowman and T.R. Seastedt, eds., Structure and Function of an Alpine Ecosystem: Niwot Ridge, Colorado. Oxford University Press, Oxford.

DeByle, N.V. 1985. Wildlife. *In* N.V. DeByle and R.P. Winokur, eds., Aspen: Ecology and Management in the Western United States. USDA USFS RMRS General Technical Report RM-119.

DeCourten, F.L. 2003. The Broken Land: Adventures in Great Basin Geology. University of Utah Press, Salt Lake City.

de Groot, P., and J.J. Turgeon. 1998. Insect-pine interactions. *In* D.M. Richardson, ed., Ecology and Biogeography of *Pinus*. Cambridge University Press, Cambridge.

Dickenson, W.R. 1987. Laramide tectonics and paleogeography inferred from sedimentary records in Laramide basins of the Central Rocky Mountain Region. Geological Society of America Abstracts with Programs 19:271.

———. 1989. Plate tectonic evolution of the southern cordillera. Arizona Geological Society Digest 14:113–135.

Dieterich, J.H. 1980. Chimney Spring forest fire history. USDA FS Research Paper RM-220.

Dobrowolski, J.P., M.M. Caldwell, and J.H. Richards. 1990. Basin hydrology and plant root systems. *In* C.B. Osmond, L.F. Pitelka, and G.M. Hidy, eds., Plant Biology of the Basin and Range. Springer-Verlag, Berlin.

Dodd, M.E., J. Silvertown, and M.W. Chase. 1999. Phylogenetic analysis of trait evolution and species diversity variation among angiosperm families. Evolution 53(3):732–744.

Donnegan, J.A., and A.J. Rebertus. 1999. Rates and mechanisms of subalpine forest succession along an environmental gradient. Ecology 80:1370–1384.

Douhovnikoff, V., J.R. McBride, and R.S. Dodd. 2005. *Salix exigua* clonal growth and population dynamics in relation to disturbance regime variation. Ecology 86(2):446–452.

Echelle, A.A. 2007. The western pupfish clade (Cyprinodontidae: *Cyprinodon*): mtDNA divergence times and drainage history. *In* M. Reheis and R. Hershler, eds., Late Cenozoic Drainage History of the Southwestern Great Basin and Lower Colorado River Region: Geologic and Biotic Perspective. Geological Society of America Special Paper.

Ehleringer, J.R., and R.K. Monson. 1993. Evolutionary and ecological aspects of photosynthetic pathway variation. Annual Review of Ecology and Systematics 24:411–439.

Emmel, J.F., T.C. Emmel, and G.F. Pratt. 1998. Five new subspecies of *Apodemia mormo* (Lepidoptera: Riodinidae) from southern California. *In* T.C. Emmel, ed., Systematics of Western North American Butterflies. Mariposa Press, Gainesville, FL.

England, A.S., L.D. Foreman, and W.F. Laudenslayer. 1984. Composition and abundance of bird populations in riparian systems of the California desert. *In* R.E. Warner and K.M. Hendrix, eds., California Riparian Systems: Ecology, Conservation, and Productive Management. University of California Press, Berkeley.

Eriksson, O., and B. Bremer. 1992. Pollination systems, dispersal modes, life forms, and diversification rates in Angiosperm families. Evolution 46:258–266.

Fahlund, A. 2000. Reoperation and decommission of hydropower dams: An opportunity for river rehabilitation. *In* R. A. Abell, D.M. Olson, E. Dinerstein, P.T. Hurley, and J.T. Diggs, eds., Freshwater Ecoregions of North America: A Conservation Assessment. Island Press, Washington, D.C.

Fautin, R.W. 1946. Biotic communities of the northern desert shrub biome in western Utah. Ecological Monographs 16:251–310.

Fechner, G.H. 1990. *Picea pungens*, blue spruce. *In* R.H. Burns and B.H. Honkala, tech. coord., Silvics of North America. Agricultural Handbook 654, USFS/USDA, Washington, D.C.

Feinsinger, P., E.E. Spears, and R.W. Poole. 1981. A simple measure of niche breadth. Ecology 62:27–32.

Fernandes, G.W., and T.G. Whitham. 1989. Selective fruit abscission by *Juniperus monosperma* as an induced defense against predators. American Midland Naturalist 121:389–392.

Fiero, W. 1986. Geology of the Great Basin. University of Nevada Press, Reno.

Fischer, J.T. 1983. Water relations of mistletoes and their hosts. *In* M. Calder and T. Bernhard, eds., The Biology of Mistletoes. Academic Press, Sydney.

Fischer, W.C., and A.F. Bradley. 1987. Fire Ecology of Western Montana Forest Habitat Types. USDA USFS GTR INT-223.

Fisher, S.G. 1995. Stream ecosystems of the western United States. *In* C.E. Cushing, K.W. Cummins, and G.W. Minshall, eds., River and Stream Ecosystems. Vol. 22 of Ecosystems of the World. Elsevier, Amsterdam.

Fitter, A.H., and R.K. Hay. 1987. Environmental Physiology of Plants. Academic Press, New York.

Fleischner, T.L. 1994. Ecological costs of livestock grazing in western North America. Conservation Biology 8:629–644.

Fletcher, R., and W.A. Robbie. 2004. Historic and current conditions of southwestern grasslands. *In* D.M. Finch, ed., Assessment of Grasslands Ecosystems in the Southwestern United States, Vol. 1. USDA USFS RMRS-GTR-135.

Flint, R. 1925. Fire resistance of northern Rocky Mountain conifers. Idaho Forester 7:40–43.

Flowers, S. 1959. Vegetation of Glen Canyon. *In* A.M. Woodbury, ed., Ecological Studies of Flora and Fauna in Glen Canyon. Anthropological Papers, Glen Canyon Series No. 7, No. 40. University of Utah, Salt Lake City.

Floyd, M.L., T.L. Fleischner, D. Hanna, and P. Whitefield. 2003. Effects of historic livestock grazing on vegetation at Chaco Culture National Historic Park, New Mexico. Conservation Biology 17(6):1703–1711.

Floyd, M.L., D.D. Hanna, and W.H. Romme. 2004. Historical and recent fire regimes in pinyon-juniper woodlands on Mesa Verde, Colorado, USA. Forest Ecology and Management 198:269–289.

Forbis, T.A. 2003. Seedling demography in an alpine ecosystem. American Journal of Botany 90:1197–1206.

Forbis, T.A., and D.F. Doak. 2004. Seedling establishment and life history trade-offs in alpine plants. American Journal of Botany 91:1147–1153.

Foxworthy, B.L., D.L. Hanneman, D.L. Coffin, and E.C. Halstead. 1988. Western mountain ranges. *In* W. Back, J.S. Rosenshein, and P.R. Seaber, eds., Hydrogeology, Vol. 0-2 of The Geology of North America. Geological Society of America, Boulder.

Franceschinelli, E.V., and K.S. Bawa. 2000. The effect of ecological factors on the mating system of a South American shrub species (*Helicteres brevispira*). Heredity 84:116–123.

Freeman, D.C., K.T. Harper, and W.K. Ostler. 1980. Ecology of plant dioecy in the intermountain region of western North America and California. Oecologia 44:410–417.

Freeman, D.C., L.G. Klikoff, and K.T. Harper. 1976. Differential resource utilization by the sexes of dioecious plants. Science 13:597–599.

Friedman, W.E. 1990. Double fertilization in *Ephedra*, a nonflowering seed plant: Its bearing on the origin of angiosperms. Science 247:951–954.

———. 2006. Sex among the flowers. Natural History (Nov.):48–53.

Fuentes, M., and E.W. Schupp. 1998. Empty seeds reduce seed predation by birds in *Juniperus osteosperma*. Evolutionary Ecology 12:823–827.

Fuhlendorf, S.D., and F.E. Smeins. 1997. Long-term vegetation dynamics mediated by herbivores, weather and fire in a *Juniperus-Quercus* savanna. Journal of Vegetation Science 8:819–828.

Fule, P.Z., W.W. Covington, and M.M. Moore. 1997. Determining reference conditions for ecosystem management of southwestern ponderosa pine forests. Ecological Applications 7:895–908.

Fule, P.Z., J.D. Springer, D.W. Huffman, and W.W. Covington. 2001. Response of a rare endemic, *Penstemon clutei*, to burning and reduced belowground competition. *In* J. Maschinski and L. Holter, tech. coord., Southwestern Rare and Endangered Plants: Proceedings of the Third Conference. USDA FS RMRS-P-23.

Furniss, R.L., and V.M. Carolin. 1977. Western Forest Insects. USDA USFS Miscellaneous Publication No. 1339.

Futuyma, D.J. 1986. Evolutionary Biology. Sinauer Associates, Sundlerland, MA.

Gali-Muhtasib, H.U., and C.C. Smith. 1992. The effect of silica in grasses on the feeding behavior of the prairie vole, *Microtus ochrogaster*. Ecology 73(5):1724–1729.

Gammonsley, J.H. 1996. Seasonal use of montane wetlands by waterbirds on the rim of the Colorado Plateau. Ph.D. dissertation in biology, University of Missouri, Columbia.

Gehring, C.A., and T.G. Whitham. 1992. Reduced mycorrhizae on *Juniperus monosperma* with mistletoe: The influence of environmental stress and tree gender on a plant parasite and a plant-fungal mutualism. Oecologia 89:298–303.

Goodwin, J.G., and C.R. Hungerford. 1979. Rodent population densities and food habits in Arizona ponderosa pine forests. *In* Rocky Mountain Forest and Range Experiment Station Research Paper RM 199-214. Fort Collins, CO.

Grand Canyon Trust. Website: grandcanyontrust. org.

Grand Canyon Wildlands Council. 2010. http://grandcanyonwildlands.org/resources.html.

Grant, V. 1992. Floral isolation between ornithophilous and sphingophilous species of *Ipomopsis* and *Aquilegia*. Proceedings of the National Academy of Sciences 89:11828–11831.

———. 1994, Historical development of ornithophily in the western North American flora. Proceedings of the National Academy of Sciences 91:10407–10411.

Graybosch, R. 1981. Grasses of the Coconino National Forest. M.S. thesis, Northern Arizona University, Flagstaff.

Grayson, D.K. 1994. The extinct Late Pleistocene mammals of the Great Basin. *In* K.T. Harper, L.L. St. Clair, K.H. Thorne, and W.M. Hess, eds., Natural History of the Colorado Plateau and Great Basin. University Press of Colorado, Niwot.

Grimaldi, D.A., and M.S. Engel. 2005. Evolution of the Insects. Cambridge University Press, Cambridge.

Griswold, T.L. 2009. The dominator: Rabbitbrush (*Ericameria* spp.) in the late summer-fall pollinator market of the Colorado Plateau. Ecological Society of America Meeting, Abstract No. COS 33-2.

Gronemeyer, P., B.J. Dilger, J.L. Bouzat, and K.N. Paige. 1997. The effects of herbivory on paternal fitness in scarlet gilia: Better moms also make better pops. American Naturalist 150:592–602.

Hambrey, M., and J. Alean. 2004. Glaciers. Cambridge University Press, Cambridge.

Hamilton, W.J. 1962. Reproductive adaptations of the red tree mouse. Journal of Mammalogy 43:486–504.

Hamrick, J.L., M.J.W. Godt, and S.L. Sherman-Boyles. 1992. Factors influencing levels of genetic diversity in woody plant species. New Forests 6:95–124.

Hamrick, J.L., Y.B. Linhart, and J.B. Mitton. 1979. Relationships between life history characteristics and electrophoretically detectable genetic variation in plants. Annual Review of Ecology and Systematics 10:173–200.

Hanks, J.P., E.L. Fitzhugh, and S.R. Hanks. 1983. A habitat type classification system for ponderosa pine forests of northern Arizona. USDA FS GTR RM-97.

Hansen, P., and J.G. Massey. 1999. Tissue distribution of excess copper in *Salix exigua* (sandbar willow). *In* J.L. Means and R.E. Hinchee, eds., Wetlands and Remediation: An International Conference, Salt Lake City, UT, Nov. 16–17. Battelle Press, Columbus, OH.

Harper, K.T. 1979. Some reproductive and life history characteristics of rare plants and implication of management. Great Basin Naturalist Memoirs 3:129–137.

Harper, K.T., J.D. Shane, and J.R. Jones. 1985. Taxonomy. *In* N.V. DeByle and R.P. Winokur, eds., Aspen: Ecology and Management in the Western United States. USDA USFS RMRS General Technical Report RM-119.

Harper, K.T., R. VanBuren, and S.G. Kitchen. 1996. Invasion of alien annuals and ecological consequences in salt desert shrublands of western Utah. *In* J.R. Barrow, E.D. McArthur, R.E. Sosebee, and R.J. Tausch, eds., Proceedings: Shrublands Ecosystem Dynamics in a Changing Environment. USDA USFS INT-GTR-338.

Harrington, T.C., and M.J. Wingfield. 1998. Diseases and the ecology of indigenous and exotic pines. *In* D.M. Richardson, ed., Ecology and Biogeography of *Pinus*. Cambridge University Press, Cambridge.

Hartnett, D.C., and K.H. Keeler. 1995. Population processes. *In* A. Joern and K.H. Keeler, eds., The Changing Prairie: North American Grasslands. Oxford University Press, Oxford.

Haskins, K.E. 2003. Mycorrhizal responses to host plant competition, facilitation and disturbance in pinyon-juniper woodlands. M.S. thesis, Northern Arizona University, Flagstaff.

Hastings, J.R., and R.M. Turner. 1965. The Changing Mile: An Ecological Study of Vegetation Change with Time in the Lower Mile of an Arid and Semiarid Region. University of Arizona Press, Tucson.

Hawksworth, F.G., and C.G. Shaw. 1984. Damage and loss caused by dwarf mistletoe in coniferous forests of North America. *In* R.K.S. Wood and C.G. Jellis, eds., Plant Diseases: Infection, Damage and Loss. Blackwell Scientific Publications, Oxford, UK.

———. 1988. Damage and control of major diseases of ponderosa pine. *In* D.M. Baumgartner and J.E. Lotan, eds., Ponderosa pine: The Species and Its Management. Washington State University Press, Pullman, pp. 99–109.

Haws, B.A., G.E. Bohart, R.W. Meadows, E.M. Coombs, and A.H. Roe. 1984. Status of information concerning insects associated with selected species of *Atriplex*. *In* A.R. Tiedemann et al., eds., Proceedings: Symposium on the Biology of *Atriplex* and Related Chenopods. USDA USFS GTR INT-172.

Heckard, L.R. 1968. Chromosome numbers and polyploidy in *Castilleja*. Brittonia 20:212–226.

Heckard, L.R., and T.I. Chuang. 1977. Chromosome numbers, polyploidy, and hybridization in *Castilleja scrophularigeae* of the Great Basin and Rocky Mountains. Brittonia 29:159–172.

Heckathorn, S.A., S.J. McNaughton, and J.S. Coleman. 1999. $C_4$ plants and herbivory. *In* R.F. Sage and R.K. Monson, eds., $C_4$ Plant Biology. Academic Press, New York.

Heidmann, L.J., T.N. Johnson, Q.W. Cole, and G. Cullum. 1982. Establishing natural regeneration of ponderosa pine in central Arizona. Journal of Forestry 80:77–79.

Hennessy, J.T., R.P. Gibbens, J.M. Tromble, and M. Cardenas. 1983. Vegetation changes from 1935 to 1980 in mesquite dunelands and former grasslands of southern New Mexico. Journal of Range Management 36:370–374.

Hereford, R., K.S. Thompson, K.J. Burke, and H.C. Fairley. 1996. Tributary debris fans and the Late Holocene alluvial chronology of the Colorado River, Eastern Grand Canyon,

Arizona. Geological Society of America Bulletin 108:3–19.

Herget, J. 2005. Reconstruction of Pleistocene ice-dammed lake outburst floods in the Altai Mountains, Siberia. Geological Society of America, Special Paper 386.

Hironaka, M. 1994. Medusahead: Natural successor to the cheatgrass type in the northern Great Basin. *In* S.B. Monsen and S.G. Kitchen, eds., Proceedings: Ecology and Management of Annual Rangelands. USFS INT-GTR-313.

Hodges, S.A. 1997. Rapid radiation due to a key innovation in columbines (Ranunculaceae: *Aquilegia*). *In* T.J. Givnish and K.J. Sytsma, eds., Molecular Evolution and Adaptive Radiation. Cambridge University Press, Cambridge.

Hodges, S.A., and M.L. Arnold. 1994. Columbines: A geographically widespread species flock. Proceedings of the National Academy of Sciences, USA 91:5129–5132.

Hodges, S.A., M. Fulton, J.Y. Yang, and J.B. Whittall. 2003. Verne Grant and evolutionary studies of *Aquilegia*. New Phytologist 161:113–120.

Hoffmeister, D.F., and V.E. Diersing. 1978. Review of the tassel-eared squirrels of the subgenus *Otosciurus*. Journal of Mammalogy 59:402–413.

Hofstetter, R.W., J.T. Cronin, K.D. Klepzig, J.C. Moser, and M.P. Ayers. 2006. Antagonisms, mutualisms and commensalisms affect outbreak dynamics of the southern pine beetle. Oecologia 147:679–691.

Holechek, J.L., R.D. Pieper, and C.H. Herbel. 1998. Range Management Principles and Practices. 3rd ed. Prentice-Hall, Englewood Cliffs, NJ.

Holmgren, N.H. 1972. Plant geography of the Intermountain region. *In* A. Cronquist, A.H. Holmgren, N.H. Holmgren, and J.L. Reveal, eds., Intermountain Flora: Vascular plants of the Intermountain West, U.S.A., Vol. 1. Hafner Publishing Co., New York.

Holmgren, C.A., J. Norris, and J.L. Betancourt. 2006. Inferences about winter temperatures and summer rains from the Late Quaternary record of $C_4$ perennial grasses and $C_3$ desert shrubs in the northern Chihuahuan Desert. Journal of Quaternary Science 22:141–161.

Hosten, P.E., and N.E. West. 1994. Cheatgrass dynamics following wildfire on a sagebrush semidesert site in central Utah. *In* S.B. Monsen and S.G. Kitchen, eds., Proceedings: Ecology and Management of Annual Rangelands. USFS INT-GTR-313.

Houghton, S.G. 1994. A Trace of Desert Waters: The Great Basin Story. University of Nevada Press, Reno.

Hrycan, W.C., and A.R. Davis. 2005. Comparative structure and pollen production of the stamens and pollinator-deceptive staminodes of *Commelina coelestis* and *C. dianthifolia* (Commelinaceae). Annals of Botany 95:1113–1130.

Hubbs, C.L., and R.R. Miller. 1948. The zoological evidence: Correlation between fish distribution and hydrographic history in the desert basins of western United States. Bulletin of the University of Utah 30:17–166.

Huckaby, L.S., M.R. Kaufmann, P.J. Fornwalt, J.M. Stoker, and C. Dennis. 2003. Identification and ecology of old ponderosa pine trees in the Colorado Front Range. Gen. Tech. Rept. RMRS-GTR-110.

Hughes, N.F. 1976. Paleobiology of angiosperm origins. Cambridge University Press, Cambridge.

Hunter, K.L., and J.R. McAuliffe. 1994. Elevational shifts of *Coleogyne ramosissima* in the Mohave Desert during the Little Ice Age. Quaternary Research 42:216–221.

Huntoon, P. 2003. Post-Precambrian tectonism in the Grand Canyon Region. *In* S.S. Beus and M. Morales, eds., Grand Canyon Geology, Oxford University Press, New York.

Hutchins, H.E., and R.M. Lanner. 1982. The central role of Clark's nutcracker in the dispersal and establishment of whitebark pine. Oecologia 55:192–201.

Ilg, B.R., K.E. Karlstrom, M.L. Williams, and D.P. Hawkins. 1996. Tectonic evolution of paleoproterozoic rocks in the Grand Canyon: Insights into middle-crustal processes. Geological Society of America Bulletin 108:1149–1166.

Izbicki, J.A., and R.L. Michel. 2004. Movement and age of ground water in the western part of the Mojave Desert, southern California, USA. USGS Water Resources Investigation Report 03-4314.

Jackson, S.T., J.L. Betancourt, M.E. Lyford, and K. Aasen Rylander. 2005. A 40,000 year woodrat-midden record of vegetational and biogeographical dynamics in north-eastern Utah, USA. Journal of Biogeography 32:1085–1106.

Jacobs, B.F., J.D. Kingston, and L.L. Jacobs. 1999. The origin of grass-dominated ecosystems. Annals of the Missouri Botanical Garden 86:590–643.

Janis, C.M., J. Damuth, and J.M. Theodor. 2000. Miocene ungulates and terrestrial primary productivity: Where have all the browsers gone? Proceedings of the National Academy of Sciences 7899–7904.

Jewett, D.G., M.L. Lord, J.R. Miller, and J.C. Chambers. 2004. Geomorphic and hydrologic controls on surface and subsurface flow regimes in riparian meadow ecosystems. *In* J.C. Chambers and J.R. Miller, eds., Great Basin Riparian Ecosystems. Island Press, Washington, D.C.

Joern, A., and K.H. Keeler, eds. 1995. The Changing Prairie: North American Grasslands. Oxford University Press, Oxford.

Johnson, D.A., and M.M. Caldwell. 1975. Gas exchange of four arctic and alpine tundra plant species in relation to atmospheric and soil moisture stress. Oecologia 21:93–108.

Johnson, D.A., M.M. Caldwell, and L.L. Tieszen. 1974. Photosynthesis in relation to leaf water potential in three alpine plant species. *In* L.C. Bliss and F.E. Wielgolaski, eds., Primary Production and Production Processes. Tundra Biome Steering Committee, Edmonton.

Johnson, D.W., L.C. Yarger, C.D. Minnemeyer, and V.E. Pace. 1976. Dwarf mistletoe as a predisposing factor for mountain pine beetle attack of ponderosa pine in the Colorado Front Range. Technical Report R2-4, USDA USFS RMR, Forest Insect and Disease Management, Denver, CO.

Johnson, R.R. 1990. Historic changes in vegetation along the Colorado River in the Grand Canyon. *In* Colorado River Ecology and Dam Management, Proceedings of a Symposium. National Academy Press, Washington, D.C.

Johnson, R.R., L.T. Haight, and J.M. Simpson. 1977. Endangered species versus endangered habitats: A concept. *In* R.R. Johnson and D.A. Jones, eds., Importance, Preservation and Management of Riparian Habitat: A symposium. USDA FS GTR RM-43, Tucson, AZ.

Johnson, S.D., and K.E. Steiner. 2000. Generalization versus specialization in plant pollination systems. TREE 15(4):140–143.

Johnston, C.A., and R.J. Naiman. 1990. Browse selection by beaver: Effects on riparian forest composition. Canadian Journal of Forestry Research 20:1036–1043.

Jones, A. 2000. Effects of cattle grazing on North American arid ecosystems: A quantitative review. Western North American Naturalist 60:155–164.

Jones, J.R. 1985. Distribution. *In* N.V. DeByle and R.P. Winokur, eds., Aspen: Ecology and Management in the Western United States. USDA USFS RMRS General Technical Report RM-119.

Jones, R.G., R.J. Gagne, and W.F. Barr. 1983. Biology and taxonomy of the *Rhopalomyia* gall midges (Diptera: Cecidomyiidae) of *Artemisia tridentata* Nuttall (Compositae) in Idaho. Contributions of the American Entomological Institute 21(1):1–80.

Juenger, T., and J. Bergelson. 1997. Pollen and resource limitation of compensation to herbivory in scarlet gilia, *Ipomopsis aggregata*. Ecology 78:1684–1695.

———. 1998. Pairwise versus diffuse natural selection and the multiple herbivores of scarlet gilia, *Ipomopsis aggregata*. Evolution 52:1583–1592.

———. 2000. The evolution of compensation to herbivory in scarlet gilia, *Ipomopsis aggregata*: Herbivore-imposed natural selection and the quantitative genetics of tolerance. Evolution 54:764–777.

Juenger, T., T.C. Morton, R.E. Miller, and J. Bergelson. 2005. Scarlet gilia resistance to insect herbivory: The effects of early season browsing, plant apparency, and phytochemistry on patterns of seed fly attack. Evolutionary Ecology 19:79–101.

Kaltenecker, J.H., M.C. Wicklow-Howard, and R. Rosentreter. 1999. Biological soil crusts in three sagebrush communities recovering from a century of livestock trampling. *In* E.D. McArthur, W.K. Ostler, and C.L. Wambolt, eds., Proceedings: Shrubland Ecotones. USDA USFS RMRS-P-11.

Kanehl, P.D., J. Lyons, and J.E. Nelson. 1997. Changes in the habitat and fish community of the Milwaukee River, Wisconsin, following removal of the Woolen Mills dam. North American Journal of Fisheries Management 17:387–400.

Kartesz, J., and A. Farstad. 1999. Multi-scale analysis of endemism of vascular plant species. *In* T.H. Ricketts, E. Dinerstein, D.M. Olson, and C. Loucks, eds., Terrestrial Ecoregions of North America: A Conservation Assessment. Island Press, Washington, D.C.

Kay, C.E. 1997. Is aspen doomed? Journal of Forestry 95:4–11.

Keeley, J.E., and P.H. Zedler. 1998. Evolution of life histories in *Pinus*. *In* D.M. Richardson, ed., Ecology and Biogeography of *Pinus*. Cambridge University Press, Cambridge.

Keigley, R.B., and M.R. Frisina. 2008. Aspen height, stem-girth and survivorship in an area of high ungulate use. Northwest Science 82:199–210.

Keith, J.O. 2003. Abert's squirrel (*Sciurus aberti*): A technical conservation assessment. Species Conservation Project. USDA USFS RMR.

Kelley, S.T., and J.B. Mitton. 1999. Strong differentiation in mitochondrial DNA of *Dendroctonus brevicomis* (Coleoptera: Scolytidae). Annals of the Entomological Society of America 92:193–197.

Kellogg, E.A. 2000. The grasses: A case study in macroevolution. Ann. Rev. Ecol. Syst. 31:217–238.

Kenagy, G.J. 1972. Salt-bush leaves: Excision of hypersaline tissue by a kangaroo rat. Science 178:1094–1096.

Kenaley, S.C. 2004. Bark beetle and dwarf mistletoe interactions in northern Arizona. Master's thesis. Northern Arizona University, Flagstaff.

Kendall, K.C., and R.E. Keane. 2001. Whitebark pine decline: Infection, mortality, and population trends. *In* D.F. Tomback, S.F. Arno, and R.E. Keane, eds., Whitebark Pine Communities: Ecology and Restoration. Island Press, Washington, D.C.

Kilgore, B.M. 1981. Fire in ecosystem distribution and structure: Western forests and scrublands. *In* H.A. Mooney, T.M. Bonnicksen, N.L. Christensen, J.E. Lotan, and W.A. Reiner, tech. eds., Fire Regimes and Ecosystem Properties, Proceedings, Honolulu, HI. USDA Forest Service GTR WO-26.

Kitchen, S.G., and G.L. Jorgensen. 2001. Winterfat decline and halogeton spread in the Great Basin. *In* E.D. McArthur and D.J. Fairbanks, eds., Shrubland Ecosystem Genetics and Biodiversity: Proceedings. UDSA USFS RMRS-P-21.

Klepzig, K.D., D.J. Robison, G. Fowler, P.R. Minchin, F.P. Hain, and H.L. Allen. 2005. Effects of mass inoculation on induced oleoresin response in intensively managed loblolly pine. Tree Physiology 25:681–688.

Knight, T.M., J.A. Steets, J.C. Vamosi, S.J. Mazer, M. Burd, D.R. Campbell, M.R. Dudash, M.O. Johnston, R.J. Mitchell, and T.L. Ashman. 2005. Pollen limitation of plant reproduction: Pattern and process. Annual Review of Ecology, Evolution and Systematics 36:467–497.

Knopf, F.L. 1992. Faunal mixing, faunal integrity, and the biopolitical template for diversity conservation. Transactions of the North American Wildlife Natural Resources Conference 57:330–342.

———. 1994. Avian assemblages on altered grasslands. Studies in Avian Biology 15:247–257.

Knopf, F.L., R.R. Johnson, T. Rich, F.B. Samson, and R.C. Szaro. 1988. Conservation of riparian ecosystems in the United States. Wilson Bulletin 100:272–284.

Kolb, T.E., K.M. Holmberg, M.R. Wagner, and J.E. Stone. 1998. Regulation of ponderosa pine foliar physiology and insect resistance mechanisms by basal area treatments. Tree Physiology 18:375–381.

Kolbert, E. 2007. Stung: Where have all the bees gone? New Yorker, August 6.

Krueger, K. 1986. Feeding relationships among bison, pronghorn, and prairie dogs: An experimental analysis. Ecology 67:760–770.

Kuchler, A.W. 1970. Potential natural vegetation (map at scale 1:7,500,000). *In* The National Atlas of the USA. U.S. Government Printing Office, Washington, D.C.

Lamb, T., T.R. Jones, and P.J. Wettstein. 1997. Evolutionary genetics and phylogeography of tassel-eared squirrels (*Sciurus aberti*). Journal of Mammalogy 78:117–133.

Landis, A.G., and J.D. Bailey. 2005. Reconstruction of age structure and spatial arrangement of pinyon-juniper woodlands and savannas of Anderson Mesa, northern Arizona. Forest Ecology and Management 204:221–236.

Lange, R.S., and P.E. Scott. 1999. Hummingbird and bee pollination of *Penstemon pseudospectabilis*. Journal of the Torrey Botanical Society 12:99–106.

Lanner, R.M. 1980. A self-pollination experiment in *Pinus edulis*. Great Basin Naturalist 40:265–267.

———. 1981. The Pinyon Pine: A Natural and Cultural History. University of Nevada Press, Reno.

———. 1996. Made for Each Other: A Symbiosis of Birds and Pines. Oxford University Press, New York.

Lanner, R.M., and S.B. Vander Wall. 1980. Dispersal of limber pine seeds by Clark's nutcracker. Journal of Forestry 78:637–639.

Lanner, R.M., and T.R. Van Devender. 1998. The recent history of pinyon pines in the American Southwest. *In* D.M. Richardson, ed., The Ecology and Biogeography of *Pinus*. Cambridge University Press, Cambridge.

Lara, J.M., and J.I. Sanders. 1970. The 1963–1964 Lake Mead Survey. REC-OCE-70-21. US Bureau of Reclamation, Denver, CO.

La Rivers, I. 1994. Fishes and Fisheries of Nevada. University of Nevada Press, Reno.

Larson, F. 1940. The role of bison in maintaining the short grass plains. Ecology 21:113–121.

Larson, G.C. 1944. More on seedlings of western aspen. Journal of Forestry 42:452.

Latta, R.G., and J.B. Mitton. 1999. Historical separation and present gene flow through a zone of secondary contact in ponderosa pine. Evolution 53(3):769–776.

Lauenroth, W.K. 1979. Grassland primary production: North American grasslands in perspective. *In* N. French, ed., Perspectives in Grassland Ecology. Ecological Studies 32. Springer-Verlag, New York.

Lauenroth, W.K., and D.G. Milchunas. 1992. Short-grass steppe. *In* R.T. Coupland, ed., Natural Grasslands: Introduction and Western Hemisphere. Ecosystems of the World, 8A. Elsevier, London.

Laycock, W.A. 1994. Implications of grazing vs. no grazing on today's rangelands. *In* M. Vavra, W.A. Laycock, and R.D. Pieper, eds., Ecological Implications of Livestock Herbivory in the West. Society for Range Management, Denver, CO.

Leatherman, D.A., and B.C. Kondratieff. 2003. Insects associated with the pinyon-Juniper woodlands of Mesa Verde Country. *In* M.L. Floyd, ed., Ancient Pinyon-Juniper Woodlands: A Natural History of Mesa Verde Country. University Press of Colorado, Boulder.

Ledig, F.T., P.D. Hodgskiss, K.V. Krutovskii, D.B. Neale, and T. Eguiluz-Piedra. 2004. Relationships among the spruces (*Picea*, Pinaceae) of southwestern North America. Systematic Botany 29:275–295.

Lei, S.A. 1997. Variation in germination response to temperature and water availability in blackbrush (*Coleogyne ramosissima*) and its ecological significance. Great Basin Naturalist 57(2):172–177.

Lei, S.A., and L.R. Walker. 1997. Biotic and abiotic factors influencing the distribution of *Coleogyne* communities in southern Nevada. Great Basin Naturalist 57(2):163–171.

Leopold, A. 1920. "Piute forestry" vs. forest fire prevention. Southwestern Magazine 2:12–13.

———. 1937. Conservationist in Mexico. American Forests 43:118–120.

Levine, M.T., and K.N. Paige. 2004. Direct and indirect effects of drought on compensation following herbivory in scarlet gilia. Ecology 85:3185–3191.

Li, P., and W.T. Adams. 1989. Range-wide patterns of allozyme variation in Douglas-fir (*Pseudotsuga menziesii*). Canadian Journal of Forest Resources 19:149–161.

Lidgard, S., and P.R. Crane. 1988. Quantitative analyses of the early angiosperm radiation. Nature 331:344–346.

Ligon, J.D. 1978. Reproductive interdependence of pinyon jays and pinyon pines. Ecological Monographs 48:111–126.

Lin, G., S. Phillips, and J.R. Ehleringer. 1996. Monsoonal precipitation responses of shrubs in a cold desert community on the Colorado Plateau. Oecologia 106:8–17.

Lindroth, R.L. 2001. Adaptations of quaking aspen for defense against damage by herbivores and related environmental agents. *In* W.D. Shepperd, D. Brinkley, D. Bartos, T.J. Stohlgren, and L.G. Eskew, eds., Sustaining Aspen in Western Landscapes: Symposium Proceedings. USDA USFS RMRS-P-18.

Linhart, Y.B. 1988. Ecological and evolutionary studies of ponderosa pine in the Rocky Mountains. *In* D.M. Baumgartner and J.E. Lotan, eds., Ponderosa Pine: The Species and Its Management. Washington State University Press, Pullman.

Linhart, Y.B., M.A. Snyder, and S.A. Habeck. 1989. The influence of animals on genetic variability within ponderosa pine stands, illustrated by the effects of Abert's squirrel and porcupine. *In* A. Tecle, W.W. Covington, and R.H. Hamre, eds., Multiresource Management of Ponderosa Pine Forests. USDA Forest Service GTR RM-185.

Linton, M.J., J.S. Sperry, and D.G. Williams. 1998. Limits to water transport in *Juniperus osteosperma* and *Pinus edulis*: Implications for drought tolerance and regulation of transpiration. Functional Ecology 12:906–911.

Loeser, M.R.R., T.E. Crews, and T.D. Sisk. 2004. Defoliation increased above-ground productivity in a semiarid grassland. Journal of Range Management 57:442–447.

Loeser, M.R.R., T.D. Sisk, and T. E. Crews. 2007. Impact of grazing intensity during drought in an Arizona grassland. Conservation Biology 21:87–97.

Loeser, M.R.R, T.D. Sisk, T.E. Crews, K. Olsen, C. Moran, and C. Hudenko. 2001. Reframing the grazing debate: Evaluating ecological sustainability and bioregional food production. *In* Proceedings, Fifth Biennial Conference on Research on the Colorado Plateau.

Loftin, S.R., C.E. Bock, J.H. Bock, and S.L. Brantley. 2000. Desert grasslands. *In* R. Jemison and C. Raish, eds., Livestock Management in the American Southwest: Ecology, Society, and Economics. Developments in Animal and Veterinary Sciences 30. Elsevier, New York.

Lotan, J.E., and W.B. Critchfield. 1990. *Pinus contorta*, lodgepole pine. *In* R.H. Burns and B.H. Honkala, tech. coord., Silvics of North America. Agricultural Handbook 654. USFS/USDA, Washington, D.C.

Loveless, M.D., and J.L. Hamrick. 1984. Ecological determinants of genetic structure in plant populations. Annual Review of Ecology and Systematics 15:65–95.

Lucash, M.S., B. Farnsworth, and W.E. Winner. 2005. Response of sagebrush steppe species to elevated $CO_2$ and soil temperature. Western North American Naturalist 65(1):80–86.

MacDonald, G.M., L.C. Cwynar, and C. Whitlock. 1998. The Late Quaternary dynamics of pines in northern North America. *In* D.M. Richardson, ed., Ecology and Biogeography of *Pinus*. Cambridge University Press, Cambridge.

MacFadden, B.J. 1997. Origin and evolution of the grazing guild in New World terrestrial mammals. Trends in Evolution and Ecology 12:182–187.

MacFadden, B.J., and R.C. Hurlbert. 1988. Explosive speciation at the base of the adaptive radiation of Miocene grazing horses. Nature 336:466–468.

Mackley, R.D. 2005. Relating bedrock strength to hydraulic driving forces along the large-scale profile of the Colorado River in Glen and Grand Canyons. M.S. thesis, Department of Geology, Utah State University, Logan.

Mahalovich, M.F., and E.D. McArthur. 2004. Sagebrush (*Artemisia* spp.), seed and plant transfer guidelines. Native Plants 5(2):141–148.

Malanson, G.P. 1993. Riparian Landscapes. Cambridge University Press, Cambridge.

Marchetti, D.W., T.E. Cerling, and E.W. Lips. 2005. A glacial chronology for the Fish Creek drainage of Boulder Mountain, Utah, USA. Quaternary Research 64:264–271.

Marchetti, M.P., and P.B. Moyle. 2001. Effects of flow regime on fish assemblages in a regulated California stream. Ecological Applications 11:530–539.

Marquis, R.J. 1992. The selective impact of herbivores. *In* R.S. Fritz and E.L. Simms, eds., Plant Resistance to Herbivores and Pathogens: Ecology, Evolution, and Genetics. University of Chicago Press, Chicago.

Martens, S.N., D.D. Breshears, and F.J. Barnes. 2001. Development of species dominance along an elevational gradient: Population dynamics of *Pinus edulis* and *Juniperus monosperma*. International Journal of Plant Sciences 162:777–783.

Martin, P.S. 1973. The discovery of America. Science 179:969–974.

Marvier, M. 1998. Parasite impacts on host communities: Plant parasitism in a California coastal prairie. Ecology 79:2616–2623.

Marzluff, J.M., and R.P. Balda. 1992. The pinyon jay: Behavioral ecology of a colonial and cooperative corvid. T. and A.D. Poyser, London.

Maschinski, J., and T.G. Whitham. 1989. The continuum of plant responses to herbivory: The influence of plant association, nutrient availability and timing. American Naturalist 143:1–19.

Mast, J. 2003. Tree health and forest structure. *In* P. Friederici, ed., Ecological Restoration of Southwestern Ponderosa Pine Forests. Island Press, Washington, D.C.

Mast, J., T.T. Veblen, and Y.B. Linhart. 1998. Disturbance and climatic influences on age structure of ponderosa pine at the pine/grassland ecotone, Colorado Front Range. Journal of Biogeography 25:743–755.

Mast, J.N., and G.L. Waring. 1996. Historical vegetation patterns along the Colorado River in Grand Canyon: Changes in Goodding willow detected with dendrochronology. *In* Proceedings of the Third Biennial Conference of Research on the Colorado Plateau, 115–127.

Matthies, D. 1997. Parasite-host interactions in *Castilleja* and *Orthocarpus*. Canadian Journal of Botany 75:1252–1260.

Mayeaux, H.S., H.B. Johnson, H.W. Polley, and S.R. Malone. 1997. Yield of wheat across a subambient carbon dioxide gradient. Global Change Biology 3:269–278.

Mayr, E. 1963. Animal species and evolution. Belknap Press of Harvard University Press, Cambridge, MA.

McAdoo, J.K., and D.A. Klebenow. 1978. Native faunal relationships in sagebrush ecosystems. *In* The Sagebrush Ecosystem: A Symposium. Utah State University, Logan.

McArthur, E.D. 1978. Sagebrush systematics and evolution. *In* The Sagebrush Ecosystem: A Symposium. Utah State University, Logan.

———. 1983. Taxonomy, origin and distribution of big sagebrush (*Artemisia tridentata*) and allies (subgenus *Tridentatae*). *In* K.L. Johnson, ed., Proceedings: First Utah Shrub Ecology Workshop, Sept. 9–10, 1981, Ephraim, UT. Utah State University, College of Natural Resources, Logan.

———. 1989. Breeding systems in shrubs. *In* C.M. McKell, ed., The Biology and Utilization of Shrubs. Academic Press, New York.

———. 1994. Ecology, distribution and values of sagebrush within the Intermountain region. *In* S.B. Monsen and S.G. Kitchen, coords., Proceedings: Ecology Management of Annual Rangelands, Ogden, UT, USDA USFS, Intermountain Research Station. INT-GTR-313.

———. 2005. Sagebrush, common and uncommon, palatable and unpalatable. Rangelands 27:47–51.

McArthur, E.D., and S.B. Monsen. 2004. Chenopod shrubs. *In* S.B. Monsen, R. Stevens, and N.L. Shaw, eds., Restoring Western Ranges and Wildlands. USDA USFS RMRS-GTR-136, Vol. 2.

McArthur, E.D., and A.P. Plummer. 1978. Biogeography and management of native western shrubs: A case study, section Tridentatae of *Artemisia*. Great Basin Naturalist Memoirs 2:229–243.

McArthur, E.D., and S.C. Sanderson. 1999. Cytogeography and chromosome evolution of subgenus Tridentatae of *Artemisia* (Asteraceae). American Journal of Botany 86:1754–1775.

McArthur, E.D., and R. Stevens. 2004. Composite shrubs. *In* S.B. Monsen, R. Stevens, and N.L. Shaw, eds., Restoring Western Ranges and Wildlands. USDA USFS RMRS GTR-136, Vol. 2.

McArthur, E.D., B.L. Welch and S.C. Sanderson. 1988. Natural and artificial hybridization between big sagebrush (*Artemisia tridentata*) subspecies. Journal of Heredity 79:268–276.

McClaran, M.P. 1995. Desert grasslands and grasses. *In* M.P. McClaran and T.R. Van Devender, eds., The Desert Grassland. University of Arizona Press, Tucson.

McCullough, D.G., R.A. Werner, and D. Newmann. 1998. Fire and insects in northern and boreal ecosystems of North America. Annual Review of Entomology 43:107–127.

McDonald, G.I., and R.J. Hoff. 2001. Blister rust: An introduced plague. *In* D.F. Tomback, S.F. Arno, and R.E. Keane, eds., Whitebark Pine Communities: Ecology and Restoration. Island Press, Washington, D.C.

McDougall, W.B. 1973. Seed Plants of Northern Arizona. Museum of Northern Arizona, Flagstaff.

McMahon, J.A. 2004. Foreword. *In* J.C. Chambers and J.R. Miller, eds., Great Basin Riparian Ecosystems. Island Press, Washington, D.C.

McNaughton, S.J., J.L. Tarrants, M.M. McNaughton, and R.H. Davis. 1985. Silica as a defense against herbivory and a growth promoter in African grasses. Ecology 66(2):528–535.

Meade, R.H., T.R. Yuzyk, and T.J. Day. 1990. Movement and storage of sediment in rivers. *In* M.G. Wolman and H.C. Riggs, eds., Surface Water Hydrology. The Geology of North America, Vol. 0-1. Geological Society of America, Boulder.

Meier, M.F. 1990. Snow and ice. *In* W.G. Wolman and H.C. Riggs, eds., Surface Water Hydrology. The Geology of North America, Vol. 0-1. Geological Society of America.

Mengel, R.M. 1970. The North American central plains as an isolating agent in bird speciation. *In* W. Dort and J.K. Jones, eds., Pleistocene and Recent Environments of the Central Great Plains. University of Kansas Press, Lawrence.

Middleton, L.T., and D.K. Elliott. 2003. Tonto Group. *In* S.S. Beus and M. Morales, eds., Grand Canyon Geology, Oxford University Press, New York.

Mifflin, M.D. 1988. Region 5, Great Basin. *In* W. Back, J.S. Rosensheim, and P.R. Seaber, eds., Hydrogeology. Geological Society of America, Boulder, pp. 69–78.

Milchunas, D.G., and W.K. Lauenroth. 1993. Quantitative effects of grazing on vegetation and soils over a global range of environments. Ecological Monographs 53:291–320.

Milchunas, D.G., W.K. Lauenroth, P.L. Chapman, and M.K. Kazempour. 1989. Effects of grazing, topography, and precipitation on the structure of a semiarid grassland. Vegetation 80:11–23.

Millar, C.I. 1998. Early evolution of pines. *In* D.M. Richardson, ed., Ecology and Biogeography of *Pinus*. Cambridge University Press, Cambridge.

Miller, C.N. 1988. The origin of modern conifer families. *In* C.B. Beck, ed., Origin and Evolution of Gymnosperms. Columbia University Press, New York.

Miller, J.R., K. House, D. Germanoski, R.J. Tausch, and J.C. Chambers. 2004. Fluvial geomorphic responses to Holocene climate change. *In* J.C. Chambers and J.R. Miller, eds., Great Basin Riparian Ecosystems. Island Press, Washington, D.C.

Miller, R.B. 1978. The pollination ecology of *Aquilegia elegantula* and *A. caerulea* (Ranunculaceae) in Colorado. American Journal of Botany 65(4):406–414.

———. 1981. Hawkmoths and the geographic patterns of floral variation in *Aquiliegia caerulea*. Evolution 35(4):763–774.

———. 1985. Hawkmoth pollination of *Aquilegia chrysantha* (Ranunculaceae) in southern Arizona. Southwestern Naturalist 30(91):69–76.

Miller, R.B., and C.L. Willard. 1983. The pollination ecology of *Aquilegia micrantha* (Ranunculaceae) in Colorado. Southwestern Naturalist 28(2):157–164.

Miller, R.F., and P.E. Wigand. 1994. Holocene changes in semi-arid pinyon-juniper woodlands. Bioscience 44:465–474.

Miller, R.R. 1948. The cyprinodont fishes of the Death Valley system of eastern California and southwestern Nevada. Miscellaneous Publications of the Museum of Zoology, University of Michigan, No. 68.

———. 1959. Origin and affinities of the freshwater fish fauna of western North America. *In* C.L. Hubbs., ed., Zoogeography. Publication 51. American Association for the Advancement of Science, Washington, D.C.

———. 1961. Speciation rates in some fresh-water fishes of western North America. *In* W.F. Blair, ed., Vertebrate Speciation. University of Texas Press, Austin.

———. 1981. Coevolution of deserts and pupfishes (Genus *Cyprinidon*) in the American Southwest. *In* R.J. Naiman and D.L. Soltz, eds., Fishes in North American Deserts. John Wiley and Sons, New York.

Minckley, W.L. 1991. Native fishes of the Grand Canyon region, an obituary? *In* National Research Council, ed., Colorado River Ecology and Dam Management, Proceedings of a Symposium. National Academy Press, Washington, D.C.

Minckley, W.L., D.A. Henderson, and C.E. Bond. 1986. Geography of western North American freshwater fishes: Descriptions and relationships to intracontinental tectonism. *In* C.H. Hocutt and E.O. Wiley, eds., The Zoogeography of North American Freshwater Fishes. John Wiley and Sons, New York.

Minckley, W.L., and G.K. Meffe. 1987. Differential selection by flooding in stream fish communities of the arid American Southwest. *In* T. Sandlund, P.J. Schei, and B.W. Barton, eds., Invasive Species and Biodiversity Management. Dordrecht, The Netherlands.

Minckley, W.L., and P.J. Unmack. 2000. Western springs: Their faunas and threats to their existence. *In* R.A. Abell, D.M. Olson, E. Dinerstein, P.T. Hurley, J.T. Diggs, W. Eichbaum, S. Walters, W. Wettengel, T. Allnlutt, C.J. Loucks, and P. Hedao, eds., Freshwater Ecoregions of North America. Island Press, Washington, D.C.

Mirov, N.T. 1967. The Genus *Pinus*. Ronald Press, New York.

Mitton, J.B. 1995. Genetics and the physiological ecology of conifers. *In* W.K. Smith and T.M. Hinckley, eds., Ecophysiology of Coniferous Forests. Academic Press, San Diego.

Mitton, J.B., and M.C. Grant. 1996. Genetic variation and the natural history of quaking aspen. Bioscience 46:25–31.

Moir, W.H. 1969. The lodgepole pine zone in Colorado. American Midland Naturalist 81:87–98.

Moir, W.H., and W.M. Block 2001. Adaptive management on public lands in the United States: Commitment or rhetoric? Environmental Management 28:141–148.

Moir, W.H., B. Geils, M.A. Benoit, and D. Scurlock. 1997. Ecology of southwestern ponderosa pine forests. *In* USDA FS GTR RM-GTR-292.

Moir, W.H., and J.A. Ludwig. 1979. A classification of spruce-fir and mixed conifer habitat types of Arizona and New Mexico. USDA USFS Research Paper RM-207.

Moldenke, A.R. 1976. California pollination ecology and vegetation types. Phytologia 34:305–361.

Monnig, E., and J. Byler. 1992. Forest health and ecological integrity in the northern Rockies. USDA Forest Service, FPM Reports 92–97.

Monroe, S.A., R.A. Antweiler, R.J. Hart, H.E. Taylor, M. Truini, J.R. Rihs, and T.J. Feger. 2005. Chemical characteristics of ground-water discharge along the South Rim of Grand Canyon in Grand Canyon National Park, 2000–2001. USGS Scientific Investigations Report 2004-5146.

Monsen, S.B. 1994. The competitive influences of cheatgrass (*Bromus tectorum*) on site restoration. *In* S.B. Monsen and S.G. Kitchen, eds., Proceedings: Ecology and Management of Annual Rangelands. USFS INT-GTR-313.

Monson, R.K., R. Mullen, and W.D. Bowman. 2001. Plant nutrient relations. *In* W.D. Bowman and T.R. Seastedt, eds., Structure and Function of an Alpine Ecosystem: Niwot Ridge, Colorado. Oxford University Press, Oxford.

Monzingo, H. 1987. Shrubs of the Great Basin. University of Nevada Press, Reno.

Mooney, K.A. 2006. The disruption of an ant-aphid mutualism increases the effects of insectivorous birds on pine herbivores. Ecology 87:1805–1815.

Mopper, S., J.B. Mitton, T.G. Whitham, N.S. Cobb, and K.M. Christensen. 1991. Genetic differentiation and heterozygosity in pinyon pine associated with resistance to herbivory and environmental stress. Evolution 45:989–999.

Morgan, C., and A.F. Hedlin. 1960. Notes on the juniper berry mite, *Trisetacus quadrisetus* (Thomas) (Acarina: Eriophyidae) in British Columbia. Canadian Entomologist 92:608–610.

Morrison, R.B. 1968. Pluvial lakes. *In* R.W. Fairbridge, ed., The Encyclopedia of

Geomorphology. Van Nostrand-Reinhold, New York.

Mortenson, S.G., P.J. Weisberg, and B.E. Ralston. 2008. Do beavers promote the invasion of non-native *Tamarix* in the Grand Canyon riparian zone? Wetlands 28:666–675.

Mueller, G.A., and P.C. Marsh. 2002. Lost, a desert river and its native fishes: A historical perspective of the lower Colorado River. Information and Technology Report USGS/BRD/ITR 2002-0010. USGS, Ft. Collins Science Center.

Mueller, I.M., and J.E. Weaver. 1942. Relative drought resistance of seedlings of dominant prairie grasses. Ecology 23:387–398.

Mueller, R.C. 2004. Dwarf mistletoe infection of pinyon pine: Environmental stress, host vigor and ectomycorrhizae. M.S. thesis, Northern Arizona University, Flagstaff.

Mueller, R.C., C.M. Scudder, M.E. Porter, R.T. Trotter, C.A. Gehring, and T.G. Whitham. 2005. Differential tree mortality in response to severe drought: Evidence for long-term vegetation shifts. Journal of Ecology 93:1085–1093.

Murawski, D.A., and J.L Hamrick. 1991. The effect of the density of flowering individuals on the mating systems of nine tropical tree species. Heredity 67:167–174.

Mutel, C.F., and J.C. Emerick. 1984. From Grassland to Glacier. Johnson Books, Boulder, CO.

Neel, M.C., J. Ross-Ibarra, and N.C. Ellstrand. 2001. Implications of mating patterns for conservation of the endangered plant *Eriogonum ovalifolium* var. *vineum* (Polygonaceae). American Journal of Botany 88:1214–1222.

Neff, J.C., A.P. Ballantine, G.L. Farmer, N.M. Mahowald, J.L. Conory, C.C. Landry, J.T. Overpeck, T.H. Painter, C.R. Lawrence, and R.L. Reynolds. 2008. Increasing eolian dust deposition in the western United States linked to human activity. Nature Geoscience 1:189–195.

Nelson, C.R. 1994. Insects of the Great Basin and Colorado Plateau. *In* K.T. Harper, L.L. St. Clair, K.T. Thorne, and W.M. Hess, eds., Natural History of the Colorado Plateau and Great Basin. University Press of Colorado, Boulder.

Newsholme, C. 1992. Willows: The Genus *Salix*. B.T. Batsford, London.

Niemeyer, L., and T.L. Fleischner. 2005. Desert Wetlands. University of New Mexico Press, Albuquerque.

Nilsson, L.A. 1988. The evolution of flowers with deep corolla tubes. Nature 334:147–149.

Nold, R. 1999. Penstemons. Timber Press, Portland, OR.

Norris, J.R., S.T. Jackson, and J.L. Betancourt. 2006. Classification tree and minimum-volume ellipsoid analyses of the distribution of ponderosa pine in the western U.S.A. Journal of Biogeography 33:342–360.

O'Connor, J.E. 1993. Hydrology, hydraulics, and geomorphology of the Bonneville Flood. Special Paper 274. Geological Society of America, Boulder, CO.

Packer, J.G. 1974. Differentiation and dispersal in alpine floras. Arctic Alpine Research 6:117–128.

Paige, K.N. 1992. Overcompensation in response to mammalian herbivory: From mutualistic to antagonistic interactions. Ecology 73:2076–2085.

Paige, K.N., and T.G. Whitham. 1985. Individual and population shifts in flower color by scarlet gilia: A mechanism for pollinator tracking. Science 227:315–317.

———. 1987. Overcompensation in response to herbivory: The advantage of being eaten. American Naturalist 129:407–416.

Paine, T.D., and F.M. Stephen. 1987. Fungi associated with the southern pine beetle: Avoidance of induced defense response in loblolly pine. Oecologia 74:377–379.

Parfit, M. 1995. The floods that carved the West. Smithsonian 26(1):48–58.

Parker, T.J. 2001. Bird communities in dwarf mistletoe infested ponderosa pine forests. M.S. thesis, Northern Arizona University, Flagstaff.

Pearson, G.A. 1923. Natural reproduction of western yellow pine in the Southwest. Bulletin No. 1105. USDA, Washington, D.C.

Peet, R.K. 1989. Forests of the Rocky Mountains. *In* M.G. Barbour and W.D. Billings, eds., North American Terrestrial Vegetation. Cambridge University Press, Cambridge.

———. 2000. Forests and meadows of the Rocky Mountains. *In* M.G. Barbour and W.D. Billings, eds., North American Terrestrial Vegetation. Cambridge University Press, Cambridge.

Pendleton, B.K., and S.E. Meyer. 2004. Habitat-correlated variation in blackbrush (*Coleogyne ramosissima*) seed germination response. Journal of Arid Environments 59:229–243.

Pendleton, B.K., and R.L. Pendleton. 1998. Pollination biology of *Coleogyne ramosissima* (Rosaceae). Southwestern Naturalist 43(3):376–380.

Pendleton, R.L., B.K. Pendleton, and K.T. Harper. 1989. Breeding systems of woody plant species in Utah. *In* A. Wallace, E.D. McArthur, and M.R. Haferkamp, eds., Proceedings: Symposium on Shrub Ecophysiology and Biotechnology. GTR INT-256.

Petersen, K.L. 1994. Modern and Pleistocene climatic patterns in the West. *In* K.T. Harper, L.L. St. Clair, K.H. Thorne, and W.M. Hess, eds., Natural History of the Colorado Plateau and Great Basin. University of Colorado Press, Niwot.

Polley, H.W., H.B. Johnson, B.D. Marinot, and H.S. Mayeaux. 1993. Increase in $C_3$ plant water-use efficiency and biomass over glacial to present $CO_2$ concentrations. Nature 316:61–64.

Pratt, G.F. 1994. Evolution of *Euphilotes* (Lepidoptera: Lycaenidae) by seasonal and host shifts. Biological Journal of the Linnaean Society 51:387–416.

Pratt, G.F., and G.R. Ballmer. 1991. Three biotypes of *Apodemia mormo* (Riodinidae) in the Mojave Desert. Journal of the Lepidopterists' Society 45:46–57.

Pratt, G.F., and J.F. Emmel. 1998. Revision of the *Euphilotes enoptes* and *E. battoides* complexes (Lepidoptera: Lycaenidae). *In* T.C. Emmel, ed., Systematics of Western North American Butterflies. Mariposa Press, Gainesville, FL.

Prave, A.R. 2002. Life on land in the proterozoic: Evidence for the torridonian dating from the Proterozoic. Geology 9:811–814.

Preisler, H.K., and R.G. Mitchell. 1993. Colonization patterns of the mountain pine beetle in thinned and unthinned lodgepole pine stands. Forest Science 39:528–545.

Price, P.W. 1982. Wild buckwheat, *Eriogonum inflatum* (Polygonaceae): An enigmatic plant. Southwestern Naturalist 27:247–253.

Pyne, S.J. 1982. Fire in America: A Cultural History of Wildland and Rural Fire. Princeton University Press, Princeton, NJ.

Ramsey, J., and D.W. Schemske. 1998. Pathways, mechanisms, and rates of polyploid formation in flowering plants. Annual Review of Ecology and Systematics 29:467–501.

Ranney, W.D. 2005. Carving Grand Canyon: Evidence, Theories, and Mystery. Grand Canyon Association, Grand Canyon, AZ.

———. 2010. Sedona Through Time. 3rd ed. Zia Interpretive Services, Flagstaff, AZ.

Rathburn, S.L. 1993. Pleistocene cataclysmic flooding along the Big Lost River. Geomorphology 8:305–319.

Read, D.J. 1998. The mycorrhizal status of *Pinus*. *In* D.M. Richardson, ed., Ecology and Biogeography of *Pinus*. Cambridge University Press, Cambridge.

Reveal, J.L. 1979. The Intermountain region: Its biogeography and its evolutionary history. Mentzelia 4:1–92.

———. N.d. *Eriogonum*. Flora of North America: www.eFloras.org.

Reynolds, D.N. 1984. Alpine annual plants: Phenology, germination, photosynthesis, and growth of three Rocky Mountain species. Ecology 65:759–766.

Richardson, D.M., and S.I. Higgins. 1998. Pines as invaders in the Southern Hemisphere. *In* D.M. Richardson, ed., Ecology and Biogeography of *Pinus*. Cambridge University Press, Cambridge.

Richardson, D.M., and P.W. Rundel. 1998. Ecology and biogeography of *Pinus*: An introduction. *In* D.M. Richardson, ed., Ecology and Biogeography of *Pinus*. Cambridge University Press, Cambridge.

Riggs, N.R., T.M. Lehman, G.E. Gehrels, and W.R. Dickinson. 1996. Detrital zircon link between headwaters and terminus of the Upper Triassic Chinle-Dockum paleoriver system. Science 273:97–100.

Rignot, E., J.L. Bamber, M.R. van de Broeke, C. Davis, Y. Li, W.J. van de Berg, and E. van Meijgaard. 2008. Recent Antarctic ice mass loss from radar interferometry and regional climate modeling. Nature Geoscience 1:106–110.

Risser, R.J., and R.R. Harris. 1989. Mitigation for impacts to riparian vegetation on western montane streams. *In* J.A. Gore and G.E. Petts, eds., Alternatives in Regulated River Management. CRC Press, Boca Raton, FL.

Ritchie, J.C., and G.M. MacDonald. 1986. The patterns of post-glacial spread of white spruce. Journal of Biogeography 13:527–540.

Robson, S.G., and E.R. Banta. 1995. Arizona, Colorado, New Mexico, Utah. Hydrological Investigations Atlas 730-C, Segment 2. Groundwater Atlas of the United States. USGS, Reston, VA.

Rolf, J.M. 2001. Aspen fencing in northern Arizona: A 15-year perspective. *In* W.D. Shepperd, D. Brinkley, D. Bartos, T.J. Stohlgren, and L.G. Eskew, eds., Sustaining aspen in western landscapes: Symposium proceedings. USDA USFS RMRS-P-18.

Romme, W.H., L. Floyd-Hanna, and D.D. Hanna. 2003. Ancient pinyon-juniper forests of Mesa Verde and the West: A cautionary note for forest restoration programs. USDA Forest Service Proceedings RMRS-P-29.

Romme, W.H., L. Floyd-Hanna, D.D. Hanna, and E. Bartlett. 2001. Aspen's ecological role in the West. *In* W.D. Shepperd, D. Brinkley, D. Bartos, T.J. Stohlgren, and L.G. Eskew. Sustaining Aspen in Western Landscapes: Symposium Proceedings. USDA USFS RMRS-P-18.

Romme, W.H., S. Oliva, and M.L. Floyd. 2003. Threats to the pinyon-Juniper woodlands. *In* M.L. Floyd, ed., Ancient Pinyon-Juniper Woodlands: A Natural History of Mesa Verde Country. University Press of Colorado, Boulder.

Rosenstock, S.S. 1998. Influence of Gambel oak on breeding birds in ponderosa pine forests of northern Arizona. Condor 100:485–492.

Rosenstock, S.S., and C. Van Riper III. 2001. Breeding bird responses to juniper woodland expansion. Journal of Range Management 54:226–232.

Rosenzweig, M.L. 1995. Species Diversity in Space and Time. Cambridge University Press, Cambridge.

Rowlands, P.G., and N.J. Brian. 2001. Fishtail Mesa: A vegetation survey of a relict area in Grand Canyon National Park, Arizona. Western North American Naturalist 61:159–181.

Rundel, P.W., and B.J. Yoder. 1998. Ecophysiology of pines. *In* D.M. Richardson, ed., The Ecology and Biogeography of *Pinus*. Cambridge University Press, Cambridge.

Rupert, M.G., and L.N. Plummer. 2004. Groundwater flow direction, water quality, recharge sources, and age, Great Sand Dunes National Monument and Preserve, south-central Colorado, 2000–2001. USGS Scientific Investigations Report 2004-5027.

Ryser, F.A. 1985. Birds of the Great Basin: A Natural History. University of Nevada Press, Reno.

Sacks, D. 2002. Fluvial linkages in Lake Bonneville subbasin integration. *In* R. Hershler, D.B. Madsen, and D.R. Currey, eds., Great Basin Aquatic Systems History. Smithsonian Contributions to the Earth Sciences, No. 33. Smithsonian Institution Press, Washington, D.C.

Sage, R.F., D.A. Wedin, and M. Li. 1999. The biogeography of $C_4$ photosynthesis: Patterns and controlling factors. *In* R.F. Sage and R.K. Monson, eds., $C_4$ Plant Biology. Academic Press, New York.

Sala, O.E., and W.K. Lauenroth. 1982. Small rainfall events: An ecological role in semiarid regions. Oecologia 53:301–304.

Salomonson, M.G., and R.P. Balda. 1977. Winter territoriality of Townsend's solitaires (*Myadestes townsendi*) in a pinyon-juniper-ponderosa pine ecotone. Condor 79:148–161.

Sampson, D.A. 1988. Pinyon-juniper seedling establishment patterns in relation to microsite. M.S. thesis, Northern Arizona University, Flagstaff.

Samson, F.B., and F.L. Knopf. 1994. Prairie conservation in North America. Bioscience 44:418–421.

Samson, F.B., F.L. Knopf, and W.R. Ostlie. 1998. Grasslands. *In* M.J. Mac, P.A. Opler, C.E. Packett Haecker, and P.D. Doran, eds., Status and Trends of the Nation's Biological Resources, Vol. 2. USDI, USGS, Reston, VA.

Samuels, M.L., and J.L. Betancourt. 1982. Modeling the long-term effects of fuelwood harvests on pinyon-juniper woodlands. Environmental Management 6:505–515.

Sanderson, S.C., and E.D. McArthur. 2004. Fourwing saltbush (*Atriplex canescens*) seed transfer zones. USDA Forest Service, Rocky Mountain Research Station. RMRS GTR-125.

Sanderson, S.C., E.D. McArthur, and H.C. Stutz. 1989. A relationship between polyploidy and habitat in western shrub species. *In* A. Wallace, E.D. McArthur, and M.R. Haferkamp, eds., Proceedings: Symposium on Shrub Ecophysiology and Biotechnology. USDA USFA GTR INT-256.

Sanderson, S.C., and H.C. Stutz. 2001. Chromosome races of four-wing saltbush (*Atriplex canescens*), Chenopodiaceae. *In* E.D. McArthur and D.J. Fairbanks, eds., Shrubland Ecosystem Genetics and Biodiversity: Proceedings. UDSA USFS RMRS-P-21.

Sanderson, S.C., H.C. Stutz, M. Stutz, and R.C. Roos. 1999. Chromosome races in *Sarcobatus* (Sarcobataceae, Carophyllales). Great Basin Naturalist 59(4):301–314.

San Miguel, G.L., and M. Colyer. 2003. Mesa Verde country's woodland avian community. *In* M.L. Floyd, ed., Ancient Pinyon-Juniper Woodlands: A Natural History of Mesa Verde Country. University Press of Colorado, Boulder.

Savage, M. 1991. Structural dynamics of a southwestern pine forest under chronic human influence. Annals of the Association of American Geographers 8:271–289.

Savage, M., P.M. Brown, and J. Feddema. 1996. The role of climate in a pine forest regeneration pulse in the southwestern United States. Ecoscience 3:310–318.

Savory, A. 1988. Holistic resource management. Island Press, Washington, D.C.

Schaack, C.G. 1983. The alpine flora: Vascular flora of Arizona. Madrono 30:79–88.

Schlesinger, W.H., J.F. Reynolds, G.L. Cunningham, L.F. Huenneke, W.M. Jarrell, R.A. Virginia, and W.G. Whitford. 1990. Biological feedbacks in global desertification. Science 247:1043–1048.

Schöning, C., X. Espadaler, I. Hensen, and F. Roces. 2004. Seed predation of the tussock-grass *Stipa tenacissima* L. by ants (*Messor* spp.) in south-eastern Spain: The adaptive value of trypanocarpy. Journal of Arid Environments 56:43–61.

Schupp, E.W., J.M. Gomez, J.E. Jimenez, and M. Fuentes. 1997. Dispersal of *Juniperus occidentalis* (western juniper) seed by frugivorous mammals on Juniper Mountain, eastern Oregon. Great Basin Naturalist 57:74–78.

Schwinning, S., B.I. Starr, and J.R. Ehleringer. 2005. Summer and winter drought in a cold desert ecosystem (Colorado Plateau), part II: Effects on plant carbon assimilation and growth. Journal of Arid Environments 61:61–78.

Scudder, R.C. 2005. Negative impacts of drought on arthropods: Community-level consequences of climate change. M.S. thesis, Northern Arizona University, Flagstaff.

Sharp, R.P. 1988. Living ice: Understanding glaciers and glaciation. Cambridge University Press, Cambridge.

Shelford, V.E. 1963. The Ecology of North America. University of Illinois Press, Urbana.

Shields, O., and J.L. Reveal. 1988. Sequential evolution of *Euphilotes* (Lycaenidae: Scolitantidini) on their plant host *Eriogonum* (Polygonaceae: Eriogonoideae). Biological Journal of the Linnaean Society 33:51–93.

Shultz, L.M. 1993. Patterns of endemism in the Utah flora. *In* R. Sivinksi and K. Lightfoot, eds., Southwestern Rare and Endangered Plants. Proceedings of the Southwestern Rare and Endangered Plant Conference. New Mexico Forestry and Resources Conservation, Santa Fe.

Siepielski, A.M., and C.W. Benkman. 2004. Interactions among moths, crossbills, squirrels, and lodgepole pine in a geographic selection mosaic. Evolution 58(1):95–101.

Sigler, W.F., and J.W. Sigler. 1996. Fishes of Utah. University of Utah Press, Salt Lake City.

Sims, P.L. 1989. Grasslands. *In* M.G. Barbour and W.D. Billings, eds., North American Terrestrial Vegetation. Cambridge University Press, New York.

Sims, P.L., and P.G. Risser. 2000. Grasslands. *In* M.G. Barbour and W.D. Billings, eds., North American Terrestrial Vegetation. Cambridge University Press, New York.

Sisk, T.D. 2007. Wild times in cow country: Working landscapes and conservation. *In* S. Silbert, G. Chandler, and G.P. Nabhan, eds., Five ways to value the working landscape of the West. Center for Sustainable Environments, Northern Arizona University, Flagstaff.

Sisk, T.D., T.F. Crews, R.T. Eisfeldt, M. King, and F. Stanley. 1999. Assessing impacts of alternative livestock management practices:

Raging debates and a role for science. *In* C. van Riper III and M.A. Stuart, eds., Proceedings: Fourth Biennial Conference of Research on the Colorado Plateau, Flagstaff, AZ. USGS FRESC Report Series.

Slobodchikoff, C.N., B.S. Perla, and J.L. Verdolin. 2009. Prairie Dogs: Communication and Community in an Animal Society. Harvard University Press, Cambridge.

Smith, G.R., and T.E. Dowling. 2008. Phylogeography of speckled dace, *Rhinichthys osculus*, in the Colorado River basin. Special Publication. Geological Society of America, Boulder, CO.

Smith, G.R., T.E. Dowling, K.W. Gobalet, T. Lugaski, D.K. Shiozawa, and R.P. Evans. 2002. Biogeography and timing of evolutionary events among Great Basin fishes. *In* R. Heshler, D.B. Madsen, and D.R. Currey, eds., Great Basin Aquatic Systems History. Smithsonian Contributions to the Earth Sciences, No. 33. Smithsonian Institution Press, Washington, D.C.

Smith, S.D., T.E. Huzman, S.F. Zitzer, T.N. Charlet, D.C. Housman, J.S. Coleman, L.K. Fenstermaker, J.R. Seeman, and R.S. Nowak. 2000. Elevated $CO_2$ increases productivity and invasive species success in an arid system. Nature 408:79–81.

Smith, S.D., and R.S. Nowak. 1990. Ecophysiology of plants in the intermountain lowlands. *In* C.B. Osmond, L.F. Pitelka, and G.M. Hidy, eds., Plant Biology of the Basin and Range. Springer-Verlag, Berlin.

Smith, S.D., and C.B. Osmond. 1987. Stem photosynthesis in a desert ephemeral, *Eriogonum inflatum*: Morphology, stomatal conductance, and water-use efficiency in field populations. Oecologia 72:533–541.

Snyder, M.A. 1998. Abert's squirrels (*Sciurus aberti*) in ponderosa pine (*Pinus ponderosa*) forests: Directional selection, diversifying selection. *In* M. A. Steele, J.F. Merritt, and D.A. Zegers, eds., Ecology and Evolutionary Biology of Tree Squirrels. Special Publication No. 6. Virginia Museum of Natural History, Martinsville.

Soltis, D.E., P.S. Soltis, and J. Tate. 2004. Advances in the study of polyploidy since *Plant Speciation*. New Phytologist 161:173–191.

Soltis, P.S., D.E. Soltis, M.W. Chase, P.K. Endress, and P.R. Crane. 2004. The diversification of flowering plants. *In* J. Cracraft and M.J. Donoghue, eds., Assembling the Tree of Life. Oxford University Press, New York.

Southwood, T.R.E. 1961. The number of species of insects associated with various trees. Journal of Animal Ecology 30:1–8.

Spence, J.R. 2008. Spring-supported vegetation along the Colorado River, Colorado Plateau: Floristics, vegetation structure and environment. *In* L.E. Stevens and V.J. Meretsky, eds., Aridland Springs in North America: Ecology and Conversion. University of Arizona Press, Tucson.

Spencer, J.E., G.R. Smith, and T.E. Dowling. 2008. Middle to Late Cenozoic evolution of topography and Late Cenozoic evolution of fish in the American Southwest, and the location of the Continental Divide. *In* M. Reheis, R. Hershler, and D. Miller, eds., Late Cenozoic Drainage History of the Southwestern Great Basin and the Lower Colorado River Region: Geologic and Biotic Perspectives. Special Publication. Geological Society of America, Boulder, CO.

Stafford, M.P., and J.B. Johnson. 1986. Phytophagous insects on green rabbitbrush in southeastern Idaho. *In* E.D. McArthur and B.L. Welch, comps., Proceedings: Symposium on the Biology of *Artemisia* and *Chrysothamnus*. USDA USFS GTR-INT-200.

Stanford, J.A., and J.V. Ward. 1986. The Colorado River system. *In* B.R. Davies and K.F. Walker, eds., The Ecology of River Systems. Monographiae Biologicae Vol. 60. Dr. W. Junk, The Hague.

Stark, R.W. 1982. Generalized ecology and life cycle of bark beetles. *In* J.B. Mitton and K.B. Sturgeon, eds., Bark Beetles in North American Conifers. University of Texas Press, Austin.

States, J.S. 1990. Mushrooms and truffles of the Southwest. University of Arizona Press, Tucson.

Stebbins, G.G. 1950. Variation and Evolution in Plants. Columbia University Press, New York.

——— . 1981. Coevolution of grasses and herbivores. Annals of the Missouri Botanical Garden 68:75–86.

Steinger, T., C. Korner, and B. Schmid. 1996. Long-term persistence in a changing climate: DNA analysis suggests very old ages of clones of alpine *Carex curvula*. Oecologia 105:94–99.

Stevens, L.E. 1985. Aspects of invertebrate herbivore community dynamics on *Tamarix chinensis* and *Salix exigua* in the Grand Canyon. M.S. thesis, Northern Arizona University, Flagstaff.

———. 1989. The status of ecological research on tamarisk (Tamaricaceae: *Tamarix ramosissima*) in Arizona. *In* M.R. Kunzman, R.R. Johnson, and P.S. Bennett, eds., Tamarisk Control in the Southwestern United States. Cooperative National Park Resources Study Unit Special Report No. 9, Tucson, AZ.

Stevens, L.E., and T.J. Ayers. 2002. The biodiversity and distribution of exotic vascular plants and animals in the Grand Canyon region. *In* B. Tellman, ed., Invasive Exotic Species in the Sonoran Region. University of Arizona Press, Tucson.

Stevens, L.E., T.J. Ayers, J.B. Bennett, K. Christensen, M.J. Kearsley, V.J. Meretsky, A.M. Phillips III, R.A. Parnell, J. Spence, M.K. Sogge, A.E. Springer, and D.L. Wegner. 2001. Planned flooding and Colorado River riparian trade-offs downstream from Glen Canyon Dam, Arizona. Ecological Applications 11:701–710.

Stevens, L.E., K.A. Buck, B.T. Brown, and N. Kline. 1997. Dam and geomorphic influences on Colorado River waterbird distribution in Grand Canyon, Arizona. Regulated Rivers: Research and Management 13:151–169.

Stevens, L.E., T.L. Griswold, O. Messenger, W.G. Abrahamson II, and T.J. Ayers. 2007. Plant and pollinator diversity in northern Arizona. Plant Press 31:5–7.

Stevens, L.E., and V.J. Meretsky. 2008. Springs ecosystem ecology and conservation. *In* L.E. Stevens and V.J. Meretsky, eds., Aridland Springs in North America: Ecology and Conservation. University of Arizona Press, Tucson.

Stevens, L.E., and G.P. Nabhan. 2002. Biodiversity: Plant and animal endemism, biotic associations, and unique habitat mosaics in living landscapes. *In* Center for Sustainable Environments, Terralingua, and Grand Canyon Wildlands Council, eds.,

Safeguarding the Uniqueness of the Colorado Plateau: An Ecoregional Assessment of Biocultural Diversity. Center for Sustainable Environments, Northern Arizona University, Flagstaff.

Stevens, L.E., and J.T. Polhemus. 2008. Biogeography of aquatic and semi-aquatic Hemiptera in the Grand Canyon ecoregion, southwestern USA. Western North American Naturalist 4:38–76.

Stevens, L.E., J.S. Schmidt, T.J. Ayers, and B.T. Brown. 1995. Geomorphic influences on fluvial marsh development along the dam-regulated Colorado River in the Grand Canyon, Arizona. Ecological Applications 5:1035–1039.

Stevens, L.E., J.P. Shannon, and D.W. Blinn. 1997. Benthic ecology of the Colorado River in Grand Canyon: Dam and geomorphic influences. Regulated Rivers: Research and Management 13:129–149.

Stevens, L.E., and A.E. Springer. 2004. A conceptual model of springs ecosystems ecology. National Park Service, Flagstaff, AZ; published online at http://www.nature.nps.gov/im/units/scpn/phase2.htm.

Stevens, L.E., and G.L. Waring. 1988. Effects of post-dam flooding on riparian substrates, vegetation and invertebrate populations in the Colorado River corridor in Grand Canyon. Glen Canyon Environmental Studies Report 19. Bureau of Reclamation, Flagstaff, AZ. NTIS PB88-183488/AS.

Sthultz, C.M., C.A. Gehring, and T.G. Whitham. 2009. Deadly combination of genes and drought: Increased mortality of herbivore-resistant trees in a foundation species. Global Change Biology 15:1949–1961.

Stocks, B.J., and R.B. Street. 1983. Forest fire weather and wildfire occurrence in the boreal forest of northwestern Ontario. *In* R.R. Riewe and I.R. Methven, eds., Resources and Dynamics of the Boreal Zone. Association of Canadian Universities Northern Studies, Ottawa.

Stohlgren, T.J., G.W. Chong, M.A Kalkhan, and L.D. Schell. 1997. Multi-scale sampling of plant diversity: Effects of minimum mapping unit size. Ecological Applications 7(3):1064–1074.

Stohlgren, T.J., D.A. Guenther, P.H. Evangelista, and N. Alley. 2005. Patterns of plant species richness, rarity, endemism, and uniqueness in an arid landscape. Ecological Applications 15:715–725.

Stone, A.M., and C.T. Mason. 1979. A study of stem inflation in wild buckwheat, *Eriogonum inflatum*. Desert Plants 1:77–81.

Sturgeon, K.B., and J.B. Mitton. 1986. Biochemical diversity of *Pinus ponderosa* and bark beetle predation. Journal of Economic Entomology 79:1064–1068.

Stutz, H.C. 1978. Explosive evolution of perennial *Atriplex* in western North America. Great Basin Naturalist Memoirs 2:161–168.

———. 1994. Evolution of weedy annuals. *In* S.B. Monsen and S.G. Kitchen, eds., Proceedings: Ecology and Management of Annual Rangelands. USFS INT-GTR-313.

Stutz, H.C., and S.C. Sanderson. 1983. Evolutionary studies of *Atriplex*: Chromosome races of *A. confertifolia* (shadscale). American Journal of Botany 70(10):1536–1547.

Suring, L.H., M.J. Wisdom, and R.J. Tauscher. 2005. Modeling threats to sagebrush and other shrubland communities. *In* M.J. Wisdom, M.M. Rowland, and L.H. Suring, eds., Habitat Threat in the Sagebrush Ecosystems: Methods of Regional Assessment and Application in the Great Basin. Alliance Communications Group, Allen Press, Lawrence, KS.

Swetnam, T.W. 1990. Fire history and climate in the southwestern United States. *In* J.S. Krammes, tech. coord., Effects of Fire Management of Southwestern Natural Resources: Proceedings. Tucson, AZ. USDA USFS RMRS GTR-191.

———. 1998. Mesoscale disturbance and ecological response to decadal climatic variability in the American Southwest. Journal of Climate 11:3128–3147.

Swetnam, T.W., and A.M. Lynch. 1993. Multicentury regional-scale patterns of western spruce budworm outbreaks. Ecological Monographs 63:399–424.

Szaro, R.C., and R.P Balda. 1979. Bird community dynamics in a ponderosa pine forest. Studies in Avian Biology 3:1–66.

Tausch, R.J., N.E. West, and A.A. Nabi. 1981. Tree age and dominance patterns in Great Basin pinyon-juniper woodlands. Journal of Range Management 34:259–264.

Teeri, J.A., and L.G. Stowe. 1976. Climatic patterns and the distribution of $C_4$ grasses in North America. Oecologia 23:1–12.

Thompson, R.S. 1990. Great Basin: Vegetation and climate. *In* J.L. Betancourt, T.R. Van Devender, and P.S. Martin, eds., Packrat Middens: The Last 40,000 Years of Biotic Change. University of Arizona Press, Tucson.

———. 1991. Pliocene environments and climates in the western United States. Quaternary Science Reviews 10:115–132.

Thompson, V. 2004. Associative nitrogen fixation, $C_4$ photosynthesis, and the evolution of spittlebugs (Hemiptera: Cercopidae) as major pests of neotropical sugarcane and forage grasses. Bulletin of Entomological Research 94:189–200.

Thomson, J.D., and P. Wilson. 2008. Explaining evolutionary shifts between bee and hummingbird pollination: Convergence, divergence, and directionality. International Journal of Plant Science 169:23–38.

Tomback, D.F. 1978. Foraging strategies of Clark's nutcracker. Living Bird (16th Annual):123–161.

———. 1988. Nutcracker-pine mutualism: Multitrunk trees and seed size. Acta International Ornithological Congress XIX:518–527.

Topping, D.J., J.C. Schmidt, and L.E. Vierra, Jr. 2003. Computation and analysis of the instantaneous-discharge record for the Colorado River at Lees Ferry, Arizona— May 8, 1921, through September 30, 2000. Professional Paper 1677. USDI USGS, Denver.

Trimble, S. 1999. The Sagebrush Ocean: A Natural History of the Great Basin. University of Nevada Press, Reno.

Trotter, R.T., III, N.S. Cobb, and T.G. Whitham. 2008. Arthropod community diversity and trophic structure: A comparison between extremes of plant stress. Ecological Entomology 33:1–11.

Turner, C.L., T.R. Seastedt ,and M.I. Dyer. 1993. Maximization of aboveground grassland production: The role of defoliation frequency, intensity, and history. Ecological Applications 3:175–186.

Turner, R.H., and M.M. Karpiscak. 1980. Recent vegetation changes along the Colorado River between Glen Canyon Dam and Lake Mead, Arizona. USGS Professional Paper No. 1132. USGS, Washington, D.C.

Ushimaru, A., T. Watanabe, and K. Nakata. 2007. Colored floral organs influence pollinator behavior and pollen transfer in *Commelina communis* (Commelinaceae). American Journal of Botany 94:249–258.

Vail, D. 1994. Symposium introduction: Management of semiarid rangelands; impact of annual weeds on resource values. *In* S.B. Monsen and S.G. Kitchen, eds., Proceedings: Ecology and Management of Annual Rangelands. USFS INT-GTR-313.

Valdez, R.A., T.L. Hoffnagle, C.C. McIvor, T. McKinney, and W.C. Liebfried. 2001. Effects of a test flood on fishes of the Colorado River in Grand Canyon, Arizona. Ecological Applications 11:686–700.

Vallentine, J.F., and A.R. Stevens. 1994. Use of livestock to control cheatgrass: A review. *In* S.B. Monsen and S.G. Kitchen, eds., Proceedings: Ecology and Management of Annual Rangelands. USFS INT-GTR-313.

Valone, T.J., M. Meyer, J.H. Brown, and R.M. Chews. 2002. Timescale of perennial grass recovery in desertified arid grasslands following livestock removal. Conservation Biology 16:995–1002.

Van Auken, O.W. 2000. Shrub invasions of North American semiarid grasslands. Annual Review of Ecology and Systematics 31:197–215.

Vander Wall, S.B. 1997. Dispersal of singleleaf pinyon pine (*Pinus monophylla*) by seed-caching rodents. Journal of Mammalogy 78:181–191.

Vander Wall, S.B., and R.P. Balda. 1977. Coadaptations of the Clark's nutcracker and the pinyon pine for efficient seed harvest and dispersal. Ecological Monographs 47:89–111.

Van Devender, T.R. 1990. Late Quaternary vegetation and climate of the Chihuahuan Desert. *In* J.L. Betancourt, T.R. Van Devender, and P.S. Martin, eds., Packrat Middens: The Last 40,000 Years of Biotic Change. University of Arizona Press, Tucson.

———. 1995. Desert grassland history: Changing climates, evolution, biogeography, and community dynamics. *In* M.P. McClaran and T.R. Van Devender, eds., The Desert Grassland. University of Arizona Press, Tucson.

Van Devender, T.R., R.S. Thompson, and J.L. Betancourt. 1987. Vegetation history of the deserts of southwestern North America: The nature and timing of the Late Wisconsin-Holocene transition. *In* W.F. Ruddiman and H.E. Wright, eds., North American and Adjacent Oceans During the Last Deglaciation. The Geology of North America Vol. K-3. Geological Society of America, Boulder, CO.

Van Haverbeke, D.R. 1990. Physio-chemical characteristics and ecology of ephemeral rock pools in northern Arizona. Master's thesis, Northern Arizona University, Flagstaff.

Vannote, R.L., G.W. Minshall, K.W. Cummins, J.R. Sedell, and C.E. Cushing. 1980. The river continuum concept. Canadian Journal of Fisheries and Aquatic Sciences 37:130–137.

Van Ommeren, R.J., and T.G. Whitham. 2002. Changes in interactions between juniper and mistletoe mediated by shared avian frugivores: Parasitism to potential mutualism. Oecologia 130:281–288.

Vaughn, T.A. 1982. Stephens's woodrat, a dietary specialist. Journal of Mammalogy 63:53–62.

Vaughn, T.A., and N.J. Czaplewski. 1985. Reproduction in Stephen's woodrat: The wages of folivory. Journal of Mammalogy 66:429–443.

Veblen, T.T., K.S. Hadley, E.M. Nel, T. Kitzberger, M. Reid, and R. Villalba. 1994. Disturbance regime and disturbance interactions in a Rocky Mountain subalpine forest. Journal of Ecology 82:125–135.

Veech, J.A., and S.H. Jenkins. 2005. Comparing the effects of granivorous rodents on persistence of Indian ricegrass (*Oryzopsis hymenoides*) seeds in mixed and monospecific seed patches. Western North American Naturalist 65(3):321–328.

Vickery, P.D., P.L. Tubaro, J.M. Cardoso da Silva, B.G. Peterjohn, J.R. Herkert, and R.B. Cavalcanti. 1999. Conservation of grassland birds in the Western Hemisphere. Studies in Avian Biology 19:2–26.

Vitousek, P.M., J.R. Gosz, C.C. Grier, J.M. Melillo, and W.A. Reiners. 1982. A comparative analysis of potential nitrification and nitrate mobility in forest ecosystems. Ecological Monographs 52:155–177.

Wagner, M.R., and R.L. Mathiasen. 1985. Dwarf mistletoe–Pandora moth interaction and its contribution to ponderosa pine mortality. Great Basin Naturalist 45:423–426.

Walker, M.D., F.J.A. Daniels, and E. Van der Maarel, eds. 1995. Circumpolar Arctic Vegetation. Special Features in Vegetation Science, No. 7. IAVS and Opulus Press, Uppsala, Sweden.

Walker, M.D., D.A. Walker, T.A. Theodose, and P.J. Webber. 2001. The vegetation: Hierarchical species–environment relationships. *In* W.D. Bowman and T.R. Seastedt, eds., Structure and Function of an Alpine Ecosystem: Niwot Ridge, Colorado. Oxford University Press, Oxford.

Ward, J.V., and B.C. Kondratieff. 1992. An Illustrated Guide to the Mountain Stream Insects of Colorado. University Press of Colorado, Niwot.

Waring, G.L. 1993. The impact of exotic plants on faunal diversity along a southwestern river. Special Report to the Navajo Natural Heritage Program, Window Rock, AZ.

———. 1996a. Current and historical riparian vegetation trends in Grand Canyon, using multitemporal remote sensing analyses of GIS sites. NAU-NPS Cooperative Agreement CA 8000-8-0002. Glen Canyon Environmental Studies, Flagstaff, AZ.

———. 1996b. Historical vegetation patterns along the Colorado River in Grand Canyon: Large-scale and species-specific trends. NAU-NPS Cooperative Agreement CA 8000-8-0002. Glen Canyon Environmental Studies, Flagstaff, AZ.

Warner, T.T. 2004. Desert Meteorology. Cambridge University Press, New York.

Warren, P.L., and C.R. Schwalbe. 1988. Lizards along the Colorado River in Grand Canyon National Park: Possible effects of fluctuating river flows. *In* Bureau of Reclamation, Glen Canyon Environmental Studies Report 19, Flagstaff, AZ. NTIS PB88-183488/AS.

Watanabe, Y., J.E. Martini, and H. Ohmoto. 2000. Geochemical evidence for terrestrial ecosystems 2.6 billion years ago. Nature 408:574–578.

Weaver, T. 2001. Whitebark pine and its environment. *In* D.F. Tomback, S.F. Arno, and R.E. Keane, eds., Whitebark Pine Communities: Ecology and Restoration. Island Press, Washington, D.C.

Webb, R.H. 1996. Grand Canyon: A Century of Change. University of Arizona Press, Tucson.

Webb, R.H., J. Belnap, and J.S. Weisheit. 2004. Cataract Canyon: A Human and Environmental History of the Rivers in Canyonlands. University of Utah Press, Salt Lake City.

Webb, R.H., J.B. Blainey, and D.W. Hyndman. 2001. Paleoflood hydrology of the Paria River, southern Utah and northern Arizona, USA. *In* P.K. House, R.H. Webb, V.R. Baker, and D.R. Levish, eds., Ancient Floods, Modern Hazards: Principles and Applications of Paleoflood Hydrology. American Geophysical Union, Washington, D.C.

Webb, R.H., S.A. Leake, and R.M. Turner. 2007. The Ribbon of Green: Change in Riparian Vegetation in the Southwestern United States. University of Arizona Press, Tucson.

Webb, S.D. 1977. A history of savanna vertebrates in the New World, Part I: North America. Annual Review of Ecology and Systematics 8:355–380.

———. 1982. The rise and fall of the Late Miocene ungulate fauna in North America. *In* M.H. Nitecki, ed., Coevolution. University of Chicago Press, Chicago.

Webb, S.D., and N.D. Opdyke. 1995. Global climate influence on Cenozoic land mammal faunas. *In* S.M. Stanley, ed., Effects of Past Global Change on Life. Studies in Geophysics. National Academy Press, Washington, D.C.

Webster, G.L. 1961. The altitudinal limits of vascular plants. Ecology 42:587–590.

Weddell, B.J. 1996. Geographic overview: Climate, phenology, and disturbance regimes in steppe and desert communities. *In* Ecosystem Disturbance and Wildlife Conservation in Western Grasslands: Symposium Proceedings. UDSA USFS RM-GTR-285.

Weixelman, D.A., D.C. Zamudio, and K.A. Zamudio. 1996. Central Nevada Riparian Field Guide. Publication No. 22.09.417.01/96. Toiyabe National Forest, USDA.

Welch, B.L. 1999. Add three more to the list of big sagebrush eaters. *In* E.D. McArthur, W.K. Ostler, and C.L. Wambolt, eds., Proceedings: Shrubland Ecotones. USDA USFS RMRS-P-11.

Welker, J.M., W.D. Bowman, and T.R. Seastedt. 2001. Environmental change and future directions. *In* W.D. Bowman and T.R. Seastedt, eds., Structure and Function of an Alpine Ecosystem: Niwot Ridge, Colorado. Oxford University Press, Oxford.

Wells, P.V., and R. Berger. 1967. Late Pleistocene history of the coniferous woodland in the Mohave Desert. Science 143:1171–1173.

Wells, P.V., and J.D. Stewart. 1987. Cordilleran-boreal taiga and fauna on the central Great Plains of North America, 14,000–18,000 years ago. American Midland Naturalist 118(1):94–106.

Welsh, S.L. 1978. Problems in plant endemism on the Colorado Plateau. Great Basin Naturalist Memoirs, Intermountain Biogeography: A Symposium 2:191–196.

Welsh, S.L., N.D. Atwood, S. Goodrich, and L.C. Higgins, eds., 1993. Utah Flora. Brigham Young University, Provo, UT.

Weltzin, J.F., S. Archer, and R.K. Heitschmidt. 1997. Small-mammal regulation of vegetation structure in a temperate savanna. Ecology 78:751–763.

West, N.E. 1983a. Intermountain salt-desert shrubland. *In* N.E. West, ed., Temperate Deserts and Semi-Deserts. Ecosystems of the World No. 5. Elsevier Scientific Publishing Co., Amsterdam.

———. 1983b. Colorado Plateau-Mohavian blackbrush semi-desert. *In* N.E. West, ed., Temperate Deserts and Semi-Deserts. Ecosystems of the World No. 5. Elsevier Scientific Publishing Co., Amsterdam.

———. 1983c. Great Basin-Colorado Plateau sagebrush semi-desert. *In* N.E. West, ed., Temperate Deserts and Semi-Deserts. Ecosystems of the World No. 5. Elsevier Scientific Publishing Co., Amsterdam.

———. 1983d. Western intermountain sagebrush steppe. *In* N.E. West, ed., Temperate Deserts and Semi-Deserts. Ecosystems of the World No. 5. Elsevier Scientific Publishing Co., Amsterdam.

———. 1989. Intermountain deserts, shrub steppes and woodlands. *In* M.G. Barbour and W.D. Billings, eds., North American Terrestrial Vegetation. Cambridge University Press, Cambridge.

———. 1994. Effects of fire on salt-desert shrub rangelands. *In* S.B. Monsen and S.G. Kitchen, eds., Proceedings: Ecology and Management of Annual Rangelands. USFS INT-GTR-313.

———. 1999. Juniper-pinyon savannas and woodlands of western North America. *In* R.C. Anderson, J.S. Fralish, and J.M. Baskin, eds., Savannas, Barrens, and Rock Outcrop Plant Communities of North America. Cambridge University Press, Cambridge.

West, N.E., and J.A. Young. 2000. Intermountain valleys and lower mountain slopes. *In* M.G. Barbour and W.D. Billings, eds., North American Terrestrial Vegetation. Cambridge University Press, New York.

Western Great Basin Coordination Center. 2004. Website: http://gacc.nifc.gov/wgbc.

Whiles, M.R., and R.E. Charlton. 2006. The ecological significance of tallgrass prairie arthropods. Annual Review of Entomology 51:387–412.

Whisenant, S.G. 1990. Changing fire frequencies on Idaho's Snake River Plains: Ecological and management implications. *In* E.D. McArthur, E.M. Romney, S.D. Smith, and P.T. Tueller, eds., Proceedings: Symposium on Cheatgrass Invasion, Shrub Die-off, and Other Aspects of Shrub Biology and Management. USDA USFA GTR INT-276.

Whitcomb, R.F., A.L. Hicks, H.D. Blocker, and D.E. Lynn. 1994. Biogeography of leafhopper specialists of the shortgrass prairie: Evidence for the role of phenology in determination of biological diversity. American Entomologist 40:19–35.

White, A.S. 1985. Presettlement regeneration patterns in a southwestern ponderosa pine stand. Ecology 66:589–594.

Whitham, T.G., and S. Mopper. 1985. Chronic herbivory: Impacts on tree architecture and sex expression on pinyon pine. Science 228:1089–1091.

Whitham, T.G., W.P. Young, G.D. Martinsen, C.A. Gehring, J.A. Schweitzer, S.M. Shuster,

G.M. Wimp, D.G. Fischer, J.K. Bailey, R.L. Lindroth, S. Woolbright, and C.R. Kuske. 2003. Community and ecosystem genetics: A consequence of the extended phenotype. Ecology 84:559–573.

Whitlock, C. 1993. Postglacial vegetation and climate of Grand Teton and southern Yellowstone National Parks. Ecological Monographs 63(2):173–198.

Whittall, J.B., and S.A. Hodges. 2007. Pollinator shifts drive increasingly long nectar spurs in columbine flowers. Nature 447:706–709.

Wiegand, T., and S.J. Milton. 1996. Vegetation change in semiarid communities. Vegetation 125:169–183.

Wildeman, G., and J.H. Brock. 2000. Grazing in the Southwest: History of land use and grazing since 1540. *In* R. Jemison and C. Raish, eds., Livestock Management in the American Southwest: Ecology, Society, and Economics. Developments in Animal and Veterinary Sciences, 30. Elsevier, New York.

Williams, J.E., and G.R. Wilde. 1981. Taxonomic status and morphology of isolated populations of the White River springfish, *Crenichthys baileyi* (Cyprinodontidae). Southwestern Naturalist 25:485–503.

Williams, N.M., and J.D. Thomson. 1998. Trapline foraging by bumble bees, III: Temporal patterning of visits. Behavioral Ecology 9: 612–621.

Willson, M.F. 1983. Plant Reproductive Ecology. Wiley Interscience, New York.

Wilson, P., M.C. Castellanos, A.D. Wolfe, and J.D. Thomson. 2006. Shifts between bee and bird pollination in penstemons. *In* N.M. Waser and J. Ollerton, eds., Plant-Pollinator Interactions: From Specialization to Generalization. University of Chicago Press, Chicago.

Wing, S.L. 2000. Evolution and expansion of flowering plants. *In* R.A. Gastaldo and W.A. DiMichele, eds., Phanerozoic Terrestrial Ecosystems. Paleontological Society Papers 6:209–231.

Winograd, I.J., and W. Thordarson. 1975. Hydrogeologic and hydrochemical framework, south-central Great Basin, Nevada-California, with special reference to the Nevada Test Site. USGS Professional Paper 712-C.

Wolfe, A.D., S.L. Datwyler, and C.P. Randle. 2002. A phylogenetic and biogeographic analysis of the Chelonae (Scrophulariaceae) based on ITS and *matK* sequence data. Systematic Botany 27:138–148.

Wolfe, A.D., C.P. Randle, S.L. Datwyler, J.J. Morawetz, N. Arguedas, and J. Diaz. 2006. Phylogeny, taxonomic affinities, and biogeography of *Penstemon* (Plantaginaceae) based on ITS and $_{CP}$DNA sequence data. American Journal of Botany 93:1699–1713.

Wolfe, J.A., and G.R. Upchurch. 1986. Vegetation, climatic and floral changes at the Cretaceous-Tertiary boundary. Nature 324:148–152.

Wolman, M.G., M. Church, R. Newbury, M. Lapointe, M. Frenette, E.D. Andrews, T.E. Lisle, J.P. Buchanan, S.A. Schumm, and B.R. Winkley. 1990. The riverscape. *In* M.G. Wolman and H.C. Riggs, eds., Surface Water Hydrology. The Geology of North America, Vol. 0-1. Geological Society of America, Boulder, CO.

Wuerthner, G., and M. Matteson, eds. 2002. Welfare Ranching: The Subsidized Destruction of the American West. Island Press, Washington, D.C.

Young, J.A. 1994. Changes in plant communities in the Great Basin induced by domestic livestock grazing. *In* K.T. Harper, L.L. St. Clair, K.H. Thorne, and W.M. Hess, eds., Natural History of the Colorado Plateau and Great Basin. University Press of Colorado, Niwot.

Young, J.A., and C.D. Clements. 2009. Cheatgrass: Fire and Forage on the Range. University of Nevada Press, Reno.

Young, J.A., and R.A. Evans. 1989. Dispersal and germination of big sagebrush (*Artemisia tridentata*). Weed Science 37:319–325.

Zwinger, A.H., and B.E. Willard. 1972. Land Above the Trees: A Guide to American Alpine Tundra. Harper and Row, New York.

# Index

Numbers in *italics* refer to figures and tables.